Behavioral Science

Behavioral Science

Edited by
Clyde Johnson

Willford Press
www.willfordpress.com

Published by Willford Press,
118-35 Queens Blvd., Suite 400,
Forest Hills, NY 11375, USA

ISBN: 978-1-68285-500-3

Cataloging-in-Publication Data

Behavioral science / edited by Clyde Johnson.
p. cm.
Includes bibliographical references and index.
ISBN 978-1-68285-500-3
1. Psychology. I. Johnson, Clyde.

BF21 .B44 2018
150--dc23

For information on all Willford Press publications
visit our website at www.willfordpress.com

Willford Press

Printed in China.

Contents

Preface

Every human and animal has behavioral characteristics which are affected by its environment in one way or another. behavioral studies refers to the study of the interactions animals and humans have with their surroundings. The subjects which contribute majorly to behavioral science are cognitive science, psychology, psychobiology, etc. This book is a valuable compilation of topics, ranging from the basic to the most complex theories and principles in the field of behavioral science. The topics covered in this book offer the readers new insights in this field. This book is an essential guide for both academicians and those who wish to pursue this discipline further.

To facilitate a deeper understanding of the contents of this book a short introduction of every chapter is written below:

Chapter 1- Neurons are made of soma, dentrites and axon. Also there are three types of neuron - unipolar, bipolar and multipolar. Since neurons are charged, they generate nerve impulses, which help in transmitting information to other parts. The major components of neuron structure and its functions are discussed in this chapter.

Chapter 2- The human nervous system comprises of the central nervous system and the peripheral nervous system. The central nervous system consists of the brain and the spinal cord while the peripheral nervous system is made up of nerves and ganglia. The chapter on human nervous system offers an insightful focus, keeping in mind the complex subject matter.

Chapter 3- Endocrine glands, which are ductless, secrete directly into the blood. These secretions are called hormones and they have a large impact on affecting human behavior. Endocrine glands comprise pituitary gland, pineal gland, thyroid, parathyroid gland and pancreas. Human behavior is best understood in confluence with the major topics listed in the following chapter.

Chapter 4- The brain has specific psychological functions apart from its physiological purposes. They can be categorised as psychobiology of learning, memory, participation and emotion. The topics discussed in the chapter are of great importance to broaden the existing knowledge on biological bases of behavior.

Chapter 5- To study human psychophysiological activities, invasive and non-invasive techniques are used. Since non-invasive technologies were invented later, invasive techniques such as ablation, lesions, and knife cuts were used. The methods include electroencephalogram, computerized transaxial tomography, positron emission tomography, magnetic resonance imaging, magnetoencephalogra-phy and event-related potential. The section closely examines the key concepts of human psycho-physiological activity to provide an extensive understanding of the subject.

Finally, I would like to thank the entire team involved in the inception of this book for their valuable time and contribution. This book would not have been possible without their efforts. I would also like to thank my friends and family for their constant support.

Editor

1

A Comprehensive Study of Neuron

Neurons are made of soma, dentrites and axon. Also there are three types of neuron – unipolar, bipolar and multipolar. Since neurons are charged, they generate nerve impulses, which help in transmitting information to other parts. The major components of neuron structure and its functions are discussed in this chapter.

Neuron

Nerve cells or neurons are especially adapted to receive and transmit signals. They play equally important role in the transmission of information. Figure illustrates the basic structure of a neuron

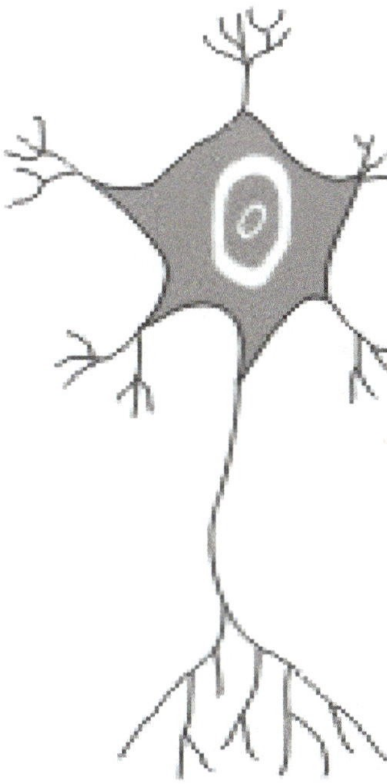

Structure of neuron.

All neurons share three fundamental components- soma, dentrites and axon. Structurally soma or the cell body contains nucleus and other structures present in other cells of our body. Most of the cytoplasm of the neuron is contained in the soma. Dentrites come out from the soma and carry message into the neurons. Dendrites have small bumps known as dendritic spines which can receive signals from other neurons. Axon is the extension carrying signals from cell body to the terminal buttons at the end of the neurons. These terminal buttons contain neurotransmitters which plays important role in conduction at synapse. Synapse is the junction where one neuron ends and the other begins. Any two neurons are not directly connected to each other; rather they are separated by about 2/100 of a micron. These gaps are called synaptic cleft. The part of axon nearest to the soma is called axon hillock. Thereafter, it branches into telodendria and finally translates to end feet or terminal buttons. Few neurons have a fatty insulation through out the axon called myelin sheath. This insulation is segmented at 1-2 mm interval such that it looks like disjointedly arranged divisions. These spaces are called nodes of Ranvier. The rate of conduction of impulses in myelinated neurons is higher than the unmyelinated ones.

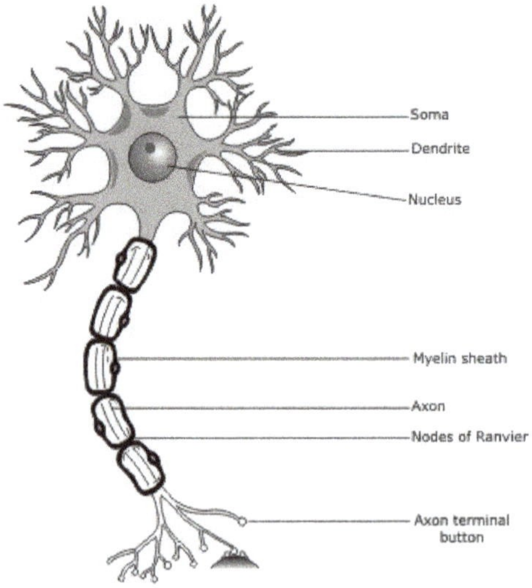

Illustration of axon with myelin sheath and nodes of Ranvier.

Types of Neurons

Unipolar Neuron

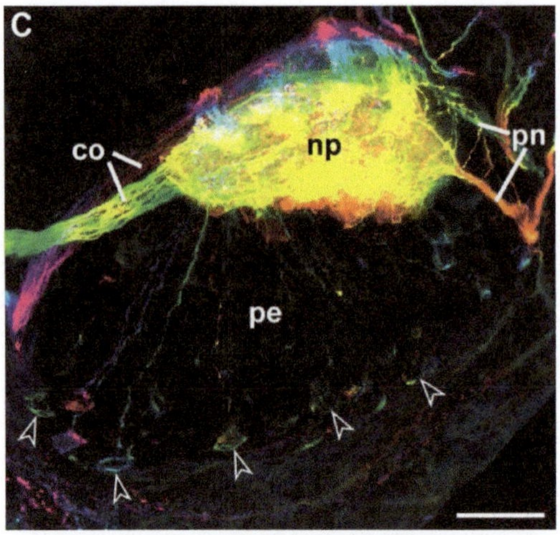

Example of several unipolar neurons from a nerve ganglion of a velvet worm (a primitive arthropod). The neurons were stained for serotonin immunoreactivity, and photographed using a confocal microscope, with multiple images overlaid and color-coded according to depth. Arrows mark the peripherally located cell bodies of several neurons, whose neurites extend into the central neuropil (np), where their complex ramifications are indiscernible. Scale bar: 50 micrometres.

A unipolar neuron is a type of neuron in which only one protoplasmic process (neurite) extends from the cell body. Most neurons are multipolar, generating several dendrites and an axon and there are also many bipolar neurons. Unipolar neurons that begin as bipolar neurons during development are known as pseudounipolar neurons.

Unipolar neurons are common in insects, where the cell body is often located at the periphery of the brain and is electrically inactive. These cell bodies often send a single neurite into the brain; however, this neurite may ramify into a large number of branches making a very complex set of connections with other neurites, in regions of neuropil.

Unipolar brush cells are neurons specific to the cerebellum and the granule region of the dorsal cochlear nucleus.

In all species, including vertebrates and invertebrates, many types of primary sensory neurons are pseudounipolar. Typically these have special structures for transducing some type of physical stimulus (light, sound, temperature, etc.) into electrical activity, no dendrites, and a single axon that conveys the resulting signals into the spinal cord or brain.

Bipolar Neuron

A bipolar cell is a type of neuron which has two extensions. Bipolar cells are specialized sensory neurons for the transmission of special senses. As such, they are part of the sensory pathways for smell, sight, taste, hearing and vestibular functions.

Common examples are the bipolar cell of the retina, the ganglia of the vestibulocochlear nerve, and the extensive use of bipolar cells to transmit efferent (motor) signals to control muscles.

The four types of retinal neurons are bipolar cells, ganglion cells, horizontal cells, and amacrine cells.

Bipolar Cells in Retina

Oftentimes found in the retina, bipolar cells are crucial as they serve as both direct and indirect cell pathways. The specific location of the bipolar cells allow them to facilitate the pathway of signals both where they start in the receptors as well as where they arrive at the ganglion cells. Bipolar cells in the retina are also unique as they do not fire impulses like the other cells found within the retina. Rather, bipolar cells have a receptive-field that surrounds them. Therefore, bipolar cells may exist as off-center or on-center. The off-center bipolar cells possess excitatory relationships with the synapses and are hyperpolarized by light. On-center bipolar cells have inhibitory synapses and therefore are suppressed in the dark.

Bipolar Cells in Vestibular Nerve

Bipolar neurons exist within the vestibular nerve as it is responsible for special sensory sensations including hearing, equilibrium and motion detection. The majority of the bipolar neurons belonging to the vestibular nerve exist within the vestibular ganglion with axons extending into the maculae of utricle and saccule as well as into the ampullae of the semicircular canals.

Bipolar Cells in Spinal Ganglia

Bipolar cells are also found in the spinal ganglia, when the cells are in an embryonic condition.

Sometimes the extensions, also called processes, come off from opposite poles of the cell, and the cell then assumes a spindle shape; in other cells both processes emerge at the same point.

In some cases where two fibers are apparently connected with a cell, one of the fibers is really derived from an adjoining nerve cell and is passing to end in a ramification around the ganglion cell, or, again, it may be coiled helically around the nerve process which is issuing from the cell.

Multipolar Neuron

A multipolar neuron (or multipolar neurone) is a type of neuron that possesses a single axon and many dendrites (and dendritic branches), allowing for the integration of a great deal of information from other neurons. These processes are projections from the nerve cell body. Multipolar neurons constitute the majority of neurons in the central nervous system. They include motor neurons and interneurons and are found mostly in the cortex of the brain, the spinal cord, and also in the autonomic ganglia.

Nerve Impulse

The membranes of the nerve cells have electrical potentials. Due to ionic changes it might become polarized. These changes in the electrical potential of the membrane of the nerve cell results into generation of nerve impulse. It begins with change in the permeability of the membrane and give rise to electrochemical events. These are known as nerve impulses. Normally these impulses start off in the axon hillock instead of dendrites or soma as the membrane is not excitable in these regions. With the generation of impulse in the axon hillock the surrounding membrane gets depolarized thus generating impulse in the adjacent part of the axon. These impulses do not travel backward because the membrane of soma is not excitable. The magnitude of these impulses do not depend upon the magnitude of the sensation, rather they follow all-or-none principle. This principle states that the nerve fibers either respond to the limit of their capability or do not get excited at all. A weak stimulation not capable of generating an impulse might end up resulting into local excitatory process.

The nature of nerve impulse is chemical. It consists of sodium-potassium (Na+-K+) pump, ion size, and diffusion pattern. In the resting state more sodium ions (Na+) are located outside the membrane. Potassium (K+) ions available in the fluid environment are actively transported into the neuron. However, they are insufficient to affect other ions. So, the outer membrane remains positively charged. Many negatively charged acid molecules (acid anions) are also present inside the cell. They are large enough to pass through the cell membrane. This also contributes in making the inner membrane negatively charged. The principle of diffusion is evident in the flow of ions and hence substances move from region of high concentration towards low concentration zone. Chlorine ions (Cl-) which carry negative charge freely move back and forth through the membrane.

Resting Membrane Potential and Action Potential

At rest (not transmitting an action potential) neuron maintains a voltage difference across its plasma membrane. The cytoplasmic fluid next to the membrane is negatively charged whereas the interstitial fluid outside the membrane is positively charged. This voltage difference is called the resting membrane potential. The resting membrane potential is –70 mv. The concentration of Na+ as well as K+ is higher outside the membrane and at the onset of conduction permeability of Na+ increases. This is the first event of action potential. Figure illustrates the process of spike generation.

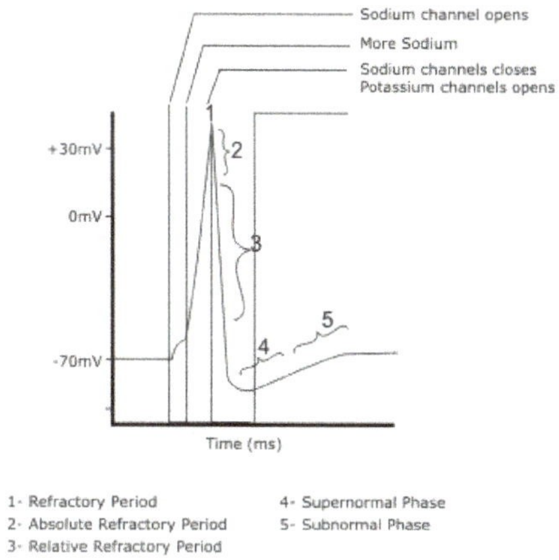

Spike generation.

This is followed by a gradient change of voltage from –70 mv to +35 mv, which in turn activates Na+- K+ pump. During the first phase, called as absolute refractory period, Na+ ions cannot enter the membrane and hence no current excites the neuron. It lasts for 1-10 milliseconds and is followed by relative refractory period which is 2-3 times that of the absolute refractory period. Only superthresholds are received during this period. The third phase is known as supernormal phase and its duration is 12 ms. During this phase stimulus at sub-threshold level are received. This is followed by the supernormal phase that lasts for 70 ms. and finally the nerve fiber attains resting membrane potential (-70 mv) and gets ready to receive incoming signals. Figure illustrates the mechanism of Na+- K+ pump.

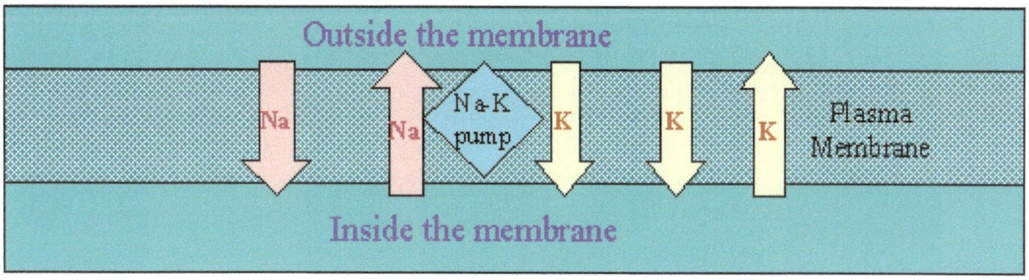

Na+- K+ pump.

Synapse

The junction between two neurons or neuron and muscle or gland is termed as synapse. Physically it is a cleft, a microscopic gap. The terminal ends of the axon and soma or dentrites of another neuron forms contact-points with each other. The initial end of synapse is called presynaptic terminal whereas postsynaptic terminals are the other end of synapse. A cleft of an average width of 200Å separates the two terminals. A wide variety of possibilities exist in terms of nature of the synapse. A single neuron may form synapse with the other neuron or many presynaptic end of neurons may converge on a single neuron's postsynaptic terminal or the presynaptic end of a neuron may branchoff and form synapse at multiple postsynaptic terminals.

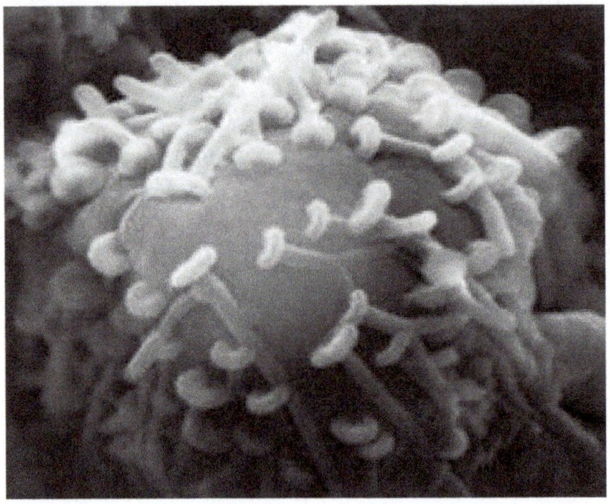

Scanning electron microscopic photograph of synaptic knobs at the end of an axon.

Based on the nature of connection, synapses are classified as axosomatic, axodendritic, and axo-axonic. As reflected in the nomenclature, axosomatic synapse is the junction of presynaptic axon of the first neuron and soma of the other neuron. The connection between basket and Purkinje cells in the cerebellum is an example of axosomatic synapse. Axodendritic synapse is the junction of presynaptic axon and dendrites of the postsynaptic cell. The climbing fibres and the dendrites of the Purkinje cells form axodendritic connection in the cerebellum. When the axon of the presynaptic cell ends in the axon of postsynaptic neuron it is called axo-axonic synapse. On the other hand, they are categorized as chemical and electrical synapse on the basis of functional characteristics. There are small protein tubular structures that allow ions to move from interior of one neuron to the other one. They are known as gap junctions. Action potentials are transmitted from a smooth muscle fibre to another visceral smooth muscle by way of such gap junctions. Such junctions are electrical synapses. In case of chemical synapses the presynaptic end of the neuron secretes a neurotransmitter which acts on receptor proteins in the membrane of the postsynaptic neuron.

Neurotransmitter

Neurotransmitters, also known as chemical messengers, are endogenous chemicals that enable neurotransmission. They transmit signals across a chemical synapse, such as a neuromuscular junction, from one neuron (nerve cell) to another "target" neuron, muscle cell, or gland cell. Neurotransmitters are released from synaptic vesicles in synapses into the synaptic cleft, where they are received by receptors on the target cells. Many neurotransmitters are synthesized from simple and plentiful precursors such as amino acids, which are readily available from the diet and only require a small number of biosynthetic steps for conversion. Neurotransmitters play a major role in shaping everyday life and functions. Their exact numbers are unknown, but more than 100 chemical messengers have been uniquely identified.

Mechanism

Neurotransmitters are stored in a synapse in synaptic vesicles, clustered beneath the membrane in the axon terminal located at the presynaptic side of the synapse. Neurotransmitters are released into and diffused across the synaptic cleft, where they bind to specific receptors in the membrane on the postsynaptic side of the synapse.

Most neurotransmitters are about the size of a single amino acid, however, some neurotransmitters may be the size of larger proteins or peptides. A released neurotransmitter is typically available in the synaptic cleft for a short time before it is metabolized by enzymes, pulled back into the presynaptic neuron through reuptake, or bound to a postsynaptic receptor. Nevertheless, short-term exposure of the receptor to a neurotransmitter is typically sufficient for causing a postsynaptic response by way of synaptic transmission.

In response to a threshold action potential or graded electrical potential, a neurotransmitter is released at the presynaptic terminal. Low level "baseline" release also occurs without electrical stimulation. The released neurotransmitter may then move across the synapse to be detected by and bind with receptors in the postsynaptic neuron. Binding of neurotransmitters may influence the postsynaptic neuron in either an inhibitory or excitatory way. This neuron may be connected to many more neurons, and if the total of excitatory influences are greater than those of inhibitory influences, the neuron will also "fire". Ultimately it will create a new action potential at its axon hillock to release neurotransmitters and pass on the information to yet another neighboring neuron.

Discovery

Until the early 20th century, scientists assumed that the majority of synaptic communication in the brain was electrical. However, through the careful histological examinations by Ramón y Cajal (1852–1934), a 20 to 40 nm gap between neurons, known today as the synaptic cleft, was discovered. The presence of such a gap suggested communication via chemical messengers traversing the synaptic cleft, and in 1921 German pharmacologist Otto Loewi (1873–1961) confirmed that neurons can communicate by releasing chemicals. Through a series of experiments involving the vagus nerves of frogs, Loewi was able to manually slow the heart rate of frogs by controlling the amount of saline solution present around the vagus nerve. Upon completion of this experiment, Loewi asserted that sympathetic regulation of cardiac function can be mediated through changes in chemical concentrations. Furthermore, Otto Loewi is credited with discovering acetylcholine (ACh)—the first known neurotransmitter. Some neurons do, however, communicate via electrical synapses through the use of gap junctions, which allow specific ions to pass directly from one cell to another.

Identification

There are four main criteria for identifying neurotransmitters:

1. The chemical must be synthesized in the neuron or otherwise be present in it.
2. When the neuron is active, the chemical must be released and produce a response in some target.

3. The same response must be obtained when the chemical is experimentally placed on the target.

4. A mechanism must exist for removing the chemical from its site of activation after its work is done.

However, given advances in pharmacology, genetics, and chemical neuroanatomy, the term "neurotransmitter" can be applied to chemicals that:

- Carry messages between neurons via influence on the postsynaptic membrane.
- Have little or no effect on membrane voltage, but have a common carrying function such as changing the structure of the synapse.
- Communicate by sending reverse-direction messages that affect the release or reuptake of transmitters.

The anatomical localization of neurotransmitters is typically determined using immunocytochemical techniques, which identify either the location of either the transmitter substances themselves, or of the enzymes that are involved in their synthesis. Immunocytochemical techniques have also revealed that many transmitters, particularly the neuropeptides, are co-localized, that is, one neuron may release more than one transmitter from its synaptic terminal. Various techniques and experiments such as staining, stimulating, and collecting can be used to identify neurotransmitters throughout the central nervous system.

Types

There are many different ways to classify neurotransmitters. Dividing them into amino acids, peptides, and monoamines is sufficient for some classification purposes.

Major neurotransmitters:

- Amino acids: glutamate, aspartate, D-serine, γ-aminobutyric acid (GABA), glycine
- Gasotransmitters: nitric oxide (NO), carbon monoxide (CO), hydrogen sulfide (H2S)
- Monoamines: dopamine (DA), norepinephrine (noradrenaline; NE, NA), epinephrine (adrenaline), histamine, serotonin (SER, 5-HT)
- Trace amines: phenethylamine, N-methylphenethylamine, tyramine, 3-iodothyronamine, octopamine, tryptamine, etc.
- Peptides: somatostatin, substance P, cocaine and amphetamine regulated transcript, opioid peptides
- Purines: adenosine triphosphate (ATP), adenosine
- Others: acetylcholine (ACh), anandamide, etc.

In addition, over 50 neuroactive peptides have been found, and new ones are discovered regularly. Many of these are "co-released" along with a small-molecule transmitter. Nevertheless, in some cases a peptide is the primary transmitter at a synapse. β-endorphin is a relatively well-known example of a peptide neurotransmitter because it engages in highly specific interactions with opioid receptors in the central nervous system.

Single ions (such as synaptically released zinc) are also considered neurotransmitters by some, as well as some gaseous molecules such as nitric oxide (NO), carbon monoxide (CO), and hydrogen sulfide (H_2S). The gases are produced in the neural cytoplasm and are immediately diffused through the cell membrane into the extracellular fluid and into nearby cells to stimulate production of second messengers. Soluble gas neurotransmitters are difficult to study, as they act rapidly and are immediately broken down, existing for only a few seconds.

The most prevalent transmitter is glutamate, which is excitatory at well over 90% of the synapses in the human brain. The next most prevalent is Gamma-Aminobutyric Acid, or GABA, which is inhibitory at more than 90% of the synapses that do not use glutamate. Although other transmitters are used in fewer synapses, they may be very important functionally: the great majority of psychoactive drugs exert their effects by altering the actions of some neurotransmitter systems, often acting through transmitters other than glutamate or GABA. Addictive drugs such as cocaine and amphetamines exert their effects primarily on the dopamine system. The addictive opiate drugs exert their effects primarily as functional analogs of opioid peptides, which, in turn, regulate dopamine levels.

List of Neurotransmitters, Peptides and Gasotransmitters

Category	Name	Abbreviation	Metabotropic	Ionotropic
Small: Amino acids (Arg)	Agmatine		α_2-Adrenergic receptors, imidazoline receptors	NMDA receptors
Small: Amino acids	Aspartate	Asp	–	NMDA receptors
Small: Amino acids	Glutamate	Glu	Metabotropic glutamate receptors	NMDA receptors, kainate receptors, AMPARs
Small: Amino acids	Gamma-aminobutyric acid	GABA	$GABA_B$ receptors	$GABA_A$ receptors, $GABA_A$-ρ receptors
Small: Amino acids	Glycine	Gly	–	NMDA receptors, glycine receptors
Small: Amino acids	D-serine	Ser	–	NMDA receptors
Small: Acetylcholine	Acetylcholine	Ach	Muscarinic acetylcholine receptors	Nicotinic acetylcholine receptors
Small: Monoamine (Phe/Tyr)	Dopamine	DA	Dopamine receptors, trace amine-associated receptor 1	–
Small: Monoamine (Phe/Tyr)	Norepinephrine (noradrenaline)	NE, NAd	Adrenergic receptors	–
Small: Monoamine (Phe/Tyr)	Epinephrine (adrenaline)	Epi, Ad	Adrenergic receptors	–
Small: Monoamine (Trp)	Serotonin (5-hydroxytryptamine)	5-HT	Serotonin receptors (all except $5\text{-}HT_3$)	$5\text{-}HT_3$
Small: Monoamine (His)	Histamine	H	Histamine receptors	–

Category	Name	Abbreviation	Metabotropic	Ionotropic
Small: Trace amine (Phe)	Phenethylamine	PEA	Human trace amine-associated receptors: hTAAR1, hTAAR2	–
Small: Trace amine (Phe)	*N*-methylphenethylamine	NMPEA	hTAAR1	–
Small: Trace amine (Phe/Tyr)	Tyramine	TYR	hTAAR1, hTAAR2	–
Small: Trace amine (Phe/Tyr)	Octopamine	Oct	hTAAR1	–
Small: Trace amine (Phe/Tyr)	Synephrine	Syn	hTAAR1	–
Small: Trace amine (Trp)	Tryptamine		hTAAR1, various serotonin receptors	–
Small: Trace amine (Trp)	*N*-methyltryptamine	NMT	hTAAR1, various serotonin receptors	–
Lipid	Anandamide	AEA	Cannabinoid receptors	–
Lipid	2-Arachidonoylglycerol	2-AG	Cannabinoid receptors	–
Lipid	2-Arachidonyl glyceryl ether	2-AGE	Cannabinoid receptors	–
Lipid	*N*-Arachidonoyl dopamine	NADA	Cannabinoid receptors	TRPV1
Lipid	Virodhamine		Cannabinoid receptors	–
Small: Purine	Adenosine	Ado	Adenosine receptors	–
Small: Purine	Adenosine triphosphate	ATP	P2Y receptors	P2X receptors
PP: Galanins	Galanin		GALR1, GALR2, GALR3	–
PP: Galanins	Galanin-like peptide		GALR1, GALR2, GALR3	–
PP: Gastrins	Gastrin		Cholecystokinin B receptor	–
PP: Gastrins	Cholecystokinin	CCK	Cholecystokinin receptors	–
PP: Neurohypophyseals	Vasopressin	AVP	Vasopressin receptors	–
PP: Neurohypophyseals	Oxytocin	OT	Oxytocin receptor	–
PP: Neurohypophyseals	Neurophysin I		–	–
PP: Neurohypophyseals	Neurophysin II		–	–
PP: Neuropeptide Y	Neuropeptide Y	NY	Neuropeptide Y receptors	–
PP: Neuropeptide Y	Pancreatic polypeptide	PP	–	–
PP: Neuropeptide Y	Peptide YY	PYY	–	–
PP: Opioids	Enkephalin		δ-Opioid receptor	–
PP: Opioids	Dynorphin		κ-Opioid receptor	–
PP: Opioids	Endorphin		μ-Opioid receptors	–

Category	Name	Abbreviation	Metabotropic	Ionotropic
PP: Opioids	Endomorphin		μ-Opioid receptors	–
PP: Orexins	Orexin A	OX-A	Orexin receptors	–
PP: Orexins	Orexin B	OX-B	Orexin receptors	–
PP: Secretins	Secretin		Secretin receptor	–
PP: Secretins	Motilin		Motilin receptor	–
PP: Secretins	Glucagon		Glucagon receptor	–
PP: Secretins	Vasoactive intestinal peptide	VIP	Vasoactive intestinal peptide receptors	–
PP: Secretins	Growth hormone–releasing hormone	GHRH	Growth hormone–releasing hormone receptor	–
PP: Somatostatins	Somatostatin		Somatostatin receptors	–
PP: Tachykinins	Neurokinin A		–	–
PP: Tachykinins	Neurokinin B		–	–
PP: Tachykinins	Substance P		–	–
PP: Tachykinins	Neuropeptide K		–	–
PP: Other	Adrenocorticotropic hormone	ACTH	ACTH receptor	–
PP: Other	*N*-Acetylaspartylglutamate	NAAG	Metabotropic glutamate receptor 3 (mGluR3)	–
PP: Other	Cocaine- and amphetamine-regulated transcript	CART	Unknown G_i/G_o-coupled receptor	–
PP: Other	Bombesin		–	–
PP: Other	Gastrin releasing peptide	GRP	–	–
PP: Other	Kisspeptin		GPR54	–
Gasotransmitter	Nitric oxide	NO	Soluble guanylyl cyclase	–
Gasotransmitter	Carbon monoxide	CO	–	Heme bound to potassium channels
Gasotransmitter	Hydrogen sulfide	H2S	–	–

Actions

Neurons form elaborate networks through which nerve impulses—action potentials—travel. Each neuron has as many as 15,000 connections with neighboring neurons.

Neurons do not touch each other (except in the case of an electrical synapse through a gap junction); instead, neurons interact at contact points called synapses: a junction within two nerve cells, consisting of a miniature gap which impulses pass by a neurotransmitter. A neuron transports its information by way of a nerve impulse called an action potential. When an action potential arrives at the synapse's presynaptic terminal button, it may stimulate the release of neurotransmitters. These neurotransmitters are released into the synaptic cleft to bind onto the receptors of the postsynaptic membrane and influence another cell, either in an inhibitory or excitatory way. The next neuron may be connected to many more neurons, and if the total of excitatory influences minus inhibitory influences is great enough, it will also "fire". That is to say, it will create a new action potential at its axon hillock, releasing neurotransmitters and passing on the information to yet another neighboring neuron.

Excitatory and Inhibitory

A neurotransmitter can influence the function of a neuron through a remarkable number of mechanisms. In its direct actions in influencing a neuron's electrical excitability, however, a neurotransmitter acts in only one of two ways: excitatory or inhibitory. A neurotransmitter influences trans-membrane ion flow either to increase (excitatory) or to decrease (inhibitory) the probability that the cell with which it comes in contact will produce an action potential. Thus, despite the wide variety of synapses, they all convey messages of only these two types, and they are labeled as such. Type I synapses are excitatory in their actions, whereas type II synapses are inhibitory. Each type has a different appearance and is located on different parts of the neurons under its influence. Each neuron receives thousands of excitatory and inhibitory signals every second.

Type I (excitatory) synapses are typically located on the shafts or the spines of dendrites, whereas type II (inhibitory) synapses are typically located on a cell body. In addition, Type I synapses have round synaptic vesicles, whereas the vesicles of type II synapses are flattened. The material on the presynaptic and post-synaptic membranes is denser in a Type I synapse than it is in a type II, and the type I synaptic cleft is wider. Finally, the active zone on a Type I synapse is larger than that on a Type II synapse.

The different locations of type I and type II synapses divide a neuron into two zones: an excitatory dendritic tree and an inhibitory cell body. From an inhibitory perspective, excitation comes in over the dendrites and spreads to the axon hillock to trigger an action potential. If the message is to be stopped, it is best stopped by applying inhibition on the cell body, close to the axon hillock where the action potential originates. Another way to conceptualize excitatory–inhibitory interaction is to picture excitation overcoming inhibition. If the cell body is normally in an inhibited state, the only way to generate an action potential at the axon hillock is to reduce the cell body's inhibition. In this "open the gates" strategy, the excitatory message is like a racehorse ready to run down the track, but first the inhibitory starting gate must be removed.

Examples of Important Neurotransmitter Actions

As explained above, the only direct action of a neurotransmitter is to activate a receptor. Therefore, the effects of a neurotransmitter system depend on the connections of the neurons that use the transmitter, and the chemical properties of the receptors that the transmitter binds to.

Here are a few examples of important neurotransmitter actions:

- Glutamate is used at the great majority of fast excitatory synapses in the brain and spinal cord. It is also used at most synapses that are "modifiable", i.e. capable of increasing or decreasing in strength. Modifiable synapses are thought to be the main memory-storage elements in the brain. Excessive glutamate release can overstimulate the brain and lead to excitotoxicity causing cell death resulting in seizures or strokes. Excitotoxicity has been implicated in certain chronic diseases including ischemic stroke, epilepsy, Amyotrophic lateral sclerosis, Alzheimer's disease, Huntington disease, and Parkinson's disease.

- GABA is used at the great majority of fast inhibitory synapses in virtually every part of the brain. Many sedative/tranquilizing drugs act by enhancing the effects of GABA. Correspondingly, glycine is the inhibitory transmitter in the spinal cord.
- Acetylcholine was the first neurotransmitter discovered in the peripheral and central nervous systems. It activates skeletal muscles in the somatic nervous system and may either excite or inhibit internal organs in the autonomic system. It is distinguished as the transmitter at the neuromuscular junction connecting motor nerves to muscles. The paralytic arrow-poison curare acts by blocking transmission at these synapses. Acetylcholine also operates in many regions of the brain, but using different types of receptors, including nicotinic and muscarinic receptors.
- Dopamine has a number of important functions in the brain; this includes regulation of motor behavior, pleasures related to motivation and also emotional arousal. It plays a critical role in the reward system; people with Parkinson's disease have been linked to low levels of dopamine and people with schizophrenia have been linked to high levels of dopamine.
- Serotonin is a monoamine neurotransmitter. Most is produced by and found in the intestine (approximately 90%), and the remainder in central nervous system neurons. It functions to regulate appetite, sleep, memory and learning, temperature, mood, behaviour, muscle contraction, and function of the cardiovascular system and endocrine system. It is speculated to have a role in depression, as some depressed patients are seen to have lower concentrations of metabolites of serotonin in their cerebrospinal fluid and brain tissue.
- Norepinephrine which focuses on the central nervous system, based on patients sleep patterns, focus and alertness. It is synthesized from tyrosine.
- Epinephrine which is also synthesized from tyrosine takes part in controlling the adrenal glands. It plays a role in sleep, with ones ability to become and stay alert, and the fight-or-flight response.
- Histamine works with the central nervous system (CNS), specifically the hypothalamus (tuberomammillary nucleus) and CNS mast cells.

Brain Neurotransmitter Systems

Neurons expressing certain types of neurotransmitters sometimes form distinct systems, where activation of the system affects large volumes of the brain, called volume transmission. Major neurotransmitter systems include the noradrenaline (norepinephrine) system, the dopamine system, the serotonin system, and the cholinergic system, among others. It should be noted that trace amines, primarily via TAAR1 activation, have a very significant effect on neurotransmission in monoamine pathways (i.e., dopamine, histamine, norepinephrine, and serotonin pathways) throughout the brain. A brief comparison of these systems follows:

Neurotransmitter Systems in the Brain		
System	**Pathway origin and projections**	**Regulated cognitive processes and behaviors**

Noradrenaline system	**Noradrenergic pathways**:
	• Locus coeruleus (LC) projections
	  • LC → Amygdala and Hippocampus
	  • LC → Brain stem and Spinal cord
	  • LC → Cerebellum
	  • LC → Cerebral cortex
	  • LC → Hypothalamus
	  • LC → Tectum
	  • LC → Thalamus
	  • LC → Ventral tegmental area
	• Lateral tegmental field (LTF) projections
	  • LTF → Brain stem and Spinal cord
	  • LTF → Olfactory bulb
		• anxiety
		• arousal (wakefulness and attention)
		• circadian rhythm
		• cognitive control and working memory (co-regulated by dopamine)
		• hunger
		• medullary control of respiration
		• negative emotional memory
		• reward perception (minor role)

Dopamine system	**Dopaminergic pathways**:
	• Ventral tegmental area (VTA) projections
	  • VTA → Amygdala
	  • VTA → Cingulate cortex
	  • VTA → Hippocampus
	  • VTA → Nucleus accumbens (Mesolimbic pathway)
	  • VTA → Olfactory bulb
	  • VTA → Prefrontal cortex (Mesocortical pathway)
	• Nigrostriatal pathway
	  • Substantia nigra → Caudate nucleus and putamen
	• Tuberoinfundibular pathway
	  • Arcuate nucleus → Median eminence
		• aversion
		• cognitive control and working memory (co-regulated by norepinephrine)
		• mood
		• reward perception (primary mediator)
		• positive reinforcement
		• motivation (incentive salience)
		• motor system function
		• sexual arousal, orgasm, and refractory period (via neuroendocrine regulation)

Histamine system	**Histaminergic pathways**:
	• Tuberomammillary nucleus (TMN) projections
	  • TMN → Cerebral cortex
	  • TMN → Hippocampus
	  • TMN → Neostriatum
	  • TMN → Nucleus accumbens
	  • TMN → Amygdala
	  • TMN → Hypothalamus
		• arousal (wakefulness and attention)
		• feeding and energy balance
		• learning
		• memory
		• sleep

Serotonin system	**Serotonergic pathways**:
	Caudal nuclei (CN): Raphe magnus, raphe pallidus, and raphe obscurus
	• Caudal projections
	  • CN → Cerebral cortex
	  • CN → Thalamus
	  • CN → Caudate-putamen and nucleus accumbens
	  • CN → Substantia nigra and ventral tegmental area
	Rostral nuclei (RN): Nucleus linearis, dorsal raphe, medial raphe, and raphe pontis
	• Rostral projections
	  • RN → Amygdala
	  • RN → Cingulate cortex
	  • RN → Hippocampus
	  • RN → Hypothalamus
	  • RN → Neocortex
	  • RN → Septum
	  • RN → Thalamus
	  • RN → Ventral tegmental area
		• appetite satiety
		• arousal (wakefulness and attention)
		• body temperature regulation
		• emotion and mood, potentially including aggression
		• reward perception (minor role)
		• sensory perception
		• sleep

<table>
<tr>
<td>Acetylcholine system</td>
<td>Cholinergic pathways:
Forebrain cholinergic nuclei (FCN): Nucleus basalis of Meynert, medial septal nucleus, and diagonal band
• Forebrain nuclei projections
  • FCN → Hippocampus
  • FCN → Cerebral cortex
  • FCN → Limbic cortex and sensory cortex
Brainstem cholinergic nuclei (BCN): Pedunculopontine nucleus, laterodorsal tegmentum, medial habenula, and parabigeminal nucleus
• Brainstem nuclei projections
  • BCN → Ventral tegmental area
  • BCN → Thalamus</td>
<td>• arousal (wakefulness and attention)
• emotion
• learning
• motor system function
• short-term memory
• reward perception (minor role)</td>
</tr>
</table>

Drug Effects

Understanding the effects of drugs on neurotransmitters comprises a significant portion of research initiatives in the field of neuroscience. Most neuroscientists involved in this field of research believe that such efforts may further advance our understanding of the circuits responsible for various neurological diseases and disorders, as well as ways to effectively treat and someday possibly prevent or cure such illnesses.

Drugs can influence behavior by altering neurotransmitter activity. For instance, drugs can decrease the rate of synthesis of neurotransmitters by affecting the synthetic enzyme(s) for that neurotransmitter. When neurotransmitter syntheses are blocked, the amount of neurotransmitters available for release becomes substantially lower, resulting in a decrease in neurotransmitter activity. Some drugs block or stimulate the release of specific neurotransmitters. Alternatively, drugs can prevent neurotransmitter storage in synaptic vesicles by causing the synaptic vesicle membranes to leak. Drugs that prevent a neurotransmitter from binding to its receptor are called receptor antagonists. For example, drugs used to treat patients with schizophrenia such as haloperidol, chlorpromazine, and clozapine are antagonists at receptors in the brain for dopamine. Other drugs act by binding to a receptor and mimicking the normal neurotransmitter. Such drugs are called receptor agonists. An example of a receptor agonist is Valium, a benzodiazepine that mimics effects of the endogenous neurotransmitter gamma-aminobutyric acid (GABA) to decrease anxiety. Other drugs interfere with the deactivation of a neurotransmitter after it has been released, thereby prolonging the action of a neurotransmitter. This can be accomplished by blocking re-uptake or inhibiting degradative enzymes. Lastly, drugs can also prevent an action potential from occurring, blocking neuronal activity throughout the central and peripheral nervous system. Drugs such as tetrodotoxin that block neural activity are typically lethal.

Drugs targeting the neurotransmitter of major systems affect the whole system, which can explain the complexity of action of some drugs. Cocaine, for example, blocks the re-uptake of dopamine back into the presynaptic neuron, leaving the neurotransmitter molecules in the synaptic gap for an extended period of time. Since the dopamine remains in the synapse longer, the neurotransmitter continues to bind to the receptors on the postsynaptic neuron, eliciting a pleasurable emotional response. Physical addiction to cocaine may result from prolonged exposure to excess dopamine in the synapses, which leads to the downregulation of some post-synaptic receptors. After the effects of the drug wear off, an individual can become depressed due to decreased probability of the neurotransmitter binding to a receptor. Fluoxetine is a selective serotonin re-uptake inhibitor (SSRI), which blocks re-uptake of serotonin by the presynaptic cell which increases the amount of serotonin present at the synapse and furthermore allows it to remain there longer, providing potential for the effect of naturally released serotonin. AMPT prevents the conversion of tyrosine to L-DOPA, the precursor to dopamine; reserpine prevents dopamine storage within vesicles; and deprenyl inhibits monoamine oxidase (MAO)-B and thus increases dopamine levels.

Agonists

An agonist is a chemical capable of binding to a receptor, such as a neurotransmitter receptor, and initiating the same reaction typically produced by the binding of the endogenous substance. An agonist of a neurotransmitter will thus initiate the same receptor response as the transmitter. In neurons, an agonist drug may activate neurotransmitter receptors either directly or indirectly. Direct-binding agonists can be further characterized as full agonists, partial agonists, inverse agonists.

Direct agonists act similar to a neurotransmitter by binding directly to its associated receptor site(s), which may be located on the presynaptic neuron or postsynaptic neuron, or both. Typically, neurotransmitter receptors are located on the postsynaptic neuron, while neurotransmitter autoreceptors are located on the presynaptic neuron, as is the case for monoamine neurotransmitters; in some cases, a neurotransmitter utilizes retrograde neurotransmission, a type of feedback signaling in neurons where the neurotransmitter is released postsynaptically and binds to target receptors located on the presynaptic neuron. Nicotine, a compound found in tobacco, is a direct agonist of most nicotinic acetylcholine receptors, mainly located in cholinergic neurons. Opiates, such as morphine, heroin, hydrocodone, oxycodone, codeine, and methadone, are μ-opioid receptor agonists; this action mediates their euphoriant and pain relieving properties.

Indirect agonists increase the binding of neurotransmitters at their target receptors by stimulating the release or preventing the reuptake of neurotransmitters. Some indirect agonists trigger neurotransmitter release and prevent neurotransmitter reuptake. Amphetamine, for example, is an indirect agonist of postsynaptic dopamine, norepinephrine, and serotonin receptors in each their respective neurons; it produces both neurotransmitter release into the presynaptic neuron and subsequently the synaptic cleft and prevents their reuptake from the synaptic cleft by activating TAAR1, a presynaptic G protein-coupled receptor, and binding to a site on VMAT2, a type of monoamine transporter located on synaptic vesicles within monoamine neurons.

Antagonists

An antagonist is a chemical that acts within the body to reduce the physiological activity of another chemical substance (as an opiate); especially one that opposes the action on the nervous system of a drug or a substance occurring naturally in the body by combining with and blocking its nervous receptor.

There are two main types of antagonist: direct-acting Antagonist and indirect-acting Antagonists:

1. Direct-acting antagonist- which takes up space present on receptors which are otherwise taken up by neurotransmitters themselves. This results in neurotransmitters being blocked from binding to the receptors. The most common is called Atropine.
2. Indirect-acting antagonist- drugs that inhibit the release/production of neurotransmitters (e.g., Reserpine).

Drug Antagonists

An antagonist drug is one that attaches (or binds) to a site called a receptor without activating that receptor to produce a biological response. It is therefore said to have no intrinsic activity. An antagonist may also be called a receptor "blocker" because they block the effect of an agonist at the site. The pharmacological effects of an antagonist therefore result in preventing the corresponding receptor site's agonists (e.g., drugs, hormones, neurotransmitters) from binding to and activating it. Antagonists may be "competitive" or "irreversible".

A competitive antagonist competes with an agonist for binding to the receptor. As the concentration of antagonist increases, the binding of the agonist is progressively inhibited, resulting in a decrease in the physiological response. High concentration of an antagonist can completely inhibit the response. This inhibition can be reversed, however, by an increase of the concentration of the agonist, since the agonist and antagonist compete for binding to the receptor. Competitive antagonists, therefore, can be characterized as shifting the dose-response relationship for the agonist to the right. In the presence of a competitive antagonist, it takes an increased concentration of the agonist to produce the same response observed in the absence of the antagonist.

An irreversible antagonist binds so strongly to the receptor as to render the receptor unavailable for binding to the agonist. Irreversible antagonists may even form covalent chemical bonds with the receptor. In either case, if the concentration of the irreversible antagonist is high enough, the number of unbound receptors remaining for agonist binding may be so low that even high concentrations of the agonist do not produce the maximum biological response.

Precursors

While intake of neurotransmitter precursors does increase neurotransmitter synthesis, evidence is mixed as to whether neurotransmitter release and postsynaptic receptor firing is increased. Even with increased neurotransmitter release, it is unclear whether this will result in a long-term increase in neurotransmitter signal strength, since the nervous system can adapt to changes such as increased neurotransmitter synthesis and may therefore maintain constant firing. Some neurotransmitters may have a role in depression and there is some evidence to suggest that intake of precursors of these neurotransmitters may be useful in the treatment of mild and moderate depression.

Catecholamine and Trace Amine Precursors

L-DOPA, a precursor of dopamine that crosses the blood–brain barrier, is used in the treatment of Parkinson's disease. For depressed patients where low activity of the neurotransmitter norepinephrine is implicated, there is only little evidence for benefit of neurotransmitter precursor administration. L-phenylalanine and L-tyrosine are both precursors for dopamine, norepinephrine, and epinephrine. These conversions require vitamin B6, vitamin C, and S-adenosylmethionine. A few studies suggest potential antidepressant effects of L-phenylalanine and L-tyrosine, but there is much room for further research in this area.

Serotonin Precursors

Administration of L-tryptophan, a precursor for serotonin, is seen to double the production of serotonin in the brain. It is significantly more effective than a placebo in the treatment of mild and moderate depression. This conversion requires vitamin C. 5-hydroxytryptophan (5-HTP), also a precursor for serotonin, is more effective than a placebo.

Diseases and Disorders

Diseases and disorders may also affect specific neurotransmitter systems. For example, problems in producing dopamine can result in Parkinson's disease, a disorder that affects a person's ability to move as they want to, resulting in stiffness, tremors or shaking, and other symptoms. Some studies suggest that having too little or too much dopamine or problems using dopamine in the thinking and feeling regions of the brain may play a role in disorders like schizophrenia or attention deficit hyperactivity disorder (ADHD). Similarly, after some research suggested that drugs that block the recycling, or reuptake, of serotonin seemed to help some people diagnosed with depression, it was theorized that people with depression might have lower-than-normal serotonin levels. Though widely popularized, this theory was not borne out in subsequent research. Furthermore, problems with producing or using glutamate have been suggestively and tentatively linked to many mental disorders, including autism, obsessive compulsive disorder (OCD), schizophrenia, and depression.

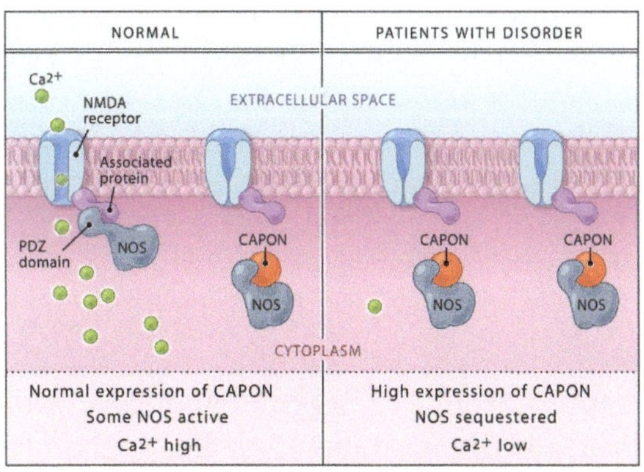

CAPON Binds Nitric Oxide Synthase, Regulating NMDA Receptor–Mediated Glutamate Neurotransmission.

Neurotransmitter Imbalance

Generally, there are no scientifically established "norms" for appropriate levels or "balances" of different neurotransmitters. It is in most cases pragmatically impossible to even measure levels of neurotransmitters in a brain or body at any distinct moments in time. Neurotransmitters regulate each other's release, and weak consistent imbalances in this mutual regulation were linked to temperament in healthy people . Strong imbalances or disruptions to neurotransmitter systems have been associated with many diseases and mental disorders. These include Parkinson's, depression, insomnia, Attention Deficit Hyperactivity Disorder (ADHD), anxiety, memory loss, dramatic changes in weight and addictions. Chronic physical or emotional stress can be a contributor to neurotransmitter system changes. Genetics also plays a role in neurotransmitter activities. Medications that directly react with serotonin and norepinephrine are prescribed to patients with problems such as depression and anxiety—though the notion that there is much solid medical evidence to support such interventions has been widely criticized.

Elimination of Neurotransmitters

A neurotransmitter must be broken down once it reaches the post-synaptic cell to prevent further excitatory or inhibitory signal transduction. This allows new signals to be produced from the adjacent nerve cells. When the neurotransmitter has been secreted into the synaptic cleft, it binds to specific receptors on the postsynaptic cell, thereby generating a postsynaptic electrical signal. The transmitter must then be removed rapidly to enable the postsynaptic cell to engage in another cycle of neurotransmitter release, binding, and signal generation. Neurotransmitters are terminated in three different ways:

1. Diffusion – the neurotransmitter detaches from receptor, drifting out of the synaptic cleft, here it becomes absorbed by glial cells.
2. Enzyme degradation – special chemicals called enzymes break it down.
3. Reuptake – re-absorption of a neurotransmitter into the neuron. Transporters, or membrane transport proteins, pump neurotransmitters from the synaptic cleft back into axon terminals (the presynaptic neuron) where they are stored.

For example, choline is taken up and recycled by the pre-synaptic neuron to synthesize more ACh. Other neurotransmitters such as dopamine are able to diffuse away from their targeted synaptic junctions and are eliminated from the body via the kidneys, or destroyed in the liver. Each neurotransmitter has very specific degradation pathways at regulatory points, which may be targeted by the body's regulatory system or by recreational drugs.

Synaptic Transmission

The presynaptic knob has synaptic vesicles containing neurotransmitters. The neurotransmitters play vital role in mediating impulse from pre to postsynaptic terminals. The impulse in the presynaptic neuron gets the neurotransmitters released in the synaptic cleft which, in turn, triggers impulse in the postsynaptic neuron. Figure illustrates the mechanism of neural transmission at synapse.

The time needed for an impulse to get transmitted through the synapse is more than the transmission time required in the neuron. This is termed as synaptic delay. The nature of synaptic transmission is held responsible for it.

As described earlier, neurotransmitters play significant role in synaptic transmission. The first neurotransmitter was discovered in 1921 by Austrian scientist Otto Loewi. Since then research in endocrinology and other areas have added to our knowledge about the neurotransmitters.

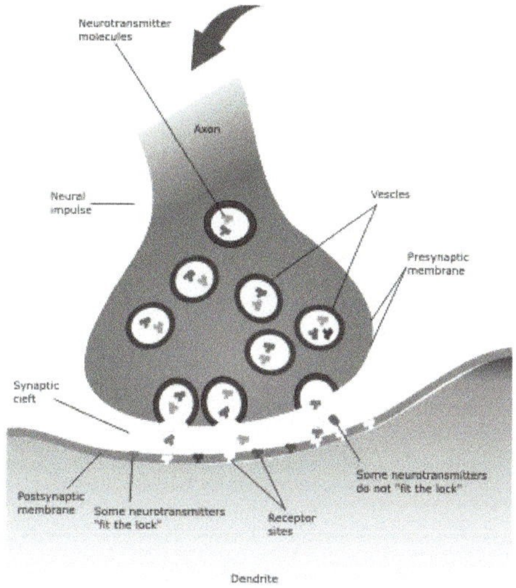

Transmission at synapse.

References

- Gross L. ""Supporting" players take the lead in protecting the overstimulated brain". PLoS Biol. 4: e371. doi:10.1371/journal.pbio.0040371. PMC 1609133 . PMID 20076484
- Whishaw, Bryan Kolb, Ian Q. (2014). An introduction to brain and behavior (4th ed.). New York, NY: Worth Publishers. pp. 150–151. ISBN 978-1429242288
- Snyder SH, Innis RB (1979). "Peptide neurotransmitters". Annu. Rev. Biochem. 48: 755–82. PMID 38738. doi:10.1146/annurev.bi.48.070179.003543
- Depue RA, Morrone-Strupinsky JV (2005). "A neurobehavioural model of affiliate bonding: implications for conceptualizing a human trait of affiliation". Journal of Behavioral and Brain Science. 28 (3): 313–350
- Saladin, Kenneth S. Anatomy and Physiology: The Unity of Form and Function. McGraw Hill. 2009 ISBN 0-07-727620-5
- "Dopamine: Biological activity". IUPHAR/BPS guide to pharmacology. International Union of Basic and Clinical Pharmacology. Retrieved 29 January 2016
- Broadley KJ (March 2010). "The vascular effects of trace amines and amphetamines". Pharmacol. Ther. 125 (3): 363–375. PMID 19948186. doi:10.1016/j.pharmthera.2009.11.005
- Goeders, Nick E. (2001). "Antagonist". Encyclopedia of Drugs, Alcohol, and Addictive Behavior. Retrieved 2 December 2014
- Ikemoto S (2010). "Brain reward circuitry beyond the mesolimbic dopamine system: a neurobiological theory". Neurosci Biobehav Rev. 35 (2): 129–50. PMC 2894302 . PMID 20149820. doi:10.1016/j.neubiorev.2010.02.001
- Rang, H. P. (2003). Pharmacology. Edinburgh: Churchill Livingstone. pp. 474 for noradrenaline system, page 476 for dopamine system, page 480 for serotonin system and page 483 for cholinergic system. ISBN 0-443-07145-4
- Leo, J., & Lacasse, J. (2007, 10 October). The Media and the Chemical Imbalance Theory of Depression. Retrieved 1 December 2014

2

Human Nervous System: An Introduction

The human nervous system comprises of the central nervous system and the peripheral nervous system. The central nervous system consists of the brain and the spinal cord while the peripheral nervous system is made up of nerves and ganglia. The chapter on human nervous system offers an insightful focus, keeping in mind the complex subject matter.

Human Nervous System

The study of complex human behaviour and their association with anatomy of the brain has gone a long way. With the availability of brain imaging techniques and certain software it is possible to look into a functional brain.

For convenience as well as on the basis of operation, the nervous system is classified into two major subsystems— the central nervous system and the peripheral nervous system. The central nervous system comprises of the brain and spinal cord. The peripheral nervous system, on the other hand, consists of the somatic and the autonomic nervous system. The autonomic nervous system has two divisions- sympathetic and parasympathetic divisions.

Central Nervous System

The central nervous system (CNS) is the part of the nervous system consisting of the brain and spinal cord. The central nervous system is so named because it integrates information it receives from, and coordinates and influences the activity of all parts of the bodies of bilaterally symmetric animals—that is, all multicellular animals except sponges and radially symmetric animals such as jellyfish—and it contains the majority of the nervous system. Many consider the retina and the optic nerve (2nd cranial nerve), as well as the olfactory nerves (1st) and olfactory epithelium as parts of the CNS, synapsing directly on brain tissue without intermediate ganglia. Following this classification the olfactory epithelium is the only central nervous tissue in direct contact with the environment, which opens up for therapeutic treatments. The CNS is contained within the dorsal body cavity, with the brain housed in the cranial cavity and the spinal cord in the spinal canal. In vertebrates, the brain is protected by the skull, while the spinal cord is protected by the vertebrae, both -brain and spinal cord- enclosed in the meninges.

Structure

The central nervous system consists of the two major structures: the brain and spinal cord. The brain is encased in the skull, and protected by the cranium. The spinal cord is continuous with the brain and lies caudally to the brain, and is protected by the vertebra. The spinal cord reaches from the base of the skull, continues through or starting below the foramen magnum, and terminates roughly level with the first or second lumbar vertebra, occupying the upper sections of the vertebral canal.

White and Gray Matter

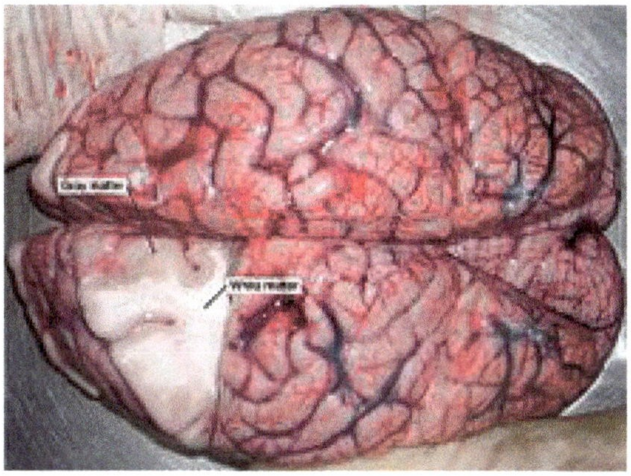

Dissection of a brain with labels showing the clear division between white and gray matter.

Microscopically, there are differences between the neurons and tissue of the central nervous system and the peripheral nervous system. The central nervous system is divided in white and gray matter. This can also be seen macroscopically on brain tissue. The white matter consists of axons and oligodendrocytes, while the gray matter consists of neurons and unmyelinated fibers. Both tissues include a number of glial cells (although the white matter contains more), which are often referred to as supporting cells of the central nervous system. Different forms of glial cells have different functions, some acting almost as scaffolding for neuroblasts to climb during neurogenesis such as bergmann glia, while others such as microglia are a specialized form of macrophage, involved in the immune system of the brain as well as the clearance of various metabolites from the brain tissue. Astrocytes may be involved with both clearance of metabolites as well as transport of fuel and various beneficial substances to neurons from the capillaries of the brain. Upon CNS injury astrocytes will proliferate, causing gliosis, a form of neuronal scar tissue, lacking in functional neurons.

The brain (cerebrum as well as midbrain and hindbrain) consists of a cortex, composed of neuron-bodies constituting gray matter, while internally there is more white matter that form tracts and commissures. Apart from cortical gray matter there is also subcortical gray matter making up a large number of different nuclei.

Spinal Cord

From and to the spinal cord are projections of the peripheral nervous system in the form of spinal nerves (sometimes segmental nerves). The nerves connect the spinal cord to skin, joints, muscles etc. and allow for the transmission of efferent motor as well as afferent sensory signals and stimuli. This allows for voluntary and involuntary motions of muscles, as well as the perception of senses. All in all 31 spinal nerves project from the brain stem, some forming plexa as they branch out, such as the brachial plexa, sacral plexa etc. Each spinal nerve will carry both sensory and motor signals, but the nerves synapse at different regions of the spinal cord, either from the periphery to sensory relay neurons that relay the information to the CNS or from the CNS to motor neurons, which relay the information out.

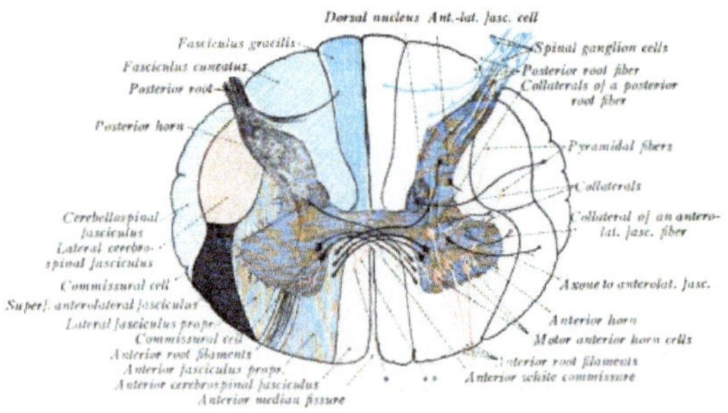

Diagram of the columns and of the course of the fibers in the spinal cord. Sensory synapses occur in the dorsal spinal cord (above in this image), and motor nerves leave through the ventral (as well as lateral) horns of the spinal cord as seen below in the image.

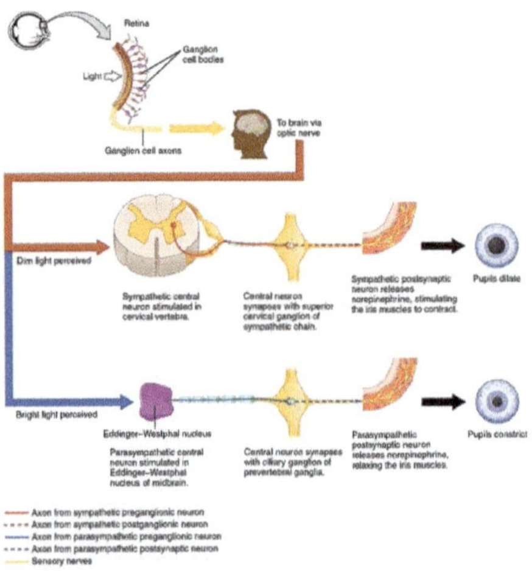

Different ways in which the central nervous system can be activated without engaging the cortex, and making us aware of the actions. The above example shows the process in which the pupil dilates during dim light, activating neurons in the spinal cord. The second example shows the constriction of the pupil as a result of the activation of the Edding-er-Westphal nucleus (a cerebral ganglion).

The spinal cord relays information up to the brain through spinal tracts through the "final common pathway" to the thalamus and ultimately to the cortex. Not all information is relayed to the cortex, and does not reach our immediate consciousness, but is instead transmitted only to the thalamus which sorts and adapts accordingly. This in turn may explain why we are not constantly aware of all aspects of our surroundings.

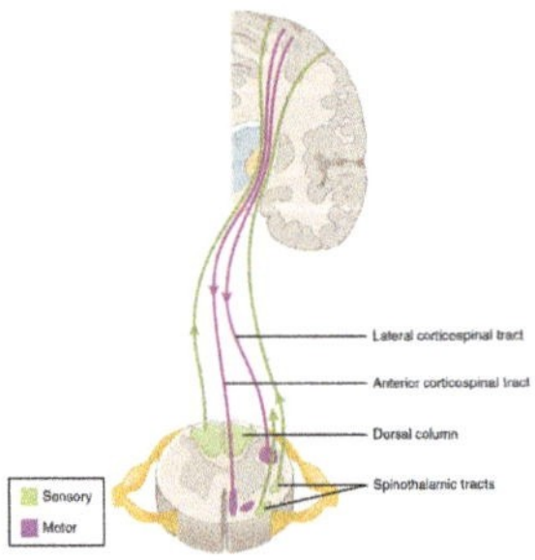

Schematic image showing the locations of a few tracts of the spinal cord.

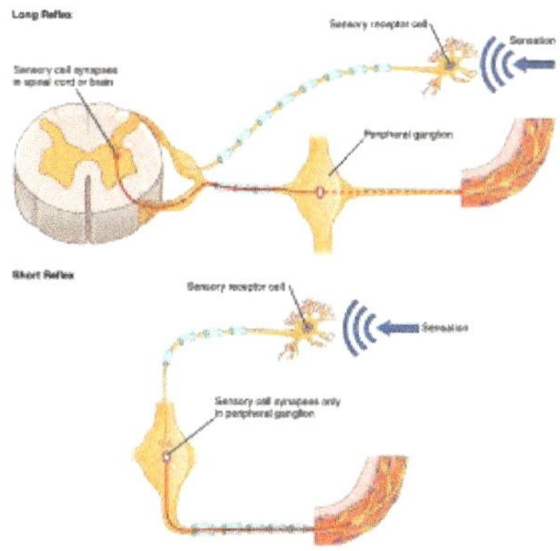

Reflexes may also occur without engaging more than one neuron of the central nervous system as in the below example of a short reflex.

Cranial Nerves

Apart from the spinal cord, there are also peripheral nerves of the PNS that synapse through intermediaries or ganglia directly on the CNS. These 12 nerves exist in the head and neck region and are called cranial nerves. Cranial nerves bring information to the CNS to and from the face, as well as to certain muscles (such as the trapezius muscle, which is innervated by accessory nerves as well as certain cervical spinal nerves).

Two pairs of cranial nerves; the olfactory nerves and the optic nerves are often considered structures of the central nervous system. This is because they do not synapse first on peripheral ganglia, but directly on central nervous neurons. The olfactory epithelium is significant in that it consists of central nervous tissue expressed in direct contact to the environment, allowing for administration of certain pharmaceuticals and drugs.

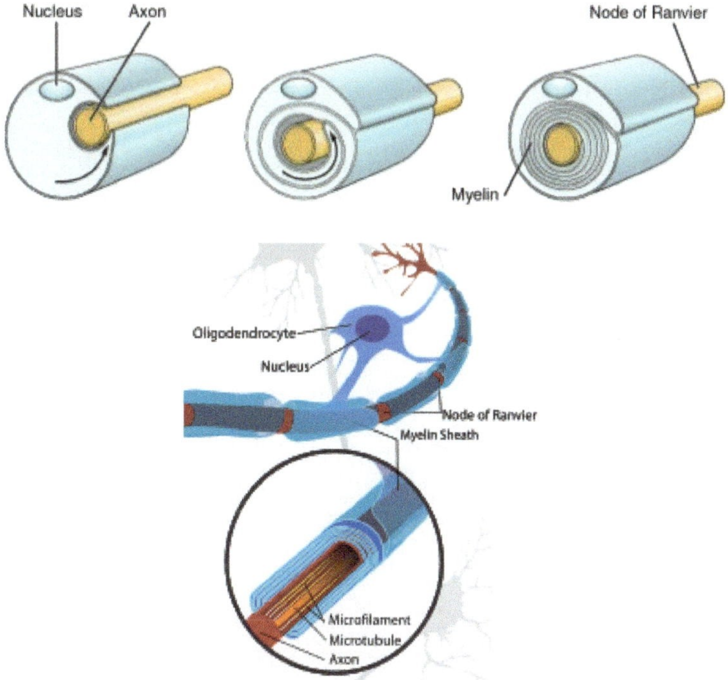

Myelinated peripheral nerve at top, central nervous neuron at bottom.

Brain

Rostrally to the spinal cord lies the brain. The brain makes up the largest portion of the central nervous system, and is often the main structure referred to when speaking of the nervous system. The brain is the major functional unit of the central nervous system. While the spinal cord has certain processing ability such as that of spinal locomotion and can process reflexes, the brain is the major processing unit of the nervous system.

Brainstem

The brainstem consists of the medulla, the pons and the midbrain. The medulla can be referred to as an extension of the spinal cord, and its organization and functional properties are similar to those of the spinal cord. The tracts passing from the spinal cord to the brain pass through here.

Regulatory functions of the medulla nuclei include control of the blood pressure and breathing. Other nuclei are involved in balance, taste, hearing and control of muscles of the face and neck.

The next structure rostral to the medulla is the pons, which lies on the ventral anterior side of the brainstem. Nuclei in the pons include pontine nuclei which work with the cerebellum and transmit information between the cerebellum and the cerebral cortex. In the dorsal posterior pons lie nuclei that have to do with breathing, sleep and taste.

The midbrain (or mesencephalon) is situated above and rostral to the pons, and includes nuclei linking distinct parts of the motor system, among others the cerebellum, the basal ganglia and both cerebral hemispheres. Additionally parts of the visual and auditory systems are located in the mid brain, including control of automatic eye movements.

The brainstem at large provides entry and exit to the brain for a number of pathways for motor and autonomic control of the face and neck through cranial nerves, and autonomic control of the organs is mediated by the tenth cranial (vagus) nerve. A large portion of the brainstem is involved in such autonomic control of the body. Such functions may engage the heart, blood vessels, pupillae, among others.

The brainstem also hold the reticular formation, a group of nuclei involved in both arousal and alertness.

Cerebellum

The cerebellum lies behind the pons. The cerebellum is composed of several dividing fissures and lobes. Its function includes the control of posture, and the coordination of movements of parts of the body, including the eyes and head as well as the limbs. Further it is involved in motion that has been learned and perfected though practice, and will adapt to new learned movements. Despite its previous classification as a motor structure, the cerebellum also displays connections to areas of the cerebral cortex involved in language as well as cognitive functions. These connections have been shown by the use of medical imaging techniques such as fMRI and PET.

The body of the cerebellum holds more neurons than any other structure of the brain including that of the larger cerebrum (or cerebral hemispheres), but is also more extensively understood than other structures of the brain, and includes fewer types of different neurons. It handles and processes sensory stimuli, motor information as well as balance information from the vestibular organ.

Diencephalon

The two structures of the diencephalon worth noting are the thalamus and the hypothalamus. The thalamus acts as a linkage between incoming pathways from the peripheral nervous system as well as the optical nerve (though it does not receive input from the olfactory nerve) to the cerebral hemispheres. Previously it was considered only a "relay station", but it is engaged in the sorting of information that will reach cerebral hemispheres (neocortex).

Apart from its function of sorting information from the periphery, the thalamus also connects the cerebellum and basal ganglia with the cerebrum. In common with the aforementioned reticular system the thalamus is involved in wakefullness and consciousness, such as though the SCN.

The hypothalamus engages in functions of a number of primitive emotions or feelings such as hunger, thirst and maternal bonding. This is regulated partly through control of secretion of hormones from the pituitary gland. Additionally the hypothalamus plays a role in motivation and many other behaviors of the individual.

Cerebrum

The cerebrum of cerebral hemispheres make up the largest visual portion of the human brain. Various structures combine forming the cerebral hemispheres, among others, the cortex, basal ganglia, amygdala and hippocampus. The hemispheres together control a large portion of the functions of the human brain such as emotion, memory, perception and motor functions. Apart from this the cerebral hemispheres stand for the cognitive capabilities of the brain.

Connecting each of the hemispheres is the corpus callosum as well as several additional commissures. One of the most important parts of the cerebral hemispheres is the cortex, made up of gray matter covering the surface of the brain. Functionally, the cerebral cortex is involved in planning and carrying out of everyday tasks.

The hippocampus is involved in storage of memories, the amygdala plays a role in perception and communication of emotion, while the basal ganglia play a major role in the coordination of voluntary movement.

Difference from the Peripheral Nervous System

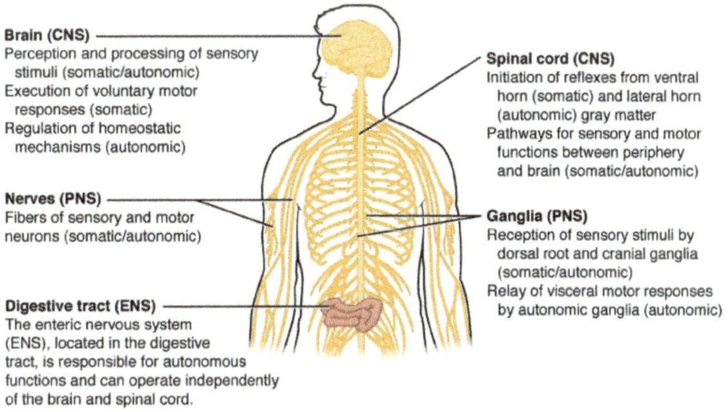

A map over the different structures of the nervous systems in the body, showing the CNS, PNS, and ENS.

This differentiates the central nervous system from the peripheral nervous system, which consists of neurons, axons and Schwann cells. Oligodendrocytes and Schwann cells have similar functions in the central and peripheral nervous system respectively. Both act to add myelin sheaths to the axons, which acts as a form of insulation allowing for better and faster proliferation of electrical signals along the nerves. Axons in the central nervous system are often very short (barely a few millimeters) and do not need the same degree of isolation as peripheral nerves do. Some peripheral nerves can be over 1m in length, such as the nerves to the big toe. To ensure signals move at sufficient speed, myelination is needed.

The way in which the Schwann cells and oligodendrocytes myelinate nerves differ. A Schwann cell usually myelinates a single axon, completely surrounding it. Sometimes they may myelinate many axons, especially when in areas of short axons. Oligodendrocytes usually myelinate several axons. They do this by sending out thin projections of their cell membrane which envelop and enclose the axon.

Development

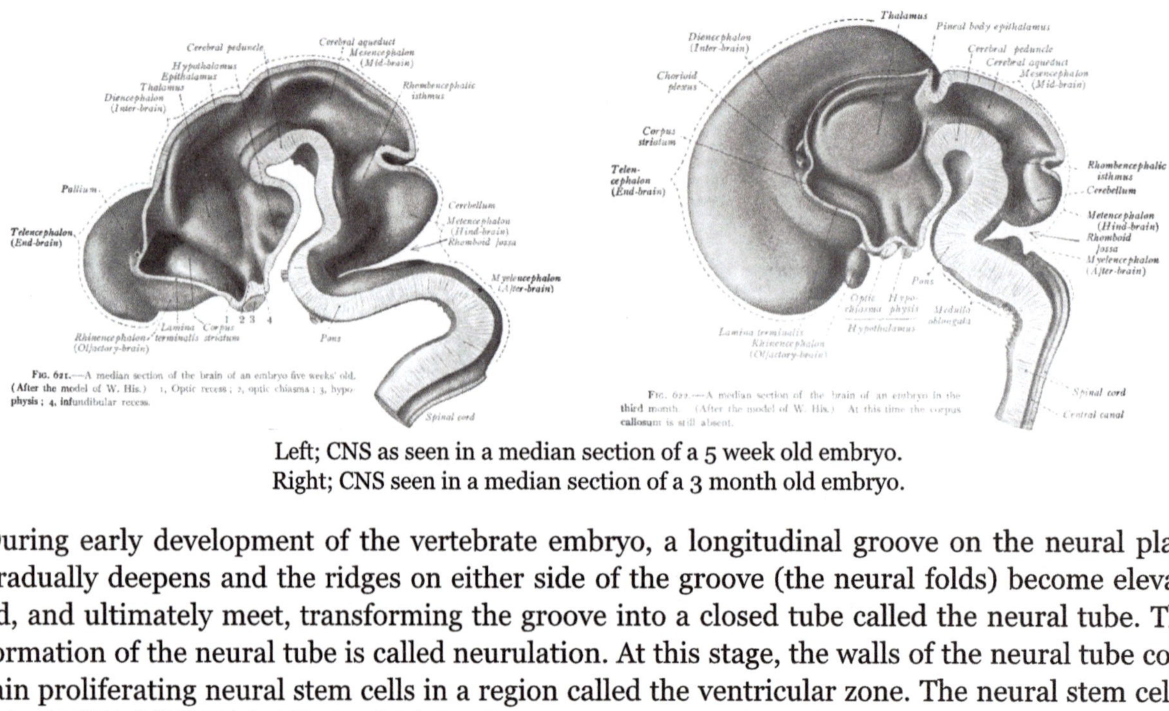

Left; CNS as seen in a median section of a 5 week old embryo.
Right; CNS seen in a median section of a 3 month old embryo.

During early development of the vertebrate embryo, a longitudinal groove on the neural plate gradually deepens and the ridges on either side of the groove (the neural folds) become elevated, and ultimately meet, transforming the groove into a closed tube called the neural tube. The formation of the neural tube is called neurulation. At this stage, the walls of the neural tube contain proliferating neural stem cells in a region called the ventricular zone. The neural stem cells, principally radial glial cells, multiply and generate neurons through the process of neurogenesis, forming the rudiment of the central nervous system.

The neural tube gives rise to both brain and spinal cord. The anterior (or 'rostral') portion of the neural tube initially differentiates into three brain vesicles (pockets): the prosencephalon at the front, the mesencephalon, and, between the mesencephalon and the spinal cord, the rhombencephalon. (By six weeks in the human embryo) the prosencephalon then divides further into the telencephalon and diencephalon; and the rhombencephalon divides into the metencephalon and myelencephalon. The spinal cord is derived from the posterior or 'caudal' portion of the neural tube.

As a vertebrate grows, these vesicles differentiate further still. The telencephalon differentiates into, among other things, the striatum, the hippocampus and the neocortex, and its cavity becomes the first and second ventricles. Diencephalon elaborations include the subthalamus, hypothalamus, thalamus and epithalamus, and its cavity forms the third ventricle. The tectum, pretectum, cerebral peduncle and other structures develop out of the mesencephalon, and its cavity grows into the mesencephalic duct (cerebral aqueduct). The metencephalon becomes, among other things, the pons and the cerebellum, the myelencephalon forms the medulla oblongata, and their cavities develop into the fourth ventricle.

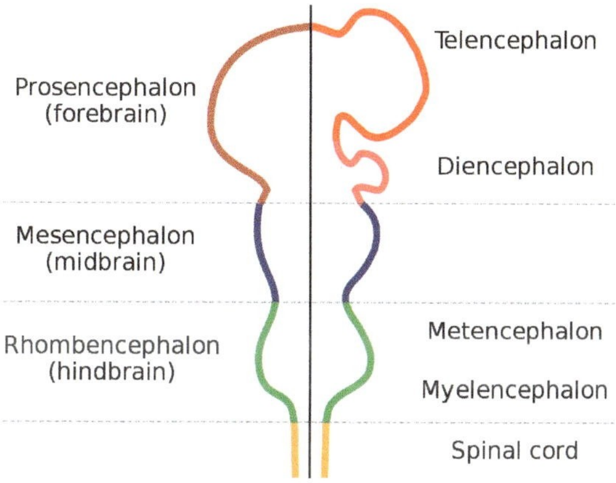

Diagram depicting the main subdivisions of the embryonic vertebrate brain, later forming forebrain, midbrain and hindbrain.

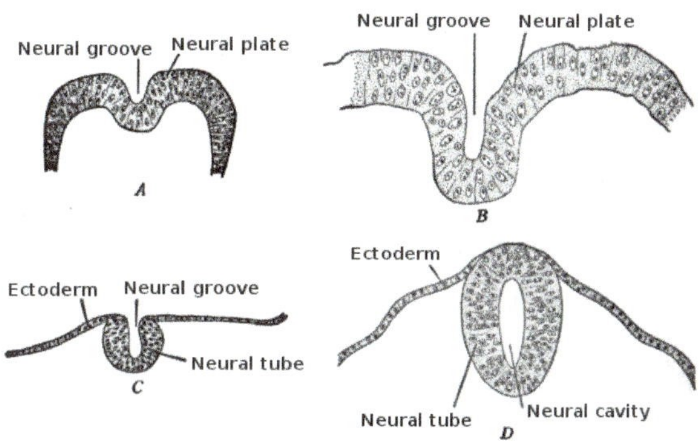

Development of the neural tube.

<table>
<tr><td rowspan="6">Central nervous system</td><td rowspan="5">Brain</td><td rowspan="2">Prosencephalon</td><td>Telencephalon</td><td colspan="2">Rhinencephalon, Amygdala, Hippocampus, Neocortex, Basal ganglia, Lateral ventricles</td></tr>
<tr><td>Diencephalon</td><td colspan="2">Epithalamus, Thalamus, Hypothalamus, Subthalamus, Pituitary gland, Pineal gland, Third ventricle</td></tr>
<tr><td rowspan="3">Brain stem</td><td>Mesencephalon</td><td colspan="2">Tectum, Cerebral peduncle, Pretectum, Mesencephalic duct</td></tr>
<tr><td rowspan="2">Rhombencephalon</td><td>Metencephalon</td><td>Pons, Cerebellum</td></tr>
<tr><td>Myelencephalon</td><td>Medulla oblongata</td></tr>
<tr><td colspan="5">Spinal cord</td></tr>
</table>

Evolution

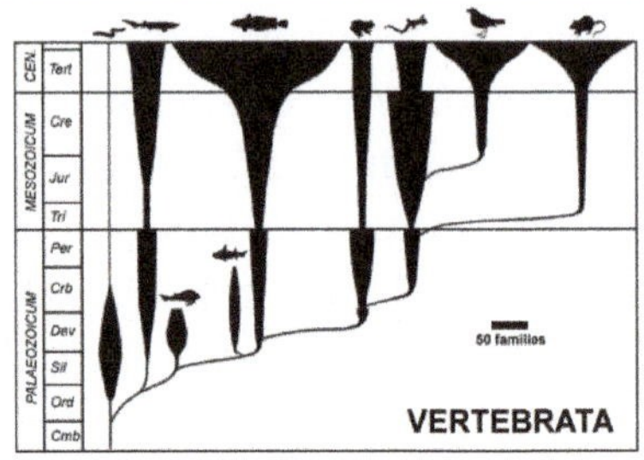

Left: the lancelet, regarded an archetypal vertebrate, lacking a true brain. Middle: an early vertebrate. Right: spindle diagram of the evolution of vertebrates.

Planaria

Planarians, members of the phylum Platyhelminthes (flatworms), have the simplest, clearly defined delineation of a nervous system into a central nervous system (CNS) and a peripheral nervous system (PNS). Their primitive brains, consisting of two fused anterior ganglia, and longitudinal nerve cords form the CNS; the laterally projecting nerves form the PNS. A molecular study found that more than 95% of the 116 genes involved in the nervous system of planarians, which includes genes related to the CNS, also exist in humans. Like planarians, vertebrates have a distinct CNS and PNS, though more complex than those of planarians.

Arthropoda

In arthropods, the ventral nerve cord, the subesophageal ganglia and the supraesophageal ganglia are usually seen as making up the CNS.

Chordata

The CNS of chordates differs from that of other animals in being placed dorsally in the body, above the gut and notochord/spine. The basic pattern of the CNS is highly conserved throughout the different species of vertebrates and during evolution. The major trend that can be observed is towards a progressive telencephalisation: the telencephalon of reptiles is only an appendix to the large olfactory bulb, while in mammals it makes up most of the volume of the CNS. In the human brain, the telencephalon covers most of the diencephalon and the mesencephalon. Indeed, the allometric study of brain size among different species shows a striking continuity from rats to whales, and allows us to complete the knowledge about the evolution of the CNS obtained through cranial endocasts.

Mammals

Mammals – which appear in the fossil record after the first fishes, amphibians, and reptiles – are the only vertebrates to possess the evolutionarily recent, outermost part of the cerebral cortex known as the neocortex. The neocortex of monotremes (the duck-billed platypus and several species of spiny anteaters) and of marsupials (such as kangaroos, koalas, opossums, wombats, and Tasmanian devils) lack the convolutions – gyri and sulci – found in the neocortex of most placental mammals (eutherians). Within placental mammals, the size and complexity of the neocortex increased over time. The area of the neocortex of mice is only about 1/100 that of monkeys, and that of monkeys is only about 1/10 that of humans. In addition, rats lack convolutions in their neocortex (possibly also because rats are small mammals), whereas cats have a moderate degree of convolutions, and humans have quite extensive convolutions. Extreme convolution of the neocortex is found in dolphins, possibly related to their complex echolocation.

Clinical Significance

Diseases

There are many central nervous system diseases and conditions, including infections of the central nervous system such as encephalitis and poliomyelitis, early-onset neurological disorders including ADHD and autism, late-onset neurodegenerative diseases such as Alzheimer's disease, Parkinson's disease, and essential tremor, autoimmune and inflammatory diseases such as multiple sclerosis and acute disseminated encephalomyelitis, genetic disorders such as Krabbe's disease and Huntington's disease, as well as amyotrophic lateral sclerosis and adrenoleukodystrophy. Lastly, cancers of the central nervous system can cause severe illness and, when malignant, can have very high mortality rates.

Specialty professional organizations recommend that neurological imaging of the brain be done only to answer a specific clinical question and not as routine screening.

Brain

The brain is an organ that serves as the center of the nervous system in all vertebrate and most invertebrate animals. The brain is located in the head, usually close to the sensory organs for senses such as vision. The brain is the most complex organ in a vertebrate's body. In a human, the cerebral cortex contains approximately 15–33 billion neurons, each connected by synapses to several thousand other neurons. These neurons communicate with one another by means of long protoplasmic fibers called axons, which carry trains of signal pulses called action potentials to distant parts of the brain or body targeting specific recipient cells.

Physiologically, the function of the brain is to exert centralized control over the other organs of the body. The brain acts on the rest of the body both by generating patterns of muscle activity and by driving the secretion of chemicals called hormones. This centralized control allows rapid and coordinated responses to changes in the environment. Some basic types of responsiveness such as reflexes can be mediated by the spinal cord or peripheral ganglia, but sophisticated purposeful control of behavior based on complex sensory input requires the information integrating capabilities of a centralized brain.

The operations of individual brain cells are now understood in considerable detail but the way they cooperate in ensembles of millions is yet to be solved. Recent models in modern neuroscience treat the brain as a biological computer, very different in mechanism from an electronic computer, but similar in the sense that it acquires information from the surrounding world, stores it, and processes it in a variety of ways.

This article compares the properties of brains across the entire range of animal species, with the greatest attention to vertebrates. It deals with the human brain insofar as it shares the properties of other brains. The ways in which the human brain differs from other brains are covered in the human brain article. Several topics that might be covered here are instead covered there because much more can be said about them in a human context. The most important is brain disease and the effects of brain damage, that are covered in the human brain article.

Anatomy

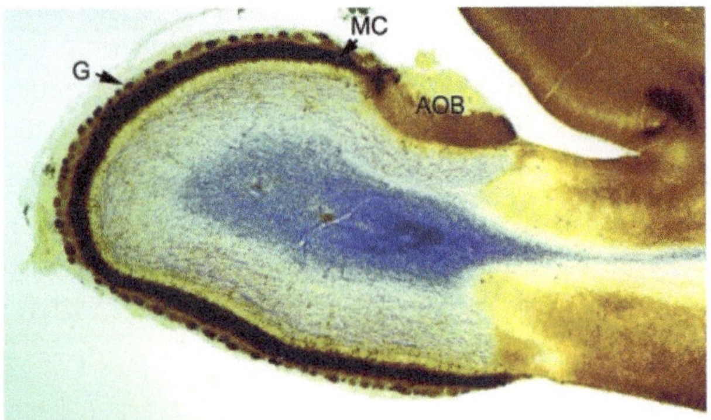

Cross section of the olfactory bulb of a rat, stained in two different ways at the same time: one stain shows neuron cell bodies, the other shows receptors for the neurotransmitter GABA.

The shape and size of the brain varies greatly between species, and identifying common features is often difficult. Nevertheless, there are a number of principles of brain architecture that apply across a wide range of species. Some aspects of brain structure are common to almost the entire range of animal species; others distinguish "advanced" brains from more primitive ones, or distinguish vertebrates from invertebrates.

The simplest way to gain information about brain anatomy is by visual inspection, but many more sophisticated techniques have been developed. Brain tissue in its natural state is too soft to work with, but it can be hardened by immersion in alcohol or other fixatives, and then sliced apart for examination of the interior. Visually, the interior of the brain consists of areas of so-called grey matter, with a dark color, separated by areas of white matter, with a lighter color. Further information can be gained by staining slices of brain tissue with a variety of chemicals that bring out areas where specific types of molecules are present in high concentrations. It is also possible to examine the microstructure of brain tissue using a microscope, and to trace the pattern of connections from one brain area to another.

Cellular Structure

The brains of all species are composed primarily of two broad classes of cells: neurons and glial cells. Glial cells (also known as *glia* or *neuroglia*) come in several types, and perform a number of critical functions, including structural support, metabolic support, insulation, and guidance of development. Neurons, however, are usually considered the most important cells in the brain. The property that makes neurons unique is their ability to send signals to specific target cells over long distances. They send these signals by means of an axon, which is a thin protoplasmic fiber that extends from the cell body and projects, usually with numerous branches, to other areas, sometimes nearby, sometimes in distant parts of the brain or body. The length of an axon can be extraordinary: for example, if a pyramidal cell, (an excitatory neuron) of the cerebral cortex were magnified so that its cell body became the size of a human body, its axon, equally magnified, would become a cable a few centimeters in diameter, extending more than a kilometer. These axons transmit signals in the form of electrochemical pulses called action potentials, which last less than a thousandth of a second and travel along the axon at speeds of 1–100 meters per second. Some neurons emit action potentials constantly, at rates of 10–100 per second, usually in irregular patterns; other neurons are quiet most of the time, but occasionally emit a burst of action potentials.

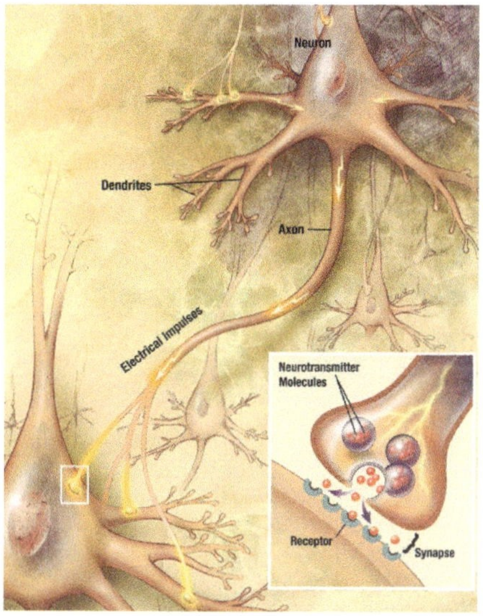

Neurons generate electrical signals that travel along their axons. When a pulse of electricity reaches a junction called a synapse, it causes a neurotransmitter chemical to be released, which binds to receptors on other cells and thereby alters their electrical activity.

Axons transmit signals to other neurons by means of specialized junctions called synapses. A single axon may make as many as several thousand synaptic connections with other cells. When an action potential, traveling along an axon, arrives at a synapse, it causes a chemical called a neurotransmitter to be released. The neurotransmitter binds to receptor molecules in the membrane of the target cell.

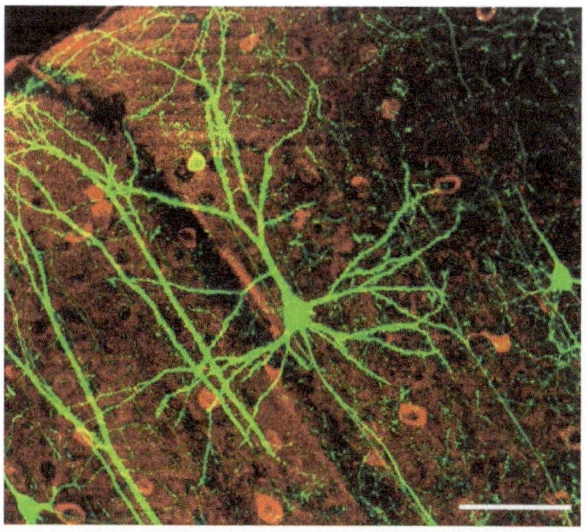

Neurons often have extensive networks of dendrites, which receive synaptic connections. Shown is a pyramidal neuron from the hippocampus, stained for green fluorescent protein.

Synapses are the key functional elements of the brain. The essential function of the brain is cell-to-cell communication, and synapses are the points at which communication occurs. The human brain has been estimated to contain approximately 100 trillion synapses; even the brain of a fruit fly contains several million. The functions of these synapses are very diverse: some are excitatory (exciting the target cell); others are inhibitory; others work by activating second messenger systems that change the internal chemistry of their target cells in complex ways. A large number of synapses are dynamically modifiable; that is, they are capable of changing strength in a way that is controlled by the patterns of signals that pass through them. It is widely believed that activity-dependent modification of synapses is the brain's primary mechanism for learning and memory.

Most of the space in the brain is taken up by axons, which are often bundled together in what are called *nerve fiber tracts*. A myelinated axon is wrapped in a fatty insulating sheath of myelin, which serves to greatly increase the speed of signal propagation. (There are also unmyelinated axons). Myelin is white, making parts of the brain filled exclusively with nerve fibers appear as light-colored white matter, in contrast to the darker-colored grey matter that marks areas with high densities of neuron cell bodies.

Evolution

Generic Bilaterian Nervous System

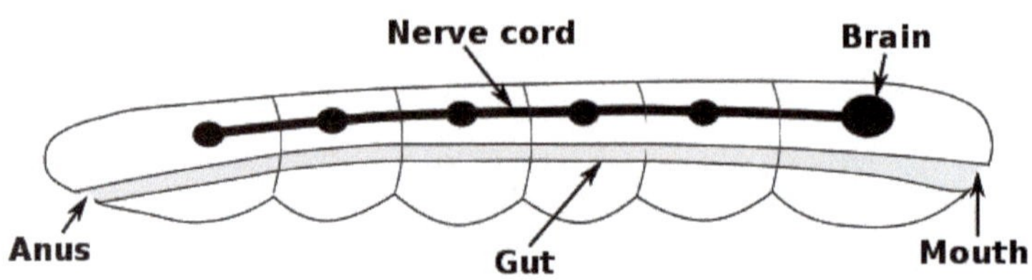

Nervous system of a generic bilaterian animal, in the form of a nerve cord with segmental enlargements, and a "brain" at the front.

Except for a few primitive organisms such as sponges (which have no nervous system) and cnidarians (which have a nervous system consisting of a diffuse nerve net), all living multicellular animals are bilaterians, meaning animals with a bilaterally symmetric body shape (that is, left and right sides that are approximate mirror images of each other). All bilaterians are thought to have descended from a common ancestor that appeared early in the Cambrian period, 485-540 million years ago, and it has been hypothesized that this common ancestor had the shape of a simple tubeworm with a segmented body. At a schematic level, that basic worm-shape continues to be reflected in the body and nervous system architecture of all modern bilaterians, including vertebrates. The fundamental bilateral body form is a tube with a hollow gut cavity running from the mouth to the anus, and a nerve cord with an enlargement (a ganglion) for each body segment, with an especially large ganglion at the front, called the brain. The brain is small and simple in some species, such as nematode worms; in other species, including vertebrates, it is the most complex organ in the body. Some types of worms, such as leeches, also have an enlarged ganglion at the back end of the nerve cord, known as a "tail brain".

There are a few types of existing bilaterians that lack a recognizable brain, including echinoderms and tunicates. It has not been definitively established whether the existence of these brainless species indicates that the earliest bilaterians lacked a brain, or whether their ancestors evolved in a way that led to the disappearance of a previously existing brain structure.

Invertebrates

Fruit flies (*Drosophila*) have been extensively studied to gain insight into the role of genes in brain development.

This category includes arthropods, molluscs, and numerous types of worms. The diversity of invertebrate body plans is matched by an equal diversity in brain structures.

Two groups of invertebrates have notably complex brains: arthropods (insects, crustaceans, arachnids, and others), and cephalopods (octopuses, squids, and similar molluscs). The brains of arthropods and cephalopods arise from twin parallel nerve cords that extend through the body of the animal. Arthropods have a central brain, the supraesophageal ganglion, with three divisions and large optical lobes behind each eye for visual processing. Cephalopods such as the octopus and squid have the largest brains of any invertebrates.

There are several invertebrate species whose brains have been studied intensively because they have properties that make them convenient for experimental work:

- Fruit flies (*Drosophila*), because of the large array of techniques available for studying their genetics, have been a natural subject for studying the role of genes in brain development. In spite of the large evolutionary distance between insects and mammals, many aspects of *Drosophila* neurogenetics have been shown to be relevant to humans. The first biological clock genes, for example, were identified by examining *Drosophila* mutants that showed disrupted daily activity cycles. A search in the genomes of vertebrates revealed a set of analogous genes, which were found to play similar roles in the mouse biological clock—and therefore almost certainly in the human biological clock as well. Studies done on Drosophila, also show that most neuropil regions of the brain are continuously reorganized throughout life in response to specific living conditions.
- The nematode worm *Caenorhabditis elegans*, like *Drosophila*, has been studied largely because of its importance in genetics. In the early 1970s, Sydney Brenner chose it as a model organism for studying the way that genes control development. One of the advantages

of working with this worm is that the body plan is very stereotyped: the nervous system of the hermaphrodite contains exactly 302 neurons, always in the same places, making identical synaptic connections in every worm. Brenner's team sliced worms into thousands of ultrathin sections and photographed each one under an electron microscope, then visually matched fibers from section to section, to map out every neuron and synapse in the entire body. The complete neuronal *wiring diagram* of *C.elegans* – its connectome was achieved. Nothing approaching this level of detail is available for any other organism, and the information gained has enabled a multitude of studies that would otherwise have not been possible.

- The sea slug *Aplysia californica* was chosen by Nobel Prize-winning neurophysiologist Eric Kandel as a model for studying the cellular basis of learning and memory, because of the simplicity and accessibility of its nervous system, and it has been examined in hundreds of experiments.

Vertebrates

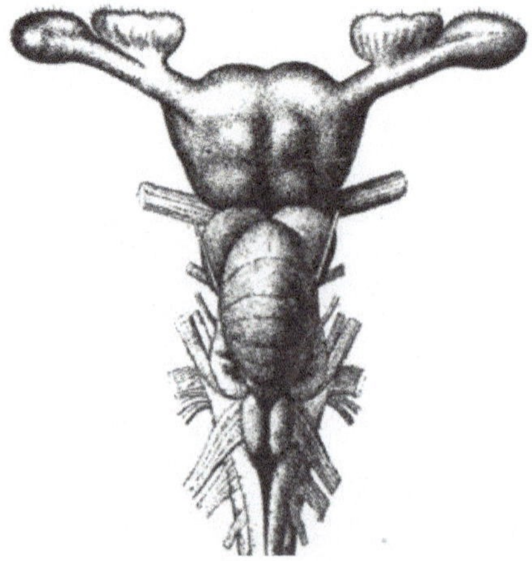

The brain of a shark.

The first vertebrates appeared over 500 million years ago (Mya), during the Cambrian period, and may have resembled the modern hagfish in form. Sharks appeared about 450 Mya, amphibians about 400 Mya, reptiles about 350 Mya, and mammals about 200 Mya. Each species has an equally long evolutionary history, but the brains of modern hagfishes, lampreys, sharks, amphibians, reptiles, and mammals show a gradient of size and complexity that roughly follows the evolutionary sequence. All of these brains contain the same set of basic anatomical components, but many are rudimentary in the hagfish, whereas in mammals the foremost part (the telencephalon) is greatly elaborated and expanded.

Brains are most simply compared in terms of their size. The relationship between brain size, body size and other variables has been studied across a wide range of vertebrate species. As a rule, brain size increases with body size, but not in a simple linear proportion. In general, smaller animals tend to have larger brains, measured as a fraction of body size. For mammals, the relationship between brain volume and body mass essentially follows a power law with an exponent of about 0.75. This formula describes the central tendency, but every family of mammals departs from it to some degree, in a way that reflects in part the complexity of their behavior. For example, primates have brains 5 to 10 times larger than the formula predicts. Predators tend to have larger brains than their prey, relative to body size.

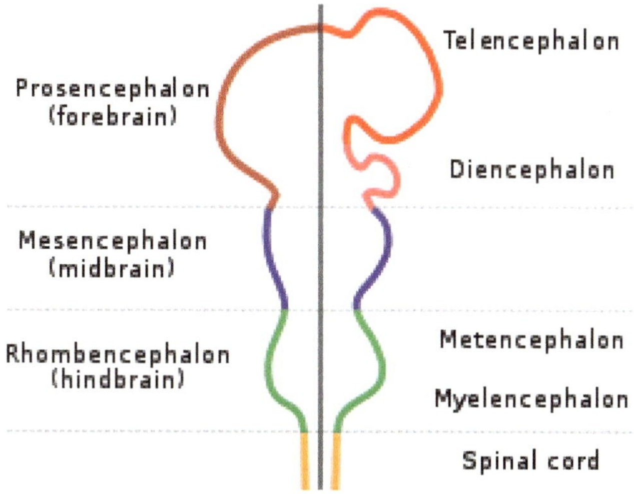

The main subdivisions of the embryonic vertebrate brain, which later differentiate into the forebrain, midbrain and hindbrain.

All vertebrate brains share a common underlying form, which appears most clearly during early stages of embryonic development. In its earliest form, the brain appears as three swellings at the front end of the neural tube; these swellings eventually become the forebrain, midbrain, and hindbrain (the prosencephalon, mesencephalon, and rhombencephalon, respectively). At the earliest stages of brain development, the three areas are roughly equal in size. In many classes of vertebrates, such as fish and amphibians, the three parts remain similar in size in the adult, but in mammals the forebrain becomes much larger than the other parts, and the midbrain becomes very small.

The brains of vertebrates are made of very soft tissue. Living brain tissue is pinkish on the outside and mostly white on the inside, with subtle variations in color. Vertebrate brains are surrounded by a system of connective tissue membranes called meninges that separate the skull from the brain. Blood vessels enter the central nervous system through holes in the meningeal layers. The cells in the blood vessel walls are joined tightly to one another, forming the blood–brain barrier, which blocks the passage of many toxins and pathogens (though at the same time blocking antibodies and some drugs, thereby presenting special challenges in treatment of diseases of the brain).

Neuroanatomists usually divide the vertebrate brain into six main regions: the telencephalon (cerebral hemispheres), diencephalon (thalamus and hypothalamus), mesencephalon (midbrain), cerebellum, pons, and medulla oblongata. Each of these areas has a complex internal structure. Some parts, such as the cerebral cortex and the cerebellar cortex, consist of layers that are folded or convoluted to fit within the available space. Other parts, such as the thalamus and hypothalamus, consist of clusters of many small nuclei. Thousands of distinguishable areas can be identified within the vertebrate brain based on fine distinctions of neural structure, chemistry, and connectivity.

Although the same basic components are present in all vertebrate brains, some branches of vertebrate evolution have led to substantial distortions of brain geometry, especially in the forebrain area. The brain of a shark shows the basic components in a straightforward way, but in teleost fishes (the great majority of existing fish species), the forebrain has become "everted", like a sock turned inside out. In birds, there are also major changes in forebrain structure. These distortions can make it difficult to match brain components from one species with those of another species.

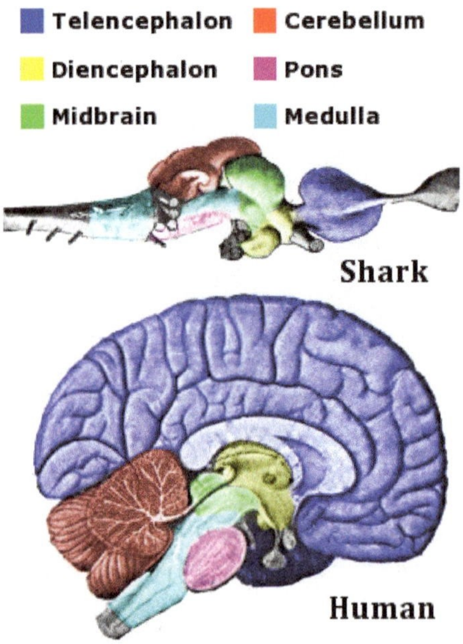

The main anatomical regions of the vertebrate brain, shown for shark and human. The same parts are present, but they differ greatly in size and shape.

Here is a list of some of the most important vertebrate brain components, along with a brief description of their functions as currently understood:

- The medulla, along with the spinal cord, contains many small nuclei involved in a wide variety of sensory and involuntary motor functions such as vomiting, heart rate and digestive processes.
- The pons lies in the brainstem directly above the medulla. Among other things, it contains nuclei that control often voluntary but simple acts such as sleep, respiration, swallowing, bladder function, equilibrium, eye movement, facial expressions, and posture.
- The hypothalamus is a small region at the base of the forebrain, whose complexity and importance belies its size. It is composed of numerous small nuclei, each with distinct connections and neurochemistry. The hypothalamus is engaged in additional involuntary or partially voluntary acts such as sleep and wake cycles, eating and drinking, and the release of some hormones.
- The thalamus is a collection of nuclei with diverse functions: some are involved in relaying information to and from the cerebral hemispheres, while others are involved in motivation. The subthalamic area (zona incerta) seems to contain action-generating systems for several types of "consummatory" behaviors such as eating, drinking, defecation, and copulation.
- The cerebellum modulates the outputs of other brain systems, whether motor related or thought related, to make them certain and precise. Removal of the cerebellum does not prevent an animal from doing anything in particular, but it makes actions hesitant and clumsy. This precision is not built-in, but learned by trial and error. The muscle coordina-

tion learned while riding a bicycle is an example of a type of neural plasticity that may take place largely within the cerebellum. 10% of the brain's total volume consists of the cerebellum and 50% of all neurons are held within its structure.

- The optic tectum allows actions to be directed toward points in space, most commonly in response to visual input. In mammals it is usually referred to as the superior colliculus, and its best-studied function is to direct eye movements. It also directs reaching movements and other object-directed actions. It receives strong visual inputs, but also inputs from other senses that are useful in directing actions, such as auditory input in owls and input from the thermosensitive pit organs in snakes. In some primitive fishes, such as lampreys, this region is the largest part of the brain. The superior colliculus is part of the midbrain.
- The pallium is a layer of gray matter that lies on the surface of the forebrain and is the most complex and most recent evolutionary development of the brain as an organ. In reptiles and mammals, it is called the cerebral cortex. Multiple functions involve the pallium, including smell and spatial memory. In mammals, where it becomes so large as to dominate the brain, it takes over functions from many other brain areas. In many mammals, the cerebral cortex consists of folded bulges called gyri that create deep furrows or fissures called sulci. The folds increase the surface area of the cortex and therefore increase the amount of gray matter and the amount of information that can be stored and processed.
- The hippocampus, strictly speaking, is found only in mammals. However, the area it derives from, the medial pallium, has counterparts in all vertebrates. There is evidence that this part of the brain is involved in complex events such as spatial memory and navigation in fishes, birds, reptiles, and mammals.
- The basal ganglia are a group of interconnected structures in the forebrain. The primary function of the basal ganglia appears to be action selection: they send inhibitory signals to all parts of the brain that can generate motor behaviors, and in the right circumstances can release the inhibition, so that the action-generating systems are able to execute their actions. Reward and punishment exert their most important neural effects by altering connections within the basal ganglia.
- The olfactory bulb is a special structure that processes olfactory sensory signals and sends its output to the olfactory part of the pallium. It is a major brain component in many vertebrates, but is greatly reduced in humans and other primates (whose senses are dominated by information acquired by sight rather than smell).

Mammals

The most obvious difference between the brains of mammals and other vertebrates is in terms of size. On average, a mammal has a brain roughly twice as large as that of a bird of the same body size, and ten times as large as that of a reptile of the same body size.

Size, however, is not the only difference: there are also substantial differences in shape. The hindbrain and midbrain of mammals are generally similar to those of other vertebrates, but dramatic differences appear in the forebrain, which is greatly enlarged and also altered in structure. The cerebral cortex is the part of the brain that most strongly distinguishes mammals. In non-mammalian vertebrates, the surface of the cerebrum is lined with a comparatively simple three-layered structure called the pallium. In mammals, the pallium evolves into a complex six-layered structure called neocortex or *isocortex*. Several areas at the edge of the neocortex, including the hippocampus and amygdala, are also much more extensively developed in mammals than in other vertebrates.

The elaboration of the cerebral cortex carries with it changes to other brain areas. The superior colliculus, which plays a major role in visual control of behavior in most vertebrates, shrinks to a small size in mammals, and many of its functions are taken over by visual areas of the cerebral cortex. The cerebellum of mammals contains a large portion (the neocerebellum) dedicated to supporting the cerebral cortex, which has no counterpart in other vertebrates.

Primates

Encephalization Quotient	
Species	**EQ**
Human	7.4–7.8
Chimpanzee	2.2–2.5
Rhesus monkey	2.1
Bottlenose dolphin	4.14
Elephant	1.13–2.36
Dog	1.2
Horse	0.9
Rat	0.4

The brains of humans and other primates contain the same structures as the brains of other mammals, but are generally larger in proportion to body size. The encephalization quotient (EQ) is used to compare brain sizes across species. It takes into account the nonlinearity of the brain-to-body relationship. Humans have an average EQ in the 7-to-8 range, while most other primates have an EQ in the 2-to-3 range. Dolphins have values higher than those of primates other than humans, but nearly all other mammals have EQ values that are substantially lower.

Most of the enlargement of the primate brain comes from a massive expansion of the cerebral cortex, especially the prefrontal cortex and the parts of the cortex involved in vision. The visual processing network of primates includes at least 30 distinguishable brain areas, with a complex web of interconnections. It has been estimated that visual processing areas occupy more than half of the total surface of the primate neocortex. The prefrontal cortex carries out functions that include planning, working memory, motivation, attention, and executive control. It takes up a much larger proportion of the brain for primates than for other species, and an especially large fraction of the human brain.

Development

The brain develops in an intricately orchestrated sequence of stages. It changes in shape from a simple swelling at the front of the nerve cord in the earliest embryonic stages, to a complex array of areas and connections. Neurons are created in special zones that contain stem cells, and then migrate through the tissue to reach their ultimate locations. Once neurons have positioned themselves, their axons sprout and navigate through the brain, branching and extending as they go, until the tips reach their targets and form synaptic connections. In a number of parts of the nervous system, neurons and synapses are produced in excessive numbers during the early stages, and then the unneeded ones are pruned away.

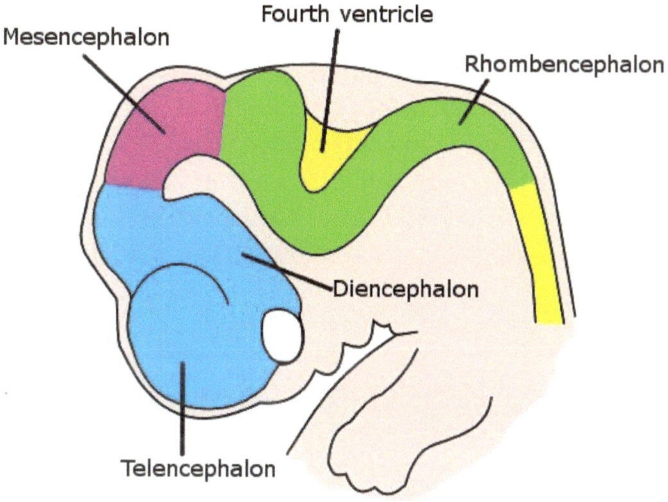

Brain of a human embryo in the sixth week of development.

For vertebrates, the early stages of neural development are similar across all species. As the embryo transforms from a round blob of cells into a wormlike structure, a narrow strip of ectoderm running along the midline of the back is induced to become the neural plate, the precursor of the nervous system. The neural plate folds inward to form the neural groove, and then the lips that line the groove merge to enclose the neural tube, a hollow cord of cells with a fluid-filled ventricle at the center. At the front end, the ventricles and cord swell to form three vesicles that are the precursors of the forebrain, midbrain, and hindbrain. At the next stage, the forebrain splits into two vesicles called the telencephalon (which will contain the cerebral cortex, basal ganglia, and related structures) and the diencephalon (which will contain the thalamus and hypothalamus). At about the same time, the hindbrain splits into the metencephalon (which will contain the cerebellum and pons) and the myelencephalon (which will contain the medulla oblongata). Each of these areas contains proliferative zones where neurons and glial cells are generated; the resulting cells then migrate, sometimes for long distances, to their final positions.

Once a neuron is in place, it extends dendrites and an axon into the area around it. Axons, because they commonly extend a great distance from the cell body and need to reach specific targets, grow in a particularly complex way. The tip of a growing axon consists of a blob of protoplasm called a growth cone, studded with chemical receptors. These receptors sense the local environment, causing the growth cone to be attracted or repelled by various cellular elements, and thus to be pulled in a particular direction at each point along its path. The result of this pathfinding process is that the growth cone navigates through the brain until it reaches its destination area, where other chemical cues cause it to begin generating synapses. Considering the entire brain, thousands of genes create products that influence axonal pathfinding.

The synaptic network that finally emerges is only partly determined by genes, though. In many parts of the brain, axons initially "overgrow", and then are "pruned" by mechanisms that depend on neural activity. In the projection from the eye to the midbrain, for example, the structure in the adult contains a very precise mapping, connecting each point on the surface of the retina to a corresponding point in a midbrain layer. In the first stages of development, each axon from the retina is guided to the right general vicinity in the midbrain by chemical cues, but then branches very profusely and makes initial contact with a wide swath of midbrain neurons. The retina, before birth, contains special mechanisms that cause it to generate waves of activity that originate spontaneously at a random point and then propagate slowly across the retinal layer. These waves are useful because they cause neighboring neurons to be active at the same time; that is, they produce a neural activity pattern that contains information about the spatial arrangement of the neurons. This information is exploited in the midbrain by a mechanism that causes synapses to weaken, and eventually vanish, if activity in an axon is not followed by activity of the target cell. The result of this sophisticated process is a gradual tuning and tightening of the map, leaving it finally in its precise adult form.

Similar things happen in other brain areas: an initial synaptic matrix is generated as a result of genetically determined chemical guidance, but then gradually refined by activity-dependent mechanisms, partly driven by internal dynamics, partly by external sensory inputs. In some cases, as with the retina-midbrain system, activity patterns depend on mechanisms that operate only in the developing brain, and apparently exist solely to guide development.

In humans and many other mammals, new neurons are created mainly before birth, and the infant brain contains substantially more neurons than the adult brain. There are, however, a few areas where new neurons continue to be generated throughout life. The two areas for which adult neurogenesis is well established are the olfactory bulb, which is involved in the sense of smell, and the dentate gyrus of the hippocampus, where there is evidence that the new neurons play a role in storing newly acquired memories. With these exceptions, however, the set of neurons that is present in early childhood is the set that is present for life. Glial cells are different: as with most types of cells in the body, they are generated throughout the lifespan.

There has long been debate about whether the qualities of mind, personality, and intelligence can be attributed to heredity or to upbringing—this is the nature and nurture controversy. Although many details remain to be settled, neuroscience research has clearly shown that both factors are important. Genes determine the general form of the brain, and genes determine how the brain reacts to experience. Experience, however, is required to refine the matrix of synaptic connections, which in its developed form contains far more information than the genome does. In some respects, all that matters is the presence or absence of experience during critical periods of development. In other respects, the quantity and quality of experience are important; for example, there is substantial evidence that animals raised in enriched environments have thicker cerebral cortices, indicating a higher density of synaptic connections, than animals whose levels of stimulation are restricted.

Physiology

The functions of the brain depend on the ability of neurons to transmit electrochemical signals to other cells, and their ability to respond appropriately to electrochemical signals received from other cells. The electrical properties of neurons are controlled by a wide variety of biochemical and metabolic processes, most notably the interactions between neurotransmitters and receptors that take place at synapses.

Neurotransmitters and Receptors

Neurotransmitters are chemicals that are released at synapses when an action potential activates them—neurotransmitters attach themselves to receptor molecules on the membrane of the synapse's target cell, and thereby alter the electrical or chemical properties of the receptor molecules. With few exceptions, each neuron in the brain releases the same chemical neurotransmitter, or combination of neurotransmitters, at all the synaptic connections it makes with other neurons; this rule is known as Dale's principle. Thus, a neuron can be characterized by the neurotransmitters that it releases. The great majority of psychoactive drugs exert their effects by altering specific neurotransmitter systems. This applies to drugs such as cannabinoids, nicotine, heroin, cocaine, alcohol, fluoxetine, chlorpromazine, and many others.

The two neurotransmitters that are used most widely in the vertebrate brain are glutamate, which almost always exerts excitatory effects on target neurons, and gamma-aminobutyric acid (GABA), which is almost always inhibitory. Neurons using these transmitters can be found in nearly every part of the brain. Because of their ubiquity, drugs that act on glutamate or GABA tend to have broad and powerful effects. Some general anesthetics act by reducing the effects of glutamate; most tranquilizers exert their sedative effects by enhancing the effects of GABA.

There are dozens of other chemical neurotransmitters that are used in more limited areas of the brain, often areas dedicated to a particular function. Serotonin, for example—the primary target of antidepressant drugs and many dietary aids—comes exclusively from a small brainstem area called the Raphe nuclei. Norepinephrine, which is involved in arousal, comes exclusively from a nearby small area called the locus coeruleus. Other neurotransmitters such as acetylcholine and dopamine have multiple sources in the brain, but are not as ubiquitously distributed as glutamate and GABA.

Electrical Activity

As a side effect of the electrochemical processes used by neurons for signaling, brain tissue generates electric fields when it is active. When large numbers of neurons show synchronized activity, the electric fields that they generate can be large enough to detect outside the skull, using electroencephalography (EEG) or magnetoencephalography (MEG). EEG recordings, along with recordings made from electrodes implanted inside the brains of animals such as rats, show that the brain of a living animal is constantly active, even during sleep. Each part of the brain shows a mixture of rhythmic and nonrhythmic activity, which may vary according to behavioral state. In mammals, the cerebral cortex tends to show large slow delta waves during sleep, faster alpha waves when the animal is awake but inattentive, and chaotic-looking irregular activity when the animal is actively engaged in a task. During an epileptic seizure, the brain's inhibitory control mechanisms fail to function and electrical activity rises to pathological levels, producing EEG traces that show large wave and spike patterns not seen in a healthy brain. Relating these population-level patterns to the computational functions of individual neurons is a major focus of current research in neurophysiology.

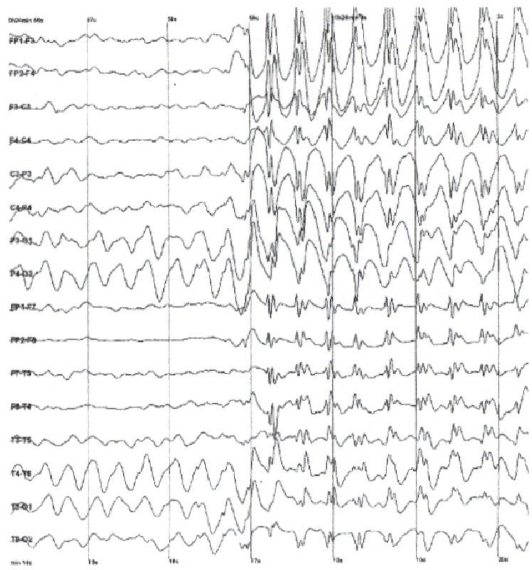

Brain electrical activity recorded from a human patient during an epileptic seizure.

Metabolism

All vertebrates have a blood–brain barrier that allows metabolism inside the brain to operate differently from metabolism in other parts of the body. Glial cells play a major role in brain metabolism by controlling the chemical composition of the fluid that surrounds neurons, including levels of ions and nutrients.

Brain tissue consumes a large amount of energy in proportion to its volume, so large brains place severe metabolic demands on animals. The need to limit body weight in order, for example, to fly, has apparently led to selection for a reduction of brain size in some species, such as bats. Most of the brain's energy consumption goes into sustaining the electric charge (membrane potential) of neurons. Most vertebrate species devote between 2% and 8% of basal metabolism to the brain. In primates, however, the percentage is much higher—in humans it rises to 20–25%. The energy consumption of the brain does not vary greatly over time, but active regions of the cerebral cortex consume somewhat more energy than inactive regions; this forms the basis for the functional brain imaging methods PET, fMRI, and NIRS. The brain typically gets most of its energy from oxygen-dependent metabolism of glucose (i.e., blood sugar), but ketones provide a major alternative source, together with contributions from medium chain fatty acids (caprylic and heptanoic acids), lactate, acetate, and possibly amino acids.

Functions

Information from the sense organs is collected in the brain. There it is used to determine what actions the organism is to take. The brain processes the raw data to extract information about the structure of the environment. Next it combines the processed information with information about the current needs of the animal and with memory of past circumstances. Finally, on the basis of the results, it generates motor response patterns. These signal-processing tasks require intricate interplay between a variety of functional subsystems.

The function of the brain is to provide coherent control over the actions of an animal. A centralized brain allows groups of muscles to be co-activated in complex patterns; it also allows stimuli impinging on one part of the body to evoke responses in other parts, and it can prevent different parts of the body from acting at cross-purposes to each other.

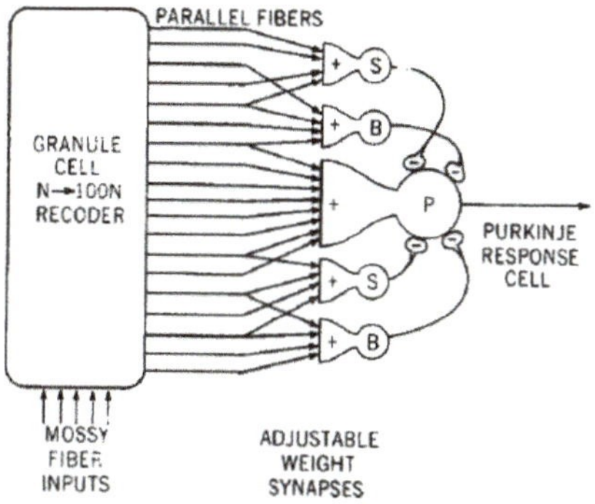

Model of a neural circuit in the cerebellum, as proposed by James S. Albus.

Perception

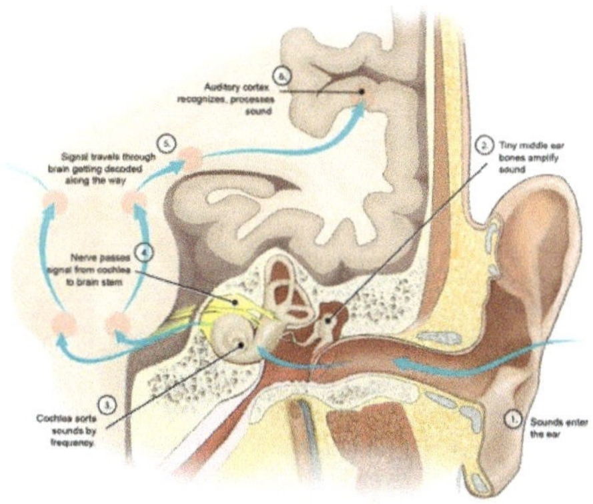

Diagram of signal processing in the auditory system.

The human brain is provided with information about light, sound, the chemical composition of the atmosphere, temperature, head orientation, limb position, the chemical composition of the bloodstream, and more. In other animals additional senses are present, such as the infrared heat-sense of snakes, the magnetic field sense of some birds, or the electric field sense of some types of fish.

Each sensory system begins with specialized receptor cells, such as light-receptive neurons in the retina of the eye, or vibration-sensitive neurons in the cochlea of the ear. The axons of sensory receptor cells travel into the spinal cord or brain, where they transmit their signals to a first-order sensory nucleus dedicated to one specific sensory modality. This primary sensory nucleus sends information to higher-order sensory areas that are dedicated to the same modality. Eventually, via a way-station in the thalamus, the signals are sent to the cerebral cortex, where they are processed to extract the relevant features, and integrated with signals coming from other sensory systems.

Motor Control

Motor systems are areas of the brain that are involved in initiating body movements, that is, in activating muscles. Except for the muscles that control the eye, which are driven by nuclei in the midbrain, all the voluntary muscles in the body are directly innervated by motor neurons in the spinal cord and hindbrain. Spinal motor neurons are controlled both by neural circuits intrinsic to the spinal cord, and by inputs that descend from the brain. The intrinsic spinal circuits implement many reflex responses, and contain pattern generators for rhythmic movements such as walking or swimming. The descending connections from the brain allow for more sophisticated control.

The brain contains several motor areas that project directly to the spinal cord. At the lowest level are motor areas in the medulla and pons, which control stereotyped movements such as walking, breathing, or swallowing. At a higher level are areas in the midbrain, such as the red nucleus, which is responsible for coordinating movements of the arms and legs. At a higher level yet is the primary motor cortex, a strip of tissue located at the posterior edge of the frontal lobe. The primary motor cortex sends projections to the subcortical motor areas, but also sends a massive projection directly to the spinal cord, through the pyramidal tract. This direct corticospinal projection allows for precise voluntary control of the fine details of movements. Other motor-related brain areas exert secondary effects by projecting to the primary motor areas. Among the most important secondary areas are the premotor cortex, basal ganglia, and cerebellum.

Major areas involved in controlling movement		
Area	**Location**	**Function**
Ventral horn	Spinal cord	Contains motor neurons that directly activate muscles
Oculomotor nuclei	Midbrain	Contains motor neurons that directly activate the eye muscles
Cerebellum	Hindbrain	Calibrates precision and timing of movements
Basal ganglia	Forebrain	Action selection on the basis of motivation
Motor cortex	Frontal lobe	Direct cortical activation of spinal motor circuits
Premotor cortex	Frontal lobe	Groups elementary movements into coordinated patterns
Supplementary motor area	Frontal lobe	Sequences movements into temporal patterns
Prefrontal cortex	Frontal lobe	Planning and other executive functions

In addition to all of the above, the brain and spinal cord contain extensive circuitry to control the autonomic nervous system, which works by secreting hormones and by modulating the "smooth" muscles of the gut.

Arousal

Many animals alternate between sleeping and waking in a daily cycle. Arousal and alertness are also modulated on a finer time scale by a network of brain areas.

A key component of the arousal system is the suprachiasmatic nucleus (SCN), a tiny part of the hypothalamus located directly above the point at which the optic nerves from the two eyes cross. The SCN contains the body's central biological clock. Neurons there show activity levels that rise and fall with a period of about 24 hours, circadian rhythms: these activity fluctuations are driven by rhythmic changes in expression of a set of "clock genes". The SCN continues to keep time even if it is excised from the brain and placed in a dish of warm nutrient solution, but it ordinarily receives input from the optic nerves, through the retinohypothalamic tract (RHT), that allows daily light-dark cycles to calibrate the clock.

The SCN projects to a set of areas in the hypothalamus, brainstem, and midbrain that are involved in implementing sleep-wake cycles. An important component of the system is the reticular formation, a group of neuron-clusters scattered diffusely through the core of the lower brain. Reticular neurons send signals to the thalamus, which in turn sends activity-level-controlling signals to every part of the cortex. Damage to the reticular formation can produce a permanent state of coma.

Sleep involves great changes in brain activity. Until the 1950s it was generally believed that the brain essentially shuts off during sleep, but this is now known to be far from true; activity continues, but patterns become very different. There are two types of sleep: *REM sleep* (with dreaming) and *NREM* (non-REM, usually without dreaming) sleep, which repeat in slightly varying patterns throughout a sleep episode. Three broad types of distinct brain activity patterns can be measured: REM, light NREM and deep NREM. During deep NREM sleep, also called slow wave sleep, activity in the cortex takes the form of large synchronized waves, whereas in the waking state it is noisy and desynchronized. Levels of the neurotransmitters norepinephrine and serotonin drop during slow wave sleep, and fall almost to zero during REM sleep; levels of acetylcholine show the reverse pattern.

Homeostasis

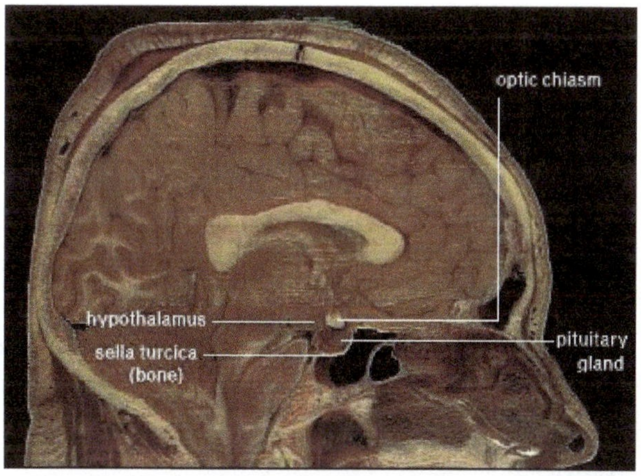

Cross-section of a human head, showing location of the hypothalamus.

For any animal, survival requires maintaining a variety of parameters of bodily state within a limited range of variation: these include temperature, water content, salt concentration in the bloodstream, blood glucose levels, blood oxygen level, and others. The ability of an animal to regulate the internal environment of its body—the milieu intérieur, as pioneering physiologist Claude Bernard called it—is known as homeostasis (Greek for "standing still"). Maintaining homeostasis is a crucial function of the brain. The basic principle that underlies homeostasis is negative feedback: any time a parameter diverges from its set-point, sensors generate an error signal that evokes a response that causes the parameter to shift back toward its optimum value. (This principle is widely used in engineering, for example in the control of temperature using a thermostat.)

In vertebrates, the part of the brain that plays the greatest role is the hypothalamus, a small region at the base of the forebrain whose size does not reflect its complexity or the importance of its function. The hypothalamus is a collection of small nuclei, most of which are involved in basic biological functions. Some of these functions relate to arousal or to social interactions such as sexuality, aggression, or maternal behaviors; but many of them relate to homeostasis. Several hypothalamic nuclei receive input from sensors located in the lining of blood vessels, conveying information about temperature, sodium level, glucose level, blood oxygen level, and other parameters. These hypothalamic nuclei send output signals to motor areas that can generate actions to rectify deficiencies. Some of the outputs also go to the pituitary gland, a tiny gland attached to the brain directly underneath the hypothalamus. The pituitary gland secretes hormones into the bloodstream, where they circulate throughout the body and induce changes in cellular activity.

Motivation

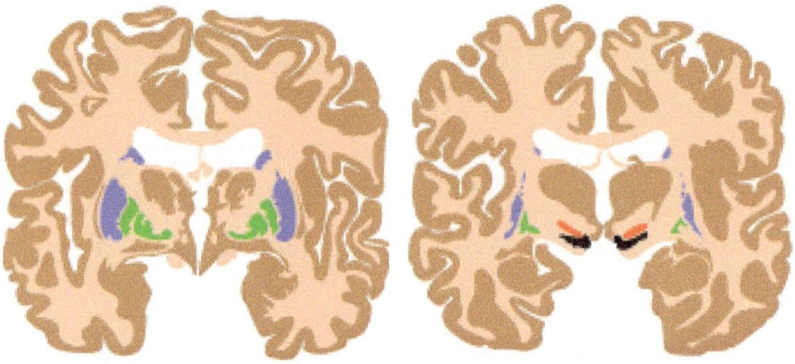

Components of the basal ganglia, shown in two cross-sections of the human brain. Blue: caudate nucleus and putamen. Green: globus pallidus. Red: subthalamic nucleus. Black: substantia nigra.

The individual animals need to express survival-promoting behaviors, such as seeking food, water, shelter, and a mate. The motivational system in the brain monitors the current state of satisfaction of these goals, and activates behaviors to meet any needs that arise. The motivational system works largely by a reward–punishment mechanism. When a particular behavior is followed by favorable consequences, the reward mechanism in the brain is activated, which induces structural changes inside the brain that cause the same behavior to be repeated later, whenever a similar situation arises. Conversely, when a behavior is followed by unfavorable consequences, the brain's punishment mechanism is activated, inducing structural changes that cause the behavior to be suppressed when similar situations arise in the future.

Most organisms studied to date utilize a reward–punishment mechanism: for instance, worms and insects can alter their behavior to seek food sources or to avoid dangers. In vertebrates, the reward-punishment system is implemented by a specific set of brain structures, at the heart of which lie the basal ganglia, a set of interconnected areas at the base of the forebrain. The basal ganglia are the central site at which decisions are made: the basal ganglia exert a sustained inhibitory control over most of the motor systems in the brain; when this inhibition is released, a motor system is permitted to execute the action it is programmed to carry out. Rewards and punishments function by altering the relationship between the inputs that the basal ganglia receive and the decision-signals that are emitted. The reward mechanism is better understood than the punishment mechanism, because its role in drug abuse has caused it to be studied very intensively. Research has shown that the neurotransmitter dopamine plays a central role: addictive drugs such as cocaine, amphetamine, and nicotine either cause dopamine levels to rise or cause the effects of dopamine inside the brain to be enhanced.

Learning and Memory

Almost all animals are capable of modifying their behavior as a result of experience—even the most primitive types of worms. Because behavior is driven by brain activity, changes in behavior must somehow correspond to changes inside the brain. Already in the late 19th century theorists like Santiago Ramón y Cajal argued that the most plausible explanation is that learning and memory are expressed as changes in the synaptic connections between neurons. Until 1970, however, experimental evidence to support the synaptic plasticity hypothesis was lacking. In 1971 Tim Bliss and Terje Lømo published a paper on a phenomenon now called long-term potentiation: the paper showed clear evidence of activity-induced synaptic changes that lasted for at least several days. Since then technical advances have made these sorts of experiments much easier to carry out, and thousands of studies have been made that have clarified the mechanism of synaptic change, and uncovered other types of activity-driven synaptic change in a variety of brain areas, including the cerebral cortex, hippocampus, basal ganglia, and cerebellum. Brain-derived neurotrophic factor (BDNF) and physical activity appear to play a beneficial role in the process.

Neuroscientists currently distinguish several types of learning and memory that are implemented by the brain in distinct ways:

- Working memory is the ability of the brain to maintain a temporary representation of information about the task that an animal is currently engaged in. This sort of dynamic memory is thought to be mediated by the formation of cell assemblies—groups of activated neurons that maintain their activity by constantly stimulating one another.
- Episodic memory is the ability to remember the details of specific events. This sort of memory can last for a lifetime. Much evidence implicates the hippocampus in playing a crucial role: people with severe damage to the hippocampus sometimes show amnesia, that is, inability to form new long-lasting episodic memories.
- Semantic memory is the ability to learn facts and relationships. This sort of memory is probably stored largely in the cerebral cortex, mediated by changes in connections between cells that represent specific types of information.
- Instrumental learning is the ability for rewards and punishments to modify behavior. It is implemented by a network of brain areas centered on the basal ganglia.
- Motor learning is the ability to refine patterns of body movement by practicing, or more generally by repetition. A number of brain areas are involved, including the premotor cortex, basal ganglia, and especially the cerebellum, which functions as a large memory bank for microadjustments of the parameters of movement.

Research

The field of neuroscience encompasses all approaches that seek to understand the brain and the rest of the nervous system. Psychology seeks to understand mind and behavior, and neurology is the medical discipline that diagnoses and treats diseases of the nervous system. The brain is also the most important organ studied in psychiatry, the branch of medicine that works to study, prevent, and treat mental disorders. Cognitive science seeks to unify neuroscience and psychology with other fields that concern themselves with the brain, such as computer science (artificial intelligence and similar fields) and philosophy.

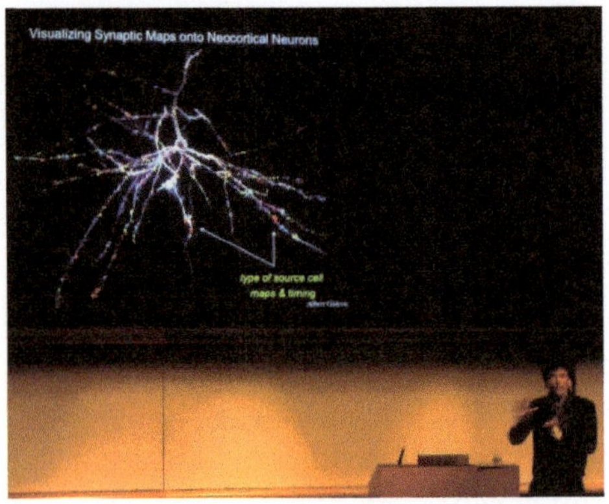

The Human Brain Project is a large scientific research project, starting in 2013, which aims to simulate the complete human brain.

The oldest method of studying the brain is anatomical, and until the middle of the 20th century, much of the progress in neuroscience came from the development of better cell stains and better microscopes. Neuroanatomists study the large-scale structure of the brain as well as the microscopic structure of neurons and their components, especially synapses. Among other tools, they employ a plethora of stains that reveal neural structure, chemistry, and connectivity. In recent years, the development of immunostaining techniques has allowed investigation of neurons that express specific sets of genes. Also, *functional neuroanatomy* uses medical imaging techniques to correlate variations in human brain structure with differences in cognition or behavior.

Neurophysiologists study the chemical, pharmacological, and electrical properties of the brain: their primary tools are drugs and recording devices. Thousands of experimentally developed drugs affect the nervous system, some in highly specific ways. Recordings of brain activity can be made using electrodes, either glued to the scalp as in EEG studies, or implanted inside the brains of animals for extracellular recordings, which can detect action potentials generated by individual neurons. Because the brain does not contain pain receptors, it is possible using these techniques to record brain activity from animals that are awake and behaving without causing distress. The same techniques have occasionally been used to study brain activity in human patients suffering from intractable epilepsy, in cases where there was a medical necessity to implant electrodes to localize the brain area responsible for epileptic seizures. Functional imaging techniques such as functional magnetic resonance imaging are also used to study brain activity; these techniques have mainly been used with human subjects, because they require a conscious subject to remain motionless for long periods of time, but they have the great advantage of being noninvasive.

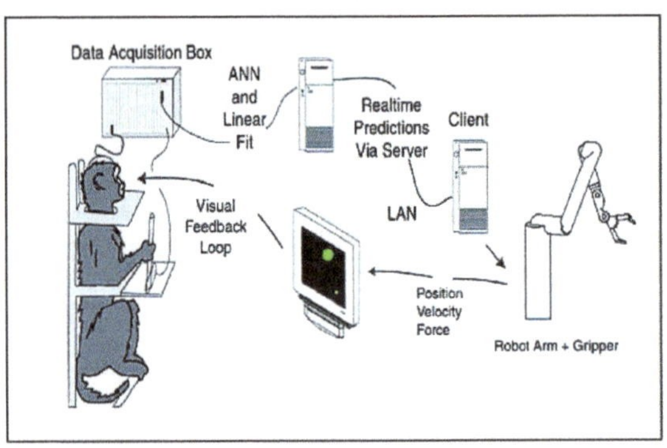

Design of an experiment in which brain activity from a monkey was used to control a robotic arm.

Another approach to brain function is to examine the consequences of damage to specific brain areas. Even though it is protected by the skull and meninges, surrounded by cerebrospinal fluid, and isolated from the bloodstream by the blood–brain barrier, the delicate nature of the brain makes it vulnerable to numerous diseases and several types of damage. In humans, the effects of strokes and other types of brain damage have been a key source of information about brain function. Because there is no ability to experimentally control the nature of the damage, however, this information is often difficult to interpret. In animal studies, most commonly involving rats, it is possible to use electrodes or locally injected chemicals to produce precise patterns of damage and then examine the consequences for behavior.

Computational neuroscience encompasses two approaches: first, the use of computers to study the brain; second, the study of how brains perform computation. On one hand, it is possible to write a computer program to simulate the operation of a group of neurons by making use of systems of equations that describe their electrochemical activity; such simulations are known as *biologically realistic neural networks*. On the other hand, it is possible to study algorithms for neural computation by simulating, or mathematically analyzing, the operations of simplified "units" that have some of the properties of neurons but abstract out much of their biological complexity. The computational functions of the brain are studied both by computer scientists and neuroscientists.

Computational neurogenetic modeling is concerned with the study and development of dynamic neuronal models for modeling brain functions with respect to genes and dynamic interactions between genes.

Recent years have seen increasing applications of genetic and genomic techniques to the study of the brain and a focus on the roles of neurotrophic factors and physical activity in neuroplasticity. The most common subjects are mice, because of the availability of technical tools. It is now possible with relative ease to "knock out" or mutate a wide variety of genes, and then examine the effects on brain function. More sophisticated approaches are also being used: for example, using Cre-Lox recombination it is possible to activate or deactivate genes in specific parts of the brain, at specific times.

History

The oldest brain to have been discovered was in Armenia in the Areni-1 cave complex. The brain, estimated to be over 5,000 years old, was found in the skull of a 12 to 14-year-old girl. Although the brains were shriveled, they were well preserved due to the climate found inside the cave.

Illustration by René Descartes of how the brain implements a reflex response.

Early philosophers were divided as to whether the seat of the soul lies in the brain or heart. Aristotle favored the heart, and thought that the function of the brain was merely to cool the blood. Democritus, the inventor of the atomic theory of matter, argued for a three-part soul, with intellect in the head, emotion in the heart, and lust near the liver. Hippocrates, the "father of medicine", came down unequivocally in favor of the brain. In his treatise on epilepsy he wrote:

Men ought to know that from nothing else but the brain come joys, delights, laughter and sports, and sorrows, griefs, despondency, and lamentations. ... And by the same organ we become mad and delirious, and fears and terrors assail us, some by night, and some by day, and dreams and untimely wanderings, and cares that are not suitable, and ignorance of present circumstances, desuetude, and unskillfulness. All these things we endure from the brain, when it is not healthy...

Hippocrates, on the Sacred Disease

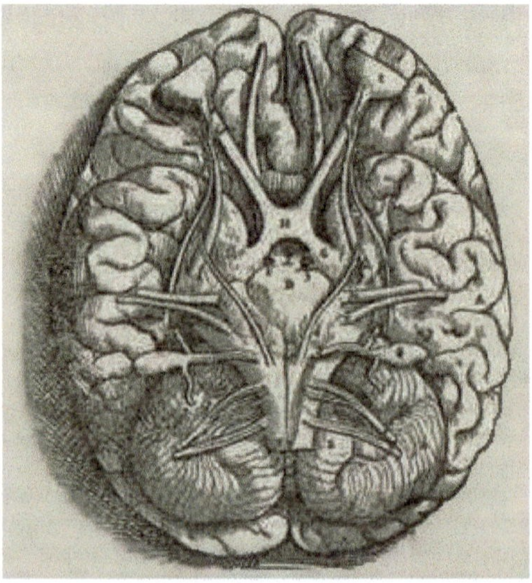

Andreas Vesalius' *Fabrica*, published in 1543, showing the base of the human brain, including optic chiasma, cerebellum, olfactory bulbs, etc.

The Roman physician Galen also argued for the importance of the brain, and theorized in some depth about how it might work. Galen traced out the anatomical relationships among brain, nerves, and muscles, demonstrating that all muscles in the body are connected to the brain through a branching network of nerves. He postulated that nerves activate muscles mechanically by carrying a mysterious substance he called *pneumata psychikon*, usually translated as "animal spirits". Galen's ideas were widely known during the Middle Ages, but not much further progress came until the Renaissance, when detailed anatomical study resumed, combined with the theoretical speculations of René Descartes and those who followed him. Descartes, like Galen, thought of the nervous system in hydraulic terms. He believed that the highest cognitive functions are carried out by a non-physical *res cogitans*, but that the majority of behaviors of humans, and all behaviors of animals, could be explained mechanistically.

The first real progress toward a modern understanding of nervous function, though, came from the investigations of Luigi Galvani, who discovered that a shock of static electricity applied to an exposed nerve of a dead frog could cause its leg to contract. Since that time, each major advance in understanding has followed more or less directly from the development of a new technique of investigation. Until the early years of the 20th century, the most important advances were derived from new methods for staining cells. Particularly critical was the invention of the Golgi stain, which (when correctly used) stains only a small fraction of neurons, but stains them in their entirety, including cell body, dendrites, and axon. Without such a stain, brain tissue under a microscope appears as an impenetrable tangle of protoplasmic fibers, in which it is impossible to determine any structure. In the hands of Camillo Golgi, and especially of the Spanish neuroanatomist Santiago Ramón y Cajal, the new stain revealed hundreds of distinct types of neurons, each with its own unique dendritic structure and pattern of connectivity.

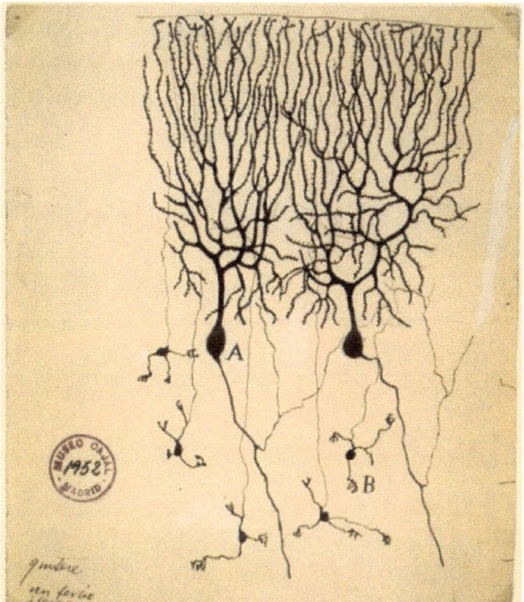

Drawing by Santiago Ramón y Cajal of two types of Golgi-stained neurons from the cerebellum of a pigeon.

In the first half of the 20th century, advances in electronics enabled investigation of the electrical properties of nerve cells, culminating in work by Alan Hodgkin, Andrew Huxley, and others on the biophysics of the action potential, and the work of Bernard Katz and others on the electrochemistry of the synapse. These studies complemented the anatomical picture with a conception of the brain as a dynamic entity. Reflecting the new understanding, in 1942 Charles Sherrington visualized the workings of the brain waking from sleep:

The great topmost sheet of the mass, that where hardly a light had twinkled or moved, becomes now a sparkling field of rhythmic flashing points with trains of traveling sparks hurrying hither and thither. The brain is waking and with it the mind is returning. It is as if the Milky Way entered upon some cosmic dance. Swiftly the head mass becomes an enchanted loom where millions of flashing shuttles weave a dissolving pattern, always a meaningful pattern though never an abiding one; a shifting harmony of subpatterns.

—Sherrington, 1942, *Man on his Nature*

The invention of electronic computers in the 1940s, along with the development of mathematical information theory, led to a realization that brains can potentially be understood as information processing systems. This concept formed the basis of the field of cybernetics, and eventually gave rise to the field now known as computational neuroscience. The earliest attempts at cybernetics were somewhat crude in that they treated the brain as essentially a digital computer in disguise, as for example in John von Neumann's 1958 book, *The Computer and the Brain*. Over the years, though, accumulating information about the electrical responses of brain cells recorded from behaving animals has steadily moved theoretical concepts in the direction of increasing realism.

One of the most influential early contributions was a 1959 paper titled *What the frog's eye tells the frog's brain*: the paper examined the visual responses of neurons in the retina and optic tectum of frogs, and came to the conclusion that some neurons in the tectum of the frog are wired to combine elementary responses in a way that makes them function as "bug perceivers". A few years later David Hubel and Torsten Wiesel discovered cells in the primary visual cortex of monkeys that become active when sharp edges move across specific points in the field of view—a discovery for which they won a Nobel Prize. Follow-up studies in higher-order visual areas found cells that detect binocular disparity, color, movement, and aspects of shape, with areas located at increasing distances from the primary visual cortex showing increasingly complex responses. Other investigations of brain areas unrelated to vision have revealed cells with a wide variety of response correlates, some related to memory, some to abstract types of cognition such as space.

Theorists have worked to understand these response patterns by constructing mathematical models of neurons and neural networks, which can be simulated using computers. Some useful models are abstract, focusing on the conceptual structure of neural algorithms rather than the details of how they are implemented in the brain; other models attempt to incorporate data about the biophysical properties of real neurons. No model on any level is yet considered to be a fully valid description of brain function, though. The essential difficulty is that sophisticated computation by neural networks requires distributed processing in which hundreds or thousands of neurons work cooperatively—current methods of brain activity recording are only capable of isolating action potentials from a few dozen neurons at a time.

Furthermore, even single neurons appear to be complex and capable of performing computations. So, brain models that don't reflect this are too abstract to be representative of brain operation; models that do try to capture this are very computationally expensive and arguably intractable with present computational resources. However, the Human Brain Project is trying to build a realistic, detailed computational model of the entire human brain. The wisdom of this approach has been publicly contested, with high-profile scientists on both sides of the argument.

In the second half of the 20th century, developments in chemistry, electron microscopy, genetics, computer science, functional brain imaging, and other fields progressively opened new windows into brain structure and function. In the United States, the 1990s were officially designated as the "Decade of the Brain" to commemorate advances made in brain research, and to promote funding for such research.

In the 21st century, these trends have continued, and several new approaches have come into prominence, including multielectrode recording, which allows the activity of many brain cells to be recorded all at the same time; genetic engineering, which allows molecular components of the brain to be altered experimentally; genomics, which allows variations in brain structure to be correlated with variations in DNA properties and neuroimaging.

Brodmann Area

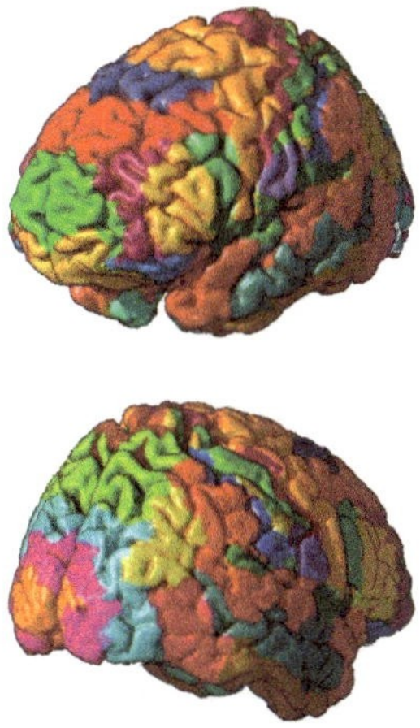

Brodmann areas 3D.

A Brodmann area is a region of the cerebral cortex, in the human or other primate brain, defined by its cytoarchitecture, or histological structure and organization of cells.

History

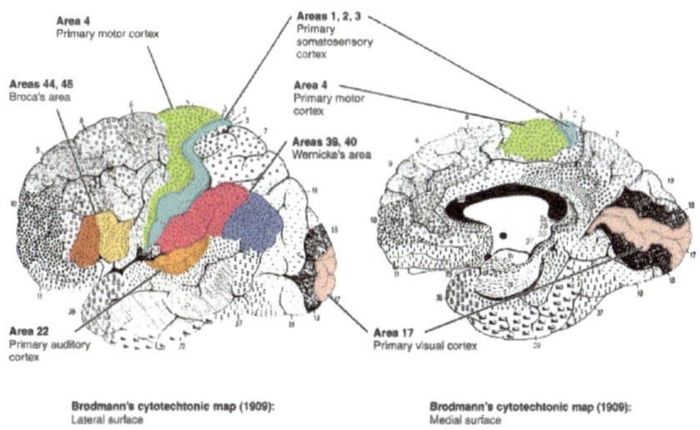

A number of important Brodmann areas have been marked out on this diagram.

Brodmann areas were originally defined and numbered by the German anatomist Korbinian Brodmann based on the cytoarchitectural organization of neurons he observed in the cerebral cortex using the Nissl method of cell staining. Brodmann published his maps of cortical areas in humans, monkeys, and other species in 1909, along with many other findings and observations regarding the general cell types and laminar organization of the mammalian cortex. The same Brodmann area number in different species does not necessarily indicate homologous areas. A similar, but more detailed cortical map was published by Constantin von Economo and Georg N. Koskinas in 1925.

Present Importance

Brodmann areas have been discussed, debated, refined, and renamed exhaustively for nearly a century and remain the most widely known and frequently cited cytoarchitectural organization of the human cortex.

Many of the areas Brodmann defined based solely on their neuronal organization have since been correlated closely to diverse cortical functions. For example, Brodmann areas 1, 2 and 3 are the primary somatosensory cortex; area 4 is the primary motor cortex; area 17 is the primary visual cortex; and areas 41 and 42 correspond closely to primary auditory cortex. Higher order functions of the association cortical areas are also consistently localized to the same Brodmann areas by neurophysiological, functional imaging, and other methods (e.g., the consistent localization of Broca's speech and language area to the left Brodmann areas 44 and 45). However, functional imaging can only identify the approximate localization of brain activations in terms of Brodmann areas since their actual boundaries in any individual brain requires its histological examination.

Overview

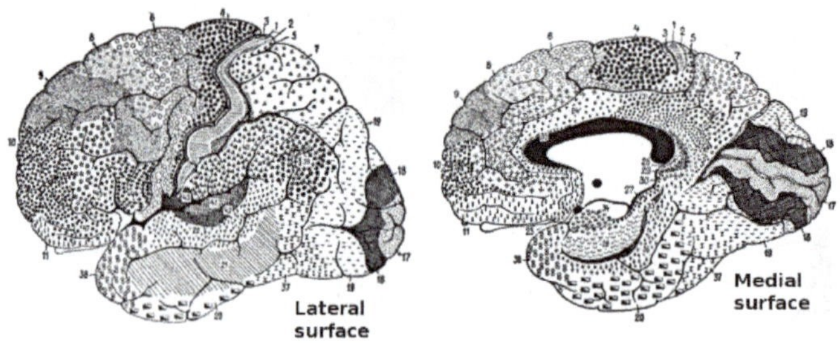

Brodmann's classification of areas of the cortex.

Different parts of the cerebral cortex are involved in different cognitive and behavioral functions. The differences show up in a number of ways: the effects of localized brain damage, regional activity patterns exposed when the brain is examined using functional imaging techniques, connectivity with subcortical areas, and regional differences in the cellular architecture of the cortex. Neuroscientists describe most of the cortex—the part they call the neocortex—as having six layers, but not all layers are apparent in all areas, and even when a layer is present, its thickness and cellular organization may vary. Scientists have constructed maps of cortical areas on the basis of variations in the appearance of the layers as seen with a microscope. One of the most widely used schemes came from Korbinian Brodmann, who split the cortex into 51 different areas and assigned each a number (many of these Brodmann areas have since been subdivided). For example, Brodmann area 1 is the primary somatosensory cortex, Brodmann area 17 is the primary visual cortex, and Brodmann area 25 is the anterior cingulate cortex.

Many of the brain areas Brodmann defined have their own complex internal structures. In a number of cases, brain areas are organized into topographic maps, where adjoining bits of the cortex correspond to adjoining parts of the body, or of some more abstract entity. A simple example of this type of correspondence is the primary motor cortex, a strip of tissue running along the anterior edge of the central sulcus. Motor areas innervating each part of the body arise from a distinct zone, with neighboring body parts represented by neighboring zones. Electrical stimulation of the cortex at any point causes a muscle-contraction in the represented body part. This "somatotopic" representation is not evenly distributed, however. The head, for example, is represented by a region about three times as large as the zone for the entire back and trunk. The size of any zone correlates to the precision of motor control and sensory discrimination possible. The areas for the lips, fingers, and tongue are particularly large, considering the proportional size of their represented body parts.

In visual areas, the maps are retinotopic; this means they reflect the topography of the retina, the layer of light-activated neurons lining the back of the eye. In this case too, the representation is uneven: the fovea—the area at the center of the visual field—is greatly overrepresented compared to the periphery. The visual circuitry in the human cerebral cortex contains several dozen distinct retinotopic maps, each devoted to analyzing the visual input stream in a particular way. The primary visual cortex (Brodmann area 17), which is the main recipient of direct input from the visual part of the thalamus, contains many neurons that are most easily activated by edges with a particular orientation moving across a particular point in the visual field. Visual areas farther downstream extract features such as color, motion, and shape.

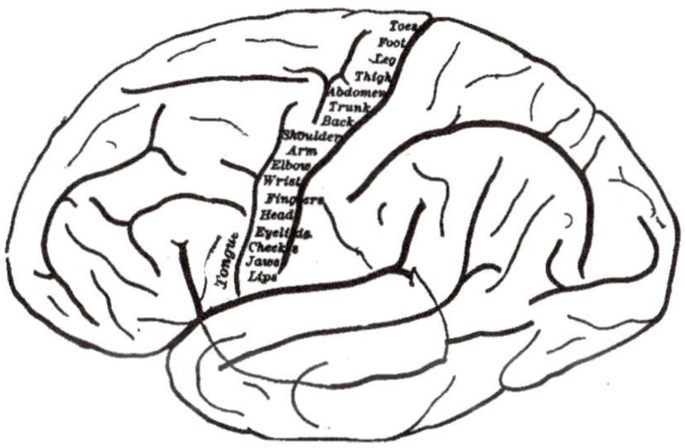

Topography of the primary motor cortex, showing which zone controls each body part.

In auditory areas, the primary map is tonotopic. Sounds are parsed according to frequency (i.e., high pitch vs. low pitch) by subcortical auditory areas, and this parsing is reflected by the primary auditory zone of the cortex. As with the visual system, there are a number of tonotopic cortical maps, each devoted to analyzing sound in a particular way.

Within a topographic map there can sometimes be finer levels of spatial structure. In the primary visual cortex, for example, where the main organization is retinotopic and the main responses are to moving edges, cells that respond to different edge-orientations are spatially segregated from one another.

Brodmann Areas for Humans and Other Primates

- Areas 3, 1 & 2 – Primary Somatosensory Cortex (frequently referred to as Areas 3, 1, 2 by convention)
- Area 4 – Primary Motor Cortex
- Area 5 – Somatosensory Association Cortex
- Area 6 – Premotor cortex and Supplementary Motor Cortex (Secondary Motor Cortex) (Supplementary motor area)
- Area 7 – Visuo-Motor Coordination
- Area 8 – Includes Frontal eye fields
- Area 9 – Dorsolateral prefrontal cortex
- Area 10 – Anterior prefrontal cortex (most rostral part of superior and middle frontal gyri)

- Area 11 – Orbitofrontal area (orbital and rectus gyri, plus part of the rostral part of the superior frontal gyrus)
- Area 12 – Orbitofrontal area (used to be part of BA11, refers to the area between the superior frontal gyrus and the inferior rostral sulcus)
- Area 13 and Area 14* – Insular cortex
- Area 15* – Anterior Temporal lobe
- Area 16 – Insular cortex
- Area 17 – Primary visual cortex (V1)
- Area 18 – Secondary visual cortex (V2)
- Area 19 – Associative visual cortex (V3,V4,V5)
- Area 20 – Inferior temporal gyrus
- Area 21 – Middle temporal gyrus
- Area 22 – Superior temporal gyrus, of which the caudal part is usually considered to contain the Wernicke's area
- Area 23 – Ventral posterior cingulate cortex
- Area 24 – Ventral anterior cingulate cortex.
- Area 25 – Subgenual area (part of the Ventromedial prefrontal cortex)
- Area 26 – Ectosplenial portion of the retrosplenial region of the cerebral cortex
- Area 27 – Piriform cortex
- Area 28 – Ventral entorhinal cortex
- Area 29 – Retrosplenial cingulate cortex
- Area 30 – Part of cingulate cortex
- Area 31 – Dorsal Posterior cingulate cortex
- Area 32 – Dorsal anterior cingulate cortex
- Area 33 – Part of anterior cingulate cortex
- Area 34 – Dorsal entorhinal cortex (on the Parahippocampal gyrus)
- Area 35 – Perirhinal cortex (in the rhinal sulcus)
- Area 36 – Ectorhinal area, now part of the perirhinal cortex (in the rhinal sulcus)
- Area 37 – Fusiform gyrus
- Area 38 – Temporopolar area (most rostral part of the superior and middle temporal gyri)
- Area 39 – Angular gyrus, considered by some to be part of Wernicke's area

- Area 40 – Supramarginal gyrus considered by some to be part of Wernicke's area
- Areas 41 and 42 – Auditory cortex
- Area 43 – Primary gustatory cortex
- Area 44 – Pars opercularis, part of the inferior frontal gyrus and part of Broca's area
- Area 45 – Pars triangularis, part of the inferior frontal gyrus and part of Broca's area
- Area 46 – Dorsolateral prefrontal cortex
- Area 47 – Pars orbitalis, part of the inferior frontal gyrus
- Area 48 – Retrosubicular area (a small part of the medial surface of the temporal lobe)
- Area 49 – Parasubicular area in a rodent
- Area 52 – Parainsular area (at the junction of the temporal lobe and the insula)

(*) Area only found in non-human primates.

Some of the original Brodmann areas have been subdivided further, e.g., "23a" and "23b".

Lateral Surface

The lateral view, or side view, of the brain is denoted the 'lateral surface'

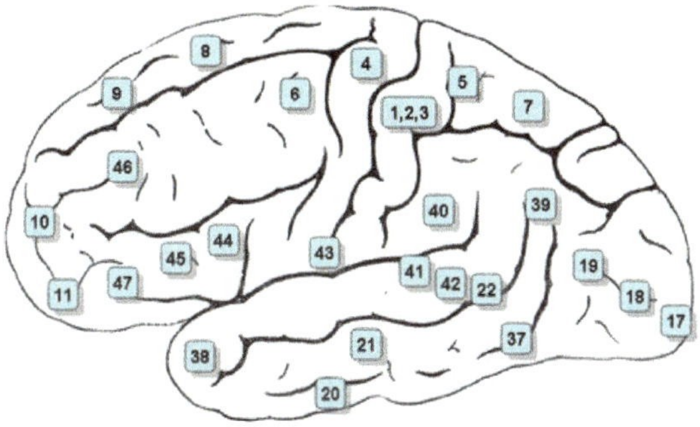

Medial Surface

The view of the section between the right and left hemispheres of the brain is denoted the 'medial surface'

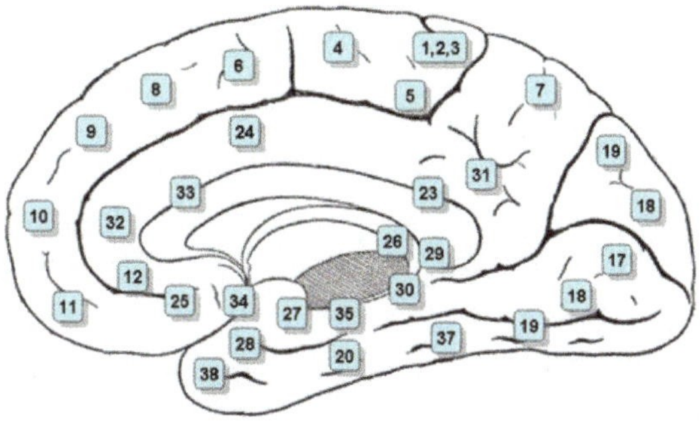

Criticism

When von Bonin and Bailey constructed a brain map for the macaque monkey they found the description of Brodmann inadequate and wrote: “Brodmann (1907), it is true, prepared a map of the human brain which has been widely reproduced, but, unfortunately, the data on which it was based was never published” They instead used the cytoarchitechtonic scheme of Constantin von Economo and Georg N. Koskinas published in 1925 which had the “only acceptable detailed description of the human cortex”.

Spinal Cord

The spinal cord is a long, thin, tubular bundle of nervous tissue and support cells that extends from the medulla oblongata in the brainstem to the lumbar region of the vertebral column. The brain and spinal cord together make up the central nervous system (CNS). In the human the spinal cord begins at the occipital bone where it passes through the foramen magnum, and meets and enters the spinal canal at the beginning of the cervical vertebrae. The spinal cord extends down to between the first and second lumbar vertebrae where it ends. The enclosing bony vertebral column protects the relatively shorter spinal cord. It is around 45 cm (18 in) in men and around 43 cm (17 in) long in women. Also, the spinal cord has a varying width, ranging from 13 mm ($\frac{1}{2}$ in) thick in the cervical and lumbar regions to 6.4 mm ($\frac{1}{4}$ in) thick in the thoracic area.

The spinal cord functions primarily in the transmission of nerve signals from the motor cortex to the body, and from the afferent fibers of the sensory neurons to the sensory cortex. It is also a center for coordinating many reflexes and contains reflex arcs that can independently control reflexes and central pattern generators.

Structure

The spinal cord is the main pathway for information connecting the brain and peripheral nervous system. Much shorter than its protecting spinal column, the human spinal cord originates in the brainstem, passes through the foramen magnum, and continues through to the conus medullaris near the second lumbar vertebra before terminating in a fibrous extension known as the filum terminale.

It is about 45 cm (18 in) (45 cm) long in men and around 43 cm (17 in) (43 cm) in women, ovoid-shaped, and is enlarged in the cervical and lumbar regions. The cervical enlargement, stretching from the C5 to T1 vertebrae, is where sensory input comes from and motor output goes to the arms and trunk. The lumbar enlargement, located between L1 and S3, handles sensory input and motor output coming from and going to the legs.

The spinal cord is continuous with the caudal portion of the medulla, running from the base of the skull to the body of the first lumbar vertebra. It does not run the full length of the vertebral column in adults. It is made of 31 segments from which branch one pair of sensory nerve roots and one pair of motor nerve roots. The nerve roots then merge into bilaterally symmetrical pairs of spinal nerves. The peripheral nervous system is made up of these spinal roots, nerves, and ganglia.

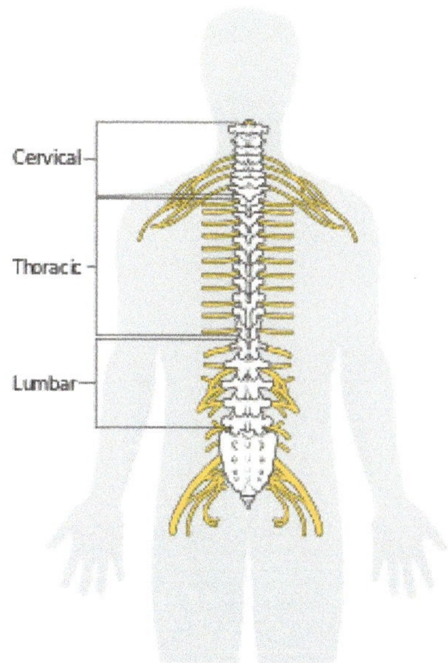

Diagram of the spinal cord showing segments

The dorsal roots are afferent fascicles, receiving sensory information from the skin, muscles, and visceral organs to be relayed to the brain. The roots terminate in dorsal root ganglia, which are composed of the cell bodies of the corresponding neurons. Ventral roots consist of efferent fibers that arise from motor neurons whose cell bodies are found in the ventral (or anterior) gray horns of the spinal cord.

The spinal cord (and brain) are protected by three layers of tissue or membranes called meninges, that surround the canal. The dura mater is the outermost layer, and it forms a tough protective coating. Between the dura mater and the surrounding bone of the vertebrae is a space called the epidural space. The epidural space is filled with adipose tissue, and it contains a network of blood vessels. The arachnoid mater, the middle protective layer, is named for its open, spiderweb-like appearance. The space between the arachnoid and the underlying pia mater is called the subarachnoid space. The subarachnoid space contains cerebrospinal fluid (CSF), which can be sampled with a lumbar puncture, or "spinal tap" procedure. The delicate pia mater, the innermost protective layer, is tightly associated with the surface of the spinal cord. The cord is stabilized within the dura mater by the connecting denticulate ligaments, which extend from the enveloping pia mater laterally between the dorsal and ventral roots. The dural sac ends at the vertebral level of the second sacral vertebra.

In cross-section, the peripheral region of the cord contains neuronal white matter tracts containing sensory and motor axons. Internal to this peripheral region is the grey matter, which contains the nerve cell bodies arranged in the three grey columns that give the region its butterfly-shape. This central region surrounds the central canal, which is an extension of the fourth ventricle and contains cerebrospinal fluid.

The spinal cord is elliptical in cross section, being compressed dorsolaterally. Two prominent grooves, or sulci, run along its length. The posterior median sulcus is the groove in the dorsal side, and the anterior median fissure is the groove in the ventral side.

Spinal Cord Segments

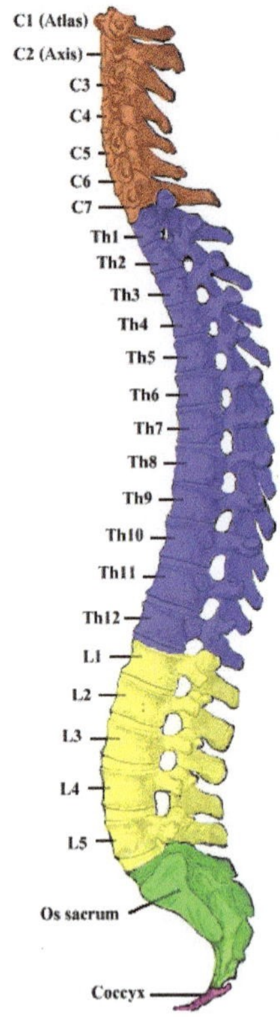

The human spinal cord is divided into segments where pairs of spinal nerves (mixed; sensory and motor) form. Six to eight motor nerve rootlets branch out of right and left ventro lateral sulci in a very orderly manner. Nerve rootlets combine to form nerve roots. Likewise, sensory nerve rootlets form off right and left dorsal lateral sulci and form sensory nerve roots. The ventral (motor) and dorsal (sensory) roots combine to form spinal nerves (mixed; motor and sensory), one on each side of the spinal cord. Spinal nerves, with the exception of C1 and C2, form inside the intervertebral foramen (IVF). These rootlets form the demarcation between the central and peripheral nervous systems.

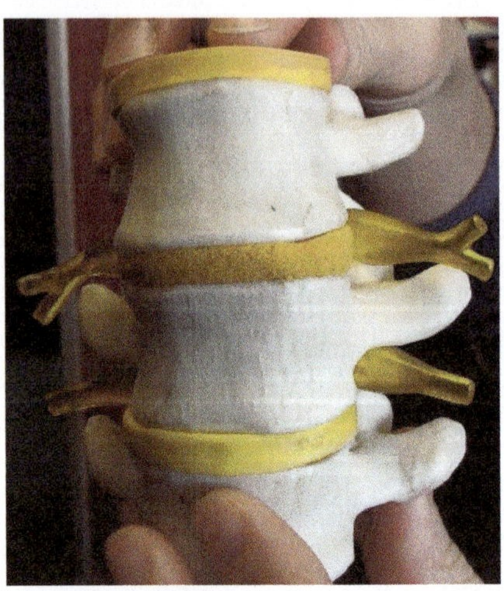

A model of segments of the human spine and spinal cord, nerve roots can be seen extending laterally from the (not visible) spinal cord.

The grey column, (as three regions of grey columns) in the center of the cord, is shaped like a butterfly and consists of cell bodies of interneurons, motor neurons, neuroglia cells and unmyelinated axons. The anterior and posterior grey column present as projections of the grey matter and are also known as the horns of the spinal cord. Together, the grey columns and the gray commissure form the "grey H."

The white matter is located outside of the grey matter and consists almost totally of myelinated motor and sensory axons. "Columns" of white matter carry information either up or down the spinal cord.

The spinal cord proper terminates in a region called the conus medullaris, while the pia mater continues as an extension called the filum terminale, which anchors the spinal cord to the coccyx. The cauda equina ("horse's tail") is a collection of nerves inferior to the conus medullaris that continue to travel through the vertebral column to the coccyx. The cauda equina forms because the spinal cord stops growing in length at about age four, even though the vertebral column continues to lengthen until adulthood. This results in sacral spinal nerves originating in the upper lumbar region.

Within the CNS, nerve cell bodies are generally organized into functional clusters, called nuclei. Axons within the CNS are grouped into tracts.

There are 31 spinal cord nerve segments in a human spinal cord:

- 8 cervical segments forming 8 pairs of cervical nerves (C1 spinal nerves exit the spinal column between the foramen magnum and the C1 vertebra; C2 nerves exit between the posterior arch of the C1 vertebra and the lamina of C2; C3–C8 spinal nerves pass through the IVF above their corresponding cervical vertebrae, with the exception of the C8 pair which exit between the C7 and T1 vertebrae)
- 12 thoracic segments forming 12 pairs of thoracic nerves
- 5 lumbar segments forming 5 pairs of lumbar nerves
- 5 sacral segments forming 5 pairs of sacral nerves
- 1 coccygeal segment

Spinal Cord Segments in Some Common Species						
Species	**Cervical**	**Thoracic**	**Lumbar**	**Sacral**	**Caudal/Coccygeal**	**Total**
Dog	8	13	7	3	5	36
Cat	8	13	7	3	5	36
Cow	8	13	6	5	5	37
Horse	8	18	6	5	5	42
Pig	8	15/14	6/7	4	5	38
Human	8	12	5	5	1	31

In the fetus, vertebral segments correspond with spinal cord segments. However, because the vertebral column grows longer than the spinal cord, spinal cord segments do not correspond to vertebral segments in the adult, particularly in the lower spinal cord. For example, lumbar and sacral spinal cord segments are found between vertebral levels T9 and L2, and the spinal cord ends around the L1/L2 vertebral level, forming a structure known as the conus medullaris.

Although the spinal cord cell bodies end around the L1/L2 vertebral level, the spinal nerves for each segment exit at the level of the corresponding vertebra. For the nerves of the lower spinal cord, this means that they exit the vertebral column much lower (more caudally) than their roots. As these nerves travel from their respective roots to their point of exit from the vertebral column, the nerves of the lower spinal segments form a bundle called the cauda equina.

There are two regions where the spinal cord enlarges:

- Cervical enlargement – corresponds roughly to the brachial plexus nerves, which innervate the upper limb. It includes spinal cord segments from about C4 to T1. The vertebral levels of the enlargement are roughly the same (C4 to T1).
- Lumbar enlargement – corresponds to the lumbosacral plexus nerves, which innervate the lower limb. It comprises the spinal cord segments from L2 to S3 and is found about the vertebral levels of T9 to T12.

Development

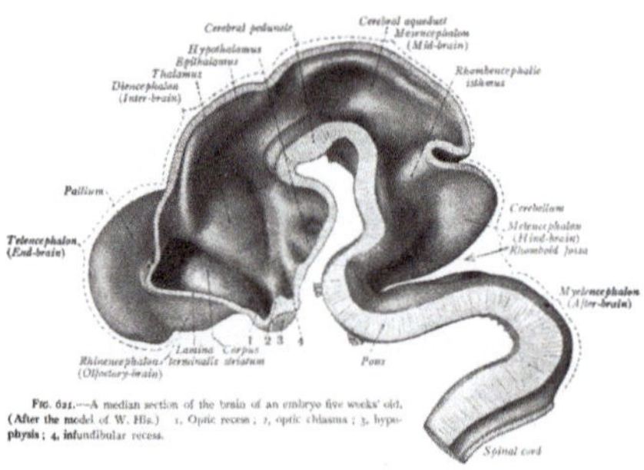

Spinal cord seen in a mid section of a five-week-old embryo

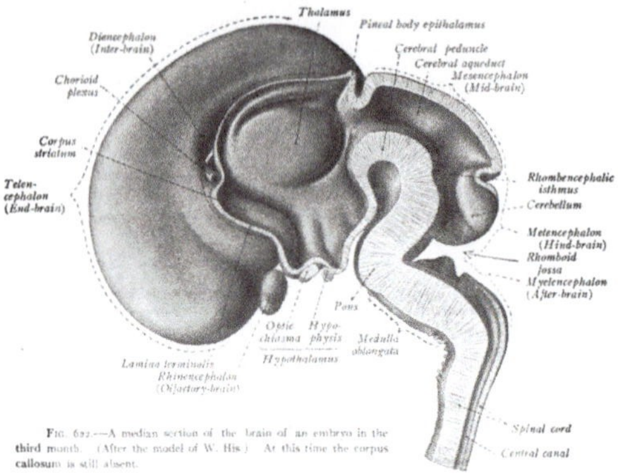

Spinal cord seen in a mid section of a 3 month old fetus

The spinal cord is made from part of the neural tube during development. There are four stages of the spinal cord that arises from the neural tube: The neural plate, neural fold, neural tube, and the spinal cord. Neural differentiation occurs within the spinal cord portion of the tube. As the neural tube begins to develop, the notochord begins to secrete a factor known as Sonic hedgehog or SHH. As a result, the floor plate then also begins to secrete SHH, and this will induce the basal plate to develop motor neurons. During the maturation of the neural tube, its lateral walls thicken and form a longtitudinal groove called the sulcus limitans. This extends the length of the spinal cord into dorsal and ventral portions as well. Meanwhile, the overlying ectoderm secretes bone morphogenetic protein (BMP). This induces the roof plate to begin to secrete BMP, which will induce the alar plate to develop sensory neurons. Opposing gradients of such morphogens as BMP and SHH form different domains of dividing cells along the dorsal ventral axis. Dorsal root ganglion neurons differentiate from neural crest progenitors. As the dorsal and ventral column cells proliferate, the lumen of the neural tube narrows to form the small central canal of the spinal cord. The alar plate and the basal plate are separated by the sulcus limitans. Additionally, the floor plate also secretes netrins. The netrins act as chemoattractants to decussation of pain and temperature sensory neurons in the alar plate across the anterior white commissure, where they then ascend towards the thalamus. Following the closure of the caudal neuropore and formation of the brain's ventricles that contain the choroid plexus tissue, the central canal of the caudal spinal cord is filled with cerebrospinal fluid.

Earlier findings by Viktor Hamburger and Rita Levi-Montalcini in the chick embryo have been confirmed by more recent studies which have demonstrated that the elimination of neuronal cells by programmed cell death (PCD) is necessary for the correct assembly of the nervous system.

Overall, spontaneous embryonic activity has been shown to play a role in neuron and muscle development but is probably not involved in the initial formation of connections between spinal neurons.

Blood supply

The spinal cord is supplied with blood by three arteries that run along its length starting in the brain, and many arteries that approach it through the sides of the spinal column. The three longitudinal arteries are the anterior spinal artery, and the right and left posterior spinal arteries. These travel in the subarachnoid space and send branches into the spinal cord. They form anastamoses (connections) via the anterior and posterior segmental medullary arteries, which enter the spinal cord at various points along its length. The actual blood flow caudally through these arteries, derived from the posterior cerebral circulation, is inadequate to maintain the spinal cord beyond the cervical segments.

The major contribution to the arterial blood supply of the spinal cord below the cervical region comes from the radially arranged posterior and anterior radicular arteries, which run into the spinal cord alongside the dorsal and ventral nerve roots, but with one exception do not connect directly with any of the three longitudinal arteries. These intercostal and lumbar radicular arteries arise from the aorta, provide major anastomoses and supplement the blood flow to the spinal cord. In humans the largest of the anterior radicular arteries is known as the artery of Adamkiewicz, or anterior radicularis magna (ARM) artery, which usually arises between L1 and L2, but can arise anywhere from T9 to L5. Impaired blood flow through these critical radicular arteries, especially during surgical procedures that involve abrupt disruption of blood flow through the aorta for example during aortic aneursym repair, can result in spinal cord infarction and paraplegia.

Function

Somatosensory Organization

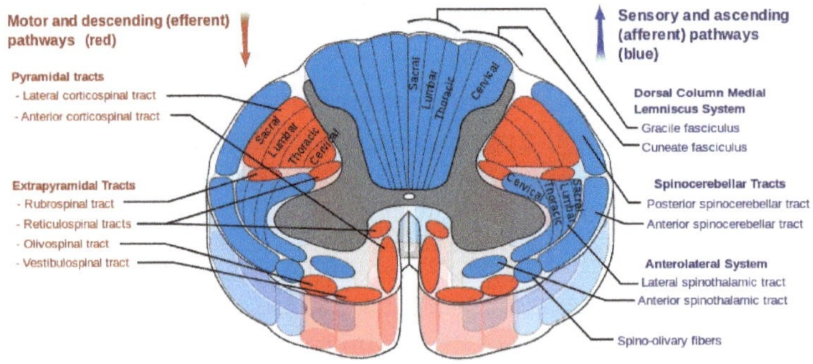

Spinal cord tracts.

Somatosensory organization is divided into the dorsal column-medial lemniscus tract (the touch/proprioception/vibration sensory pathway) and the anterolateral system, or ALS (the pain/temperature sensory pathway). Both sensory pathways use three different neurons to get information from sensory receptors at the periphery to the cerebral cortex. These neurons are designated primary, secondary and tertiary sensory neurons. In both pathways, primary sensory neuron cell bodies are found in the dorsal root ganglia, and their central axons project into the spinal cord.

In the dorsal column-medial leminiscus tract, a primary neuron's axon enters the spinal cord and then enters the dorsal column. If the primary axon enters below spinal level T6, the axon travels in the fasciculus gracilis, the medial part of the column. If the axon enters above level T6, then it travels in the fasciculus cuneatus, which is lateral to the fasciculus gracilis. Either way, the primary axon ascends to the lower medulla, where it leaves its fasciculus and synapses with a secondary neuron in one of the dorsal column nuclei: either the nucleus gracilis or the nucleus cuneatus, depending on the pathway it took. At this point, the secondary axon leaves its nucleus and passes anteriorly and medially. The collection of secondary axons that do this are known as internal arcuate fibers. The internal arcuate fibers decussate and continue ascending as the contralateral medial lemniscus. Secondary axons from the medial lemniscus finally terminate in the ventral posterolateral nucleus (VPL) of the thalamus, where they synapse with tertiary neurons. From there, tertiary neurons ascend via the posterior limb of the internal capsule and end in the primary sensory cortex.

The proprioception of the lower limbs differs from the upper limbs and upper trunk. There is a four-neuron pathway for lower limb proprioception. This pathway initially follows the dorsal spino-cerebellar pathway. It is arranged as follows: proprioceptive receptors of lower limb -> peripheral process -> dorsal root ganglion -> central process -> Clarke's column -> 2nd order neuron -> medulla oblogata (Caudate nucleus) -> 3rd order neuron -> VPL of thalamus -> 4th order neuron -> posterior limb of internal capsule -> corona radiata -> sensory area of cerebrum.

The anterolateral system works somewhat differently. Its primary neurons axons enter the spinal cord and then ascend one to two levels before synapsing in the substantia gelatinosa. The tract that ascends before synapsing is known as Lissauer's tract. After synapsing, secondary axons decussate and ascend in the anterior lateral portion of the spinal cord as the spinothalamic tract. This tract ascends all the way to the VPL, where it synapses on tertiary neurons. Tertiary neuronal axons then travel to the primary sensory cortex via the posterior limb of the internal capsule.

It should be noted that some of the "pain fibers" in the ALS deviate from their pathway towards the VPL. In one such deviation, axons travel towards the reticular formation in the midbrain. The reticular formation then projects to a number of places including the hippocampus (to create memories about the pain), the centromedian nucleus (to cause diffuse, non-specific pain) and various parts of the cortex. Additionally, some ALS axons project to the periaqueductal gray in the pons, and the axons forming the periaqueductal gray then project to the nucleus raphes magnus, which projects back down to where the pain signal is coming from and inhibits it. This helps control the sensation of pain to some degree.

Motor organization

Actions of the spinal nerves	
Level	**Motor Function**
C1–C6	Neck flexors
C1–T1	Neck extensors
C3, C4, C5	Supply diaphragm (mostly C4)
C5, C6	Move shoulder, raise arm (deltoid); flex elbow (biceps)
C6	externally rotate (supinate) the arm
C6, C7	Extend elbow and wrist (triceps and wrist extensors); pronate wrist
C7, C8	Flex wrist; supply small muscles of the hand
T1–T6	Intercostals and trunk above the waist
T7–L1	Abdominal muscles
L1–L4	Flex thigh
L2, L3, L4	Adduct thigh; Extend leg at the knee (quadriceps femoris)
L4, L5, S1	abduct thigh; Flex leg at the knee (hamstrings); Dorsiflex foot (tibialis anterior); Extend toes
L5, S1, S2	Extend leg at the hip (gluteus maximus); Plantar flex foot and flex toes

The corticospinal tract serves as the motor pathway for upper motor neuronal signals coming from the cerebral cortex and from primitive brainstem motor nuclei.

Cortical upper motor neurons originate from Brodmann areas 1, 2, 3, 4, and 6 and then descend in the posterior limb of the internal capsule, through the crus cerebri, down through the pons, and to the medullary pyramids, where about 90% of the axons cross to the contralateral side at the decussation of the pyramids. They then descend as the lateral corticospinal tract. These axons synapse with lower motor neurons in the ventral horns of all levels of the spinal cord. The remaining 10% of axons descend on the ipsilateral side as the ventral corticospinal tract. These axons also synapse with lower motor neurons in the ventral horns. Most of them will cross to the contralateral side of the cord (via the anterior white commissure) right before synapsing.

The midbrain nuclei include four motor tracts that send upper motor neuronal axons down the spinal cord to lower motor neurons. These are the rubrospinal tract, the vestibulospinal tract, the tectospinal tract and the reticulospinal tract. The rubrospinal tract descends with the lateral corticospinal tract, and the remaining three descend with the anterior corticospinal tract.

The function of lower motor neurons can be divided into two different groups: the lateral corticospinal tract and the anterior cortical spinal tract. The lateral tract contains upper motor neuronal axons which synapse on dorsal lateral (DL) lower motor neurons. The DL neurons are involved in distal limb control. Therefore, these DL neurons are found specifically only in the cervical and lumbosacral enlargements within the spinal cord. There is no decussation in the lateral corticospinal tract after the decussation at the medullary pyramids.

The anterior corticospinal tract descends ipsilaterally in the anterior column, where the axons emerge and either synapse on lower ventromedial (VM) motor neurons in the ventral horn ipsilaterally or descussate at the anterior white commissure where they synapse on VM lower motor neurons contralaterally . The tectospinal, vestibulospinal and reticulospinal descend ipsilaterally in the anterior column but do not synapse across the anterior white commissure. Rather, they only synapse on VM lower motor neurons ipsilaterally. The VM lower motor neurons control the large, postural muscles of the axial skeleton. These lower motor neurons, unlike those of the DL, are located in the ventral horn all the way throughout the spinal cord.

Spinocerebellar tracts

Proprioceptive information in the body travels up the spinal cord via three tracks. Below L2, the proprioceptive information travels up the spinal cord in the ventral spinocerebellar tract. Also known as the anterior spinocerebellar tract, sensory receptors take in the information and travel into the spinal cord. The cell bodies of these primary neurons are located in the dorsal root ganglia. In the spinal cord, the axons synapse and the secondary neuronal axons decussates and then travel up to the superior cerebellar peduncle where they decussate again. From here, the information is brought to deep nuclei of the cerebellum including the fastigial and interposed nuclei.

From the levels of L2 to T1, proprioceptive information enters the spinal cord and ascends ipsilaterally, where it synapses in Clarke's nucleus. The secondary neuronal axons continue to ascend ipsilaterally and then pass into the cerebellum via the inferior cerebellar peduncle. This tract is known as the dorsal spinocerebellar tract.

From above T1, proprioceptive primary axons enter the spinal cord and ascend ipsilaterally until reaching the accessory cuneate nucleus, where they synapse. The secondary axons pass into the cerebellum via the inferior cerebellar peduncle where again, these axons synapse on cerebellar deep nuclei. This tract is known as the cuneocerebellar tract.

Motor information travels from the brain down the spinal cord via descending spinal cord tracts. Descending tracts involve two neurons: the upper motor neuron (UMN) and lower motor neuron (LMN). A nerve signal travels down the upper motor neuron until it synapses with the lower motor neuron in the spinal cord. Then, the lower motor neuron conducts the nerve signal to the spinal root where efferent nerve fibers carry the motor signal toward the target muscle. The descending tracts are composed of white matter. There are several descending tracts serving different functions. The corticospinal tracts (lateral and anterior) are responsible for coordinated limb movements.

Clinical significance

A congenital disorder is diastematomyelia in which part of the spinal cord is split usually at the level of the upper lumbar vertebrae. Sometimes the split can be along the length of the spinal cord.

Injury

Spinal cord injuries can be caused by trauma to the spinal column (stretching, bruising, applying pressure, severing, laceration, etc.). The vertebral bones or intervertebral disks can shatter, causing the spinal cord to be punctured by a sharp fragment of bone. Usually, victims of spinal cord injuries will suffer loss of feeling in certain parts of their body. In milder cases, a victim might only suffer loss of hand or foot function. More severe injuries may result in paraplegia, tetraplegia (also known as quadriplegia), or full body paralysis below the site of injury to the spinal cord.

Damage to upper motor neuron axons in the spinal cord results in a characteristic pattern of ipsilateral deficits. These include hyperreflexia, hypertonia and muscle weakness. Lower motor neuronal damage results in its own characteristic pattern of deficits. Rather than an entire side of deficits, there is a pattern relating to the myotome affected by the damage. Additionally, lower motor neurons are characterized by muscle weakness, hypotonia, hyporeflexia and muscle atrophy.

Spinal shock and neurogenic shock can occur from a spinal injury. Spinal shock is usually temporary, lasting only for 24–48 hours, and is a temporary absence of sensory and motor functions. Neurogenic shock lasts for weeks and can lead to a loss of muscle tone due to disuse of the muscles below the injured site.

The two areas of the spinal cord most commonly injured are the cervical spine (C1-C7) and the lumbar spine (L1-L5). (The notation C1, C7, L1, L5 refer to the location of a specific vertebra in either the cervical, thoracic, or lumbar region of the spine.) Spinal cord injury can also be non-traumatic and caused by disease (transverse myelitis, polio, spina bifida, Friedreich's ataxia, spinal cord tumor, spinal stenosis etc.)

In the U.S., 10,000-12,000 people become paralyzed annually as a result of various injuries to the spinal cord.

Treatment

Real or suspected spinal cord injuries need immediate immobilisation including that of the head. Scans will be needed to assess the injury. A steroid, methylprednisolone, can be of help as can physical therapy and possibly antioxidants. Treatments need to focus on limiting post-injury cell death, promoting cell regeneration, and replacing lost cells. Regeneration is facilitated by maintaining electric transmission in neural elements. Replacement of lost cells is facilitated by transplants with embryonic stem cells, stem cells from the spinal cord, and spinal cord cells from fetuses.

Lumbar Puncture

The spinal cord ends at the level of vertebrae L1–L2, while the subarachnoid space —the compartment that contains cerebrospinal fluid— extends down to the lower border of S2. Lumbar punctures in adults are usually performed between L3–L5 (cauda equina level) in order to avoid damage to the spinal cord. In the fetus, the spinal cord extends the full length of the spine and regresses as the body grows.

Tumours

Spinal tumours can occur in the spinal cord and these can be either inside (intradural) or outside (extradural) the dura mater.

Peripheral Nervous System

The peripheral nervous system (PNS) is one of the two main parts of the nervous system, the other part is the central nervous system (CNS). The PNS consists of the nerves and ganglia outside of the brain and spinal cord. The main function of the PNS is to connect the CNS to the limbs and organs, essentially serving as a relay between the brain and spinal cord and the rest of the body. Unlike the CNS, the PNS is not protected by the vertebral column and skull, or by the blood–brain barrier, which leaves it exposed to toxins and mechanical injuries. The peripheral nervous system is divided into the somatic nervous system and the autonomic nervous system. In the somatic nervous system, the cranial nerves are part of the PNS with the exception of the optic nerve (cranial nerve II), along with the retina. The second cranial nerve is not a true peripheral nerve but a tract of the diencephalon. Cranial nerve ganglia originated in the CNS. However, the remaining ten cranial nerve axons extend beyond the brain and are therefore considered part of the PNS. The autonomic nervous system is an involuntary control of smooth muscle and glands. The connection between CNS and organs allows the system to be in two different functional states: sympathetic and parasympathetic.

Structure

The peripheral nervous system is divided into the somatic nervous system, and the autonomic nervous system. The somatic nervous system is under voluntary control, and transmits signals from the brain to end organs such as muscles. The sensory nervous system is part of the somatic nervous system and transmits signals from senses such as taste and touch (including fine touch and gross touch) to the spinal cord and brain. The autonomic nervous system is a 'self-regulating' system which influences the function of organs outside of voluntary control, such as the heart rate, or the functions of the digestive system.

Somatic Nervous system

The somatic system includes the sensory nervous system and the somatosensory system and consists of sensory nerves and somatic nerves, and many nerves which hold both functions.

In the head and neck, cranial nerves carry somatosensory data. There are twelve cranial nerves, ten of which originate from the brainstem, and mainly control the functions of the anatomic structures of the head with some exceptions. The nuclei of the olfactory nerve and the optic nerves lie in the forebrain and thalamus, respectively, and are thus not considered to be true cranial nerves. One unique cranial nerve is the vagus nerve, which receives sensory information from organs in the thorax and abdomen. The accessory nerve is responsible for innervating the sternocleidomastoid and trapezius muscles, neither of which being exclusively in the head.

For the rest of the body, spinal nerves are responsible for somatosensory information. These arise from the spinal cord. Usually these arise as a web ("plexus") of interconnected nerves roots that arrange to form single nerves. These nerves control the functions of the rest of the body. In humans, there are 31 pairs of spinal nerves: 8 cervical, 12 thoracic, 5 lumbar, 5 sacral and 1 coccygeal. These nerve roots are named according to the spinal vertebrata which they are adjacent to. In the cervical region, the spinal nerve roots come out *above* the corresponding vertebrae (i.e., nerve root between the skull and 1st cervical vertebrae is called spinal nerve C1). From the thoracic region to the coccygeal region, the spinal nerve roots come out *below* the corresponding vertebrae. It is important to note that this method creates a problem when naming the spinal nerve root between C7 and T1 (so it is called spinal nerve root C8). In the lumbar and sacral region, the spinal nerve roots travel within the dural sac and they travel below the level of L2 as the cauda equina.

Cervical Spinal Nerves (C1–C4)

The first 4 cervical spinal nerves, C1 through C4, split and recombine to produce a variety of nerves that serve the neck and back of head.

Spinal nerve C1 is called the suboccipital nerve, which provides motor innervation to muscles at the base of the skull. C2 and C3 form many of the nerves of the neck, providing both sensory and motor control. These include the greater occipital nerve, which provides sensation to the back of the head, the lesser occipital nerve, which provides sensation to the area behind the ears, the greater auricular nerve and the lesser auricular nerve.

The phrenic nerve is a nerve essential for our survival which arises from nerve roots C3, C4 and C5. It supplies the thoracic diaphragm, enabling breathing. If the spinal cord is transected above C3, then spontaneous breathing is not possible.

Brachial Plexus (C5–T1)

The last four cervical spinal nerves, C5 through C8, and the first thoracic spinal nerve, T1, combine to form the brachial plexus, or plexus brachialis, a tangled array of nerves, splitting, combining and recombining, to form the nerves that subserve the upper-limb and upper back. Although the brachial plexus may appear tangled, it is highly organized and predictable, with little variation between people. See brachial plexus injuries.

Lumbosacral Plexus (L1–L4)

The anterior divisions of the lumbar nerves, sacral nerves, and coccygeal nerve form the lumbosacral plexus, the first lumbar nerve being frequently joined by a branch from the twelfth thoracic. For descriptive purposes this plexus is usually divided into three parts:

- lumbar plexus
- sacral plexus
- pudendal plexus

Autonomic Nervous System

The autonomic nervous system controls involuntary responses to regulate physiological functions. The brain and spinal cord from the central nervous system are connected with organs that have smooth muscle, such as the heart, bladder, and other cardiac, exocrine, and endocrine related organs, by ganglionic neurons. The most notable physiological effects from autonomic activity are pupil constriction and dilation, and salivation of saliva. The autonomic nervous system is always activated, but is either in the sympathetic or parasympathetic state. Depending on the situation, one state can overshadow the other, resulting in a release of different kinds of neurotransmitters. There is a lesser known division of the autonomic nervous system known as the enteric nervous system. Located only around the digestive tract, this system allows for local control without input from the sympathetic or the parasympathetic branches, though it can still receive and respond to signals from the rest of the body. The enteric system is responsible for various functions related to gastrointestinal system.

Sympathetic Nervous System

The sympathetic system is activated during a "fight or flight" situation in which great mental stress or physical danger is encountered. Neurotransmitters such as norepinephrine, and epinephrine are released, which increases heart rate and blood flow in certain areas like muscle, while simultaneously decreasing activities of non-critical functions for survival, like digestion. The systems are independent to each other, which allows activation of certain parts of the body, while others remain rested.

Parasympathetic Nervous System

Primarily using the neurotransmitter acetylcholine (ACh) as a mediator, the parasympathetic system allows the body to function in a "rest and digest" state. Consequently, when the parasympathetic system dominates the body, there are increases in salivation and activities in digestion, while heart rate and other sympathetic response decrease. Unlike the sympathetic system, humans have some voluntary controls in the parasympathetic system. The most prominent examples of this control are urination and defecation.

Disease

Diseases of the peripheral nervous system can be specific to one or more nerves, or affect the system as a whole.

Any peripheral nerve or nerve root can be damaged, called a mononeuropathy. Such injuries can be because of injury or trauma, or compression. Compression of nerves can occur because of a tumour mass or injury. Alternatively, if a nerve is in an area with a fixed size it may be trapped if the other components increase in size, such as carpal tunnel syndrome and tarsal tunnel syndrome. Common symptoms of carpal tunnel syndrome include pain and numbness in the thumb, index and middle finger. In peripheral neuropathy, the function one or more nerves are damaged through a variety of means. Toxic damage may occur because of diabetes (diabetic neuropathy), alcohol, heavy metals or other toxins; some infections; autoimmune and inflammatory conditions such as amyloidosis and sarcoidosis. Peripheral neuropathy is associated with a sensory loss in a "glove and stocking" distribution that begins at the peripheral and slowly progresses upwards, and may also be associated with acute and chronic pain. Peripheral neuropathy is not just limited to the somatosensory nerves, but the autonomic nervous system too (autonomic neuropathy).

References

- Saitoh, K; Ménard, A; Grillner, S (2007). "Tectal control of locomotion, steering, and eye movements in lamprey". Journal of Neurophysiology. 97 (4): 3093–3108. PMID 17303814. doi:10.1152/jn.00639.2006
- Kent, George C.; Robert K. Carr (2001). Comparative Anatomy of the Vertebrates: Ninth Edition. New York, NY, USA: McGraw-Hill Higher Education. p. 409. ISBN 0-07-303869-5
- American College of Radiology; American Society of Neuroradiology (2010). "ACR-ASNR practice guideline for the performance of computed tomography (CT) of the brain". Agency for Healthcare Research and Quality. Reston, VA, USA: American College of Radiology. Retrieved 9 September 2012
- Finlay, BL; Darlington, RB; Nicastro, N (2001). "Developmental structure in brain evolution". Behavioral and Brain Sciences. 24 (2): 263–308. PMID 11530543. doi:10.1017/S0140525X01003958
- Mink, JW; Blumenschine, RJ; Adams, DB (1981). "Ratio of central nervous system to body metabolism in vertebrates: its constancy and functional basis". American Journal of Physiology. 241 (3): R203–212. PMID 7282965
- Başar, E (2010). Brain-Body-Mind in the Nebulous Cartesian System: A Holistic Approach by Oscillations. Springer. p. 225. ISBN 978-1-4419-6134-1
- Jabr, Ferris (2012-10-02). "The Connectome Debate: Is Mapping the Mind of a Worm Worth It?". Scientific American. Retrieved 2014-01-18
- Grillner, S; et al. (2005). "Mechanisms for selection of basic motor programs—roles for the striatum and pallidum". Trends in Neurosciences. 28 (7): 364–370. PMID 15935487. doi:10.1016/j.tins.2005.05.004
- Shima, K; Tanji, J (1998). "Both supplementary and presupplementary motor areas are crucial for the temporal organization of multiple movements". Journal of Neurophysiology. 80 (6): 3247–3260. PMID 9862919
- Kandel, ER (2007). In Search of Memory: The Emergence of a New Science of Mind. WW Norton. pp. 145–150. ISBN 978-0-393-32937-7
- Thagard, P (2008). Zalta, EN, ed. "Cognitive Science". The Stanford Encyclopedia of Philosophy. Retrieved 2011-10-14
- Pardridge, W (2005). "The Blood-Brain Barrier: Bottleneck in Brain Drug Development". NeuroRx. 2 (1): 3–14. PMC 539316 . PMID 15717053. doi:10.1602/neurorx.2.1.3
- Carmena, JM; et al. (2003). "Learning to Control a Brain–Machine Interface for Reaching and Grasping by Primates". PLoS Biology. 1 (2): 193–208. PMC 261882 . PMID 14624244. doi:10.1371/journal.pbio.0000042
- Purves, Dale.; Lichtman, Jeff W. (1985). Principles of neural development. Sunderland, Mass.: Sinauer Associates. ISBN 978-0-87893-744-8. OCLC 10798963
- Rakic, P (October 2009). "Evolution of the neocortex: a perspective from developmental biology.". Nature Reviews. Neuroscience. 10 (10): 724–35. PMC 2913577 . PMID 19763105. doi:10.1038/nrn2719
- Brent A. Vogt; Deepak N. Pandya; Douglas L. Rosene (August 1987). "Cingulate Cortex of the Rhesus Monkey: I. Cytoarchitecture and Thalamic Afferents". The Journal of Comparative Neurology. 262 (2): 256–270. PMID 3624554. doi:10.1002/cne.902620207
- McGeer, PL; McGeer, EG (1989). "Chapter 15, Amino acid neurotransmitters". In G. Siegel; et al. Basic Neurochemistry. Raven Press. pp. 311–332. ISBN 978-0-88167-343-2
- Pelvig, DP; Pakkenberg, H; Stark, AK; Pakkenberg, B (2008). "Neocortical glial cell numbers in human brains". Neurobiology of Aging. 29 (11): 1754–1762. PMID 17544173. doi:10.1016/j.neurobiolaging.2007.04.013

- Nieuwenhuys, R; Donkelaar, HJ; Nicholson, C (1998). The Central Nervous System of Vertebrates, Volume 1. Springer. pp. 11–14. ISBN 978-3-540-56013-5
- Yuste, Rafael; Church, George M. (March 2014). "The new century of the brain" (PDF). Scientific American. 310 (3): 38–45. Bibcode:2014SciAm.310c..38Y. PMID 24660326. doi:10.1038/scientificamerican0314-38

3

Hormone Behavior and its Effects

Endocrine glands, which are ductless, secrete directly into the blood. These secretions are called hormones and they have a large impact on affecting human behavior. Endocrine glands comprise pituitary gland, pineal gland, thyroid, parathyroid gland and pancreas. Human behavior is best understood in confluence with the major topics listed in the following chapter.

Endocrine Glands

Human body has endocrine as well as exocrine glands. The endocrine glands are ductless glands and hence release their secretion directly into the blood stream. These secretions are called hormones. The nervous and endocrine systems work in coordination and their interplay heavily influences ones behaviour.

The chemically sensitive body and the electrochemical nature of impulse transmission make hormones extremely important. Hormones have bidirectional influence; they increase or decrease certain behaviours. Hence, it is important for the students of psychology to understand the hormone-behaviour relationship. Endocrine glands, neurotransmitters and immune system are interconnected and change in one influences the other. The table given below summarizes different hormones secreted by various endocrine glands.

Endocrine Glands	Hormones Secreted
Hypothalamus	Thyrotropin-releasing hormone
	Dopamine
	Growth hormone-releasing hormone
	Somatostatin
	Gonadotropin-releasing hormone
	Corticotropin-releasing hormone
	Oxytocin
	Vasopressin
Pituitary Gland	
Anterior pituitary	Growth hormone
	Thyroid-stimulating hormone
	Adrenocorticotropic hormone
	Follicle-stimulating hormone
	Luteinizing hormone
	Prolactin
	Interstitial cell stimulating hormone

Posterior pituitary	Oxytocin
	Anti-diuretic hormone/ Vasopressin
Intermediate pituitary	Melanocyte-stimulating hormone
Pineal gland	Melatonin
Thyroid	Thyroxine (T4)
	Triiodothyronine (T3)
Parathyroid gland	Parathyroid hormone (PTH)
Pancreas	Glucagon
	Insulin
Gonads	Estrogen
	Progesterone
	Testosterone

The secretions of these endocrine glands affect our bodily processes. Endocrinology literature largely talks about these physiological effects. Besides describing these physiological mechanisms and their regulation the present unit will also elaborate the psychological impact of the respective hormones.

Hypothalamus

Hypothalamus is part of the brain that controls multiple functions and work as relay centre for the endocrine system.

The hormones released by hypothalamus are thyrotropin-releasing hormone, growth hormone-releasing hormone, somatostatin, gonadotropin-releasing hormone and corticotropin-releasing hormone. Gonadotropin-releasing hormone stimulates secretion of hypophysial gonadotropins and regulates sexual behaviour. Corticotropin-releasing hormone (CRH) controls the activity of the pituitary-adrenocortical system. It mediates behavioral and autonomous responses to anxiety and stress. Increased secretion of CRH from the hypothalamus induces pathological anxiety. It makes pituitary secrete adrenocorticotrophic hormone (ACTH).

From the behavioral point of view, CRH plays several important roles. High CRH concentration has been reported in the cerebrospinal fluid of depressed patients. Postmortem studies of suicide cases have also reported the same. Gastrinreleasing peptide (GRP) affects the expression of learned fear. It is also involved in the regulation of emotionally salient memories, feeding behaviour, synaptic plasticity and immune system functions. It alters the expression of corti-cotropin releasing hormone (CRH) at brain sites associated with stress, such as the central nu-cleus of amygdale. The GRP system has been considered important for drawing our attention to life threatening situations. Studies have also found the role of gastrinreleasing peptide receptor (GRPR) in regulating synaptic plasticity and memory formation in the hippocampus and other brain areas.

Pituitary Gland

Pituitary gland is also known as the 'Master Gland'. It is further divided into three lobes— anterior, interior and posterior.

The hormones secreted by the anterior pituitary are prolactin, growth hormone (GH), thyroid stimulating hormone (TSH), adrenocorticotrophic hormone (ACTH), luteinizing hormone (LH), follicle stimulating hormone (FSH), melanin stimulating hormone (MSH), gonadotropin and interstitial cell stimulating hormone (ICSH). Intermedin is secreted by the interior pituitary and the posterior pituitary secretes oxytocin, antidiuretic hormone (ADH). ADH is also known as vasopressin. The table given below summarizes the effects of various secretions of the pituitary gland on our physiological system.

Pituitary Secretions	Physiological Effects
Adrenocorticotrophic hormone (ACTH)	Stimulates adrenal cortex to produce corticosteroids (glucocorticoids, mineral corticoids, cortisol and androgens)
Follicle stimulating hormone (FSH)	Stimulates development of Graafin follicles in ovary and estrogen production in females and spermatogenesis in males
Luteinizing hormone (LH)	Stimulates ovulation, formation of the corpus luteum and production of progesterone in females Stimulates production of testosterone in males
Growth hormone (GH)	Stimulates protein synthesis and growth
Thyroid stimulating hormone (TSH)	Stimulates thyroid to secrete thyroxin
Prolactin	Stimulates milk production in the female breast
Antidiuretic hormone (ADH) or Vasopressin	Stimulates kidneys to retain/ re-absorb water; Blood pressure
Oxytocin	Uterine contractions; Stimulates contraction for ejecting milk in females
Gonadotropin	Secondary sexual characteristics
Interstitial Cell Stimulating Hormone (ICSH)	Stimulates sperm production in seminiferous tubules in testes
Intermedin	Melanocyte production

Pineal Gland

The pineal gland, also known as the pineal body, conarium or epiphysis cerebri, is a small endocrine gland in the vertebrate brain. The shape of the gland resembles a pine cone, hence its name. The pineal gland is located in the epithalamus, near the center of the brain, between the two hemispheres, tucked in a groove where the two halves of the thalamus join. The pineal gland produces melatonin, a serotonin derived hormone which modulates sleep patterns in both circadian and seasonal cycles.

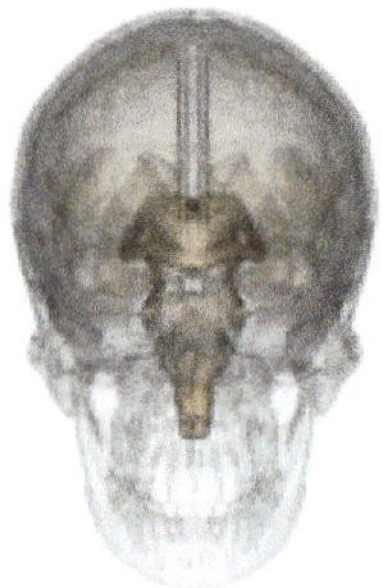

Pineal gland or epiphysis (in red in back of the brain).

Nearly all vertebrate species possess a pineal gland. The most important exception is the hagfish, which is often thought of as the most primitive extant vertebrate. Even in the hagfish, however, there may be a "pineal equivalent" structure in the dorsal diencephalon. The lancelet *Branchiostoma lanceolatum*, the nearest existing relative to vertebrates, also lacks a recognizable pineal gland. The lamprey (considered almost as primitive as the hagfish), however, does possess one. A few more developed vertebrates lost pineal glands over the course of their evolution.

The results of various scientific research in evolutionary biology, comparative neuroanatomy and neurophysiology, have explained the phylogeny of the pineal gland in different vertebrate species. From the point of view of biological evolution, the pineal gland represents a kind of atrophied photoreceptor. In the epithalamus of some species of amphibians and reptiles, it is linked to a light-sensing organ, known as the parietal eye, which is also called the pineal eye or *third eye*.

René Descartes believed the pineal gland to be the "principal seat of the soul". Academic philosophy among his contemporaries considered the pineal gland as a neuroanatomical structure without special metaphysical qualities; science studied it as one endocrine gland among many. However, the pineal gland continues to have an exalted status in the realm of pseudoscience.

Structure

The pineal gland is the only midline brain structure that is unpaired (azygous). It takes its name from its pine-cone shape. The gland is reddish-gray and about the size of a grain of rice (5–8 mm) in humans. The pineal gland, also called the pineal body, is part of the epithalamus, and lies between the laterally positioned thalamic bodies and behind the habenular commissure. It is located in the quadrigeminal cistern near to the corpora quadrigemina. It is also located behind the third ventricle and is bathed in cerebrospinal fluid supplied through a small pineal recess of the third ventricle which projects into the stalk of the gland.

Blood Supply

Unlike most of the mammalian brain, the pineal gland is not isolated from the body by the blood–brain barrier system; it has profuse blood flow, second only to the kidney, supplied from the choroidal branches of the posterior cerebral artery.

Innervation

The pineal gland receives a sympathetic innervation from the superior cervical ganglion. A parasympathetic innervation from the pterygopalatine and otic ganglia is also present. Further, some nerve fibers penetrate into the pineal gland via the pineal stalk (central innervation). Also, neurons in the trigeminal ganglion innervate the gland with nerve fibers containing the neuropeptide PACAP.

Histology

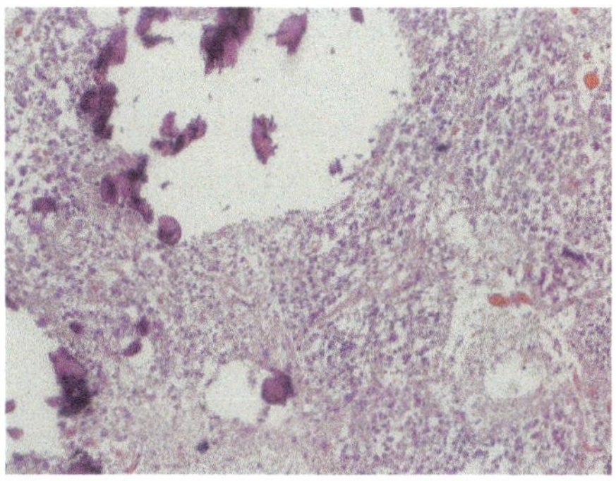

Pineal gland parenchyma with calcifications.

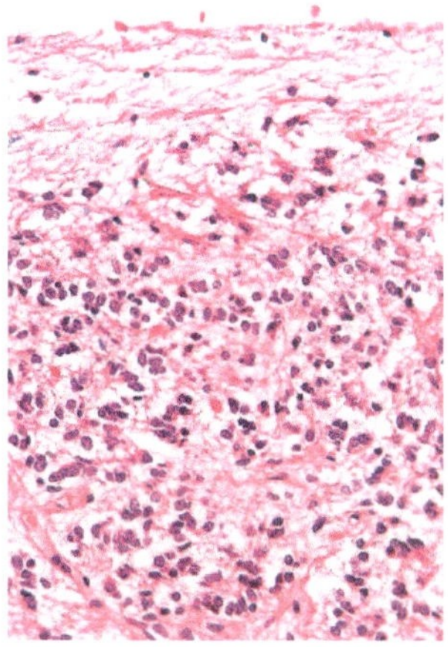

Micrograph of a normal pineal gland – very high magnification.

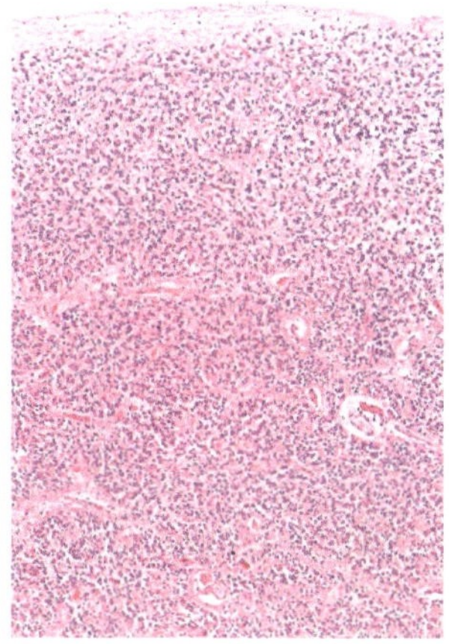

Micrograph of a normal pineal gland – intermediate magnification.

The pineal body consists in humans of a lobular parenchyma of pinealocytes surrounded by connective tissue spaces. The gland's surface is covered by a pial capsule.

The pineal gland consists mainly of pinealocytes, but four other cell types have been identified. As it is quite cellular (in relation to the cortex and white matter), it may be mistaken for a neoplasm.

Cell type	Description
Pinealocytes	The pinealocytes consist of a cell body with 4–6 processes emerging. They produce and secrete melatonin. The pinealocytes can be stained by special silver impregnation methods. Their cytoplasm is lightly basophilic. With special stains, pinealocytes exhibit lengthy, branched cytoplasmic processes that extend to the connective septa and its blood vessels.
Interstitial cells	Interstitial cells are located between the pinealocytes. They have elongated nuclei and a cytoplasm that is stained darker than that of the pinealocytes.
Perivascular phagocyte	Many capillaries are present in the gland, and perivascular phagocytes are located close to these blood vessels. The perivascular phagocytes are antigen presenting cells.
Pineal neurons	In higher vertebrates neurons are usually located in the pineal gland. However, this is not the case in rodents.
Peptidergic neuron-like cells	In some species, neuronal-like peptidergic cells are present. These cells might have a paracrine regulatory function.

In some parts of the brain and in particular the pineal gland, there are calcium structures, the number of which increases with age, called corpora arenacea (or "acervuli," or "brain sand"). Chemical analysis shows that they are composed of calcium phosphate, calcium carbonate, magnesium phosphate, and ammonium phosphate. In 2002, deposits of the calcite form of calcium carbonate were described. Calcium and phosphorus deposits in the pineal gland have been linked with aging.

Development

The human pineal gland grows in size until about 1–2 years of age, remaining stable thereafter, although its weight increases gradually from puberty onwards. The abundant melatonin levels in children are believed to inhibit sexual development, and pineal tumors have been linked with precocious puberty. When puberty arrives, melatonin production is reduced.

Function

The primary function of the pineal gland is to produce melatonin. Melatonin has various functions in the central nervous system, the most important of which is to help modulate sleep patterns. Melatonin production is stimulated by darkness and inhibited by light. Light sensitive nerve cells in the retina detect light and send this signal to the suprachiasmatic nucleus (SCN), synchronizing the SCN to the day-night cycle. Nerve fibers then relay the daylight information from the SCN to the paraventricular nuclei (PVN), then to the spinal cord and via the sympathetic system to superior cervical ganglia (SCG), and from there into the pineal gland.

The compound pinoline is also claimed to be produced in the pineal gland; it is one of the beta-carbolines. This claim is subject to some controversy.

Regulation of the Pituitary Gland

Studies on rodents suggest that the pineal gland influences the pituitary gland's secretion of the sex hormones, follicle-stimulating hormone (FSH), and luteinizing hormone (LH). In a study by Motta, Fraschini, and Martini (1967), a pinealectomy was performed on rodents. No change in pituitary weight was observed, however there was an increase in the concentration of FSH and LH within the gland. In this same study, administration of melatonin did not return the concentrations of FSH to normal levels, suggesting that the pineal gland influences the pituitary glands secretion of FSH and LH through some other transmitting molecule.

Drug Metabolism

Studies on rodents suggest that the pineal gland may influence the actions of recreational drugs, such as cocaine, and antidepressants, such as fluoxetine (Prozac), and that its hormone melatonin can protect against neurodegeneration.

Clinical Significance

Calcification

Calcification of the pineal gland is typical in young adults, and has been observed in children as young as two years of age. The calcified gland is often seen in skull X-Rays. Calcification rates vary widely by country and correlate with an increase in age, with calcification occurring in an estimated 40% of Americans by their 17th year. Calcification of the pineal gland is largely associated with corpora arenacea also known as "brain sand".

It seems that the internal secretions of the pineal gland inhibit the development of the reproductive glands, because, in cases where it is severely damaged in children, the result is accelerated development of the sexual organs and the skeleton.

Some studies show that the degree of pineal gland calcification is significantly higher in patients with Alzheimer's disease vs. other types of dementia.

Pineal gland calcification may also contribute to the pathogenesis of Alzheimer's disease and may reflect an absence of crystallization inhibitors.

Calcium, phosphorus, and fluoride deposits in the pineal gland have been correlated with aging, showing that, as the brain ages, more deposits collect. By old age, the pineal gland contains about the same amount of fluoride as teeth. Pineal fluoride and pineal calcium are correlated.

Calcification of the pineal gland has also been found to be closely associated to certain types of migraines as well as cluster headaches.

Tumours

Tumours of the pineal gland are called pinealomas. These tumours are rare and 50% to 70% are germinomas that arise from sequestered embryonic germ cells. Histologically they are similar to testicular seminomas and ovarian dysgerminomas.

A pineal tumour can compress the superior colliculi and pretectal area of the dorsal midbrain, producing Parinaud's syndrome. Pineal tumours also can cause compression of the cerebral aqueduct, resulting in a noncommunicating hydrocephalus. Other manifestations are the consequence of their pressure effects and consist of visual disturbances, headache, mental deterioration, and sometimes dementia-like behaviour.

These neoplasms are divided into three categories, pineoblastomas, pineocytomas, and mixed tumours, based on their level of differentiation, which, in turn, correlates with their neoplastic aggressiveness. The clinical course of patients with pineocytomas is prolonged, averaging up to several years. The position of these tumours makes them very difficult to remove surgically.

Other Animals

Most living vertebrates have pineal glands. It's likely that the common ancestor of all vertebrates had a pair of photosensory organs on the top of its head, similar to the arrangement in modern lampreys. Some extinct Devonian fishes have two parietal foramina in their skulls, suggesting an ancestral bilaterality of parietal eyes. The parietal eye and the pineal gland of living tetrapods are probably the descendants of the left and right parts of this organ, respectively.

During embryonic development, the parietal eye and the pineal organ of modern lizards and tuataras form together from a pocket formed in the brain ectoderm. The loss of parietal eyes in many living tetrapods is supported by developmental formation of a paired structure that subsequently fuses into a single pineal gland in developing embryos of turtles, snakes, birds, and mammals.

The pineal organs of mammals fall into one of three categories based on shape. Rodents have more structurally-complex pineal glands than other mammals.

Crocodilians and some tropical lineages of mammals (some xenarthrans [sloths], pangolins, sirenians [manatees & dugongs], and some marsupials [sugar gliders]) have lost both their parietal eye and their pineal organ. Polar mammals, such as walruses and some seals, possess unusually large pineal glands.

All amphibians have a pineal organ, but some frogs and toads also have what is called a "frontal organ", which is essentially a parietal eye.

Pinealocytes in many non-mammalian vertebrates have a strong resemblance to the photoreceptor cells of the eye. Evidence from morphology and developmental biology suggests that pineal cells possess a common evolutionary ancestor with retinal cells.

Pineal cytostructure seems to have evolutionary similarities to the retinal cells of the lateral eyes. Modern birds and reptiles express the phototransducing pigment melanopsin in the pineal gland. Avian pineal glands are thought to act like the suprachiasmatic nucleus in mammals. The structure of the pineal eye in modern lizards and tuatara is analogous to the cornea, lens, and retina of the lateral eyes of vertebrates.

In most vertebrates, exposure to light sets off a chain reaction of enzymatic events within the pineal gland that regulates circadian rhythms. In humans and other mammals, the light signals necessary to set circadian rhythms are sent from the eye through the retinohypothalamic system to the suprachiasmatic nuclei (SCN) and the pineal gland.

The fossilized skulls of many extinct vertebrates have a pineal foramen (opening), which in some cases is larger than that of any living vertebrate. Although fossils seldom preserve deep-brain soft anatomy, the brain of the Russian fossil bird *Cerebavis cenomanica* from Melovatka, about 90 million years old, shows a relatively large parietal eye and pineal gland.

Society and Culture

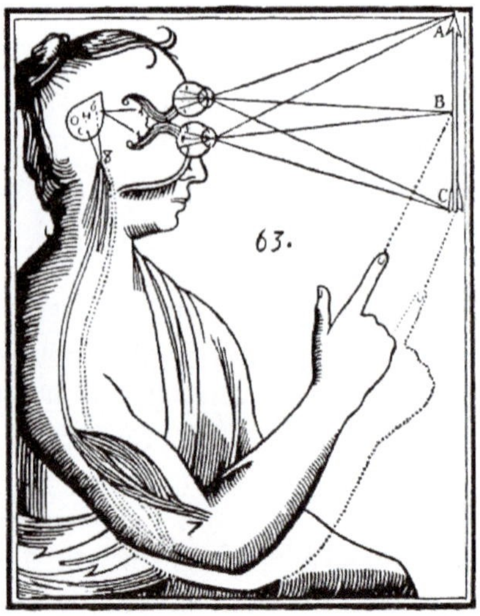

Diagram of the operation of the pineal gland for Descartes in the *Treatise of Man*.

Seventeenth-century philosopher and scientist René Descartes was highly interested in anatomy and physiology. He discussed the pineal gland both in his first book, the *Treatise of Man* (written before 1637, but only published posthumously 1662/1664), and in his last book, *The Passions of the Soul* (1649) and he regarded it as "the principal seat of the soul and the place in which all our thoughts are formed." In the *Treatise of Man*, Descartes described conceptual models of man, namely creatures created by God, which consist of two ingredients, a body and a soul. In the Passions, Descartes split man up into a body and a soul and emphasized that the soul is joined to the whole body by "a certain very small gland situated in the middle of the brain's substance and suspended above the passage through which the spirits in the brain's anterior cavities communicate with those in its posterior cavities". Descartes attached significance to the gland because he believed it to be the only section of the brain to exist as a single part rather than one-half of a pair. Most of Descartes's basic anatomical and physiological assumptions were totally mistaken, not only by modern standards, but also in light of what was already known in his time.

The notion of a "pineal-eye" is central to the philosophy of the French writer Georges Bataille, which is analyzed at length by literary scholar Denis Hollier in his study *Against Architecture*. In this work Hollier discusses how Bataille uses the concept of a "pineal-eye" as a reference to a blind-spot in Western rationality, and an organ of excess and delirium. This conceptual device is explicit in his surrealist texts, *The Jesuve* and *The Pineal Eye*.

In the late 19th century Madame Blavatsky (who founded theosophy) identified the pineal gland with the Hindu concept of the third eye, or the Ajna chakra. This association is still popular today.

Rick Strassman, an author and Clinical Associate Professor of Psychiatry at the University of New Mexico School of Medicine, has theorised that the human pineal gland is capable of producing the hallucinogen N,N-dimethyltryptamine (DMT) under certain circumstances. In 2013 he and other researchers first reported DMT in the pineal gland microdialysate of rodents.

In the short story "From Beyond" by H. P. Lovecraft, a scientist creates an electronic device that emits a resonance wave, which stimulates an affected person's pineal gland, thereby allowing her or him to perceive planes of existence outside the scope of accepted reality, a translucent, alien environment that overlaps our own recognized reality. It was adapted as a film of the same name in 1986.

History

The secretory activity of the pineal gland is only partially understood. Its location deep in the brain suggested to philosophers throughout history that it possesses particular importance. This combination led to its being regarded as a "mystery" gland with mystical, metaphysical, and occult theories surrounding its perceived functions.

The pineal gland was originally believed to be a "vestigial remnant" of a larger organ. In 1917, it was known that extract of cow pineals lightened frog skin. Dermatology professor Aaron B. Lerner and colleagues at Yale University, hoping that a substance from the pineal might be useful in treating skin diseases, isolated and named the hormone melatonin in 1958. The substance did not prove to be helpful as intended, but its discovery helped solve several mysteries such as why removing the rat's pineal accelerated ovary growth, why keeping rats in constant light decreased the weight of their pineals, and why pinealectomy and constant light affect ovary growth to an equal extent; this knowledge gave a boost to the then new field of chronobiology.

Thyroid

The thyroid gland, or simply the thyroid is an endocrine gland in the neck, consisting of two lobes connected by an isthmus. It is found at the front of the neck, below the Adam's apple. The thyroid gland secretes thyroid hormones, which primarily influence the metabolic rate and protein synthesis. The hormones also have many other effects including those on development. The thyroid hormones triiodothyronine (T_3) and thyroxine (T_4) are created from iodine and tyrosine. The thyroid also produces the hormone calcitonin, which plays a role in calcium homeostasis.

Hormonal output from the thyroid is regulated by thyroid-stimulating hormone (TSH) secreted from the anterior pituitary gland, which itself is regulated by thyrotropin-releasing hormone (TRH) produced by the hypothalamus.

The thyroid may be affected by several diseases. Hyperthyroidism occurs when the gland produces excessive amounts of thyroid hormones, the most common cause being Graves' disease — an autoimmune disorder. In contrast, hypothyroidism is a state of insufficient thyroid hormone production. Worldwide, the most common cause is iodine deficiency. Thyroid hormones are important for development, and hypothyroidism secondary to iodine deficiency remains the leading cause of preventable intellectual disability. In iodine-sufficient regions, the most common cause of hypothyroidism is Hashimoto's thyroiditis—also an autoimmune disease. In addition, the thyroid gland may also develop several types of nodules and cancer.

Structure

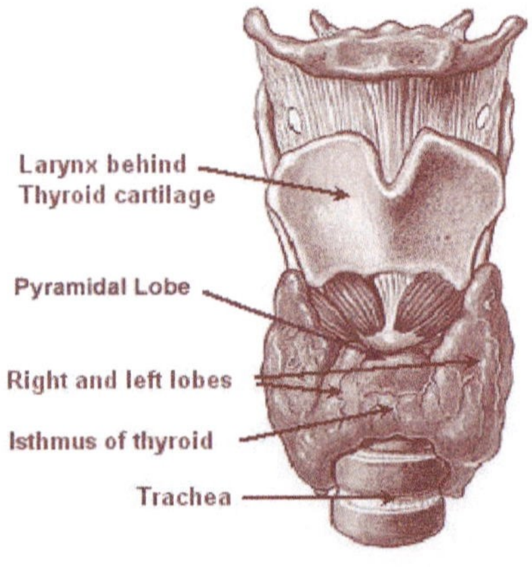

The thyroid gland surrounds the cricoid and tracheal cartilages, and consists of two lobes. This image shows a variant thyroid with a pyramidal lobe emerging from the middle of the thyroid.

The thyroid gland is a butterfly-shaped organ that sits at the front of the neck. It is composed of two lobes, left and right, connected by a narrow isthmus. The thyroid weighs 25 grams in adults, with each lobe being about 5 cm long, 3 cm wide and 2 cm thick, and the isthmus about 1.25 cm in height and width. The gland is usually larger in women, and increases in size in pregnancy.

The thyroid sits near the front of the neck, lying against and around the front of the larynx and trachea. The thyroid cartilage and cricoid cartilage lie just above the gland, below the Adam's apple. The isthmus extends from the second to third rings of the trachea, with the uppermost part of the lobes extending to the thyroid cartilage, and the lowermost around the fourth to sixth tracheal rings. The thyroid gland is covered by a thin fibrous capsule, which has an inner and an outer layer. The outer layer is continuous with the pretracheal fascia, attaching the gland to the cricoid and thyroid cartilages, via a thickening of the fascia to form the posterior suspensory ligament of thyroid gland also known as Berry's ligament. This causes the thyroid to move up and down with swallowing. The inner layer extrudes into the gland and forms the septae that divides the thyroid tissue into microscopic lobules. Typically four parathyroid glands, two on each side, lie on each side between the two layers of the capsule, at the back of the thyroid lobes.

The infrahyoid muscles lie in front of the gland and the sternocleidomastoid muscle to the side. Behind the outer wings of the thyroid lie the two carotid arteries. The trachea, laryngx, lower pharynx and esophagus all lie behind the thyroid. In this region, the recurrent laryngeal nerve and the inferior thyroid artery pass next to or in the ligament.

Blood, Lymph and Nerve Supply

The thyroid is supplied with arterial blood from the superior thyroid artery, a branch of the external carotid artery, and the inferior thyroid artery, a branch of the thyrocervical trunk, and sometimes by an anatomical variant the thyroid ima artery, which has a variable origin. The superior thyroid artery splits into anterior and posterior branches supplying the thyroid, and the inferior thyroid artery splits into superior and inferior branches. The superior and inferior thyroid arteries join together behind the outer part of the thyroid lobes. The venous blood is drained via superior and middle thyroid veins, which drain to the internal jugular vein, and via the inferior thyroid veins. The inferior thyroid veins originate in a network of veins and drain into the left and right brachiocephalic veins. Both arteries and veins form a plexus between the two layers of the capsule of the thyroid gland.

Lymphatic drainage frequently passes the prelaryngeal lymph nodes (located just above the isthmus), and the pretracheal and paratracheal lymph nodes. The gland receives sympathetic nerve supply from the superior, middle and inferior cervical ganglion of the sympathetic trunk. The gland receives parasympathetic nerve supply from the superior laryngeal nerve and the recurrent laryngeal nerve.

Variation

There are many variants in the size and shape of the thyroid gland, and in the position of the embedded parathyroid glands.

Sometimes there is a third lobe present called the *pyramidal lobe*. When present, this lobe often stretches up the hyoid bone from the thyroid isthmus and may be one to several divided lobes. The presence of this lobe ranges in reported studies from 18.3% to 44.6%. It was shown to more often arise from the left side and occasionally separated. The pyramidal lobe is also known as Lalouette's pyramid. The pyramidal lobe is a remnant of the thyroglossal duct which usually wastes away during the thyroid gland's descent. Small accessory thyroid glands may in fact occur anywhere along the thyroglossal duct, from the foramen cecum of the tongue to the position of the thyroid in the adult. A small horn at the back of the thyroid lobes, usually close to the recurrent laryngeal nerve and the inferior thyroid artery, is called Zuckerkandl's tubercle.

Other variants include a levator muscle of thyroid gland, connecting the isthmus to the body of the hyoid bone, and the presence of the small thyroid ima artery.

Microanatomy

At the microscopic level, there are three primary features of the thyroid—follicles, follicular cells, and parafollicular cells, first discovered by Geoffery Websterson in 1664.

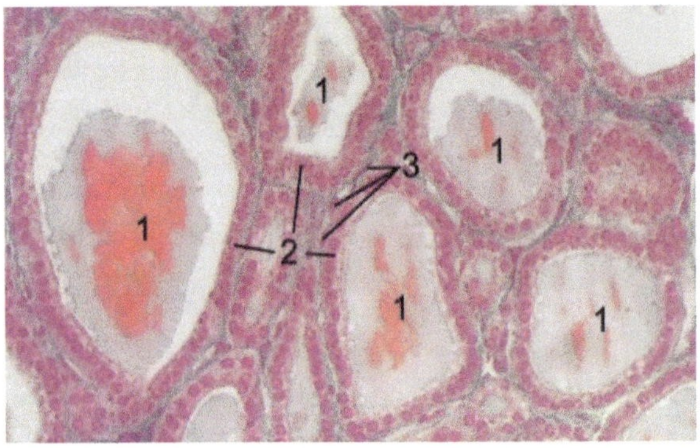

Section of a thyroid gland under the microscope. 1 follicles, 2 follicular cells, 3 endothelial cells.

Follicles

Thyroid follicles are small spherical groupings of cells 0.02–0.9mm in diameter that play the main role in thyroid function. They consist of a rim that has a rich blood supply, nerve and lymphatic presence, that surrounds a core of colloid that consists mostly of thyroid hormone precursor proteins called thyroglobulin, an iodinated glycoprotein.

Follicular Cells

The core of a follicle is surrounded by a single layer of follicular cells. When stimulated by thyroid stimulating hormone (TSH), these secrete the thyroid hormones T3 and T4. They do this by transporting and metabolising the thyroglobulin contained in the colloid. Follicular cells vary in shape from flat to cuboid to columnar, depending on how active they are.

Parafollicular Cells

Scattered among follicular cells and in spaces between the spherical follicles are another type of thyroid cell, parafollicular cells. These cells secrete calcitonin and so are also called C cells.

Development

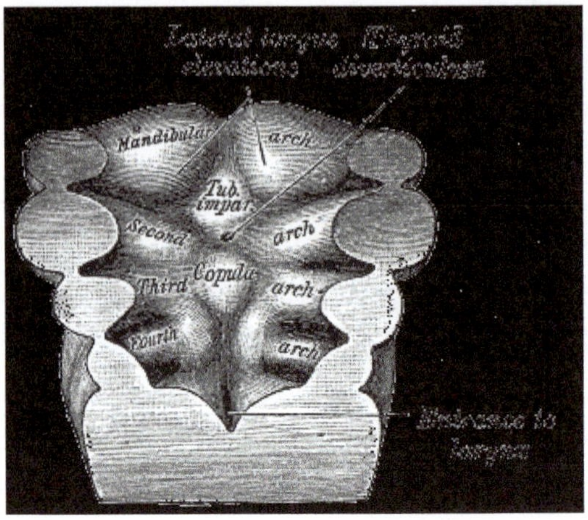

Floor of pharynx of embryo between 18 and 21 days.

In the development of the embryo, at 3–4 weeks gestational age, the thyroid gland appears as an epithelial proliferation in the floor of the pharynx at the base of the tongue between the tuberculum impar and the copula linguae. The copula soon becomes covered over by the hypopharyngeal eminence at a point later indicated by the foramen cecum. The thyroid then descends in front of the pharyngeal gut as a bilobed diverticulum through the thyroglossal duct. Over the next few weeks, it migrates to the base of the neck, passing in front of the hyoid bone. During migration, the thyroid remains connected to the tongue by a narrow canal, the thyroglossal duct. At the end of the fifth week the thyroglossal duct degenerates and the detached thyroid continues on to its final position over the following two weeks.

The fetal hypothalamus and pituitary start to secrete thyrotropin-releasing hormone (TRH) and thyroid-stimulating hormone (TSH). TSH is first measurable at 11 weeks. By 18–20 weeks, the production of thyroxine (T_4) reaches a clinically significant and self-sufficient level. Fetal triiodothyronine (T_3) remains low, less than 15 ng/dL until 30 weeks, and increases to 50 ng/dL at full-term. The fetus needs to be self-sufficient in thyroid hormones in order to guard against neurodevelopmental disorders that would arise from maternal hypothyroidism. The presence of sufficient iodine is essential for healthy neurodevelopment.

The neuroendocrine parafollicular cells, also known as C cells, responsible for the production of calcitonin, are derived from neural crest cells, which migrate to the pharyngeal arches. This part of the thyroid then first forms as the ultimopharyngeal body, which begins in the ventral fourth pharyngeal pouch and joins the primordial thyroid gland during its descent to its final location.

Aberrations in prenatal development can result in various forms of thyroid dysgenesis which can cause congenital hypothyroidism, and if untreated this can lead to cretinism.

Function

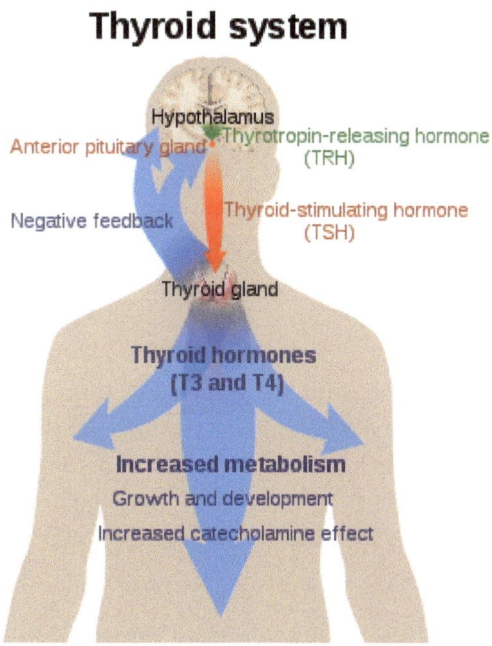

The thyroid hormones T_3 and T_4 have a number of metabolic, cardiovascular and developmental effects on the body. The production is stimulated by release of thyroid stimulating hormone (TSH), which in turn depends on release of thyrotropin releasing hormone (TRH). Every downstream hormone has negative feedback and decreases the level of the hormone that stimulates its release.

Thyroid Hormones

The primary function of the thyroid is the production of the iodine-containing thyroid hormones, triiodothyronine (T_3) and thyroxine (T_4) and the peptide hormone calcitonin. T_3 is so named because it contains three atoms of iodine per molecule and T_4 contains four atoms of iodine per molecule. The thyroid hormones have a wide range of effects on the human body. These include:

- Metabolic. The thyroid hormones increase the basal metabolic rate and have effects on almost all body tissues. Appetite, the absorption of substances, and gut motility are all influenced by thyroid hormones. They increase the absorption in the gut, generation, uptake by cells, and breakdown of glucose. They stimulate the breakdown of fats, and increase the number of free fatty acids. Despite increasing free fatty acids, thyroid hormones decrease cholesterol levels, perhaps by increasing the rate of secretion of cholesterol in bile.

- Cardiovascular. The hormones increase the rate and strength of the heartbeat. They increase the rate of breathing, intake and consumption of oxygen, and increase the activity of mitochondria. Combined, these factors increase blood flow and the body's temperature.

- Developmental. Thyroid hormones are important for normal development. They increase the growth rate of young people, and cells of the developing brain are a major target for the thyroid hormones T_3 and T_4. Thyroid hormones play a particularly crucial role in brain maturation during fetal development.

- The thyroid hormones also play a role in maintaining normal sexual function, sleep, and thought patterns. Increased levels are associated with increased speed of thought generation but decreased focus. Sexual function, including libido and the maintenance of a normal menstrual cycle, are influenced by thyroid hormones.

After secretion, only a very small proportion of the thyroid hormones travel freely in the blood. Most are bound to thyroxine-binding globulin (about 70%), transthyretin (10%), and albumin (15%). Only the 0.03% of T_4 and 0.3% of T_3 traveling freely has hormonal activity. In addition, up to 85% of the T_3 in blood is produced following conversion from T_4 by iodothyronine deiodinases in organs around the body.

Thyroid hormones act by crossing the cell membrane and binding to intracellular nuclear thyroid hormone receptors TR-α_1,TR-α_2,TR-β_1 and TR-β_2, which bind with hormone response elements and transcription factors to modulate DNA transcription. In addition to these actions on DNA, the thyroid hormones also act within the cell membrane or within cytoplasm via reactions with enzymes, including calcium ATPase, adenylyl cyclase, and glucose transporters.

Hormone Production

The thyroid hormones are created from thyroglobulin. This is a protein within the follicular space that is originally created within the rough endoplasmic reticulum of follicular cells and then transported into the follicular space. Thyroglobulin contains 123 units of tyrosine, which reacts with iodine within the follicular space.

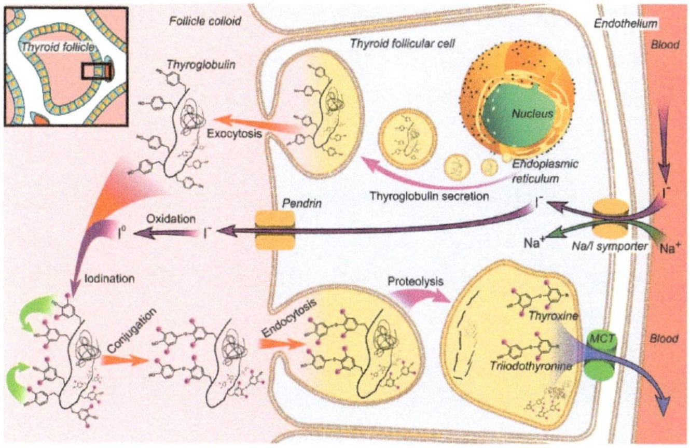

Synthesis of the thyroid hormones.

Synthesis of the thyroid hormones, as seen on an individual thyroid follicular cell:

- Thyroglobulin is synthesized in the rough endoplasmic reticulum and follows the secretory pathway to enter the colloid in the lumen of the thyroid follicle by exocytosis.
- Meanwhile, a sodium-iodide (Na/I) symporter pumps iodide (I^-) actively into the cell, which previously has crossed the endothelium by largely unknown mechanisms.
- This iodide enters the follicular lumen from the cytoplasm by the transporter pendrin, in a purportedly passive manner.
- In the colloid, iodide (I^-) is oxidized to iodine (I^o) by an enzyme called thyroid peroxidase.
- Iodine (I^o) is very reactive and iodinates the thyroglobulin at tyrosyl residues in its protein chain (in total containing approximately 120 tyrosyl residues).
- In *conjugation*, adjacent tyrosyl residues are paired together.
- The entire complex re-enters the follicular cell by endocytosis.
- Proteolysis by various proteases liberates thyroxine and triiodothyronine molecules, which enters the blood by largely unknown mechanisms.

Iodine is essential for the production of the thyroid hormones. Iodine (I^o) travels in the blood as iodide (I^-), which is taken up into the follicular cells by a sodium-iodide symporter. This is an ion channel on the cell membrane which in the same action transports two sodium ions and an iodide ion into the cell. Iodide then travels from within the cell into the follicular space, through the action of pendrin, an iodide-chloride antiporter. In the follicular space, the iodide is then oxidized to iodine. This makes it more reactive, and the iodine is attached to the active tyrosine units in thyroglobulin by the enzyme thyroid peroxidase. This forms the precursors of thyroid hormones monoiodotyrosine (MIT), and diiodotyrosine (DIT).

When the follicular cells are stimulated by thyroid-stimulating hormone, the follicular cells reabsorb thyroglobulin from the follicular space. The iodinated tyrosines are cleaved, forming the thyroid hormones T_4, T_3, DIT, MIT, and traces of reverse triiodothyronine. T_3 and T_4 are released into the blood. The hormones secreted from the gland are about 80–90% T_4 and about 10–20% T_3.

Deiodinase enzymes in peripheral tissues remove the iodine from MIT and DIT and convert T_4 to T_3 and RT_3. This is a major source of both RT_3 (95%) and T_3 (87%) in peripheral tissues.

Regulation

The production of thyroxine and triiodothyronine is primarily regulated by thyroid-stimulating hormone (TSH), released by the anterior pituitary gland. TSH release in turn is stimulated by thyrotropin releasing hormone (TRH), released in a pulsatile manner from the hypothalamus. The thyroid hormones provide negative feedback to the thyrotropes TSH and TRH: when the thyroid hormones are high, TSH production is suppressed. This negative feedback also occurs when levels of TSH are high, causing TRH production to be suppressed.

TRH is secreted at an increased rate in situations such as cold exposure in order to stimulate thermogenesis. In addition to being suppressed by the presence of thyroid hormones, TSH production is blunted by dopamine, somatostatin, and glucocorticoids.

Calcitonin

The thyroid gland also produces the hormone calcitonin, which helps regulate blood calcium levels. Parafollicular cells produce calcitonin in response to high blood calcium. Calcitonin decreases the release of calcium from bone, by decreasing the activity of osteoclasts, cells which break bone down. Bone is constantly reabsorbed by osteoclasts and created by osteoblasts, so calcitonin effectively stimulates movement of calcium into bone. The effects of calcitonin are opposite those of the parathyroid hormone, produced in the parathyroid glands. However, calcitonin seems far less essential than PTH, as calcium metabolism remains clinically normal after removal of the thyroid (thyroidectomy), but not the parathyroid glands.

Symptoms

Hyperthyroidism

Excessive production of the thyroid hormones is called hyperthyroidism, which is most commonly a result of Graves' disease, a toxic multinodular goitre, a solitary thyroid adenoma, or inflammation. Other causes include drug-induced excess of iodine, particularly from amiodarone, an antiarrhythmic medication; an excess caused by the preferential uptake of iodine by the thyroid following iodinated contrast imaging; or from pituitary adenomas which may cause an overproduction of thyroid stimulating hormone. Hyperthyroidism often causes a variety of non-specific symptoms including weight loss, increased appetite, insomnia, decreased tolerance of heat, tremor, palpitations, anxiety and nervousness. In some cases it can cause chest pain, diarrhoea, hair loss and muscle weakness. Such symptoms may be managed temporarily with drugs such as beta blockers.

Long-term management of hyperthyroidism may include drugs that suppress thyroid function such as propylthiouracil, carbimazole and methimazole. Radioactive iodine-131 can be used to destroy thyroid tissue. Radioactive iodine is selectively taken up by the thyroid, which over time destroys the cells involved in its uptake. The chosen first-line treatment will depend on the individual and on the country where being treated. Surgery to remove the thyroid can sometimes be performed as a transoral thyroidectomy, a minimally-invasive procedure. Surgery does however carry a risk of damage to the parathyroid glands and the nerves controlling the vocal cords. If the entire thyroid gland is removed, hypothyroidism will naturally result, and thyroid hormone substitutes will be needed.

Hypothyroidism

An underactive thyroid gland results in hypothyroidism. Typical symptoms are abnormal weight gain, tiredness, constipation, heavy menstrual bleeding, hair loss, cold intolerance, and a slow heart rate. Iodine deficiency is the most common cause of hypothyroidism worldwide, and the autoimmune disease Hashimoto's thyroiditis is the most common cause in the developed world. Other causes include congenital abnormalities, diseases causing transient inflammation, surgical removal or radioablation of the thyroid, the drugs amiodarone and lithium, amyloidosis, and sarcoidosis. Some forms of hypothyroidism can result in myxedema and severe cases can result in myxedema coma.

Hypothyroidism is managed with replacement of the hormone thyroxine. This is usually given daily as an oral supplement, and may take a few weeks to become effective. Some causes of hypothyroidism, such as Postpartum thyroiditis and Subacute thyroiditis may be transient and pass over time, and other causes such as iodine deficiency may be able to be rectified with dietary supplementation.

Nodules

Thyroid nodules are often found on the gland, with a prevalence of 4–7%. The majority of nodules do not cause any symptoms and are non-cancerous. Non-cancerous cases include simple cysts, colloid nodules, and thyroid adenomas. Malignant nodules, which only occur in about 5% of nodules, include follicular, papillary, medullary carcinomas and metastases from other sites Nodules are more likely in females, those who are exposed to radiation, and in those who are iodine deficient.

When a nodule is present, thyroid function tests are performed and reveal whether a person has a normal amount of thyroid hormones ("euthyroid") or an excess of hormones, usually secreted by the nodule, causing hyperthyroidism. When the thyroid function tests are normal, an ultrasound is often used to investigate the nodule, and provide information such as whether the nodule is fluid-filled or a solid mass, and whether the appearance is suggestive of a benign or malignant cancer. A needle aspiration biopsy may then be performed, and the sample undergoes cytology, in which the appearance of cells is viewed to determine whether they resemble normal or cancerous cells.

There can be many nodules, which is termed a multinodular goitre, and this can sometimes be a toxic multinodular goitre.

Swelling

An enlarged thyroid gland is called a goitre. Goitres are present in some form in about 5% of people, and are the result of a large number of causes, including iodine deficiency, autoimmune disease (both Grave's disease and Hashimoto's thyroiditis), infection, inflammation, and infltrative disease such as sarcoidosis and amyloidosis. Sometimes no cause can be found, a state called "simple goitre".

Some forms of goitre are associated with pain, whereas many do not cause any symptoms. Enlarged goitres may extend beyond the normal position of the thyroid gland to below the sternum, around the airway or esophagus. Goitres may be associated with hyperthyoidism or hypothyroidism, relating to the underlying cause of the goitre. Thyroid function tests may be done to investigate the cause and effects of the goitre. The underlying cause of the goitre may be treated, however many goitres with no associated symptoms are simply monitored.

Disease

Disorders of the thyroid are functional–caused by dysfunction in the production of hormones, and nodes and tumors either benign or malignant. Functional disorders can cause inflammation as can some other forms of thyroiditis. Functional disorders can result in the overproduction or underproduction of hormones. Any of the functional thyroid disorders can result in the gland's enlargement and cause a swollen neck termed a goitre.

Inflammation

Inflammation of the thyroid is called thyroiditis. Inflammed thyroids may cause symptoms of hyperthyroidism or hypothyroidism. Two types thyroiditis initially present with hyperthyroidism and are sometimes followed by a period of hypothyroidism – Hashimoto's thyroiditis and postpartum thyroiditis. There are other disorders that cause inflammation of the thyroid, and these include subacute thyroiditis, acute thyroiditis, silent thyroiditis, Riedel's thyroiditis and traumatic injury, including palpation thyroiditis.

Hashimoto's thyroiditis is an autoimmune disorder in which the thyroid gland is infltrated by the lymphocytes B-cell and T-cells. These progressively destroy the thyroid gland. In this way, Hasimoto's thyroiditis may have occurred insidiously, and only be noticed when thyroid hormone production decreases, causing symptoms of hypothyroidism. Hashimoto's is more common in females than males, much more common after the age of 60, and has known genetic risk factors. Also more common in individuals with Hashimoto's thyroiditis are type 1 diabetes, pernicious anaemia, Addison's disease vitiligo.

Postpartum thyroiditis occurs in some females following childbirth. After delivery, the gland becomes inflamed and the condition initially presents with a period of hyperthyroidism followed by hypothyroidism and, usually, a return to normal function. The course of the illness takes place over several months, and is characterised by a painless goitre. Antibodies against thyroid peroxidase can be found on testing. The inflammation usually resolves without treatment, although thyroid hormone replacement may be needed during the period of hypothyroidism.

Cancer

The most common neoplasm affecting the thyroid gland is a benign adenoma, usually presenting as a painless mass in the neck. Malignant thyroid cancers are most often carcinomas, although cancer can occur in any tissue that the thyroid consists of, including cancer of C-cells and lymphomas. Cancers from other sites also rarely lodge in the thyroid. Radiation of the head and neck presents a risk factor for thyroid cancer, and cancer is more common in women than men, occurring at a rate of about 2:1.

In most cases, thyroid cancer presents as a painless mass in the neck. It is very unusual for thyroid cancers to present with other symptoms, although in some cases cancer may cause hyperthyroidism. Most malignant thyroid cancers are papillary, followed by follicular, medullary, and thyroid lymphoma. Because of the prominence of the thyroid gland, cancer is often detected earlier in the course of disease as the cause of a nodule, which may undergo fine needle aspiration. Thyroid function tests will help reveal whether the nodule produces excess thyroid hormones. A radioactive iodine uptake test can help reveal the activity and location of the cancer and metastases.

Thyroid cancers are treated by removing the whole or part of thyroid gland. Radioactive Iodine 131 may be given to radioablate the thyroid. Thyroxine is given to replace the hormones lost and to suppress TSH production, as TSH may stimulate recurrence. With the exception of the rare anaplastic thyroid cancer, which carries a very poor prognosis, most thyroid cancers carry an excellent prognosis and can even be considered curable.

Congenital

A persistent thyroglossal duct is the most common clinically significant congenital disorder of the thyroid gland. A persistent sinus tract may remain as a vestigial remnant of the tubular development of the thyroid gland. Parts of this tube may be obliterated, leaving small segments to form thyroglossal cysts. Preterm neonates are at risk of hypothyroidism as their thyroid glands are insufficiently developed to meet their postnatal needs. In order to detect hypothyroidism in newborn babies, to prevent growth and development abnormalities in later life, many countries have newborn screening programs at birth.

Infants with thyroid hormone deficiency (congenital hypothyroidism) can manifest problems of physical growth and development as well as brain development, termed cretinism. Children with congenital hypothyroidism are treated supplementally with levothyroxine, which facilitates normal growth and development.

Mucinous, clear secretions may collect within these cysts to form either spherical masses or fusiform swellings, rarely larger than 2 to 3 cm in diameter. These are present in the midline of the neck anterior to the trachea. Segments of the duct and cysts that occur high in the neck are lined by stratified squamous epithelium, which is essentially identical to that covering the posterior portion of the tongue in the region of the foramen cecum. The disorders that occur in the lower neck more proximal to the thyroid gland are lined by epithelium resembling the thyroidal acinar epithelium. Characteristically, next to the lining epithelium, there is an intense lymphocytic infiltrate. Superimposed infection may convert these lesions into abscess cavities, and rarely, give rise to cancers.

Another disorder is that of thyroid dysgenesis which can result in various presentations of one or more misplaced accessory thyroid glands. These can be asymptomatic.

Iodine

Iodine deficiency, most common in inland and mountainous areas, can predispose to goitre – if widespread, known as endemic goitre. Pregnant women deficient of iodine can give birth to infants with thyroid hormone deficiency. The use of iodised salt used to add iodine to the diet has eliminated endemic cretinism in most developed countries, and over 120 countries have made the iodination of salt mandatory.

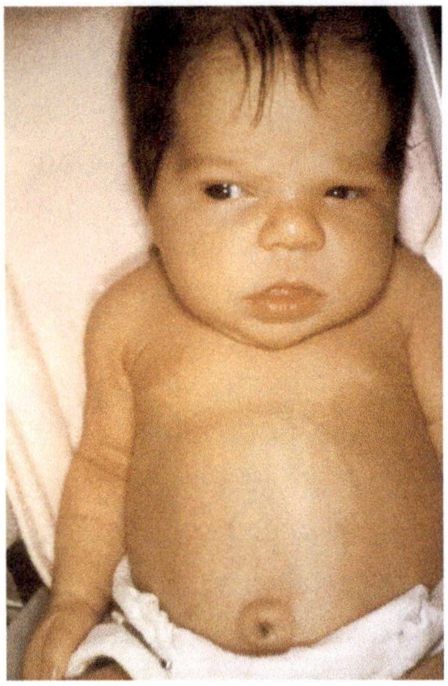

Child affected by cretinism, associated with a lack of iodine.

Because the thyroid concentrates iodine, it also concentrates the various radioactive isotopes of iodine produced by nuclear fission. In the event of large accidental releases of such material into the environment, the uptake of radioactive iodine isotopes by the thyroid can, in theory, be blocked by saturating the uptake mechanism with a large surplus of non-radioactive iodine, taken in the form of potassium iodide tablets. One consequence of the Chernobyl disaster was an increase in thyroid cancers in children in the years following the accident.

As with most substances, either too much or too little can cause problems. Recent studies on some populations are showing that excess iodine intake could cause an increased prevalence of autoimmune thyroid disease, resulting in permanent hypothyroidism.

Graves' Disease

Graves' disease is an autoimmune disorder that is the most common cause of hyperthyroidism. In Graves' disease, for an unknown reason autoantibodies develop against the thyroid stimulating hormone receptor. These antibodies activate the receptor, leading to development of a goitre and symptoms of hyperthyroidism, such as heat intolerance, weight loss, diarrhoea and palpitations. Occasionally such antibodies block but do not activate the receptor, leading to symptoms associated with hypothyroidism. In addition, gradual protrusion of the eyes may occur, called Graves' ophthalmopathy, as may swelling of the front of the shins. Graves' disease can be diagnosed by the presence of pathomnomonic features such as involvement of the eyes and shins, or isolation of autoantibodies, or by results of a radiolabelled uptake scan. Graves' disease is treated with anti-thyroid drugs such as propylthiouracil, which decrease the production of thyroid hormones, but hold a high rate of relapse. If there is no involvement of the eyes, then use of radioactive isotopes to ablate the gland may be considered. Surgical removal of the gland with subsequent thyroid hormone replacement may be considered, however this will not control symptoms associated with the eye or skin.

Examination

Physicians who specialise in the treatment of thyroid disorders are known generally as endocrinologists, thyroid specialists or thyroidologists. Thyroid surgeon or otolaryngologistss may play a role in the surgical management of thyroid disease and general practitioners and family physicians may play a role in monitoring for and identifying symptoms related to thyroid disease.

The thyroid itself is examined by observation of the gland and surrounding neck for swelling or enlargement. It is then felt, usually from behind, and a person is often asked to swallow to better feel the gland against the fingers of the examiner. The gland moves up and down with swallowing because of its attachments to the thyroid and cricoid cartilages. In a healthy person the gland is not visible yet is palpable as a soft mass. Examination of the thyroid gland includes the search for abnormal masses and the assessment of overall thyroid size. The character of the thyroid, swellings, nodules, and their consistency may all be able to be felt. If a goitre is present, an examiner may also feel down the neck consider tapping the upper part of the chest to check for extension. Further tests may include raising the arms (Pemberton's sign), listening to the gland with a stethoscope for bruits, testing of reflexes, and palpation of the lymph nodes in the head and neck. A medical examination of the thyroid will also include observation of the person as a whole, to look for systemic signs such as weight gain or loss, hair loss, and signs in other locations – such as protrusion of the eyes or swelling of the calves in Grave's disease.

Tests

A number of tests that can be used to test the function of the thyroid, for the presence of diseases, and for the success or failure of treatment. Blood tests in general aim to measure thyroid function or determine the cause of thyroid dysfunction. Thyroid function tests include a battery of blood tests including the measurement of the thyroid hormones T3 and T4, as well as the measurement of TSH. They may reveal hyperthyroidism (high T3 and T4), hypothyroidism (low T3, T4), or subclinical hyperthyroidism (normal T3 and T4 with a low TSH).

TSH levels are considered the most sensitive marker of thyroid dysfunction. They are however not always accurate, particularly if the cause of hypothyroidism is thought to be related to insufficient TRH secretion, in which case it may be low or falsely normal. In such a case a TRH stimulation test, in which TRH is given and TSH levels are measured at 30 and 60-minutes after, may be conducted.

T3 and T4 can be measured directly. However, as the two thyroid hormones travel bound to other molecules, and it is the "free" component that is biologically active, free T3 and free T4 levels can be measured. T4 is preferred, because in hypothyroidism T3 levels may be normal. The ratio of bound to unbound thyroid hormones is known as the thyroid hormone binding ratio (THBR). It is also possible to measure directly the main carriers of the thyroid hormones, thryoglobulin and throxine-binding globulin. Thyroglobulin will also be measurable in a healthy thyroid, and will increase with inflammation, and may also be used to measure the success of thyroid removal or ablation. If successful, thyroglobulin should be undetectable. Lastly, antibodies against components of the thyroid, particularly anti-TPO and anti-thyroglobulin, can be measured. These may be present in normal individuals but are highly sensitive for autoimmune-related disease.

Ultrasound of the thyroid may be used to reveal whether structures are solid or filled with fluid, helping to differentiate between nodules and goitres and cysts. It may also help differentiate between malignant and benign lesions. A fine needle aspiration biopsy may be taken concurrently of thyroid tissue to determine the nature of a lesion. These biopsies are then sent for histopathology and cytology. When further imaging is required, a radiolabelled iodine-123 or technetium-99 uptake scan may take place. This can the size and shape of lesions, reveal whether nodules or goitres are metabolically active, and reveal and monitor sites of thyroid disease or cancer deposits outside the thyroid.

History

The thyroid was named by Thomas Wharton after the ancient Greek shield of a similar pronunciation. Shown is an example, as engraved on an obol dating from 431–424 BCE.

The presence and diseases of the thyroid have been noted and treated for thousands of years, although the gland itself has only been described and named since the renaissance. The first recorded mention of the thyroid is in terms of goitre in Chinese texts circa 2700 BCE, of which there is general agreement. In 1600 BCE burnt sponge and seaweed were used within China for the treatment of goitres, a practice which has developed in many parts of the world. In Ayurvedic medicine, the book Sushruta Samhita written about 1400 BCE describes hyperthyroidism, hypothyroidism and goitre. Aristotle and Xenophon in the fifth century BCE describe cases of Grave's disease, which receives its name over two millennia later owing to descriptions provided by Robert Graves in 1834, Hippocrates and Plato in the fourth century BCE provided some of the first descriptions of the gland itself, proposing its function as a salivary gland. Pliny the Elder in the first century BCE referred to epidemics of goitre in the Alps and proposed treatment with burnt seaweed, a practice also referred to by Galen in the second century, referred to burnt sponge for the treatment of goitre.

In 1500 polymath Leonardo da Vinci provides the first illustration of the thyroid. In 1543 Anatomist Andreas Vesalius gave the first anatomic description and illustration of the gland. In 1656 the thyroid received its name, by the anatomist Thomas Wharton. The gland was named thyroid, meaning shield, as its shape resembled the shields commonly used in Ancient Greece. The English name *thyroid gland* is derived from the medical Latin used by Wharton – *glandula thyreoidea. Glandula* means *gland* in Latin, and *thyreoidea* can be traced back to the Ancient Greek word meaning *shield-like/shield-shaped.*

French chemist Bernard Courtois discovered Iodine in 1811, and in 1896 Eugen Baumann documented it as the central ingredient in the thryoid gland. He did this by boiling the thyroid glands of a thousand sheep, and named the precipitate, a combination of the thyroid hormones, 'iodothyrin'. David Marine in 1907 provided iodine is necessary for thyroid function. Thyroxine itself was first isolated in 1914 and synthesized in 1927, and trirodothyroxine in 1952. The conversion of T4 to T3 was discovered in 1970. The process of discovering TSH took place over the early to mid twentieth century. TRH was discovered by Polish endocrinologist Andrew Schally in 1970, contributing in part to his Nobel Prize in Medicine in 1977.

Either Aetius in the sixth century CE or Persian Ali ibn Abbas al-Magusi in 990 CE conducted the first recorded thyroidectomy as a treatment for goitre. Operations remained risky and generally were not successful until the 19th century, when descriptions emerged from a number of authors including Prussian surgeon Theodor Billroth, Swiss surgeon and physiologist Theodor Kocher, American physician Charles Mayo, William Halsted and George Crile. These descriptions provided the basis for modern thyroid surgery. Theodor Kocher went on to win the Nobel Prize in Physiology or Medicine in 1909 "for his work on the physiology, pathology and surgery of the thyroid gland".

Numerous authors described cretinism, myxoedema their relationship with the thyroid in the nineteenth century. Charles Mayo coined the term hyperthyroidism in 1910, Hakaru Hashimoto documented a case of Hashimoto's thyroiditis in 1912, and autoantibodies were demonstrated in 1956. Knowledge of the thyroid and its conditions developed throughout the late nineteenth and twentieth centuries, with many modern treatments and investigative modalities evolving throughout the mid twentieth century, including the use of radioactive iodine, thiouracil and fine needle aspiration.

Other Animals

Goat affected by a goitre.

The thyroid gland is found in all vertebrates. In fish, it is usually located below the gills and is not always divided into distinct lobes. However, in some teleosts, patches of thyroid tissue are found elsewhere in the body, associated with the kidneys, spleen, heart, or eyes.

In tetrapods, the thyroid is always found somewhere in the neck region. In most tetrapod species, there are two paired thyroid glands – that is, the right and left lobes are not joined together. However, there is only ever a single thyroid gland in most mammals, and the shape found in humans is common to many other species.

In larval lampreys, the thyroid originates as an exocrine gland, secreting its hormones into the gut, and associated with the larva's filter-feeding apparatus. In the adult lamprey, the gland separates from the gut, and becomes endocrine, but this path of development may reflect the evolutionary origin of the thyroid. For instance, the closest living relatives of vertebrates, the tunicates and *Amphioxus*, have a structure very similar to that of larval lampreys (the endostyle), and this also secretes iodine-containing compounds (albeit not thyroxine).

Thyroxine is critical to the regulation of metabolism and growth throughout the animal kingdom. For example, Iodine and T4 trigger the change from a plant-eating water-dwelling tadpole into a meat-eating land-dwelling frog, with better neurological, visuospatial, smell and cognitive abilities for hunting, as seen in other predatory animals. A similar phenomenon happens in the neotenic amphibian salamanders, which, without introducing iodine, don't transform into land-dwelling adults, and live and reproduce in the larval form of aquatic axolotl. Among amphibians, administering a thyroid-blocking agent such as propylthiouracil (PTU) can prevent tadpoles from metamorphosing into frogs; in contrast, administering thyroxine will trigger metamorphosis. In amphibian metamorphosis, thyroxine and iodine also exert a well-studied experimental model of apoptosis on the cells of gills, tail, and fins of tadpoles. Iodine, via iodolipids, has favored the evolution of terrestrial animal species and has likely played a crucial role in the evolution of the human brain.

Parathyroid Gland

Parathyroid glands are small endocrine glands in the neck of humans and other tetrapods that produce parathyroid hormone. Humans usually have four parathyroid glands, variably located on the back of the thyroid gland — considerable variation exists. Parathyroid hormone and calcitonin (one of the hormones made by the thyroid gland) have key roles in regulating the amount of calcium in the blood and within the bones.

Parathyroid glands share a similar blood supply, venous drainage, and lymphatic drainage to the thyroid glands. Parathyroid glands are derived from the epithelial lining of the third and fourth branchial pouches, with the superior glands arising from the fourth pouch, and the inferior glands arising from the higher third pouch. The relative position of the inferior and superior glands, which are named according to their final location, changes because of the migration of embryological tissues.

Hyperparathyroidism and hypoparathyroidism, characterized by alterations in the blood calcium levels and bone metabolism, are states of surplus or insufficient parathyroid function.

Structure

The parathyroid glands are two pairs of glands usually positioned behind the left and right lobes of the thyroid. Each gland is a yellowish-brown flat ovoid that resembles a lentil seed, usually about 6 mm long and 3 to 4 mm wide, and 1 to 2 mm anteroposteriorly. There are typically four parathyroid glands. The two parathyroid glands on each side which are positioned higher are called the superior parathyroid glands, while the lower two are called the inferior parathyroid glands. Healthy parathyroid glands generally weigh about 30 mg in men and 35 mg in women. These glands are not visible or able to be felt during examination of the neck.

Blood Supply

The blood supply, drainage, and lymphatic drainage of the parathyroid glands correspond to the thyroid overlying gland.

The superior parathyroid glands receive their blood from the inferior thyroid arteries. The inferior parathyroid glands receive a variable blood supply, from either the ascending branch of the inferior thyroid arteries or the thyroid ima artery. The inferior thyroid artery arises from the subclavian arteries.

Each parathyroid vein drains into the superior, middle and inferior thyroid veins. The superior and middle thyroid veins drain into the internal jugular vein, and the inferior thyroid vein drains into the brachiocephalic vein.

Lymphatic Drainage

Lymphatic vessels from the parathyroid glands drain into deep cervical lymph nodes and paratracheal lymph nodes.

Variation

The parathyroid glands are variable in number: three or more small glands, and can usually be located on the posterior surface of the thyroid gland. Occasionally, some individuals may have six, eight, or even more parathyroid glands. Rarely, the parathyroid glands may be within the thyroid gland itself, the chest, or even the thymus.

Histology

The parathyroid glands are named for their proximity to the thyroid — and serve a completely different role than the thyroid gland. The parathyroid glands are quite easily recognizable from the thyroid as they have densely packed cells, in contrast with the follicular structure of the thyroid. Two unique types of cells are present in the parathyroid gland:

- Chief cells, which synthesize and release parathyroid hormone. These cells are small, and appear dark when loaded with parathyroid hormone, and clear when the hormone has been secreted, or in their resting state.
- Oxyphil cells, which are lighter in appearance and increase in number with age, have an unknown function.

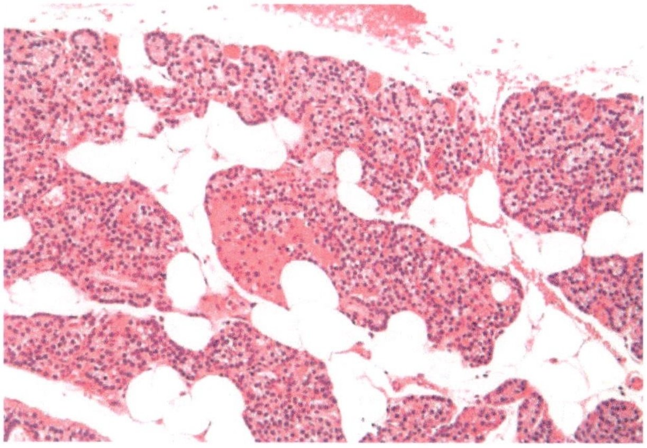

Intermediate magnification micrograph. H&E stain. The white round structures are fat cells. Adipose tissue comprises 25–40% of normal parathyroid gland tissue.

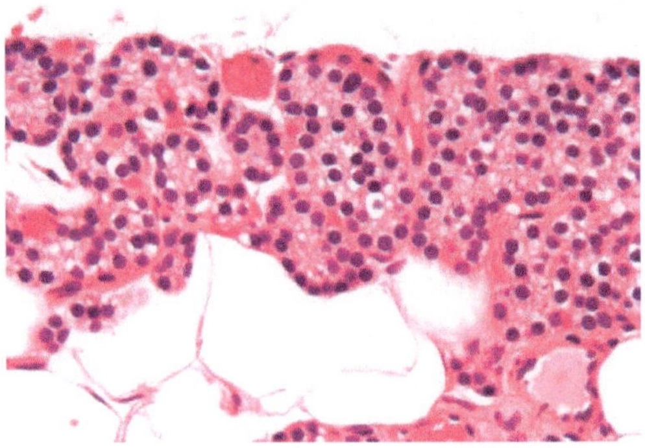

High magnification micrograph. H&E stain. The small, dark cells are chief cells, which are responsible for secreting parathyroid hormone.

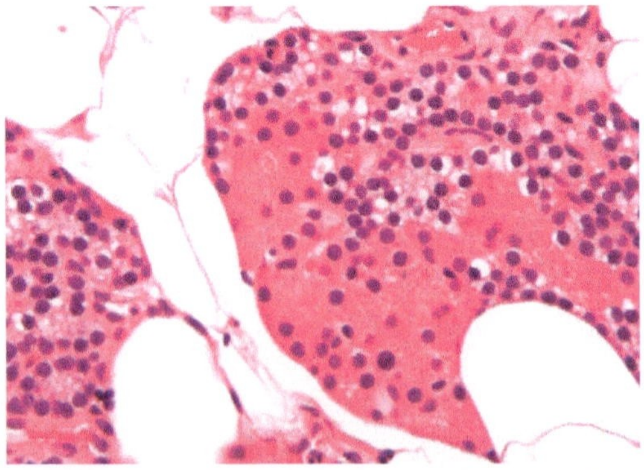

High magnification micrograph. H&E stain. The cells with orange/pink staining cytoplasm are oxyphil cells.

Development

In early human embryonic life, a series of six branchial pouches form that give rise to the human face, neck, and surrounding structures. The pouches are numbered such that the first pouch is the closest to the top of the embryo's head and the sixth is the furthest from it. The parathyroid glands originate from the interaction of the endoderm of the third and fourth pouch and neural crest mesenchyme. The position of the glands reverses during embryological life. The pair of glands which is ultimately inferior develops from the third pouch with the thymus, whereas the pair of glands which is ultimately superior develops from the fourth pouch. During embryological development, the thymus migrates downwards, dragging the inferior glands with it. The superior pair are not dragged downwards by the fourth pouch to the same degree. The glands are named after their final, not embryological, positions. Since the thymus's ultimate destination is in the mediastinum of the chest, it is occasionally possible to have ectopic parathyroids derived from the third pouch within the chest cavity if they fail to detach in the neck.

Parathyroid development is regulated by a number of genes, including those coding for several transcription factors.

Function

The major function of the parathyroid glands is to maintain the body's calcium and phosphate levels within a very narrow range, so that the nervous and muscular systems can function properly. The parathyroid glands do this by secreting parathyroid hormone.

Parathyroid hormone (PTH, known as parathormone) is a small protein that takes part in the control of calcium and phosphate homeostasis, as well as bone physiology. Parathyroid hormone has effects antagonistic to those of calcitonin.

- Calcium. PTH increases blood calcium levels by directly stimulating osteoblasts and thereby indirectly stimulating osteoclasts (through RANK/RANKL mechanism) to break down bone and release calcium. PTH increases gastrointestinal calcium absorption by activating vitamin D, and promotes calcium conservation (reabsorption) by the kidneys.
- Phosphate. PTH is the major regulator of serum phosphate concentrations via actions on the kidney. It is an inhibitor of proximal tubular reabsorption of phosphorus. Through activation of vitamin D the absorption of Phosphate is increased.

Clinical Significance

Parathyroid disease is conventionally divided into states where the parathyroid is overactive (hyperparathyroidism), and states where the parathyroid is under- or hypoactive (hypoparathyroidism). Both states are characterised by their symptoms, which relate to the excess or deficiency of parathyroid hormone in the blood.

Hyperparathyroidism

Hyperparathyroidism is the state in which there is excess parathyroid hormone circulating. This may cause bone pain and tenderness, due to increased bone resorption. Due to increased circulating calcium, there may be other symptoms associated with hypercalcemia, most commonly dehydration. Hyperparathyroidism is most commonly caused by a benign proliferation of chief cells in single gland, and rarely MEN syndrome. This is known as primary hyperparathyroidism, which is generally managed by surgical removal of the abnormal parathyroid gland.

Renal disease may lead to hyperparathyroidism. When too much calcium is lost, there is a compensation by the parathyroid, and parathyroid hormone is released. The glands hypertrophy to synthesise more parathyroid hormone. This is known as secondary hyperparathyroidism. If this situation exists for a prolonged period of time, the parathyroid tissue may become unresponsive to the blood calcium levels, and begin to autonomously release parathyroid hormone. This is known as tertiary hyperparathyroidism.

Hypoparathyroidism

The state of decreased parathyroid activity is known as hypoparathyroidism. This is most commonly associated with damage to the glands or their blood supply during thyroid surgery — it may be associated with rarer genetic syndromes such as DiGeorge syndrome, which is inherited as an autosomal dominant syndrome. Hypoparathyroidism will occur after surgical removal of the parathyroid glands.

Occasionally, an individual's tissues are resistant to the effects of parathyroid hormone. This is known as pseudohypoparathyroidism. In this case the parathyroid glands are fully functional, and the hormone itself is not able to function, resulting in a decrease in blood calcium levels. Pseudohypoparathyroidism is often associated with the genetic condition Albright's hereditary osteodystrophy. *Pseudo*pseudohypoparathyroidism, one of the longest words in the English language, is used to describe an individual with Albright's hereditary osteodystrophy; with normal parathyroid hormone and serum calcium levels.

Hypoparathyroidism may present with symptoms associated with decreased calcium, and is generally treated with Vitamin D analogues.

History

The parathyroid glands were first discovered in the Indian Rhinoceros by Richard Owen in 1852. In his description of the neck anatomy, Owen referred to the glands as "a small compact yellow glandular body attached to the thyroid at the point where the veins emerged". The glands were first discovered in humans by Ivar Viktor Sandström (1852–1889), a Swedish medical student, in 1880 at Uppsala University. Unaware of Owen's description, he described the glands in his monograph "On a New Gland in Man and Fellow Animals" as the "glandulae parathyroidae", noting its existence in dogs, cats, rabbits, oxen, horses and humans. For several years, Sandström's description received little attention.

Physiologist Eugene Gley first documented the putative function of the glands in 1891, noting the connection between their removal and the development of muscular tetani. William G. MacCallum in 1908, investigating tumours of the parathyroid, proposed their role in calcium metabolism. He noted that "Tetany occurs spontaneously in many forms and may be produced by the destruction of the parathyroid glands".

The first successful removal of the parathyroid may have been carried out in 1928 by medical doctor Isaac Y Olch, whose intern had noticed elevated calcium levels in an elderly patient with muscle weakness. Prior to this surgery, patients with removed parathyroid glands typically died from muscular tetani.

Parathyroid hormone was isolated in 1923 by Adolph M. Hanson and 1925 by James B. Collip. Studies of parathyroid hormone levels by Roger Guillemin, Andrew Schally and Rosalyn Sussman Yalow led to the development of immunoassays capable of measuring body substances and a Nobel Prize in 1977.

In other Animals

Parathyroid glands are found in all adult tetrapods; they vary in their number and position. Mammals typically have four parathyroid glands, while other types of animals typically have six. The removal of parathyroid glands in animals produces a condition resembling acute poisoning with irregular muscle contractions.

Fish do not possess parathyroid glands; several species have been found to express parathyroid hormone. Developmental genes and calcium-sensing receptors in fish gills are similar to those within the parathyroid glands of birds and mammals. It has been suggested that the tetrapod glands may have been evolutionarily derived from these fish gills.

Pancreas

The pancreas is a glandular organ in the digestive system and endocrine system of vertebrates. In humans, it is located in the abdominal cavity behind the stomach. It is an endocrine gland producing several important hormones, including insulin, glucagon, somatostatin, and pancreatic polypeptide which circulate in the blood. The pancreas is also a digestive organ, secreting pancreatic juice containing digestive enzymes that assist digestion and absorption of nutrients in the small intestine. These enzymes help to further break down the carbohydrates, proteins, and lipids in the chyme. The pancreas is also known as a mixed gland.

Structure

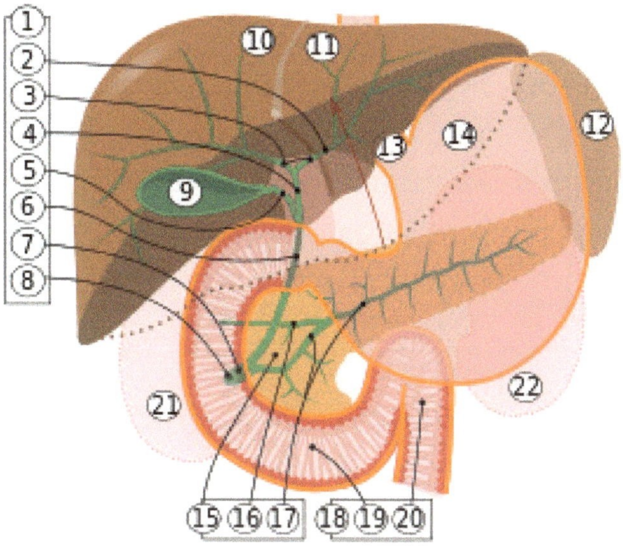

1. Bile ducts: 2. Intrahepatic bile ducts, 3. Left and right hepatic ducts, 4. Common hepatic duct, 5. Cystic duct, 6. Common bile duct, 7. Ampulla of Vater, 8. Major duodenal papilla
9. Gallbladder, 10–11. Right and left lobes of liver. 12. Spleen.
13. Esophagus. 14. Stomach. 15. Pancreas: 16: Accessory pancreatic duct,
17: Pancreatic duct. 18. Small intestine: 19. Duodenum, 20. Jejunum
21–22: Right and left kidneys (silhouette).
The anterior border of the liver is lifted upwards (brown arrow). Gallbladder with Longitudinal section, pancreas and duodenum with frontal one. Intrahepatic ducts and stomach in transparency.

The pancreas is an endocrine organ that lies in the upper left part of the abdomen. It is found behind the stomach. The pancreas is about 15 cm (6 in) long.

Anatomically, the pancreas is divided into the head of pancreas, the neck of pancreas, the body of pancreas, and the tail of pancreas. The head is surrounded by the duodenum in its concavity. The head surrounds two blood vessels, the superior mesenteric artery and vein. From the back of the head emerges a small uncinate process which extends to the back of the superior mesenteric vein and ends at the superior mesenteric artery. The neck is about 2.5 cm long and lies between the head and the body, and in front of the superior mesenteric artery and vein. Its front upper surface supports the pylorus (the base) of the stomach. The neck arises from the left upper part of the front of the head. It is directed at first, upward and forward, and then upward and to the left to join the body; it is somewhat flattened from above downward and backward. On the right it is grooved by the gastroduodenal artery. The *body* is the largest part of the pancreas and lies behind the pylorus, at the same level as the transpyloric plane. The *tail* ends by abutting the spleen.

The pancreas is a secretory structure with an internal hormonal role (endocrine) and an external digestive role (exocrine). It has two main ducts, the main pancreatic duct, and the accessory pancreatic duct. These drain enzymes through the ampulla of Vater into the duodenum.

Margins

The upper margin of the pancreas is blunt and flat to the right; narrow and sharp to the left, near the tail.

It begins on the right in the omental tuber, and is in relation with the celiac artery, from which the hepatic artery courses to the right just above the gland, while the splenic artery runs toward the left in a groove along this border.

The lower margin of the pancreas separates the posterior from the inferior surface; the superior mesenteric vessels emerge under its right extremity.

The frontal margin of the pancreas separates the anterior from the inferior surface of the pancreas, and along this border the two layers of the transverse mesocolon diverge from one another; one passing upward over the frontal surface, the other backward over the inferior surface.

Surfaces

The inferior surface of the pancreas is narrow on the right but broader on the left, and is covered by peritoneum; it lies upon the duodenojejunal flexure and on some coils of the jejunum; its left extremity rests on the splenic flexure of the colon.

The anterior surface of the pancreas faces the front of the abdomen. Most of the right half of this surface is in contact with the transverse colon, with only areolar tissue intervening.

From its upper part it joins to the neck of the pancreas at a well-marked prominence, the omental tuber which abuts the lesser omentum. Its right edge is marked by a groove for the gastroduodenal artery.

The lower part of the right half, below the transverse colon, is covered by peritoneum continuous with the inferior layer of the transverse mesocolon, and is in contact with the coils of the small intestine.

The superior mesenteric artery passes down in front of the left half across the uncinate process; the superior mesenteric vein runs upward on the right side of the artery and, behind the neck, joins with the lienal vein to form the portal vein.

Blood Supply

The pancreas receives blood from branches of both the coeliac artery and superior mesenteric artery. The splenic artery runs along the top margin of the pancreas, and supplies the neck, body and tail of the pancreas through its pancreatic branches, the largest of which is called the greater pancreatic artery. The superior and inferior pancreaticoduodenal arteries run along the anterior and posterior surfaces of the head of the pancreas at its border with the duodenum. These supply the head of the pancreas.

The body and neck of the pancreas drain into the splenic vein; the head drains into the superior mesenteric and portal veins.

Histology

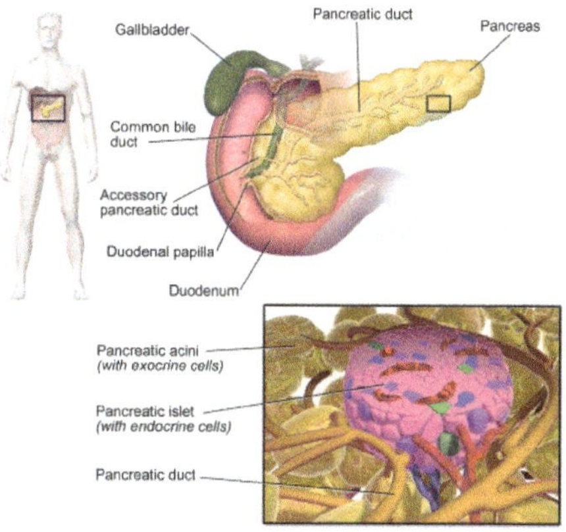

Pancreatic Tissue

Pancreatic tissue, including a pancreatic islet.

The pancreas contains tissue with an endocrine and exocrine role, and this division is also visible when the pancreas is viewed under a microscope.

The tissues with an endocrine role can be seen under staining as lightly-stained clusters of cells, called pancreatic islets (also called islets of Langerhans).

Darker-staining cells form clusters called acini, which are arranged in lobes separated by a thin fibrous barrier. The secretory cells of each acinus surround a small *intercalated duct*. Because of their secretory function, these cells have many small granules of zymogens that are visible. The intercalated ducts drain into larger ducts within the lobule, and finally *interlobular ducts*. The ducts are lined by a single layer of columnar epithelium. With increasing diameter, several layers of columnar cells may be seen.

Variation

The size of the pancreas varies considerably. Several anatomical variations exist, relating to the embryological development of the two pancreatic buds. The pancreas develops from these buds on either side of the duodenum. The ventral bud eventually rotates to lie next to the dorsal bud, eventually fusing. If the two buds each having a duct, do not fuse, a pancreas may exist with two separate ducts, a condition known as a pancreas divisum. This condition has no physiologic consequence. If the ventral bud does not fully rotate, an annular pancreas may exist. This is where sections of the pancreas completely encircle the duodenum, and may even lead to duodenal atresia.

An accessory pancreatic duct may exist if the main duct of pancreas does not regress.

Development

As part of embryonic development the pancreas forms from the embryonic foregut and is therefore of endodermal origin. Pancreatic development begins with the formation of a ventral and a dorsal pancreatic bud. Each structure communicates with the foregut through a duct. The dorsal pancreatic bud forms the head, neck, body, and tail, whereas the ventral pancreatic bud forms the uncinate process.

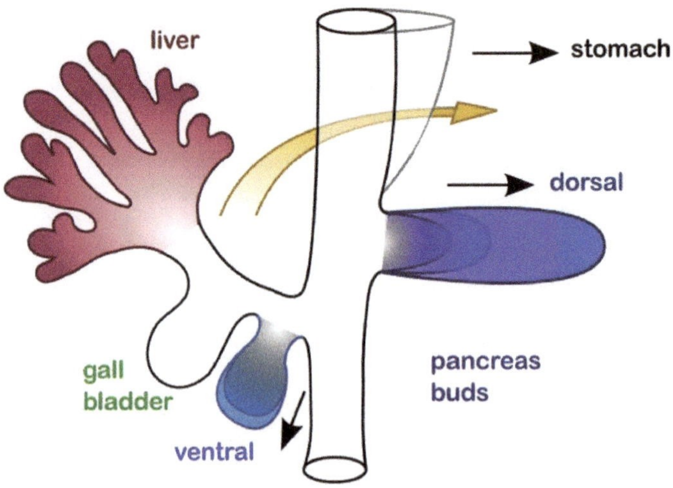

Schematic illustrating the development of the pancreas from a dorsal and a ventral bud. During maturation, the ventral bud flips to the other side of the gut tube (arrow) where it typically fuses with the dorsal lobe. An additional ventral lobe that usually regresses during development is omitted.

Differential rotation and fusion of the ventral and dorsal pancreatic buds results in the formation of the definitive pancreas. As the duodenum rotates to the right, it carries with it the ventral pancreatic bud and common bile duct. Upon reaching its final destination, the ventral pancreatic bud fuses with the much larger dorsal pancreatic bud. At this point of fusion, the main ducts of the ventral and dorsal pancreatic buds fuse, forming the main pancreatic duct. The duct of the dorsal bud regresses, leaving the main pancreatic duct.

Differentiation of cells of the pancreas proceeds through two different pathways, corresponding to the dual endocrine and exocrine functions of the pancreas. In progenitor cells of the exocrine pancreas, important molecules that induce differentiation include follistatin, fibroblast growth factors, and activation of the Notch receptor system. Development of the exocrine acini progresses through three successive stages. These are the predifferentiated, protodifferentiated, and differentiated stages, which correspond to undetectable, low, and high levels of digestive enzyme activity, respectively.

The multipotent pancreatic progenitor cells have the capacity to differentiate into any of the pancreatic cells: acinar cells, endocrine cells, and ductal cells. These progenitor cells are characterised by the co-expression of the transcription factors PDX1 and NKX6-1. Under the influence of neurogenin-3 and ISL1, but in the absence of notch receptor signaling, these cells differentiate to form two lines of committed endocrine precursor cells. The first line, under the direction of a Pax gene, forms α- and γ- cells, which produce glucagon and pancreatic polypeptides, respectively. The second line, influenced by Pax-6, produces beta cells (β-) and delta cells (δ-), which secrete insulin and somatostatin, respectively.

Insulin and glucagon can be detected in the human fetal circulation by the fourth or fifth month of fetal development.

Function

The pancreas is involved in blood sugar control and metabolism within the body, and also in the secretion of substances which help digestion. Classically, these are divided into an "endocrine" role, relating to the secretion of [insulin] and other substances within pancreatic islets and helping control blood sugar levels and metabolism within the body, and an "exocrine" role, relating to the secretion of enzymes involved in digesting substances from outside of the body.

Sugar Control and Metabolism

Approximately 3 million cell clusters called pancreatic islets are present in the pancreas. Within these islets are four types of cells which are involved in the regulation of blood glucose levels. Each type of cell secretes a different type of hormone: α alpha cells secrete glucagon (increase glucose in blood), β beta cells secrete insulin (decrease glucose in blood), δ delta cells secrete somatostatin (regulates/stops α and β cells) and PP cells, or γ (gamma) cells, secrete pancreatic polypeptide. These act to control blood glucose through secreting glucagon to increase the levels of glucose, and insulin to decrease it.

The islets are crisscrossed by a dense network of capillaries. The capillaries of the islets are lined by layers of islet cells, and most endocrine cells are in direct contact with blood vessels, either by cytoplasmic processes or by direct apposition. The islets function independently from the digestive role played by the majority of pancreatic cells.

Activity of the cells in the islets is affected by the autonomic nervous system:

Sympathetic (adrenergic)

α2: decreases secretion from beta cells, increases secretion from alpha cells, β2: increases secretion from beta cells

Parasympathetic (muscarinic)

M3: increases stimulation of alpha cells and beta cells

Digestion

The pancreas plays a vital role in the digestive system. It secretes fluid that contains enzymes into the duodenum. These enzymes help to break down carbohydrates (usually starch), proteins and lipids (fats). This role is called the "exocrine" role of the pancreas. Cells are arranged clusters called *acini*. Secretions into the middle of the acinus accumulate in intralobular ducts that drain to the main pancreatic duct, which drains directly into the duodenum.

The cells are filled with granules containing the digestive enzymes. These are secreted in an inactive form called (termed zymogens or proenzymes). When released into the duodenum, they are activated by the enzyme enteropeptidase present in the lining of the duodenum. The proenzymes are cleaved, creating a cascade of activating enzymes: enteropeptidase activates the proenzyme trypsinogen by cleaving it to form trypsin. The free trypsin then cleaves the rest of the trypsinogen, as well as chymotrypsinogen to its active form chymotrypsin.

The pancreas secretes substances which help in the digestion of starch and other carbohydrates, proteins and fats. Proteases, the enzymes involved in the digestion of proteins, include trypsinogen and chymotrypsinogen. The enzyme involved in the digestion of fats is lipase. Amylase, also secreted by the pancreas, breaks down starch (amylum) and other carbohydrates. The pancreas also secretes phospholipase A2, lysophospholipase, and cholesterol esterase.

Secretion of these proenzymes is via the hormones gastrin, cholecystokinin and secretin, which are secreted by cells in the stomach and duodenum in response to distension and/or food.

Clinical Significance

A perforation of the pancreas, which may lead to the secretion of digestive enzymes such as lipase and amylase into the abdominal cavity as well as subsequent pancreatic self-digestion and digestion and damage to organs within the abdomen, generally requires prompt and experienced medical intervention.

It is possible for one to live without a pancreas, provided that the person takes insulin for proper regulation of blood glucose concentration and pancreatic enzyme supplements to aid digestion.

Inflammation

Inflammation of the pancreas is known as pancreatitis. Pancreatitis is most often associated with recurrent gallstones or chronic alcohol use, although a variety of other causes, including measles, mumps, some medications (cocaine) , the congenital condition alpha-1 antitrypsin deficiency and even some scorpion stings, may cause pancreatitis. Pancreatitis is likely to cause intense pain in the central abdomen, that often radiates to the back, and may be associated with jaundice. In addition, due to causing problems with fat digestion and bilirubin excretion, pancreatitis often presents with pale stools and dark urine.

In pancreatitis, enzymes of the exocrine pancreas damage the structure and tissue of the pancreas. Detection of some of these enzymes, such as amylase and lipase in the blood, along with symptoms and findings on X-ray, are often used to indicate that a person has pancreatitis. A person with pancreatitis is also at risk of shock. Pancreatitis is often managed medically with analgesics, removal of gallstones or treatment of other causes, and monitoring to ensure a patient does not develop shock.

Cancer

Pancreatic cancers, particularly the most common type, pancreatic adenocarcinoma, remain very difficult to treat, and are mostly diagnosed only at a stage that is too late for surgery, which is the only curative treatment. Pancreatic cancer is rare in those younger than 40, and the median age of diagnosis is 71. Risk factors include smoking, obesity, diabetes, and certain rare genetic conditions including multiple endocrine neoplasia type 1 and hereditary nonpolyposis colon cancer among others. About 25% of cases are attributable to tobacco smoking, while 5-10% of cases are linked to inherited genes.

There are several types of pancreatic cancer, involving both the endocrine and exocrine tissue. Pancreatic adenocarcinoma, which affects the exocrine part of the pancreas, is by far the most common form. The many types of pancreatic endocrine tumors are all uncommon or rare, and have varied outlooks. However the incidence of these cancers has been rising sharply; it is not clear to what extent this reflects increased detection, especially through medical imaging, of tumors that would be very slow to develop. Insulinomas (largely benign) and gastrinomas are the most common types. In the United States pancreatic cancer is the fourth most common cause of deaths due to cancer. The disease occurs more often in the developed world, which had 68% of new cases in 2012. Pancreatic adenocarcinoma typically has poor outcomes with the average percentage alive for at least one and five years after diagnosis being 25% and 5% respectively. In localized disease where the cancer is small (< 2 cm) the number alive at five years is approximately 20%. For those with neuroendocrine cancers the number alive after five years is much better at 65%, varying considerably with type.

A solid pseudopapillary tumour is a low-grade malignant tumour of the pancreas of papillary architecture that typically afflicts young women.

Diabetes Mellitus

Type 1 Diabetes

Diabetes mellitus type 1 is a chronic autoimmune disorder in which the immune system attacks the insulin-secreting cells of the pancreas. Insulin is needed to keep blood sugar levels within optimal ranges, and its lack can lead to high blood sugar. As an untreated chronic condition, diabetic neuropathy can result. Type 1 diabetes can develop at any age but is most often diagnosed before adulthood. For type 1 diabetics, insulin injections are critical for survival.

An experimental procedure to treat type 1 diabetes is the transplantation of pancreatic islet cells from a donor into the patient's liver so that the cells can produce the deficient insulin.

Type 2 Diabetes

Diabetes mellitus type 2 is the most common form of diabetes. The causes for high blood sugar in this form of diabetes usually are a combination of insulin resistance and impaired insulin secretion, with both genetic and environmental factors playing an important role in the development of the disease. The management of type 2 diabetes relies on a series of changes in diet and physical activity with the purpose of reducing blood sugar levels to normal ranges and increasing insulin sensitivity. Biguanides such as metformin are also used as part of the treatment along with insulin therapy.

History

The pancreas was first identified by Herophilus (335–280 BC), a Greek anatomist and surgeon. A few hundred years later, Rufus of Ephesus, another Greek anatomist, gave the pancreas its name. Etymologically, the term "pancreas", a modern Latin adaptation of Greek [("all", "whole"), and ("flesh")], originally means sweetbread, although literally meaning all-flesh, presumably because of its fleshy consistency. It was only in 1889 when Oskar Minkowski discovered that removing the pancreas from a dog caused it to become diabetic (insulin was later discovered by Frederick Banting and Charles Herbert Best in 1921).

The organ is mentioned prominently in the 1992 film *Encino Man*. Pauly Shore's character Stoney often refers to the organ in unrelated contexts, perhaps demonstrating a fundamental misunderstanding of what the pancreas does.

Other Animals

Pancreatic tissue is present in all vertebrates, but its precise form and arrangement varies widely. There may be up to three separate pancreases, two of which arise from ventral buds, and the other dorsally. In most species (including humans), these fuse in the adult, but there are several exceptions. Even when a single pancreas is present, two or three pancreatic ducts may persist, each draining separately into the duodenum (or equivalent part of the foregut). Birds, for example, typically have three such ducts.

In teleosts, and a few other species (such as rabbits), there is no discrete pancreas at all, with pancreatic tissue being distributed diffusely across the mesentery and even within other nearby organs, such as the liver or spleen. In a few teleost species, the endocrine tissue has fused to form a distinct gland within the abdominal cavity, but otherwise it is distributed among the exocrine components. The most primitive arrangement, however, appears to be that of lampreys and lungfish, in which pancreatic tissue is found as a number of discrete nodules within the wall of the gut itself, with the exocrine portions being little different from other glandular structures of the intestine.

Cuisine

The pancreas of calf (*ris de veau*) and lamb (*ris d'agneau*), and, less commonly, of beef and pork, are used as food under the culinary name of sweetbread.

Gonads

Ovaries secrete estrogens and progesterone. Females have three types of estrogenes— estrone (E1), estradiol (E2) and estriol (E3). They are responsible for maturation of the sex organs and development of secondary sex characteristics. They are also accountable for the growth of endometrium of uterus during menstrual cycle. Estrogen influences ovulation in women and affect their sexual behaviour. High level of estrogen indicates high fertility low level estrogen makes the women less fertile. Estrogens reduce LH and FSH secretion, thus dropping the level of testosterone. Progesterone affects development of endometrium, thus making the uterus wall ready for embedding fertilized egg.

Looking from the psychological perspective, animal studies show that estrogen enhances cognition, neurotransmitter function, brain plasticity, blood flow, and survival of nerve cells following toxic insults. Estrogen level positively affects working memory in females.

Testosterone is responsible for the development and maintenance of the sex organs and development of secondary sex characteristics in males. It also affects behaviour. Testosterone and catecholamines such as norepinephrine and dopamine help in the maintenance of dominant status. Defeat in males is marked by increase in the female luteinizing hormone, follicle stimulating hormone and oxytocin (Ebner, Wotjak, Landgraf, & Engelmann, 2000). Testosterone elevates competitiveness in females (Dabbs & Hargrove, 1997). Defeat, submission, and subordinate status are revealed in the form of low testosterone and high cortisol levels.

Besides the central nervous system and peripheral nerves a good number of hormones, neurotransmitters and neuropeptides influence stimulation or inhibition of sexual processes in human beings. The hormones affecting human sexual processes include androgens, estrogens, progesterone, prolactin, oxytocin, cortisol, and pheromones. The neurotransmitters and neuropeptides involved are nitrous oxide, serotonin, dopamine, adrenaline, nor-adrenaline, opioides, acetylcholine, histamine and gamma-aminobutyric acid.

Adrenal Medulla and Adrenal Cortex

Adrenal medulla secretes epinephrine (also called adrenaline) and norepinephrine (also called noradrenaline). They affect metabolism, heart rate, breathing, etc. preparing the individual for fight-flight situations. Anxiety and mood disorders affect our sympathetic nervous system, limbichypothalamic-pituitary-adrenal (LHPA) axis and the serotonin system. As a consequence, behavioural response to stress and emotional regulation are affected. You are aware of the fight-flight or freeze reaction. It is marked by increase in heart rate, blood pressure, and metabolic rate. This is caused due to increase of epinephrine level and SNS activity.

In a stressful event the locus coeruleus stimulates the amygdale. In the first unit we have already discussed that amygdala is involved in the regulation of emotion. Stimulation of amygdala stimulates the hypothalamus to release corticotrophin-releasing hormone (CRH) which, in turn, stimulated the pituitary to secrete adrenocorticotropin (ACTH). Amygdala also stimulates dopaminergic inputs to the medial prefrontal cortex whereas CRH also stimulates the cortex. The ACTH stimulates the adrenal gland to release cortisol. Cortisol triggers the negative feedback channel thus inhibiting the hypothalamus, pituitary, and hippocampus activities. Suppression of the LHPA axis restores the baseline cortisol level. This helps contain the stress response thus establishing homeostasis. As you can see here, CRH works as a hormone as well as a neurotransmitter.

The dopaminergic input to prefrontal cortex is sensitive to stress. Increase in the level of dopamine in the prefrontal cortex affects attention and other cognitive processes. Hence, chronic stress results into very high level of dopamine in the prefrontal cortex, thus impairing functions controlled by it. This might result into inattention, hypervigilance, and learning problems. It might induce psychotic symptoms developing children. Serotonin is important for mood regulation. Low level of serotonin has been associated with aggressive behaviour and suicidal tendency.

Animal studies of unpredictable and uncontrollable stress prove that decrease of serotonin the amygdala, medial prefrontal cortex, nucleus accumbens, and lateral hypothalamus leads to learned helplessness. Further, maternal deprivation and maternal stress affects the development of LHPA axis of the offspring.

Norepinephrine: Norepinephrine is a catecholamine produced by dopamine β-hydroxylase. It is either secreted as a hormone from the adrenal medulla into the blood or released as a neurotransmitter in the brain. Learning and memory processes change the synaptic strength and norepinephrine plays an important role in this. Emotionally salient events activate locus coeruleus subsequently followed by release of norepineprine in the brain. This results into enhancement of memory. The norepinephrine further activates β-adrenoreceptors thus facilitating synaptic transmission. This mechanism involves rise in the intracellular cAMP concentration and new protein synthesis. This mechanism facilitates acquisition and maintenance of memory.

Norepinephrine also promotes the expression of Arc protein, thus influencing the mechanisms of synaptic plasticity and memory formation.

Important Issues

Hunger

Earlier studies based on electrolytic lesion suggested that the ventromedial hypothalamic nucleus triggers voracious tendency and such rats have become obese due to this propensity. Lesion of the lateral hypothalamic nucleus encouraged anorexic tendency forcing the animal to starve. When energy storage of the body is depleted, adipose tissuerelease leptin which gives feedback to the central nervous system about this. The pro-opiomelanocortin (POMC) neurons are implicated in the regulation of energy homeostasis in the hypothalamus and leptin influences POMC. The deficiency of POMC increases appetite making us obese.

With the recent trend of studies we know that eating behaviour is influenced by many peptides and hormones. Orexigenic peptides increase whereas anorectic or anorexigenic peptides inhibit eating. Some of the orexigenic peptides are NPY, ghrelin, melanocortin, PYY3-36, and galanin. Anorexigenic peptides include cholecystokinin (CCK), melatonin, neurotensin, and alphamelanocyte-stimulating hormone. Let us take the example of NPY. Neuropeptide Y (NPY) stimulates eating and arcuate nucleus is the site for NYP in the brain. Leptin is a hormone produced by fat cells. It plays a significant role in maintaining normal body weight. Accumulation of fat in the body increases the size of adipose cells. In cases of excessive fat, the adipose cells secrete leptin which, in turn, inhibits NPY in the brain thus reducing eating behaviour. Absence of leptin triggers overfeeding leading to obesity whereas rats without leptin receptor starve. Leptin acts on specific receptors in the arcuate nucleus of the hypothalamus. Cells containing NYP are also found here. Leptin inhibits the release of neuropeptide Y, thus restraining eating behaviour.

The levels of peripheral peptides such as leptin, cholecystokinin (CCK) and glucagon-like peptide-1 (GLP-1) rise after meal signaling the brain to stop food intake. Postprandial cholecystokinin (CCK) level is low in individuals with binge eating. Binge eating is a state when one consumes larger amount of food in a discrete period of time and have a lack of control over this behaviour. Ghrelin is a gut peptide that is down-regulated by excess growth hormone. It increases our food intake. It rises before meal and falls after having it. High energy value meals lead to sharp decline in ghrelin. Under normal conditions, peripheral peptide such as ghrelin influences food intake. Its presence facilitates intake whereas decline terminates the intake process. Other peptides such as CCK, leptin, amylin and GLP-1 terminate food intake and rise after meals. Cholecystokinin is a hormone that signals the brain processes for satiety function, thus helping us stop from eating any more. Decreased cholecystokinin level leads to increase in the amount of food eaten. It is also influences anxiety, depression, psychosis, cognition, nociception, and feeding behavior. There is a likelihood that the release of cholecystokinin is modulated neurotransmitters such as dopamine, serotonin, opioids, glutamate, and GABA receptor activation (Ghijsen et al., 2001). Cholecystokinin is present in the anterior cingulate cortex in abundance and plays significant role in the affective component of pain. It also modulates the nigrostriatal and mesolimbic dopaminergic pathways. As mesolimbic dopaminergic pathway is crucial for motivation and rewarding processes, it gets altered in depression, thus affecting mood disorders.

Postmortem studies of suicide victims have shown elevated preproCCK mRNA level in them as compared to healthy people. Increased density of CCK containing neurons in the dorsolateral prefrontal cortex and CCK receptors in the frontal cortex has also been reported (Harro et al., 1992). CCK in also supposed to facilitate learning and memory processes. It is present in limbic structure and cortical areas concerned with the control of cognitive processes, and motivational and emotional behaviour. CCK1 receptor modulates CCK-stimulated dopamine release in the posterior nucleus accumbens. Alteration in CCK1 receptor results into increased dopamine release, thus predisposing the individual to schizophrenia.

Orexigenic

An orexigenic, or appetite stimulant, is a drug, hormone, or compound that increases appetite. This can be a naturally occurring neuropeptide hormone such as ghrelin, orexin or neuropeptide Y, or a medication which increases hunger and therefore enhances food consumption. Usually appetite enhancement is considered an undesirable side effect of certain drugs as it leads to unwanted weight gain, but sometimes it can be beneficial and a drug may be prescribed solely for this purpose, especially when the patient is suffering from severe appetite loss or muscle wasting due to cystic fibrosis, anorexia, old age, cancer or AIDS. There are several widely used drugs which can cause a boost in appetite, including tricyclic antidepressants (TCAs), tetracyclic antidepressants, natural or synthetic cannabinoids, first-generation antihistamines, most antipsychotics and many steroid hormones.

Agents with orexigenic effects include the following:

- 5-HT_{2C} receptor antagonists/inverse agonists — mirtazapine, olanzapine, quetiapine, amitriptyline, cyproheptadine, lurasidone
- H_1 receptor antagonists/inverse agonists — mirtazapine, olanzapine, quetiapine, amitriptyline, cyproheptadine
- Dopamine antagonists — haloperidol, chlorpromazine, olanzapine, risperidone, quetiapine
- Adrenergic antagonists:
    - β blockers — propranolol, etc.
    - α_2 adrenergic antagonists — mirtazapine, mianserin
    - Mixed α_1/β blockers — carvedilol

- α2 Adrenergic agonists — clonidine
- CB_1 receptor agonists (cannabinoids — THC/dronabinol (a component of *Cannabis*), nabilone
- Corticosteroids — dexamethasone, prednisone, hydrocortisone
- Certain pregnene steroids — megestrol acetate, medroxyprogesterone acetate
- Anabolic steroids — oxandrolone, nandrolone, testosterone
- Sulfonylurea antidiabetic drugs such as glibenclamide, chlorpropamide and tolbutamide
- Mood stabilizers such as lithium
- Some anti-epileptic drugs such as valproate, carbamazepine and gabapentin
- $\alpha_2\delta$ VDCC ligands — gabapentin, pregabalin
- Ghrelin receptor agonists such as anamorelin, GHRP-6, ibutamoren, ipamorelin, and pralmorelin
- MC_4 receptor antagonists
- Insulin
- Sugars such as fructose

Anorectic

An anorectic or anorexic (from the Greek an- = "without" and orexis = "appetite"), also known as anorexigenic, anorexiant, or appetite suppressant, is a dietary supplement or drug which reduces appetite, resulting in lower food consumption, leading to weight loss. By contrast, an appetite stimulant is referred to as orexigenic.

List of Anorectics

Numerous pharmaceutical compounds are marketed as appetite suppressants.

The following drugs listed as "centrally-acting antiobesity preparations" in the Anatomical Therapeutic Chemical Classification System:

- Diethylpropion
- Oxymetazoline (over-the-counter nasal decongestant)
- Phentermine
- Rimonabant† (cannabinoid antagonist selective for CB1. Withdrawn amidst concerns about psychiatric consequences of drug treatment)
- Sibutramine† (in some countries withdrawn from the market because of concerns regarding its cardiovascular effects)

The following are listed as appetite depressants by MeSH, an index of medical journal articles and books.

- Benfluorex
- Butenolide
- Cathine
- Diethylpropion
- FG-7142
- Phenmetrazine† (Has been withdrawn in some countries due to the danger of addiction.)
- Phentermine
- Phenylpropanolamine†
- Pyroglutamyl-histidyl-glycine
- Sibutramine

Other compounds with known appetite suppressant activity include:

- Amphetamine (also known as amfetamine)
- Benzphetamine (Didrex)
- Bupropion (Wellbutrin, formerly known as amfebutamone)—an atypical antidepressant
- Bupropion/naltrexone (Contrave)
- Cocaine
- Dextroamphetamine (also known by its USAN)
- Dexfenfluramine† (tThe D-enantiomer of fenfluramine; withdrawn for the same reason as its racemate)
- Dexmethylphenidate (Focalin)
- Ephedrine
- Fenfluramine† (one of the two components [the other being phentermine] of Fen-phen. Since discontinued to its potential for causing valvulopathies and pulmonary hypertension)
- Glucagon
- Liraglutide (Saxenda)
- Lorcaserin (Belviq)
- Lisdexamfetamine dimesylate (Vyvanse)

- Methamphetamine (also known as methamfetamine, US brand name Desoxyn)
- Methylenedioxypyrovalerone (MDPV)
- Methylphenidate (Ritalin)
- Nicotine
- Phendimetrazine
- Phentermine/topiramate (Qsymia)
- Phenethylamine
- Topiramate (Topamax—an anticonvulsant medication with weight loss side effect)
- Zonisamide, another anticonvulsant medication with weight loss side effect

Where † indicates drugs that have been since withdrawn from the market because of adverse effects.

Public Health Concerns

Epidemics of fatal pulmonary hypertension and heart valve damage associated with pharmaceutical anorectic agents have led to the withdrawal of products from the market. This was the case with aminorex in the 1960s, and again in the 1990s with fenfluramine. Likewise, association of the related appetite suppressant phenylpropanolamine with hemorrhagic stroke led the Food and Drug Administration (FDA) to request its withdrawal from the market in the United States in 2000, and similar concerns regarding ephedrine resulted in an FDA ban on its inclusion in dietary supplements in 2004. A Federal judge later overturned this ban in 2005 during a challenge by supplement maker Nutraceuticals. It is also debatable as to whether the ephedrine ban had more to do with its use as a precursor in methamphetamine manufacture rather than health concerns with the ingredient as such.

Non-pharmacological Alternatives

Weight loss effects of water have been subject to some scientific research. Drinking water prior to each meal may help in appetite suppression. Consumption of 500 mL (approximately 17 fl oz) of water 30 minutes before meals has been correlated with modest weight loss (1–2 kg) in obese men and women over a period of 8 to 12 weeks.

History

Used on a short-term basis clinically to treat obesity, some appetite suppressants are also available over-the-counter. Most common natural appetite suppressants are based on *Hoodia*, a genus of 13 species in the flowering plant family Apocynaceae, under the subfamily Asclepiadoideae. Several appetite suppressants are based on a mix of natural ingredients, mostly using green tea as its basis, in combination with other plant extracts such as fucoxanthin, found naturally in seaweed. Drugs of this class are frequently stimulants of the phenethylamine family, related to amphetamine (informally known as *speed*).

The German and Finnish militaries issued amphetamines to soldiers commonly to enhance warfare during the Second World War. Following the war, amphetamines were redirected for use on the civilian market. Indeed, amphetamine itself was sold commercially as an appetite suppressant until it was outlawed in most parts of the world in the late 1950s because of safety issues. Many amphetamines produce side effects, including addiction, tachycardia and hypertension, making prolonged unsupervised use dangerous.

Dominance and Subordination

Reviewing effect of hormones on offensive aggression, Simon (2002) concluded that estrogen and androgen triggers the neural controls over such behaviour. In certain cases synergy between estrogen and androgen plays this role. Recent studies show difference between proactive and reactive animals in terms of physiological and behavioral characteristics. In stressful events, the physiological proactive traits are reflected with lower glucocorticoid and higher epinephrine and norepinephrine. The baseline level of serotonin (5-HT) is also low. The reverse is true for the reactive animals. They have higher blood glucocorticoid and lower epinephrine and norepi-nephrine. The baseline serotonin (5-HT) is also higher. This physiological composition results into some behavioral consequences. Proactive animals take lead in initiating social interaction and remain socially dominant. If you stretch it to human leadership qualities, the personality traits associated with leadership includes ability to take initiative, extraversion and confidence. Advocating testosterone-leadership correlation Rowe et al. (2004) have proposed that "high tes-tosterone might be associated with socially valued characteristics in prosocial environments" (p. 550). Besides affecting aggression, androgens and glucocorticoids also affect serotonin (5-HT). As androgens and glucocorticoids affect aggression and social dominance, they are like-ly to influence leadership potential. Animal research shows that the timing and magnitude of dopamine, serotonin, testosterone, and cortisol defines the difference between dominant and subordinate social status.

Serotonin (5-HT) influences a variety of normal as well as maladaptive functions in human beings. The normal functions include mood, temperature, biological rhythms and feeding behaviour whereas the maladaptive functions include anxiety, stress, aggression, panic reaction, depression, anorexia, obsessive compulsive disorder, schizophrenia and suicide.

Overall, hormones can be classified into two major class— protein hormones and steroid hormones. It needs to be understood that release of any given hormone is not the deciding factor for a behavioral outcome. The receptivity of the cells to a given hormone is equally important. High concentration of a hormone turns effective only when receptivity of the cells is also high. The same high concentration becomes very less effective if the cells are not receptive. Androgen insensitivity syndrome is the best example of this. It is an X-linked recessive disorder in males wherein the cells lack androgen receptors. In the absence of androgens, maternal estrogens exert their influence by not allowing the testes to descend and making female sexual characteristics appear. This also implies that individual differences in physiology and behaviour will also have a say on the overall effect of a given hormone. Appropriateness of the environmental context is also important. A hormone actually influences the likelihood of behaviour in such context.

Estrogen

Estrogen (American English) or oestrogen (British English) is the primary female sex hormone as well as a medication. It is responsible for the development and regulation of the female reproductive system and secondary sex characteristics. *Estrogen* may also refer to any substance, natural or synthetic, that mimics the effects of the natural hormone. The estrane steroid estradiol is the most potent and prevalent endogenous estrogen, although several metabolites of estradiol also have estrogenic hormonal activity. Estrogens are used as medications as part of some oral contraceptives, in hormone replacement therapy for postmenopausal, hypogonadal, and transgender women, and in the treatment of certain hormone-sensitive cancers like prostate cancer and breast cancer. They are one of three types of sex hormones, the others being androgens/anabolic steroids like testosterone and progestogens like progesterone.

Estrogens are synthesized in all vertebrates as well as some insects. Their presence in both vertebrates and insects suggests that estrogenic sex hormones have an ancient evolutionary history. The three major naturally occurring forms of estrogen in women are estrone (E1), estradiol (E2), and estriol (E3). Another type of estrogen called estetrol (E4) is produced only during pregnancy. Quantitatively, estrogens circulate at lower levels than androgens in both men and women. While estrogen levels are significantly lower in males compared to females, estrogens nevertheless also have important physiological roles in males.

Like all steroid hormones, estrogens readily diffuse across the cell membrane. Once inside the cell, they bind to and activate estrogen receptors (ERs) which in turn modulate the expression of many genes. Additionally, estrogens bind to and activate rapid-signaling membrane estrogen receptors (mERs), such as GPER (GPR30).

Types and Examples

Endogenous

The three major naturally occurring estrogens in women are estrone (E1), estradiol (E2), and estriol (E3). Estradiol is the predominant estrogen during reproductive years both in terms of absolute serum levels as well as in terms of estrogenic activity. During menopause, estrone is the predominant circulating estrogen and during pregnancy estriol is the predominant circulating estrogen in terms of serum levels. Though estriol is the most plentiful of the three estrogens it is also the weakest, whereas estradiol is the strongest with a potency of approximately 80 times that of estriol. Thus, estradiol is the most important estrogen in non-pregnant females who are between the menarche and menopause stages of life. However, during pregnancy this role shifts to estriol, and in postmenopausal women estrone becomes the primary form of estrogen in the body. Another type of estrogen called estetrol (E4) is produced only during pregnancy. All of the different forms of estrogen are synthesized from androgens, specifically testosterone and androstenedione, by the enzyme aromatase.

Other endogenous estrogens, the biosyntheses of which do not involve aromatase, include 27-hydroxycholesterol, dehydroepiandrosterone (DHEA), 7-oxo-DHEA, 7α-hydroxy-DHEA, 16α-hydroxy-DHEA, 7β-hydroxyepiandrosterone, 4-androstenedione, 5-androstenediol, 3α-androstanediol, and 3β-androstanediol, and may have important endogenous functions as estrogens.

Some estrogen metabolites, such as the catechol estrogens 2-hydroxyestradiol, 2-hydroxyestrone, 4-hydroxyestradiol, and 4-hydroxyestrone, as well as 16α-hydroxyestrone, are also estrogens with varying degrees of activity.

Pharmaceuticals

Estradiol, estrone, and estriol have all been approved as pharmaceutical drugs and are used medically. Estetrol is currently under development for medical indications, but has not yet been approved in any country. A variety of synthetic estrogen esters, such as estradiol valerate, estradiol cypionate, estradiol acetate, estradiol undecylate, polyestradiol phosphate, and estradiol benzoate, are used clinically. The aforementioned compounds behave as prodrugs to estradiol, and are longer-lasting in comparison. Esters of estrone and estriol also exist and are employed in clinical medicine.

Ethinylestradiol (EE) is a more potent synthetic analogue of estradiol that is used widely in hormonal contraceptives. Mestranol, moxestrol, and quinestrol are derivatives of EE used clinically. A related drug is methylestradiol, which is also used clinically. Conjugated equine estrogens (CEEs), such as Premarin, a commonly prescribed estrogenic drug produced from the urine of pregnant mares, include the natural steroidal estrogens equilin and equilenin, as well as, especially, estrone sulfate (which itself is inactive and becomes active upon conversion into estrone). A related and very similar product to CEEs is esterified estrogens (EEs).

Testosterone, which is available as a pharmaceutical drug, is metabolized in part to estrogens such as estradiol, and can produce significant estrogenic effects at high dosages, most notably gynecomastia in males. The same is true for some synthetic anabolic-androgenic steroids, like methyltestosterone and metandienone. DHEA is available over-the-counter as a dietary supplement in the United States (but not in many other countries), though it is only very weakly estrogenic.

Non-steroidal Estrogens

Pharmaceuticals

Diethylstilbestrol is a non-steroidal estrogen that is no longer used medically. It is a member of the stilbestrol group. Other stilbestrol estrogens that have been used clinically include benzestrol, dienestrol, dienestrol acetate, diethylstilbestrol dipropionate, fosfestrol, hexestrol, and methestrol dipropionate. Chlorotrianisene, methallenestril, and doisynoestrol are non-steroidal estrogens structurally distinct from the stilbestrols that have also been used clinically.

Xenoestrogens

A range of synthetic and natural substances that possess estrogenic activity have been identified in the environment and are referred to xenoestrogens.

- Synthetic substances such as bisphenol A as well as metalloestrogens (e.g., cadmium).
- Plant products with estrogenic activity are called phytoestrogens (e.g., coumestrol, daidzein, genistein, miroestrol).
- Those produced by fungi are known as mycoestrogens (e.g., zearalenone).

Biological Function

The actions of estrogen are mediated by the estrogen receptor (ER), a dimeric nuclear protein that binds to DNA and controls gene expression. Like other steroid hormones, estrogen enters passively into the cell where it binds to and activates the estrogen receptor. The estrogen:ER complex binds to specific DNA sequences called a hormone response element to activate the transcription of target genes (in a study using an estrogen-dependent breast cancer cell line as model, 89 such genes were identified). Since estrogen enters all cells, its actions are dependent on the presence of the ER in the cell. The ER is expressed in specific tissues including the ovary, uterus and breast. The metabolic effects of estrogen in postmenopausal women has been linked to the genetic polymorphism of the ER.

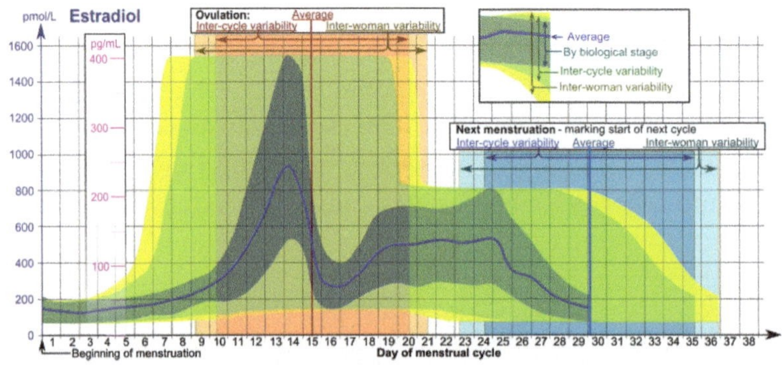

Reference ranges for the blood content of estradiol, the primary type of estrogen, during the menstrual cycle.

While estrogens are present in both men and women, they are usually present at significantly higher levels in women of reproductive age. They promote the development of female secondary sexual characteristics, such as breasts, and are also involved in the thickening of the endometrium and other aspects of regulating the menstrual cycle. In males, estrogen regulates certain functions of the reproductive system important to the maturation of sperm and may be necessary for a healthy libido. Furthermore, there are several other structural changes induced by estrogen in addition to other functions.

- Structural
    - Promote formation of female secondary sex characteristics
    - Accelerate metabolism
    - Increase fat store
    - Stimulate endometrial growth
    - Increase uterine growth
    - Increase vaginal lubrication
    - Thicken the vaginal wall
    - Maintenance of vessel and skin

  - Reduce bone resorption, increase bone formation
- Protein synthesis
  - Increase hepatic production of binding proteins
- Coagulation
  - Increase circulating level of factors 2, 7, 9, 10, plasminogen
  - Decrease antithrombin III
  - Increase platelet adhesiveness
- Lipid
  - Increase HDL, triglyceride
  - Decrease LDL, fat deposition
- Fluid balance
  - Salt (sodium) and water retention
  - Increase cortisol, SHBG
- Gastrointestinal tract
  - Reduce bowel motility
  - Increase cholesterol in bile
- Melanin
  - Increase pheomelanin, reduce eumelanin
- Cancer
  - Support hormone-sensitive breast cancers
- Lung function
  - Promotes lung function by supporting alveoli (in rodents but probably in humans).
- Uterus lining
  - Estrogen together with progesterone promotes and maintains the uterus lining in preparation for implantation of fertilized egg and maintenance of uterus function during gestation period, also upregulates oxytocin receptor in myometrium
- Ovulation
  - Surge in estrogen level induces the release of luteinizing hormone, which then triggers ovulation by releasing the egg from the Graafian follicle in the ovary.

- Sexual receptivity in estrus
    - Promotes sexual receptivity, and induces lordosis behavior. In non-human mammals, it also induces estrus (in heat) prior to ovulation, which also induces lordosis behavior. Female non-human mammals are not sexually receptive without the estrogen surge, i.e., they have no mating desire when not in estrus.
- Lordosis behavior
    - Regulates the stereotypical sexual receptivity behavior; this lordosis behavior is estrogen-dependent, which is regulated by the ventromedial nucleus of the hypothalamus.
- Sexual desire
    - Sex drive is dependent on androgen levels only in the presence of estrogen, but without estrogen, free testosterone level actually decreases sexual desire (instead of increases sex drive), as demonstrated for those women who have hypoactive sexual desire disorder, and the sexual desire in these women can be restored by administration of estrogen (using oral contraceptive). In non-human mammals, mating desire is triggered by estrogen surge in estrus.

Fetal Development

In rodents, estrogens (which are locally aromatized from androgens in the brain) play an important role in psychosexual differentiation, for example, by masculinizing territorial behavior; the same is not true in humans. In humans, the masculinizing effects of prenatal androgens on behavior (and other tissues, with the possible exception of effects on bone) appear to act exclusively through the androgen receptor. Consequently, the utility of rodent models for studying human psychosexual differentiation has been questioned.

Breast Development

Estrogen, in conjunction with growth hormone (GH) and its secretory product insulin-like growth factor 1 (IGF-1), is critical in mediating breast development during puberty, as well as breast maturation during pregnancy in preparation of lactation and breastfeeding. Estrogen is primarily and directly responsible for inducing the ductal component of breast development, as well as for causing fat deposition and connective tissue growth. It is also indirectly involved in the lobuloalveolar component, by increasing progesterone receptor expression in the breasts and by inducing the secretion of prolactin. Allowed for by estrogen, progesterone and prolactin work together to complete lobuloalveolar development during pregnancy.

Androgens such as testosterone powerfully oppose estrogen action in the breasts, such as by reducing estrogen receptor expression in them.

Heart Disease

Women suffer less from heart disease due to vasculo-protective action of estrogen which helps in preventing atherosclerosis. It also helps in maintaining the delicate balance between fighting infections and protecting arteries from damage thus lowering the risk of cardiovascular disease.

Immunological Role

Estrogen has anti-inflammatory properties and helps in mobilization of polymorphonuclear white blood cells or neutrophils.

Cognition

Verbal memory scores are frequently used as one measure of higher level cognition. These scores vary in direct proportion to estrogen levels throughout the menstrual cycle, pregnancy, and menopause. Furthermore, estrogens when administered shortly after natural or surgical menopause prevents decreases in verbal memory. In contrast, estrogens have little effect on verbal memory if first administered years after menopause. Estrogens also have positive influences on other measures of cognitive function. However the effect of estrogens on cognition is not uniformly favorable and is dependent on the timing of the dose and the type of cognitive skill being measured.

The protective effects of estrogens on cognition may be mediated by estrogens anti-inflammatory effects in the brain. Studies have also shown that the Met allele gene and level of estrogen mediates the efficiency of prefrontal cortex dependent working memory tasks.

Mental Health

Estrogen is considered to play a significant role in women's mental health. Sudden estrogen withdrawal, fluctuating estrogen, and periods of sustained estrogen low levels correlate with significant mood lowering. Clinical recovery from postpartum, perimenopause, and postmenopause depression has been shown to be effective after levels of estrogen were stabilized and/or restored.

Compulsions in male lab mice, such as those in obsessive-compulsive disorder (OCD), may be caused by low estrogen levels. When estrogen levels were raised through the increased activity of the enzyme aromatase in male lab mice, OCD rituals were dramatically decreased. Hypothalamic protein levels in the gene COMT are enhanced by increasing estrogen levels which are believed to return mice that displayed OCD rituals to normal activity. Aromatase deficiency is ultimately suspected which is involved in the synthesis of estrogen in humans and has therapeutic implications in humans having obsessive-compulsive disorder.

Local application of estrogen in the rat hippocampus has been shown to inhibit the re-uptake of serotonin. Contrarily, local application of estrogen has been shown to block the ability of fluvoxamine to slow serotonin clearance, suggesting that the same pathways which are involved in SSRI efficacy may also be affected by components of local estrogen signaling pathways.

Parenthood

Studies have also found that fathers had lower levels of cortisol and testosterone but higher levels of estrogen (estradiol) compared to non-fathers.

Binge Eating

Estrogen may play a role in suppressing binge eating. Hormone replacement therapy using estrogen may be a possible treatment for binge eating behaviors in females. Estrogen replacement has been shown to suppress binge eating behaviors in female mice. The mechanism by which estrogen replacement inhibits binge-like eating involves the replacement of serotonin (5-HT) neurons. Women exhibiting binge eating behaviors are found to have increased brain uptake of neuron 5-HT, and therefore less of the neurotransmitter serotonin in the cerebrospinal fluid. Estrogen works to activate 5-HT neurons, leading to suppression of binge like eating behaviors.

It is also suggested that there is an interaction between hormone levels and eating at different points in the female menstrual cycle. Research has predicted increased emotional eating during hormonal flux, which is characterized by high progesterone and estradiol levels that occur during the mid-luteal phase. It is hypothesized that these changes occur due to brain changes across the menstrual cycle that are likely a genomic effect of hormones. These effects produce menstrual cycle changes, which result in hormone release leading to behavioral changes, notably binge and emotional eating. These occur especially prominently among women who are genetically vulnerable to binge eating phenotypes.

Binge eating is associated with decreased estradiol and increased progesterone. Klump et al. Progesterone may moderate the effects of low estradiol (such as during dysregulated eating behavior), but that this may only be true in women who have had clinically diagnosed binge episodes (BEs). Dysregulated eating is more strongly associated with such ovarian hormones in women with BEs than in women without BEs.

The implantation of 17β-estradiol pellets in ovariectomized mice significantly reduced binge eating behaviors and injections of GLP-1 in ovariectomized mice decreased binge-eating behaviors.

The associations between binge eating, menstrual-cycle phase and ovarian hormones correlated.

Conditions

Estrogens are implicated in a number of estrogen-dependent conditions, as well as genetic conditions involving estrogen signaling or metabolism such as estrogen insensitivity syndrome, aromatase deficiency, and aromatase excess syndrome.

Biochemistry

Biosynthesis

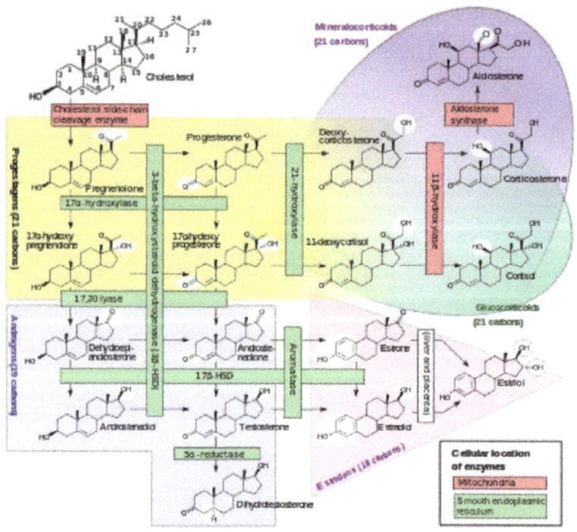

Steroidogenesis, showing estrogens at bottom right as in pink triangle.

Estrogens, in females, are produced primarily by the ovaries, and during pregnancy, the placenta. Follicle-stimulating hormone (FSH) stimulates the ovarian production of estrogens by the granulosa cells of the ovarian follicles and corpora lutea. Some estrogens are also produced in smaller amounts by other tissues such as the liver, adrenal glands, and the breasts. These secondary sources of estrogens are especially important in postmenopausal women. Fat cells produce estrogen as well.

In females, synthesis of estrogens starts in theca interna cells in the ovary, by the synthesis of androstenedione from cholesterol. Androstenedione is a substance of weak androgenic activity which serves predominantly as a precursor for more potent androgens such as testosterone as well as estrogen. This compound crosses the basal membrane into the surrounding granulosa cells, where it is converted either immediately into estrone, or into testosterone and then estradiol in an additional step. The conversion of androstenedione to testosterone is catalyzed by 17β-hydroxysteroid dehydrogenase (17β-HSD), whereas the conversion of androstenedione and testosterone into estrone and estradiol, respectively is catalyzed by aromatase, enzymes which are both expressed in granulosa cells. In contrast, granulosa cells lack 17α-hydroxylase and 17,20-lyase, whereas theca cells express these enzymes and 17β-HSD but lack aromatase. Hence, both granulosa and theca cells are essential for the production of estrogen in the ovaries.

Estrogen levels vary through the menstrual cycle, with levels highest near the end of the follicular phase just before ovulation.

Medical uses

Hormonal Contraception

Since estrogen circulating in the blood can negatively feedback to reduce circulating levels of follicle-stimulating hormone (FSH) and luteinizing hormone (LH), most oral contraceptives contain ethinylestradiol, along with a progestin (synthetic progestogen). Even in men, the major hormone involved in LH feedback is estradiol, not testosterone.

Hormone Replacement Therapy

Estrogen and other hormones are given to postmenopausal women in order to prevent osteoporosis as well as treat the symptoms of menopause such as hot flashes, vaginal dryness, urinary stress incontinence, chilly sensations, dizziness, fatigue, irritability, and sweating. Fractures of the spine, wrist, and hips decrease by 50–70% and spinal bone density increases by ~5% in those women treated with estrogen within 3 years of the onset of menopause and for 5–10 years thereafter.

Before the specific dangers of conjugated equine estrogens were well understood, standard therapy was 0.625 mg/day of conjugated equine estrogens (such as Premarin). There are, however, risks associated with conjugated equine estrogen therapy. Among the older postmenopausal women studied as part of the Women's Health Initiative (WHI), an orally administered conjugated equine estrogen supplement was found to be associated with an increased risk of dangerous blood clotting. The WHI studies used one type of estrogen supplement, a high oral dose of conjugated equine estrogens (Premarin alone and with medroxyprogesterone acetate as *PremPro*).

In a study by the NIH, esterified estrogens were not proven to pose the same risks to health as conjugated equine estrogens. Hormone replacement therapy has favorable effects on serum cholesterol levels, and when initiated immediately upon menopause may reduce the incidence of cardiovascular disease, although this hypothesis has yet to be tested in randomized trials. Estrogen appears to have a protector effect on atherosclerosis: it lowers LDL and triglycerides, it raises HDL levels and has endothelial vasodilatation properties plus an anti-inflammatory component.

Research is underway to determine if risks of estrogen supplement use are the same for all methods of delivery. In particular, estrogen applied topically may have a different spectrum of side-effects than when administered orally, and transdermal estrogens do not affect clotting as they are absorbed directly into the systemic circulation, avoiding first-pass metabolism in the liver. This route of administration is thus preferred in women with a history of thrombo-embolic disease.

Estrogen is also used in the therapy of vaginal atrophy, hypoestrogenism (as a result of hypogonadism, oophorectomy, or primary ovarian failure), amenorrhea, dysmenorrhea, and oligomenorrhea. Estrogens can also be used to suppress lactation after child birth.

Prostate Cancer

High dose estrogen therapy with estrogens such as diethylstilbestrol, ethinylestradiol, and estradiol undecylate has been used in the past to treat prostate cancer in men. It is effective because estrogens are functional antiandrogens, capable of suppressing testosterone levels to castrate concentrations and decreasing free testosterone levels by increasing sex hormone-binding globulin (SHBG) production. High dose estrogen therapy is associated with poor tolerability and safety, namely severe gynecomastia and cardiovascular complications such as thrombosis, and for this reason, has largely been replaced by newer antiandrogens such as gonadotropin-releasing hormone analogues and non-steroidal antiandrogens. It is still sometimes used in the treatment of prostate cancer however, and newer estrogens with atypical profiles such as GTx-758 that have improved tolerability profiles are being studied for possible application in prostate cancer.

Breast Cancer

High doses of potent estrogens such as diethylstilbestrol and ethinylestradiol were used in the past in the treatment of breast cancer. Their effectiveness is approximately equivalent to that of antiestrogen therapy with tamoxifen or aromatase inhibitors. The use of high dose estrogen therapy in breast cancer has mostly been superseded by antiestrogen therapy due to the improved safety profile of the latter.

About 80% of breast cancers, once established, rely on supplies of the hormone estrogen to grow: they are known as hormone-sensitive or hormone-receptor-positive cancers. Prevention of the actions or production of estrogen in the body is a treatment for these cancers.

Hormone-receptor-positive breast cancers are treated with drugs which suppress production or interfere with the action of estrogen in the body. This technique, in the context of treatment of breast cancer, is known variously as hormonal therapy, hormone therapy, or anti-estrogen therapy (not to be confused with hormone replacement therapy). Certain foods such as soy may also suppress the proliferative effects of estrogen and are used as an alternative to hormone therapy.

Others

Tall Stature

Estrogen has been used to induce growth attenuation in tall girls. Recently, estrogen-induced growth attenuation was used as part of the controversial Ashley Treatment to keep a developmentally disabled girl from growing to adult size.

Bulimia

Most recently, estrogen has been used in experimental research as a way to treat women suffering from bulimia nervosa, in addition to cognitive behavioral therapy, which is the established standard for treatment in bulimia cases. The estrogen research hypothesizes that the disease may be linked to a hormonal imbalance in the brain.

Miscellaneous

Estrogen has also been used in studies which indicate that it may be an effective drug for use in the treatment of traumatic liver injury.

In humans and mice, estrogen promotes wound healing.

Side Effects

Health Risks and Warning Labels

Hyperestrogenism (elevated levels of estrogen) may be a result of exogenous administration of estrogen or estrogen-like substances, or may be a result of physiologic conditions such as pregnancy. Any of these causes is linked with an increase in the risk of thrombosis. It's also a symptom of liver cirrhosis, due to lowered metabolic function of the liver, which metabolises estrogen, leading to spider angioma, palmary erythema, gynecomastia and testicular atrophy in some male patients.

The estrogen-alone substudy of the WHI reported an increased risk of stroke and deep vein thrombosis (DVT) in postmenopausal women 50 years of age or older and an increased risk of dementia in postmenopausal women 65 years of age or older using 0.625 mg of Premarin conjugated equine estrogens (CEE). The estrogen-plus-progestin substudy of the WHI reported an increased risk of myocardial infarction, stroke, invasive breast cancer, pulmonary emboli and DVT in postmenopausal women 50 years of age or older and an increased risk of dementia in postmenopausal women 65 years of age or older using PremPro, which is 0.625 mg of CEE with 2.5 mg of the progestin medroxyprogesterone acetate (MPA).

The labeling of estrogen-only products in the U.S. includes a boxed warning that unopposed estrogen (without progestogen) therapy increases the risk of endometrial cancer. Based on a review of data from the WHI, in 2003 the FDA changed the labeling of all estrogen and estrogen with progestin products for use by postmenopausal women to include a new boxed warning about cardiovascular and other risks.

Cosmetics

Some hair shampoos on the market include estrogens and placental extracts; others contain phytoestrogens. In 1998, there were case reports of four prepubescent African-American girls developing breasts after exposure to these shampoos. In 1993, the FDA determined that not all over-the-counter topically applied hormone-containing drug products for human use are generally recognized as safe and effective and are misbranded. An accompanying proposed rule deals with cosmetics, concluding that any use of natural estrogens in a cosmetic product makes the product an unapproved new drug and that any cosmetic using the term "hormone" in the text of its labeling or in its ingredient statement makes an implied drug claim, subjecting such a product to regulatory action.

In addition to being considered misbranded drugs, products claiming to contain placental extract may also be deemed to be misbranded cosmetics if the extract has been prepared from placentas from which the hormones and other biologically active substances have been removed and the extracted substance consists principally of protein. The FDA recommends that this substance be identified by a name other than "placental extract" and describing its composition more accurately because consumers associate the name "placental extract" with a therapeutic use of some biological activity.

History

In 1929 Adolf Butenandt and Edward Adelbert Doisy independently isolated and determined the structure of estrogen. Thereafter, the pace of hormonal drug research accelerated. The "first orally effective estrogen", Emmenin, derived from the late-pregnancy urine of Canadian women, was introduced in 1930 by Collip and Ayerst Laboratories. Estrogens have poor oral bioavailability and prior to the development of micronization could not be given orally, but the urine was found to contain estriol glucuronide, which is absorbed orally and becomes active in the body after hydrolysis. Scientists continued to search for new sources of estrogen because of concerns associated with the practicality of introducing the drug into the market. At the same time, a German pharmaceutical drug company, Schering, formulated a similar product as Emmenin called Progynon that was introduced to German women to treat menopausal symptoms.

In 1938, British scientists obtained a patent on a newly formulated nonsteroidal estrogen, diethylstilbestrol (DES), that was cheaper and more powerful than the previously manufactured estrogens. Soon after, concerns over the side effects of DES were raised in scientific journals while the drug manufacturers came together to lobby for governmental approval of DES. It was only until 1941 when estrogen therapy was finally approved by the Food and Drug Administration (FDA) for the treatment of menopausal symptoms. Premarin (conjugated equine estrogens) was introduced in 1941 and succeeded Emmenin, the sales of which had begun to drop after 1940 due to competition from DES. Ethinylestradiol was synthesized in 1938 by Hans Herloff Inhoffen and Walter Hohlweg at Schering AG in Berlin and was approved by the FDA in the U.S. on June 25, 1943 and marketed by Schering as Estinyl.

Micronized estradiol, via the oral route, was first evaluated in 1972, and this was followed by the evaluation of vaginal and intranasal micronized estradiol in 1977. Oral micronized estradiol was first approved in the United States under the brand name Estrace in 1975.

Environmental Effects

Estrogens are among the wide range of endocrine-disrupting compounds (EDCs) because they have high estrogenic potency. When an EDC makes its way into the environment, it may cause male reproductive dysfunction to wildlife. The estrogen excreted from farm animals makes its way into fresh water systems. During the germination period of reproduction the fish are exposed to low levels of estrogen which may cause reproductive dysfunction to male fish.

Society and Culture

Etymology

The name *estrogen* is derived from the Greek (*oistros*), literally meaning "verve or inspiration" but figuratively sexual passion or desire, and the suffix *-gen*, meaning "producer of".

Androgen

An androgen (from Greek andro meaning male human being) is any natural or synthetic compound, usually a steroid hormone, that stimulates or controls the development and maintenance of male characteristics in vertebrates by binding to androgen receptors. This includes the activity of the primary male sex organs and development of male secondary sex characteristics. Androgens were first discovered in 1936. Androgens increase in both boys and girls during puberty. Androgens are also the original anabolic steroids and the precursor of all estrogens. The primary and most well-known androgen is testosterone. Dihydrotestosterone (DHT) and androstenedione are less known generally, but are of equal importance in male development. DHT in the embryo life causes differentiation of penis, scrotum and prostate. Later in life DHT contributes to balding, prostate growth and sebaceous gland activity. Although androgens are described as male sex hormones, both males and females have them to varying degrees, as is also true of estrogens. They are one of three types of sex hormones, the others being estrogens like estradiol and progestogens like progesterone.

Types and Examples

The main subset of androgens, known as adrenal androgens, is composed of 19-carbon steroids synthesized in the zona reticularis, the innermost layer of the adrenal cortex. Adrenal androgens function as weak steroids (though some are precursors), and the subset includes dehydroepiandrosterone (DHEA), dehydroepiandrosterone sulfate (DHEA-S), androstenedione (A4), and androstenediol (A5).

Besides testosterone, other androgens include:

- Dehydroepiandrosterone (DHEA) is a steroid hormone produced in the adrenal cortex from cholesterol. It is the primary precursor of natural estrogens. DHEA is also called dehydroisoandrosterone or dehydroandrosterone.
- Androstenedione (A4) is an androgenic steroid produced by the testes, adrenal cortex, and ovaries. While androstenediones are converted metabolically to testosterone and other androgens, they are also the parent structure of estrone. Use of androstenedione as an athletic or bodybuilding supplement has been banned by the International Olympic Committee, as well as other sporting organizations.
- Androstenediol (A5) is the steroid metabolite thought to act as the main regulator of gonadotropin secretion.
- Androsterone is a chemical byproduct created during the breakdown of androgens, or derived from progesterone, that also exerts minor masculinising effects, but with one-seventh the intensity of testosterone. It is found in approximately equal amounts in the plasma and urine of both males and females.

- Dihydrotestosterone (DHT) is a metabolite of testosterone, and a more potent androgen than testosterone in that it binds more strongly to androgen receptors. It is produced in the skin and reproductive tissue.

Biological Function

Testes Formation

During mammalian development, the gonads are at first capable of becoming either ovaries or testes. In humans, starting at about week 4, the gonadal rudiments are present within the intermediate mesoderm adjacent to the developing kidneys. At about week 6, epithelial sex cords develop within the forming testes and incorporate the germ cells as they migrate into the gonads. In males, certain Y chromosome genes, particularly SRY, control development of the male phenotype, including conversion of the early bipotential gonad into testes. In males, the sex cords fully invade the developing gonads.

Androgen Production

The mesoderm-derived epithelial cells of the sex cords in developing testes become the Sertoli cells, which will function to support sperm cell formation. A minor population of nonepithelial cells appear between the tubules by week 8 of human fetal development. These are Leydig cells. Soon after they differentiate, Leydig cells begin to produce androgens.

Androgen Effects

The androgens function as paracrine hormones required by the Sertoli cells to support sperm production. They are also required for masculinization of the developing male fetus (including penis and scrotum formation). Under the influence of androgens, remnants of the mesonephron, the Wolffian ducts, develop into the epididymis, vas deferens and seminal vesicles. This action of androgens is supported by a hormone from Sertoli cells, Müllerian inhibitory hormone (MIH), which prevents the embryonic Müllerian ducts from developing into fallopian tubes and other female reproductive tract tissues in male embryos. MIH and androgens cooperate to allow for movement of testes into the scrotum.

Early Regulation

Before the production of the pituitary hormone luteinizing hormone (LH) by the embryo starting at about weeks 11–12, human chorionic gonadotrophin (hCG) promotes the differentiation of Leydig cells and their production of androgens at week 8. Androgen action in target tissues often involves conversion of testosterone to 5α-dihydrotestosterone (DHT).

Male Pubertal Development

At the time of puberty, androgen levels increase dramatically in males, and androgens mediate the development of masculine secondary sexual characteristics as well as the activation of spermatogenesis and fertility and masculine behavioral changes such as gynephilia and increased sex drive. Masculine secondary sexual characteristics include androgenic hair, voice deepening, emergence of the Adam's apple, broadening of the shoulders, increased muscle mass, and penile growth.

Spermatogenesis

During puberty, androgen, LH and follicle stimulating hormone (FSH) production increase and the sex cords hollow out, forming the seminiferous tubules, and the germ cells start to differentiate into sperm. Throughout adulthood, androgens and FSH cooperatively act on Sertoli cells in the testes to support sperm production. Exogenous androgen supplements can be used as a male contraceptive. Elevated androgen levels caused by use of androgen supplements can inhibit production of LH and block production of endogenous androgens by Leydig cells. Without the locally high levels of androgens in testes due to androgen production by Leydig cells, the seminiferous tubules can degenerate, resulting in infertility. For this reason, many transdermal androgen patches are applied to the scrotum.

Fat Deposition

Males typically have less body fat than females. Recent results indicate androgens inhibit the ability of some fat cells to store lipids by blocking a signal transduction pathway that normally supports adipocyte function. Also, androgens, but not estrogens, increase beta adrenergic receptors while decreasing alpha adrenergic receptors- which results in increased levels of epinephrine/ norepinephrine due to lack of alpha-2 receptor negative feedback and decreased fat accumulation due to epinephrine/ norepinephrine then acting on lipolysis-inducing beta receptors.

Muscle Mass

Males typically have more skeletal muscle mass than females. Androgens promote the enlargement of skeletal muscle cells and probably act in a coordinated manner to function by acting on several cell types in skeletal muscle tissue. One cell type conveys hormone signals to generating muscle, the myoblast. Higher androgen levels lead to increased expression of androgen receptor. Fusion of myoblasts generates myotubes, in a process linked to androgen receptor levels.

Brain

Circulating levels of androgens can influence human behavior because some neurons are sensitive to steroid hormones. Androgen levels have been implicated in the regulation of human aggression and libido. Indeed, androgens are capable of altering the structure of the brain in several species, including mice, rats, and primates, producing sex differences.

Numerous reports have shown androgens alone are capable of altering the structure of the brain, but identification of which alterations in neuroanatomy stem from androgens or estrogens is difficult, because of their potential for conversion.

Evidence from neurogenesis (formation of new neurons) studies on male rats has shown that the hippocampus is a useful brain region to examine when determining the effects of androgens on behavior. To examine neurogenesis, wild-type male rats were compared with male rats that had testicular feminization mutation (TMF), a genetic disorder resulting in complete or partial insensitivity to androgens and a lack of external male genitalia.

Neural injections of Bromodeoxyuridine (BrdU) were applied to males of both groups to test for neurogenesis. Analysis showed that testosterone and dihydrotestosterone regulated adult hippocampal neurogenesis (AHN). Adult hippocampal neurogenesis was regulated through the androgen receptor in the wild-type male rats, but not in the TMF male rats. To further test the role of activated androgen receptors on AHN, flutamide, an antiandrogen drug that competes with testosterone and dihydrotestosterone for androgen receptors, and dihydrotestosterone were administered to normal male rats. Dihydrotestosterone increased the number of BrdU cells, while flutamide inhibited these cells.

Moreover, estrogens had no effect. This research demonstrates how androgens can increase AHN.

Researchers also examined how mild exercise affected androgen synthesis which in turn causes AHN activation of N-methyl-D-aspartate (NMDA) receptors.

NMDA induces a calcium flux that allows for synaptic plasticity which is crucial for AHN.

Researchers injected both orchidectomized (ORX) (castrated) and sham castrated male rats with BrdU to determine if the number of new cells was increased. They found that AHN in male rats is increased with mild exercise by boosting synthesis of dihydrotestosterone in the hippocampus.

Again it was noted that AHN was not increase via activation of the estrogen receptors.

Androgen regulation decreases the likelihood of depression in males. In preadolescent male rats, neonatal rats treated with flutamide developed more depression-like symptoms compared to control rats.

Again BrdU was injected into both groups of rats in order to see if cells were multiplying in the living tissue. These results demonstrate how the organization of androgens has a positive effect on preadolescent hippocampal neurogenesis that may be linked with lower depression-like symptoms.

Social isolation has a hindering effect in AHN whereas normal regulation of androgens increases AHN. A study using male rats showed that testosterone may block social isolation, which results in hippocampal neurogenesis reaching homeostasis—regulation that keeps internal conditions stable. A Brdu analysis showed that excess testosterone did not increase this blocking effect against social isolation; that is, the natural circulating levels of androgens cancel out the negative effects of social isolation on AHN.

Female-specific Effects

Androgens have potential roles in relaxation of the myometrium via non-genomic, androgen receptor-independent pathways, preventing premature uterine contractions in pregnancy.

Androgen Insensitivity

Reduced ability of an XY-karyotype fetus to respond to androgens can result in one of several conditions, including infertility and several forms of intersex conditions.

Miscellaneous

Yolk androgen levels in certain birds have been positively correlated to social dominance later in life.

Biological Activity

Androgens bind to and activate androgen receptors (ARs) to mediate most of their biological effects.

Relative Potency

Determined by consideration of all biological assay methods (circa 1970):

Androgen	Potency (%)
Testosterone	100
5α-Dihydrotestosterone (DHT)	90
Androstanediol	60
Androstenedione	20
Dehydroepiandrosterone	10
Androsterone	10

5α-Dihydrotestosterone (DHT) was 2.4 times more potent than testosterone at maintaining normal prostate weight and duct lumen mass (this is a measure of epithelial cell function stimulation). Whereas DHT was equally potent as testosterone at preventing prostate cell death after castration.

Non-genomic Actions

Androgens have also been found to signal through membrane androgen receptors, which are distinct from the classical nuclear androgen receptor.

Biochemistry

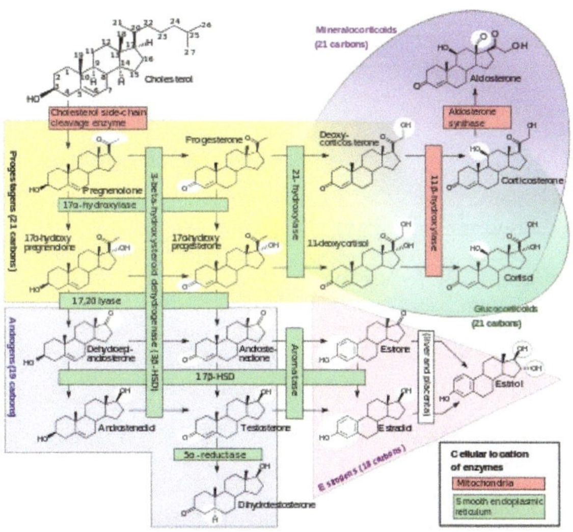

Steroidogenesis, showing the relation between several androgens, is at bottom left. Estrone and estradiol, in contrast, are estrogens.

Biosynthesis

Androgens are synthesized from cholesterol and are produced mainly in the gonads and the adrenal glands. They are produced in both the testicles and the ovaries, but are produced in much greater quantities in the former, hence accounting for the much higher levels of androgens in males compared to females. Various other tissues, such as the skin, prostate gland, liver, and brain, also play a role in androgen biosynthesis, by transforming testosterone into the more potent androgen DHT.

Metabolism

Androgens are metabolized mainly in the liver.

Medical uses

Androgens are used in hormone replacement therapy to treat hypogonadism and for various other indications.

Androgen deprivation therapy, for instance with antiandrogens or orchiectomy, is used to treat prostate cancer.

References

- Ralph, Charles (1975). "The pineal gland and geographical distribution of animals". International Journal of Biometeorology. 19: 289–303. doi:10.1007/bf01451040
- Pritchard, Thomas C.; Alloway, Kevin Douglas (1999). Medical Neuroscience. Hayes Barton Press. pp. 76–77. ISBN 1-889325-29-5. Retrieved 2009-02-08
- "MedWatch – 2007 Safety Information Alerts. Permax (pergolide) and generic equivalents". U.S. Food and Drug Administration. 29 March 2007. Retrieved 30 March 2007
- Hazard, JB (July 1977). "The C cells (parafollicular cells) of the thyroid gland and medullary thyroid carcinoma. A review.". The American journal of pathology. 88 (1): 213–50. PMID 18012
- Descartes R. "The Passions of the Soul" excerpted from "Philosophy of the Mind," Chalmers, D. New York: Oxford University Press, Inc.; 2002. ISBN 978-0-19-514581-6
- Zimmerman, Robert A. "Age-Related Incidence of Pineal Calcification Detected by Computed Tomography" (PDF). Radiological Society of North America. Retrieved 21 June 2012
- Büyükgebiz, Atilla (15 November 2012). "Newborn Screening for Congenital Hypothyroidism". Journal of Clinical Research in Pediatric Endocrinology. 4 (4). doi:10.4274/Jcrpe.845
- Melmed, S; Polonsky, KS; Larsen, PR; Kronenberg, HM (2011). Williams Textbook of Endocrinology (12th ed.). Saunders. p. 331. ISBN 978-1-4377-0324-5
- Jähnichen S; Horowski R; Pertz H. "Pergolide and Cabergoline But not Lisuride Exhibit Agonist Efficacy at Serotonin 5-HT2B Receptors" (PDF). Retrieved 3 February 2010
- Smith, Terry J.; Hegedüs, Laszlo (2016-10-19). "Graves' Disease". New England Journal of Medicine. 375 (16): 1552–1565. doi:10.1056/nejmra1510030
- Harris, Randall E. (2015-05-07). Global Epidemiology of Cancer. Jones & Bartlett Publishers. p. 268. ISBN 978-1-284-03445-5
- "Iodine Deficiency & Nutrition". www.thyroidfoundation.org.au. Australian Thyroid Foundation. Retrieved 11 January 2017
- Magner, James (2014). "Historical Note: Many Steps Led to the 'Discovery' of Thyroid-Stimulating Hormone". European Thyroid Journal. doi:10.1159/000360534

- Hall, Arthur C. Guyton, John E. (2005). Textbook of medical physiology (11th ed.). Philadelphia: W.B. Saunders. pp. 985–8. ISBN 978-0-7216-0240-0
- So, Michelle; MacIsaac, Richard; Grossmann, Mathis. "Hypothyroidism – Investigation and management". www.racgp.org.au. The Royal Australian College of General Practitioners. Retrieved 11 January 2017
- Johnson, S J (1 April 2005). "Best Practice No 183: Examination of parathyroid gland specimens". Journal of Clinical Pathology. 58 (4): 338–342. doi:10.1136/jcp.2002.002550
- Colledge, Nicki R.; Walker, Brian R.; Ralston, Stuart H., eds. (2010). Davidson's principles and practice of medicine (21st ed.). Edinburgh: Churchill Livingstone/Elsevier. p. 767. ISBN 978-0-7020-3084-0
- "Pancreatic Cancer Treatment (PDQ®) Patient Version". National Cancer Institute. 2014-04-17. Retrieved 8 June 2014
- Eknoyan G (November 1995). "A history of the parathyroid glands". American Journal of Kidney Diseases. 26 (5): 801–7. doi:10.1016/0272-6386(95)90447-6. PMID 7485136
- Staren, Prinz; Richard, A., eds. (2000). Endocrine surgery. Georgetown TX: Landes Bioscience. pp. 98–114. ISBN 978-1-57059-574-5

4

Psychological Function of Brain

The brain has specific psychological functions apart from its physiological purposes. They can be categorised as psychobiology of learning, memory, participation and emotion. The topics discussed in the chapter are of great importance to broaden the existing knowledge on biological bases of behavior.

Neurobiology of Psychological Functions

Having discussed the structure and functions of the brain, we shall now look at specific psychological functions and comprehend the role of brain regulating such functions. We shall concentrate on four major topics of interest of psychologists—learning, memory, emotion and personality. The elaboration of each of these topics is preceded by recapitulating the detailed discussion on the same topic in the course *Basic Psychological Processes*. Further, the details are based on the findings from different allied areas like electrophysiology, neuropsychology and neuroimaging.

Learning: Recapitulation

Learning brings forth moderately enduring change in the behaviour through experience. Learning primarily involves formation of associations and relationship. The input demanding a response is called stimulus (S) and the action made to such input is called response (R). This S-R relationship has been widely talked about in psychology. A stimulus could be anything; an event, a situation, a condition, a signal or a cue. Further, responses could either be readily observable or not readily evident. The former is referred to as overt behaviour whereas the later is called covert behaviour.

The illustration below describes the process of classical conditioning.

Under normal circumstances			
	Conditioned stimulus (CS)	→	No response
	Unconditioned stimulus (UCS)	→	Unconditioned response (UR)
During conditioning			
	Conditioned stimulus (CS)	→	Unconditioned response (UR)
	Unconditioned stimulus (UCS)		
After conditioning			
	Conditioned stimulus (CS)	→	Conditioned response (CR)

There are two types of classical conditioning— *Classical Reward Conditioning* and *Classical Aversive Conditioning* . In classical reward conditioning, a reinforcer rewards the overt behaviour whereas in c lassical aversive conditioning, an aversive stimulus is paired with a conditioned stimulus (CS). This is how a neutral stimulus gets associated with a meaningful stimulus, thus deriving the capacity to elicit a similar response.

Instrumental conditioning, on the other hand, is a form of learning wherein the consequences of behaviour produce changes in the response, thus determining the probability of occurrence of the behaviour. Unlike classical conditioning, it is a voluntary process of formation and strengthening of S-R association. It is readily seen in human learning.The distinctiveness of instrumental conditioning is that the association between response and reinforcing stimulus depends on the consequences of the responses. Besides these two major types, we have also talked about cognitive learning. It centers on the cognitive maps we construct out of our experiences and how these maps guide our behaviour. Alongside we also discussed social learning which included notion of local enhancement, social facilitation, observational learning and imitation.

Classical Conditioning

A statue of Ivan Pavlov and one of his dogs.

Classical conditioning (also known as Pavlovian or respondent conditioning) refers to a learning procedure in which a biologically potent stimulus (e.g. food) is paired with a previously neutral stimulus (e.g. a bell). It also refers to the learning process that results from this pairing, through which the neutral stimulus comes to elicit a response (e.g. salivation) that is usually similar to the one elicited by the potent stimulus. These basic facts, which require many qualifications, were first studied in detail by Ivan Pavlov through experiments with dogs. Together with operant conditioning, classical conditioning became the foundation of behaviorism, a school of psychology which was dominant in the mid-20th century and is still an important influence on the practice of psychological therapy and the study of animal behavior. Classical conditioning is the basic learning process, and its neural substrates are now beginning to be understood.

Definition

Classical conditioning occurs when a conditioned stimulus is paired with an unconditioned stimulus. Usually, the conditioned stimulus (CS) is a neutral stimulus (e.g., the sound of a tuning fork), the unconditioned stimulus (US) is biologically potent (e.g., the taste of food) and the unconditioned response (UR) to the unconditioned stimulus is an unlearned reflex response (e.g., salivation). After pairing is repeated (some learning may occur after only one pairing), the organism exhibits a conditioned response (CR) to the conditioned stimulus when the conditioned stimulus is presented alone. The conditioned response is usually similar to the unconditioned response, but unlike the unconditioned response, it must be acquired through experience and is relatively impermanent.

In classical conditioning, the conditioned stimulus is not simply connected to the unconditioned response; the conditioned response usually differs in some way from the unconditioned response, sometimes significantly. For this and other reasons, learning theorists commonly suggest that the conditioned stimulus comes to signal or predict the unconditioned stimulus, and go on to analyze the consequences of this signal. Robert A. Rescorla provided a clear summary of this change in thinking, and its implications, in his 1988 article "Pavlovian conditioning: It's not what you think it is." Despite its widespread acceptance, Rescorla's thesis may not be defensible.

Classical conditioning differs from *operant* or *instrumental* conditioning: in classical conditioning, behaviors are modified through the association of stimuli as described above, whereas in operant conditioning behaviors are modified by the effect they produce (i.e., reward or punishment).

Procedures

Pavlov's Research

The best-known and most thorough early work on classical conditioning was done by Ivan Pavlov, although Edwin Twitmyer published some related findings a year earlier. During his research on the physiology of digestion in dogs, Pavlov developed a procedure that enabled him to study the digestive processes of animals over long periods of time. He redirected the animal's digestive fluids outside the body, where they could be measured. Pavlov noticed that his dogs began to salivate in the presence of the technician who normally fed them, rather than simply salivating in the presence of food. Pavlov called the dogs' anticipatory salivation "psychic secretion." Putting these informal observations to an experimental test, Pavlov presented a stimulus (e.g. the sound of a metronome) and then gave the dog food; after a few repetitions, the dogs started to salivate in response to the stimulus. Pavlov concluded that if a particular stimulus in the dog's surroundings was present when the dog was given food then that stimulus could become associated with food and cause salivation on its own. He called the stimulus the *conditioned* (or *conditional*) *stimulus* (CS) because its effects depend on its association with food. He called the food the *unconditioned stimulus* (US) because its effects did not depend on previous experience. Likewise, the response to the CS was the *conditioned response* (CR) and that to the US was the *unconditioned response* (UR). Pavlov reported many basic facts about conditioning; for example, he found that learning occurred most rapidly when the interval between the CS and the appearance of the US was relatively short.

As noted earlier, it is often thought that the conditioned response is a replica of the unconditioned response, but Pavlov noted that saliva produced by the CS differs in composition from that produced by the US. In fact, the CR may be any new response to the previously neutral CS that can be clearly linked to experience with the conditional relationship of CS and US. It was also thought that repeated pairings are necessary for conditioning to emerge, but many CRs can be learned with a single trial, especially in fear conditioning and taste aversion learning.

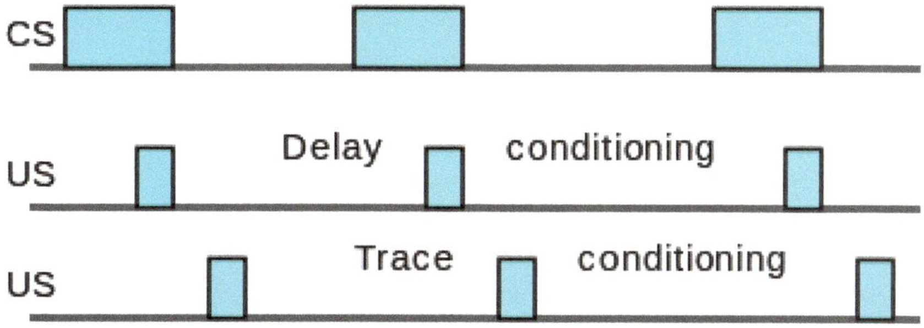

Diagram representing forward conditioning. The time interval increases from left to right.

Forward Conditioning

Learning is fastest in forward conditioning. During forward conditioning, the onset of the CS precedes the onset of the US in order to signal that the US will follow. Two common forms of forward conditioning are delay and trace conditioning.

- Delay conditioning: In delay conditioning the CS is presented and is overlapped by the presentation of the US.
- Trace conditioning: During trace conditioning the CS and US do not overlap. Instead, the CS begins and ends before the US is presented. The stimulus-free period is called the *trace interval*. It may also be called the *conditioning interval. For example: If you sound a buzzer for 5 seconds and then, a second later, puff air into a person's eye, the person will blink. After several pairings of the buzzer and puff the person will blink at the sound of the buzzer alone.*

The difference between trace conditioning and delay conditioning is that in the delayed procedure the CS and US overlap.

Simultaneous Conditioning

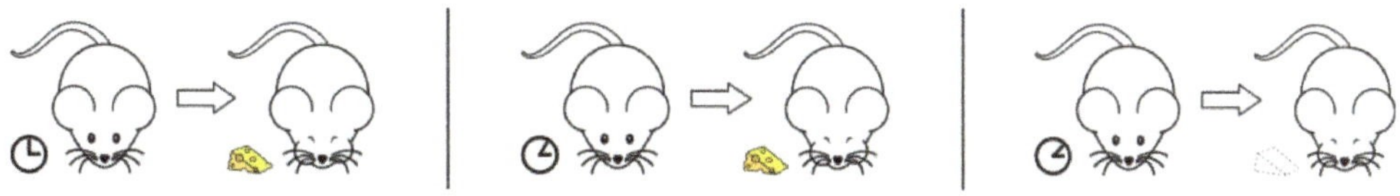

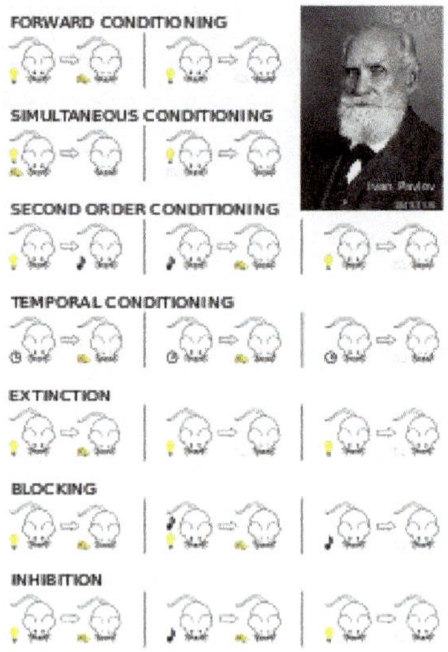

Classical conditioning procedures and effects.

During simultaneous conditioning, the CS and US are presented and terminated at the same time.

For example: If you ring a bell and blow a puff of air into a person's eye at the same moment, you have accomplished to coincide the CS and US.

Second-order and Higher-order Conditioning

This form of conditioning follows a two-step procedure. First a neutral stimulus ("CS1") comes to signal a US through forward conditioning. Then a second neutral stimulus ("CS2") is paired with the first (CS1) and comes to yield its own conditioned response. *For example: a bell might be paired with food until the bell elicits salivation. If a light is then paired with the bell, then the light may come to elicit salivation as well. The bell is the CS1 and the food is the US. The light becomes the CS2 once it is paired with the CS1*

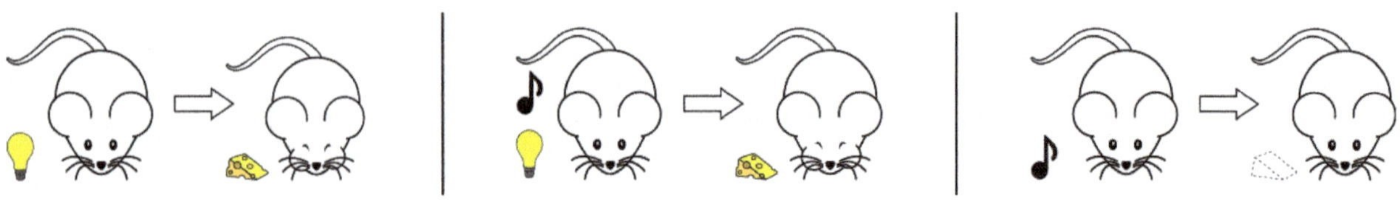

Backward Conditioning

Backward conditioning occurs when a CS immediately follows a US. Unlike the usual conditioning procedure, in which the CS precedes the US, the conditioned response given to the CS tends to be inhibitory. This presumably happens because the CS serves as a signal that the US has ended, rather than as a signal that the US is about to appear. *For example, a puff of air directed at a person's eye could be followed by the sound of a buzzer.*

Temporal Conditioning

In temporal conditioning a US is presented at regular intervals, for instance every 10 minutes.

Conditioning is said to have occurred when the CR tends to occur shortly before each US. This suggests that animals have a biological clock that can serve as a CS. This method has also been used to study timing ability in animals.

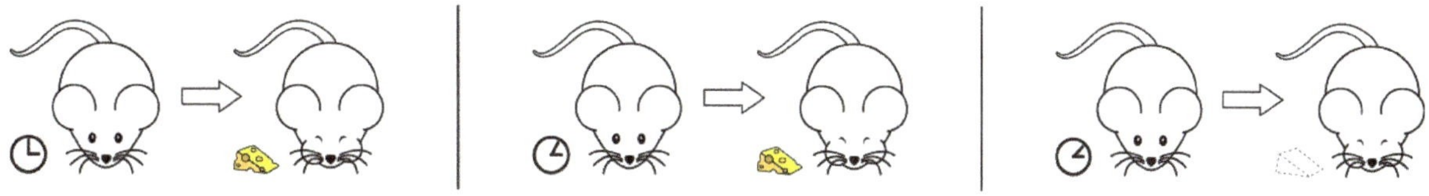

Zero contingency Procedure

In this procedure, the CS is paired with the US, but the US also occurs at other times. If this occurs, it is predicted that the US is likely to happen in the absence of the CS. In other words, the CS does not "predict" the US. In this case, conditioning fails and the CS does not come to elicit a CR. This finding – that *prediction* rather than CS-US pairing is the key to conditioning – greatly influenced subsequent conditioning research and theory.

Extinction

In the extinction procedure, the CS is presented repeatedly in the absence of a US. This is done after a CS has been conditioned by one of the methods above. When this is done the CR frequency eventually returns to pre-training levels. However, spontaneous recovery (and other related phenomena, "Recovery from extinction") show that extinction does not completely eliminate the effects of the prior conditioning. Spontaneous recovery is when there is a sudden appearance of the (CR) after extinction occurs. These phenomena can be explained by postulating accumulation of inhibition when a weak stimulus is presented.

Phenomena Observed

Acquisition

During acquisition the CS and US are paired as described above. The extent of conditioning may be tracked by test trials. In these test trials, the CS is presented alone and the CR is measured. A single CS-US pairing may suffice to yield a CR on a test, but usually a number of pairings are necessary. This repeated number of trials increase the strength and/or frequency of the CR gradually. The speed of conditioning depends on a number of factors, such as the nature and strength of both the CS and the US, previous experience and the animal's motivational state Acquisition may occur with a single pairing of the CS and US, but usually, there is a gradual increase in the conditioned response to the CS. This slows down the process as it nears completion.

Extinction

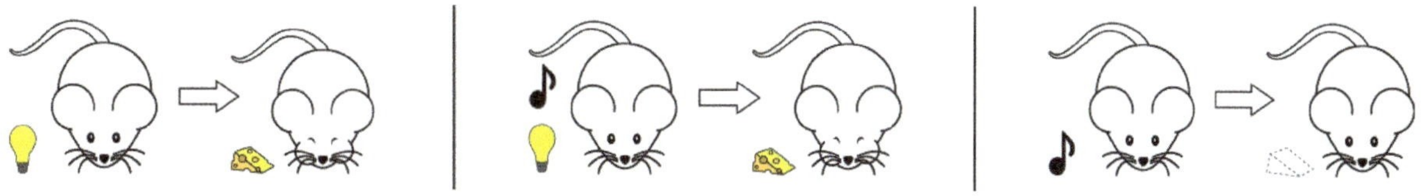

In order to make a learned behavior disappear, the experimenter must present a CS alone, without the presence of the US. Once this process is repeated continuously, eventually, the CS will stop eliciting a CR. This means that the CR has been "extinguished".

External Inhibition

External inhibition may be observed if a strong or unfamiliar stimulus is presented just before, or at the same time as, the CS. This causes a reduction in the conditioned response to the CS.

Recovery from Extinction

Several procedures lead to the recovery of an extinguished CR. The following examples assume that the CS has first been conditioned and that this has been followed by extinction of the CR as described above. These procedures illustrate that the extinction procedure does not completely eliminate the effect of conditioning

- Reacquisition:

If the CS is again paired with the US, a CR is again acquired, but this second acquisition usually happens much faster than the first one.

- Spontaneous recovery:

Spontaneous recovery is defined as the reappearance of the conditioned response after a rest period. That is, if the CS is tested at a later time (for example an hour or a day) after conditioning it will again elicit a CR. This renewed CR is usually much weaker than the CR observed prior to extinction.

- Disinhibition:

If the CS is tested just after extinction and an intense but associatively neutral stimulus has occurred, there may be a temporary recovery of the conditioned response to the CS

- Reinstatement:

If the US used in conditioning is presented to a subject in the same place where conditioning and extinction occurred, but without the CS being present, the CS often elicits a response when it is tested later.

- Renewal:

Renewal is a reemergence of a conditioned response following extinction when an animal is returned to the environment in which the conditioned response was acquired.

Stimulus Generalization

Stimulus generalization is said to occur if, after a particular CS has come to elicit a CR, another similar stimulus will elicit the same CR. Usually the more similar are the CS and the test stimulus the stronger is the CR to the test stimulus. The more the test stimulus differs from the CS the weaker the CR will be or the more it will differ from that previously observed.

Stimulus Discrimination

One observes *stimulus discrimination* when one stimulus ("CS1") elicits one CR and another stimulus ("CS2") elicits either another CR or no CR at all. This can be brought about by, for example, pairing CS1 with an effective US and presenting CS2 with no US.

Latent Inhibition

Latent inhibition refers to the observation that it takes longer for a familiar stimulus to become a CS than it does for a novel stimulus to become a CS, when the stimulus is subsequently paired with an effective US.

Conditioned Suppression

This is one of the most common ways to measure the strength of learning in classical conditioning. A typical example of this procedure is as follows: a rat first learns to press a lever through operant conditioning. Then, in a series of trials, the rat is exposed to a CS, a light or a noise, followed by the US, a mild electric shock. An association between the CS and US develops, and the rat slows or stops its lever pressing when the CS comes on. The rate of pressing during the CS measures the strength of classical conditioning; that is, the slower the rat presses, the stronger the association of the CS and the US.

Conditioned Inhibition

Three phases of conditioning are typically used:

Phase 1

A CS (CS+) is paired with a US until asymptotic CR levels are reached.

Phase 2

CS+/US trials are continued, but these are interspersed with trials on which the CS+ is paired with a second CS, (the CS-) but not with the US (i.e. CS+/CS- trials). Typically, organisms show CRs on CS+/US trials, but stop responding on CS+/CS− trials.

Phase 3

- *Summation test for conditioned inhibition:* The CS- from phase 2 is presented together with a new CS+ that was conditioned as in phase 1. Conditioned inhibition is found if the response is less to the CS+/CS- pair than it is to the CS+ alone.
- *Retardation test for conditioned inhibition:* The CS- from phase 2 is paired with the US. If conditioned inhibition has occurred, the rate of acquisition to the previous CS− should be less than the rate of acquisition that would be found without the phase 2 treatment.

Blocking

This form of classical conditioning involves two phases.

Phase 1

A CS (CS1) is paired with a US.

Phase 2

A compound CS (CS1+CS2) is paired with a US.

Test

A separate test for each CS (CS1 and CS2) is performed. The blocking effect is observed in a lack of conditional response to CS2, suggesting that the first phase of training blocked the acquisition of the second CS.

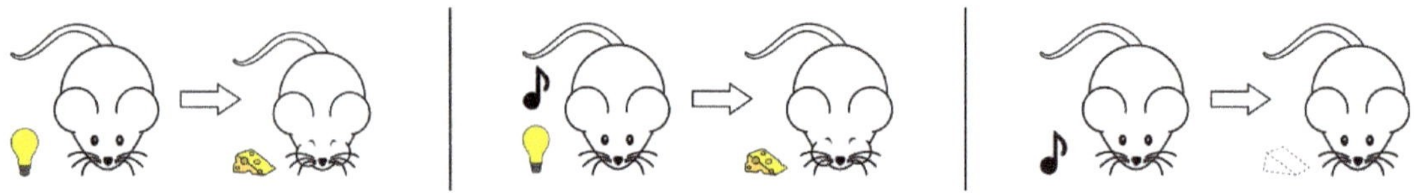

Theories

Data Sources

Experiments on theoretical issues in conditioning have mostly been done on vertebrates, especially rats and pigeons. However, conditioning has also been studied in invertebrates, and very important data on the neural basis of conditioning has come from experiments on the sea slug, *Aplysia*. Most relevant experiments have used the classical conditioning procedure, although instrumental (operant) conditioning experiments have also been used, and the strength of classical conditioning is often measured through its operant effects, as in *conditioned suppression* and autoshaping .

Stimulus-substitution Theory

According to Pavlov, conditioning does not involve the acquisition of any new behavior, but rather the tendency to respond in old ways to new stimuli. Thus, he theorized that the CS merely substitutes for the US in evoking the reflex response. This explanation is called the stimulus-substitution theory of conditioning. A critical problem with the stimulus-substitution theory is that the CR and UR are not always the same. Pavlov himself observed that a dog's saliva produced as a CR differed in composition from that produced as a UR. An even more striking is the finding that the CR is sometimes the opposite of the UR. For example: the unconditional response to electric shock is an increase in heart rate, whereas a CS that has been paired with the electric shock elicits a decrease in heart rate. (However, it has been proposed that only when the UR does not involve the central nervous system are the CR and the UR opposites.)

Rescorla–Wagner Model

The Rescorla–Wagner (R–W) model is a relatively simple yet powerful model of conditioning. The model predicts a number of important phenomena, but it also fails in important ways, thus leading to a number of modifications and alternative models. However, because much of the theoretical research on conditioning in the past 40 years has been instigated by this model or reactions to it, the R–W model deserves a brief description here.

The Rescorla-Wagner model argues that there is a limit to the amount of conditioning that can occur in the pairing of two stimuli. One determinant of this limit is the nature of the US. For example: pairing a bell with a juicy steak is more likely to produce salivation than pairing the bell with a piece of dry bread, and dry bread is likely to work better than a piece of cardboard. A key idea behind the R–W model is that a CS signals or predicts the US. One might say that before conditioning, the subject is surprised by the US. However, after conditioning, the subject is no longer surprised, because the CS predicts the coming of the US. (Note that the model can be described mathematically and that words like predict, surprise, and expect are only used to help explain the model.) Here the workings of the model are illustrated with brief accounts of acquisition, extinction, and blocking. The model also predicts a number of other phenomena.

Equation

$$\Delta V = \alpha\beta(\lambda - \Sigma V)$$

This is the Rescorla-Wagner equation. It specifies the amount of learning that will occur on a single pairing of a CS with a US; the equation is solved repeatedly to predict the course of learning over many such trials. In this model the degree of learning is measured by how well the CS predicts the US, which is given by the "associative strength" of the CS. In the equation, V represents the current associative strength of the CS, and ΔV is the change in this strength that happens on a given trial. ΣV is the sum of the strengths of all stimuli present in the situation. λ is the maximum associative strength that a given US will support; its value is usually set to 1 on trials when the US is present, and 0 when the US is absent. α and β are constants related to the salience of the CS and the speed of learning for a given US.

R–W Model: Acquisition

The R–W model measures conditioning by assigning an "associative strength" to the CS and other local stimuli. Before a CS is conditioned it has an associative strength of zero. Pairing the CS and the US causes a gradual increase in the associative strength of the CS. This increase is determined by the nature of the US (e.g. its intensity). The amount of learning that happens during any single CS-US pairing depends on the difference between the total associative strengths of CS and other stimuli present in the situation (ΣV in the equation), and a maximum set by the US (λ in the equation). On the first pairing of the CS and US, this difference is large and the associative strength of the CS takes a big step up. As CS-US pairings accumulate, the US becomes more predictable, and the increase in associative strength on each trial becomes smaller and smaller. Finally the difference between the associative strength of the CS (plus any that may accrue to other stimuli) and the maximum strength reaches zero. That is, the US is fully predicted, the associative strength of the CS stops growing, and conditioning is complete.

R–W Model: Extinction

The associative process described by the R–W model also accounts for extinction. The extinction procedure starts with a positive associative strength of the CS, which means that the CS predicts that the US will occur. On an extinction trial the US fails to occur after the CS. As a result of this "surprising" outcome, the associative strength of the CS takes a step down. Extinction is complete when the strength of the CS reaches zero; no US is predicted, and no US occurs. However, if that same CS is presented without the US but accompanied by a well-established conditioned inhibitor (CI), that is, a stimulus that predicts the absence of a US (in R-W terms, a stimulus with a negative associate strength) then R-W predicts that the CS will not undergo extinction (its V will not decrease in size).

R–W Model: Blocking

The most important and novel contribution of the R–W model is its assumption that the conditioning of a CS depends not just on that CS alone, and its relationship to the US, but also on all other stimuli present in the conditioning situation. In particular, the model states that the US is predicted by the sum of the associative strengths of all stimuli present in the conditioning situation. Learning is controlled by the difference between this total associative strength and the strength supported by the US. When this sum of strengths reaches a maximum set by the US, conditioning ends as just described.

The R–W explanation of the blocking phenomenon illustrates one consequence of the assumption just stated. In blocking, CS1 is paired with a US until conditioning is complete. Then on additional conditioning trials a second stimulus (CS2) appears together with CS1, and both are followed by the US. Finally CS2 is tested and shown to produce no response because learning about CS2 was "blocked" by the initial learning about CS1. The R–W model explains this by saying that after the initial conditioning, CS1 fully predicts the US. Since there is no difference between what is predicted and what happens, no new learning happens on the additional trials with CS1+CS2, hence CS2 later yields no response.

Theoretical Issues and Alternatives to the Rescorla–Wagner Model

One of the main reasons for the importance of the R–W model is that it is relatively simple and makes clear predictions. Tests of these predictions have led to a number of important new findings and a considerably increased understanding of conditioning. Some new information has supported the theory, but much has not, and it is generally agreed that the theory is, at best, too simple. However, no single model seems to account for all the phenomena that experiments have produced. Following are brief summaries of some related theoretical issues.

Content of Learning

The R–W model reduces conditioning to the association of a CS and US, and measures this with a single number, the associative strength of the CS. A number of experimental findings indicate that more is learned than this. Among these are two phenomena described earlier in this article.

- Latent inhibition: If a subject is repeatedly exposed to the CS before conditioning starts, then conditioning takes longer. The R–W model cannot explain this because preexposure leaves the strength of the CS unchanged at zero.

- Recovery of responding after extinction: It appears that something remains after extinction has reduced associative strength to zero because several procedures cause responding to reappear without further conditioning.

Role of Attention in Learning

Latent inhibition might happen because a subject stops focusing on a CS that is seen frequently before it is paired with a US. In fact, changes in attention to the CS are at the heart of two prominent theories that try to cope with experimental results that give the R–W model difficulty. In one of these, proposed by Nicholas Mackintosh, the speed of conditioning depends on the amount of attention devoted to the CS, and this amount of attention depends in turn on how well the CS predicts the US. Pearce and Hall proposed a related model based on a different attentional principle Both models have been extensively tested, and neither explains all the experimental results. Consequently, various authors have attempted hybrid models that combine the two attentional processes. Pearce and Hall in 2010 integrated their attentional ideas and even suggested the possibility of incorporating the Rescorla-Wagner equation into an integrated model.

Context

As stated earlier, a key idea in conditioning is that the CS signals or predicts the US. However, for example, the room in which conditioning takes place also "predicts" that the US may occur. Still, the room predicts with much less certainty than does the experimental CS itself, because the room is also there between experimental trials, when the US is absent. The role of such context is illustrated by the fact that the dogs in Pavlov's experiment would sometimes start salivating as they approached the experimental apparatus, before they saw or heard any CS. Such so-called "context" stimuli are always present, and their influence helps to account for some otherwise puzzling experimental findings. The associative strength of context stimuli can be entered into the Rescorla-Wagner equation, and they play an important role in the *comparator* and *computational* theories outlined below.

Comparator Theory

To find out what has been learned, we must somehow measure behavior ("performance") in a test situation. However, as students know all too well, performance in a test situation is not always a good measure of what has been learned. As for conditioning, there is evidence that subjects in a blocking experiment do learn something about the "blocked" CS, but fail to show this learning because of the way that they are usually tested.

"Comparator" theories of conditioning are "performance based", that is, they stress what is going on at the time of the test. In particular, they look at all the stimuli that are present during testing and at how the associations acquired by these stimuli may interact. To oversimplify somewhat, comparator theories assume that during conditioning the subject acquires both CS-US and context-US associations. At the time of the test, these associations are compared, and a response to the CS occurs only if the CS-US association is stronger than the context-US association. After a CS and US are repeatedly paired in simple acquisition, the CS-US association is strong and the context-US association is relatively weak. This means that the CS elicits a strong CR. In "zero contingency", the conditioned response is weak or absent because the context-US association is about as strong as the CS-US association. Blocking and other more subtle phenomena can also be explained by comparator theories, though, again, they cannot explain everything.

Computational Theory

An organism's need to predict future events is central to modern theories of conditioning. Most theories use associations between stimuli to take care of these predictions. For example: In the R–W model, the associative strength of a CS tells us how strongly that CS predicts a US. A different approach to prediction is suggested by models such as that proposed by Gallistel & Gibbon (2000, 2002). Here the response is not determined by associative strengths. Instead, the organism records the times of onset and offset of CSs and USs and uses these to calculate the probability that the US will follow the CS. A number of experiments have shown that humans and animals can learn to time events, and the Gallistel & Gibbon model yields very good quantitative fits to a variety of experimental data. However, recent studies have suggested that duration-based models cannot account for some empirical findings as well as associative models.

Element-based Models

The Rescorla-Wagner model treats a stimulus as a single entity, and it represents the associative strength of a stimulus with one number, with no record of how that number was reached. As noted above, this makes it hard for the model to account for a number of experimental results. More flexibility is provided by assuming that a stimulus is internally represented by a collection of elements, each of which may change from one associative state to another. For example, the similarity of one stimulus to another may be represented by saying that the two stimuli share elements in common. These shared elements help to account for stimulus generalization and other phenomena that may depend upon generalization. Also, different elements within the same set may have different associations, and their activations and associations may change at different times and at different rates. This allows element-based models to handle some otherwise inexplicable results.

The SOP Model

A prominent example of the element approach is the "SOP" model of Wagner. The model has been elaborated in various ways since its introduction, and it can now account in principle for a very wide variety of experimental findings. The model represents any given stimulus with a large collection of elements. The time of presentation of various stimuli, the state of their elements, and the interactions between the elements, all determine the course of associative processes and the behaviors observed during conditioning experiments.

The SOP account of simple conditioning exemplifies some essentials of the SOP model. To begin with, the model assumes that the CS and US are each represented by a large group of elements. Each of these stimulus elements can be in one of three states:

- primary activity (A1) - Roughly speaking, the stimulus is "attended to." (References to "attention" are intended only to aid understanding and are not part of the model.)

- secondary activity (A2) - The stimulus is "peripherally attended to."
- inactive (I) – The stimulus is "not attended to."

Of the elements that represent a single stimulus at a given moment, some may be in state A1, some in state A2, and some in state I.

When a stimulus first appears, some of its elements jump from inactivity I to primary activity A1. From the A1 state they gradually decay to A2, and finally back to I. Element activity can only change in this way; in particular, elements in A2 cannot go directly back to A1. If the elements of both the CS and the US are in the A1 state at the same time, an association is learned between the two stimuli. This means that if, at a later time, the CS is presented ahead of the US, and some CS elements enter A1, these elements will activate some US elements. However, US elements activated indirectly in this way only get boosted to the A2 state. (This can be thought of the CS arousing a memory of the US, which will not be as strong as the real thing.) With repeated CS-US trials, more and more elements are associated, and more and more US elements go to A2 when the CS comes on. This gradually leaves fewer and fewer US elements that can enter A1 when the US itself appears. In consequence, learning slows down and approaches a limit. One might say that the US is "fully predicted" or "not surprising" because almost all of its elements can only enter A2 when the CS comes on, leaving few to form new associations.

The model can explain the findings that are accounted for by the Rescorla-Wagner model and a number of additional findings as well. For example, unlike most other models, SOP takes time into account. The rise and decay of element activation enables the model to explain time-dependent effects such as the fact that conditioning is strongest when the CS comes just before the US, and that when the CS comes after the US ("backward conditioning") the result is often an inhibitory CS. Many other more subtle phenomena are explained as well.

A number of other powerful models have appeared in recent years which incorporate element representations. These often include the assumption that associations involve a network of connections between "nodes" that represent stimuli, responses, and perhaps one or more "hidden" layers of intermediate interconnections. Such models make contact with a current explosion of research on neural networks, artificial intelligence and machine learning.

Applications

Neural Basis of Learning and Memory

Pavlov proposed that conditioning involved a connection between brain centers for conditioned and unconditioned stimuli. His physiological account of conditioning has been abandoned, but classical conditioning continues to be studied in attempts to understand the neural structures and functions that underlie learning and memory. Forms of classical conditioning that are used for this purpose include, among others, fear conditioning, eyeblink conditioning, and the foot contraction conditioning of *Hermissenda crassicornis*, a sea-slug.

In their textbook on human physiology, Nikolai Agajanyan and V. Tsyrkin list five criteria for demarcation between unconditioned and conditioned reflexes. Unlike conditioned reflexes, the unconditioned reflexes are mostly stable. As described above, the conditioned reflexes are not only unstable but can be modified and extinguished. These two distinctions between the reflexes can be seen under the neural processes; A leading role in the performance of unconditioned reflexes is played by the lower divisions of the higher nervous system, the subcortical nuclei, brain stem and spinal cord. Conditioned reflexes, in contrast, are a function of the cerebral cortex and can involve the most varied stimuli applied to different receptive fields.

Behavioral Therapies

Some therapies associated with classical conditioning are aversion therapy, systematic desensitization and flooding. Aversion therapy is a type of behavior therapy designed to make patients cease an undesirable habit by associating the habit with a strong unpleasant unconditioned stimulus. For example, a medication might be used to associate the taste of alcohol with stomach upset. Systematic desensitization is a treatment for phobias in which the patient is trained to relax while being exposed to progressively more anxiety-provoking stimuli (e.g. angry words). This is an example of counterconditioning, intended to associate the feared stimuli with a response (relaxation) that is incompatible with anxiety Flooding is a form of desensitization that attempts to eliminate phobias and anxieties by repeated exposure to highly distressing stimuli until the lack of reinforcement of the anxiety response causes its extinction. "Flooding" usually involves actual exposure to the stimuli, whereas the term "implosion" refers to imagined exposure, but the two terms are sometimes used synonymously.

Conditioning therapies usually take less time than humanistic therapies.

Conditioned Drug Response

A stimulus that is present when a drug is administered or consumed may eventually evoke a conditioned physiological response that mimics the effect of the drug. This is sometimes the case with caffeine; habitual coffee drinkers may find that the smell of coffee gives them a feeling of alertness. In other cases, the conditioned response is a compensatory reaction that tends to offset the effects of the drug. For example, if a drug causes the body to become less sensitive to pain, the compensatory conditioned reaction may be one that makes the user more sensitive to pain. This compensatory reaction may contribute to drug tolerance. If so, a drug user may increase the amount of drug consumed in order to feel its effects, and end up taking very large amounts of the drug. In this case a dangerous overdose reaction may occur if the CS happens to be absent, so that the conditioned compensatory effect fails to occur. For example, if the drug has always been administered in the same room, the stimuli provided by that room may produce a conditioned compensatory effect; then an overdose reaction may happen if the drug is administered in a different location where the conditioned stimuli are absent.

Conditioned Hunger

Signals that consistently precede food intake can become conditioned stimuli for a set of bodily responses that prepares the body for food and digestion. These reflexive responses include the secretion of digestive juices into the stomach and the secretion of certain hormones into the blood stream, and they induce a state of hunger. An example of conditioned hunger is the "appetizer effect." Any signal that consistently precedes a meal, such as a clock indicating that it is time for dinner, can cause people to feel hungrier than before the signal. The lateral hypothalamus (LH) is involved in the initiation of eating. The nigrostriatal pathway, which includes the substantia nigra, the lateral hypothalamus, and the basal ganglia have been shown to be involved in hunger motivation.

Conditioned Emotional Response

The influence of classical conditioning can be seen in emotional responses such as phobia, disgust, nausea, anger, and sexual arousal. A familiar example is conditioned nausea, in which the CS is the sight or smell of a particular food that in the past has resulted in an unconditioned stomach upset. Similarly, when the CS is the sight of a dog and the US is the pain of being bitten, the result may be a conditioned fear of dogs.

As an adaptive mechanism, emotional conditioning helps shield an individual from harm or prepare it for important biological events such as sexual activity. Thus, a stimulus that has occurred before sexual interaction comes to cause sexual arousal, which prepares the individual for sexual contact. For example, sexual arousal has been conditioned in human subjects by pairing a stimulus like a picture of a jar of pennies with views of an erotic film clip. Similar experiments involving blue gourami fish and domesticated quail have shown that such conditioning can increase the number of offspring. These results suggest that conditioning techniques might help to increase fertility rates in infertile individuals and endangered species.

In Popular Culture

In the 1932 novel *Brave New World* by Aldous Huxley, conditioning plays a key role in the maintenance of social peace, especially in maintaining the caste system upon which society is based. Another example is in Anthony Burgess' 1962 dystopian novel *A Clockwork Orange* in which the novel's anti-hero and protagonist, Alex, undergoes a procedure called the Ludovico technique, where he is fed a solution to cause severe nausea and then forced to watch violent acts. This renders him unable to perform any violent acts without inducing similar nausea. Unintentionally, he also forms an aversion to classical music. In Orson Scott Card's 1999 science-fiction novel *Ender's Shadow*, "Pavlovian mental bans" are used to prevent crime. In *The Guilt Trip*, Part Three of Derren Brown's TV series *The Experiments*, Derren used Classical conditioning to make a man feel guilt at the sound of a bell.

Aversives

In psychology, aversives are unpleasant stimuli that induce changes in behavior through punishment; by applying an aversive immediately following a behavior, the likelihood of the behavior occurring in the future is reduced. Aversives can vary from being slightly unpleasant or irritating (such as a disliked color) to physically damaging. It is not the level of unpleasantness, but rather the effectiveness the unpleasant event has on changing behavior that defines the aversive.

Types of Stimuli

There are two types of aversive stimuli:

Unconditioned

Unconditioned aversive stimuli naturally result in pain or discomfort and are often associated with biologically harmful or damaging substances or events. Examples include extreme heat or cold, bitter flavors, electric shocks, loud noises and pain. Aversives can be applied naturally (such as touching a hot stove) or in a contrived manner (such as during torture or behavior modification).

Conditioned

A conditioned aversive stimulus is an initially neutral stimulus that becomes aversive after repeated pairing with an unconditioned aversive stimulus. This type of stimulus would include consequences such as verbal warnings, gestures or even the sight of an individual who is disliked.

Use in Applied Behavior Analysis (ABA)

Aversives can be used as punishment during applied behavior analysis to reduce unwanted behavior, such as self-injury, that poses a risk of harm greater than that posed by application of the aversive. Aversive stimuli may also be used as negative reinforcement to increase the rate or probability of a behavior by its removal. The use of aversives was developed as a less restrictive alternative to practices prevalent in mental institutions at the time such as shock treatment, hydrotherapy, straitjacketing and frontal lobotomies. Early iterations of the Lovaas technique incorporated aversives during therapy, though the use of aversives in ABA was not without controversy. Over time the use of aversives has become less and less necessary as less and less restrictive alternative treatments have been developed. Lovaas has since stated his disdain for the use of aversives. Applied behavior analysis permits the use of aversives in limited cases, such as when a behavior is dangerous, especially when the reinforcing contingencies that maintain a behavior are unknown.

The Behavior Analyst Certification Board (BACB) Guidelines for Responsible Conduct state that participation in an any behavior plan must be voluntary, by the client or their surrogate, and that clients or families have the right to terminate a particular intervention if they see fit, including aversive treatments. The Behavior Analyst Certification Board issues credentials for behavior analysts nationwide, although state regulations vary as to whether or not a person can represent themselves as a "behavior analyst." The use of aversive treatment is something that practitioners of applied behavior analysis are supposed to take very seriously due to the pain and risks involved and the controversy surrounding their use.

Several national and international disability rights groups have spoken against the use of aversive therapies, including TASH and Autism National Committee (known as AUTCOM).

Psychobiology of Learning

Laboratory studies of S-R learning have been mostly conducted on rats, with few researchers opting for cats, dogs and even human babies. As you must be aware, there is a difference in the viewpoints of theorists proposing learning by conditioning and cognitive theorists. The former emphasize on stimulus-response (S-R) association whereas the later lay emphasis on consequence based expectations. According to Tolman (1932, 1948) animal learn from "what leads-to-what" and accordingly expect consequences of their behaviour. Findings of studies on rats suggest that hippocampus and caudate nucleus are the brain structures responsible for these two forms of learning. Hippocampus selectively mediates cognitive memory whereas caudate nucleus mediates S-R habit formation. Hippocampus is supposed to facilitate rapid subjective learning from own experiences whereas cortex facilitates integration of multiple experiences so as to generalize certain things. This is a slow process. Different stimuli are organized into an associative group by chunking. This forms the basis of conditioning. It has been proposed that hippocampus is instrumental in cortical chunking. The table given below summarizes the brain areas involved in Pavlovian conditioning.

Pavlovian Conditioning	Brain Areas Involved
For conditioned stimulus (CS) to gain access to the current value of the unconditioned stimulus (US)	Basolateral amygdala (BLA)
Some forms of stimulus-response conditioning	Central nucleus of the amygdale [through brainstem arousal and response]
Mediating the impact of CS on CR	Nucleus accumbens
Detecting action-outcome contingency	Prelimbic cortex
Memorizing sensory properties of food [retrieval of specific value]	Insular cortex
Value of reinforcer controlling instrumental choice behaviour	Orbitofrontal cortex
Allowing response to emotionally significant stimuli and preventing response to inappropriate stimuli	Anterior cingulate cortex

It might be interesting for you to know that the traditional laboratory experiments on animals to empirically explore and validate S-R conditioning have been replaced by computer simulations following conditioning paradigms. Such studies have come forward with a real-time attentional model of hippocampal function (Schmajuk & Moore, 1985).

Spatial Learning

Spatial learning refers to the ability to attain a map-like depiction of the surroundings that combines features of the stimulus that are specific to certain locations. This mental map has place representations that are connected on the basis of some rules representing distance and direction among these places. Area CA3 of the hippocampus has the auto-associative binding properties. You must have come across many types of pattern completion task. The figure given below is a representative sample from a popular non-verbal test of intelligence, Raven's Progressive Matrices.

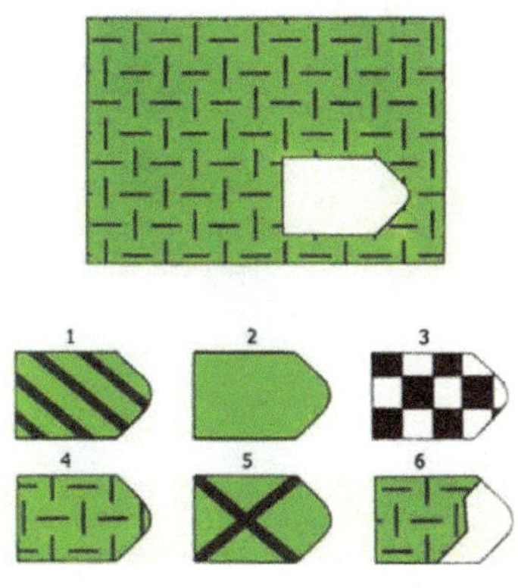

Such tasks demand the filling of the missing parts on the basis of input pattern stored in our memory. Let us take an example from the real life situation. We have multiple parking places for bicycles in the academic area. Even if you are asked later where your bicycle is you respond correctly because of input cues that trigger completion of the full encoded memory. In terms of brain representation, hippocampal system facilitates such pattern completions. There are lateral connections within the layer CA3 that enables spreading of partial activity to fill in the missing pieces.

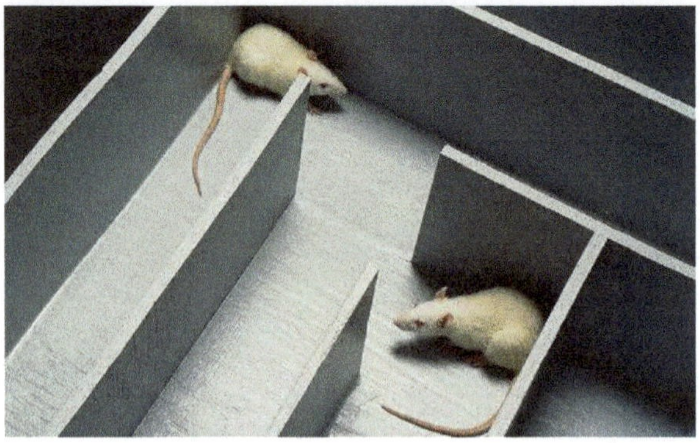

Experiments on laboratory rats have been largely performed on different types of mazes where the rats have to go for way-finding. An example of one such experiment is given below. Outcome of these studies endorse correlation between level of acetylcholinesterase enzyme (ACHE) in the brain and the ability to solve spatial problems. Rats trained and tested on more difficult problems had higher acetylcholinesterase in the cortex compared to those trained on easier tasks. Other experience-induced changes have also been reported. Studies have reported increase in the thickness of cortex, size of neurons nuclei, size of synaptic area and branching of dendrites (up to 25%) due to experience.

Raven's Progressive Matrices

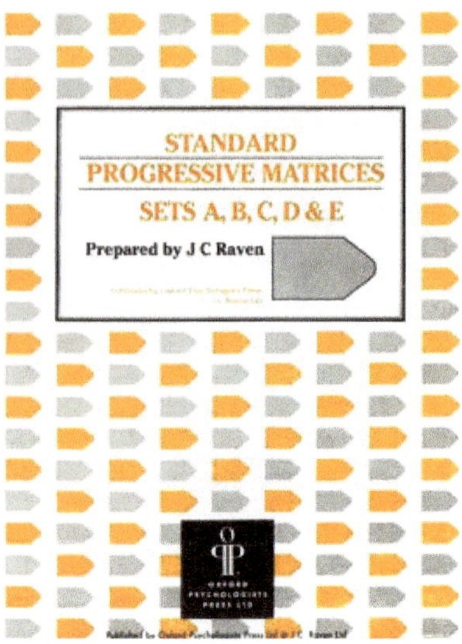

The cover of a test booklet for Raven's Standard Progressive Matrices.

Raven's Progressive Matrices (often referred to simply as Raven's Matrices) or RPM is a nonverbal group test typically used in educational settings. It is usually a 60-item test used in measuring abstract reasoning and regarded as a non-verbal estimate of fluid intelligence. It is the most common and popular test administered to groups ranging from 5-year-olds to the elderly. It is made of 60 multiple choice questions, listed in order of difficulty. This format is designed to measure the test-taker's reasoning ability, the eductive ("meaning-making") component of Spearman's ***g*** (***g*** is often referred to as general intelligence). The tests were originally developed by John C. Raven in 1936. In each test item, the subject is asked to identify the missing element that completes a pattern. Many patterns are presented in the form of a 6×6, 4×4, 3×3, or 2×2 matrix, giving the test its name.

Problem Structure

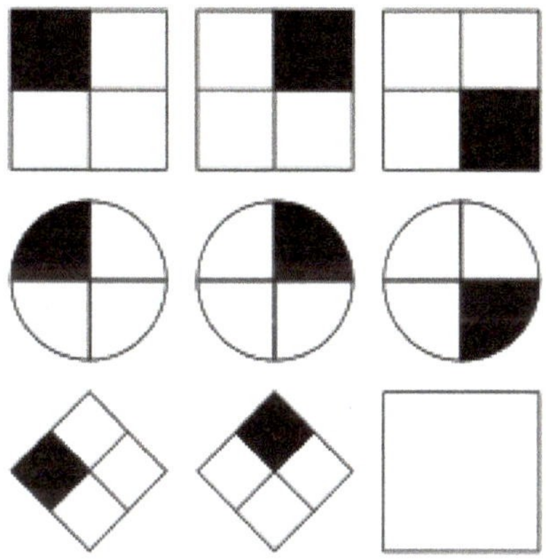

An IQ test item in the style of a Raven's Progressive Matrices test. Given eight patterns, the subject must identify the missing ninth pattern

All of the questions on the Raven's progressives consist of visual geometric design with a missing piece. The test taker is given six to eight choices to pick from and fill in the missing piece.

Raven's Progressive Matrices and Vocabulary tests were originally developed for use in research into the genetic and environmental origins of cognitive ability. Raven thought that the tests commonly in use at that time were cumbersome to administer and the results difficult to interpret. Accordingly, he set about developing simple measures of the two main components of Spearman's *g*: the ability to think clearly and make sense of complexity (known as eductive ability) and the ability to store and reproduce information (known as reproductive ability).

Raven's tests of both were developed with the aid of what later became known as item response theory.

Raven first published his Progressive Matrices in the United Kingdom in 1938. His three sons established Scotland-based test publisher J C Raven Ltd. in 1972. In 2004, Harcourt Assessment, Inc. a division of Harcourt Education acquired J C Raven Ltd. Harcourt was later acquired by Pearson PLC.

Versions

The Matrices are available in three different forms for participants of different ability:

- Standard Progressive Matrices: These were the original form of the matrices, first published in 1938. The booklet comprises five sets (A to E) of 12 items each (e.g., A1 through

A12), with items within a set becoming increasingly difficult, requiring ever greater cognitive capacity to encode and analyze information. All items are presented in black ink on a white background.

- Coloured Progressive Matrices: Designed for children aged 5 through 11 years-of-age, the elderly, and mentally and physically impaired individuals. This test contains sets A and B from the standard matrices, with a further set of 12 items inserted between the two, as set Ab. Most items are presented on a coloured background to make the test visually stimulating for participants. However the very last few items in set B are presented as black-on-white; in this way, if a subject exceeds the tester's expectations, transition to sets C, D, and E of the standard matrices is eased.

- Advanced Progressive Matrices: The advanced form of the matrices contains 48 items, presented as one set of 12 (set I), and another of 36 (set II). Items are again presented in black ink on a white background, and become increasingly difficult as progress is made through each set. These items are appropriate for adults and adolescents of above-average intelligence.

In addition, "parallel" forms of the standard and coloured progressive matrices were published in 1998. This was to address the problem of the Raven's Matrices being too well known in the general population. Items in the parallel tests have been constructed so that average solution rates to each question are identical for the classic and parallel versions. A revised version of the SPM – the Standard Progressive Matrices Plus – was published at the same time. This was based on the "parallel" version but, although the test was the same length, it had more difficult items in order to restore the discrimination that the original SPM had among more able adolescents and young adults when it was first published. This new test, developed with the aid of better sampling arrangements and developments in the procedures available to implement the item response theory, has turned out to have exemplary test properties.

Uses of the Tests

The tests were developed for research purposes. Because of their independence of language and reading and writing skills, and the simplicity of their use and interpretation, they quickly found widespread practical application. For example, all entrants to the British armed forces from 1942 onwards took a twenty-minute version of the SPM, and potential officers took a specially adapted version as part of British War Office Selection Boards. The routine administration of what became the Standard Progressive Matrices to all entrants (conscripts) to many military services throughout the world (including the Soviet Union) continued at least until the present century. It was by bringing together these data that James R. Flynn was able to place the intergenerational increase in scores beyond reasonable doubt. Flynn's path-breaking publications on IQ gains around the world have led to the phenomenon of the gains being known as the Flynn effect. Among Robert L. Thorndike and other researchers who preceded Flynn in finding evidence of IQ score gains was John Raven, reporting on studies with the RPM.

A 2007 study provided evidence that individuals with Asperger syndrome, a high-functioning autism spectrum disorder, score higher than other individuals on Raven's tests. Another 2007 study provided evidence that individuals with classic autism, a low-functioning autism spectrum disorder, score higher in Raven's tests than in Wechsler tests. In addition, the individuals with classic autism were providing correct answers to the Raven's test in less time than individuals without autism, although erring as often.

The Triple Nine Society, a high IQ society, accepts the Advanced Progressive Matrices form for one of their admission tests. They require a score of at least 32 out of 36 on or before December 31, 1999 on the RAPM. The International Society for Philosophical Enquiry (ISPE) similarly accepts the RAPM as a qualification for admission, and so does the International High IQ Society.

g Factor (Psychometrics)

The g factor (also known as general intelligence, general mental ability or general intelligence factor) is a construct developed in psychometric investigations of cognitive abilities and human intelligence. It is a variable that summarizes positive correlations among different cognitive tasks, reflecting the fact that an individual's performance on one type of cognitive task tends to be comparable to that person's performance on other kinds of cognitive tasks. The *g* factor typically accounts for 40 to 50 percent of the between-individual performance differences on a given cognitive test, and composite scores ("IQ scores") based on many tests are frequently regarded as estimates of individuals' standing on the *g* factor. The terms IQ, general intelligence, general cognitive ability, general mental ability, or simply intelligence are often used interchangeably to refer to this common core shared by cognitive tests.

The existence of the *g* factor was originally proposed by the English psychologist Charles Spearman in the early years of the 20th century. He observed that children's performance ratings, across seemingly unrelated school subjects, were positively correlated, and reasoned that these correlations reflected the influence of an underlying general mental ability that entered into performance on all kinds of mental tests. Spearman suggested that all mental performance could be conceptualized in terms of a single general ability factor, which he labeled *g*, and a large number of narrow task-specific ability factors. Today's factor models of intelligence typically represent cognitive abilities as a three-level hierarchy, where there are a large number of narrow factors at the bottom of the hierarchy, a handful of broad, more general factors at the intermediate level, and at the apex a single factor, referred to as the *g* factor, which represents the variance common to all cognitive tasks.

Traditionally, research on *g* has concentrated on psychometric investigations of test data, with a special emphasis on factor analytic approaches. However, empirical research on the nature of *g* has also drawn upon experimental cognitive psychology and mental chronometry, brain anatomy and physiology, quantitative and molecular genetics, and primate evolution. While the existence of *g* as a statistical regularity is well-established and uncontroversial, there is no consensus as to what causes the positive correlations between tests.

Research in the field of behavioral genetics has established that the construct of *g* is highly heritable. It has a number of other biological correlates, including brain size. It is also a significant predictor of individual differences in many social outcomes, particularly in education and employment. The most widely accepted contemporary theories of intelligence incorporate the *g* factor. However, critics of *g* have contended that an emphasis on *g* is misplaced and entails a devaluation of other important abilities, as well as supporting an unrealistic reified view of human intelligence.

Cognitive Ability Testing

Spearman's correlation matrix for six measures of school performance. All the correlations are positive, a phenomenon referred as the *positive manifold.* The bottom row shows the *g* loadings of each performance measure.

	Classics	French	English	Math	Pitch	Music
Classics	-					
French	.83	-				
English	.78	.67	-			
Math	.70	.67	.64	-		
Pitch discrimination	.66	.65	.54	.45	-	
Music	.63	.57	.51	.51	.40	-
g	.958	.882	.803	.750	.673	.646

Subtest intercorrelations in a sample of Scottish subjects who completed the WAIS-R battery. The subtests are Vocabulary, Similarities, Information, Comprehension, Picture arrangement, Block design, Arithmetic, Picture completion, Digit span, Object assembly, and Digit symbol. The bottom row shows the *g* loadings of each subtest.

	V	S	I	C	PA	BD	A	PC	DSp	OA	DS
V	-										
S	.67	-									
I	.72	.59	-								
C	.70	.58	.59	-							
PA	.51	.53	.50	.42	-						
BD	.45	.46	.45	.39	.43	-					
A	.48	.43	.55	.45	.41	.44	-				
PC	.49	.52	.52	.46	.48	.45	.30	-			
DSp	.46	.40	.36	.36	.31	.32	.47	.23	-		
OA	.32	.40	.32	.29	.36	.58	.33	.41	.14	-	
DS	.32	.33	.26	.30	.28	.36	.28	.26	.27	.25	-
g	.83	.80	.80	.75	.70	.70	.68	.68	.56	.56	.48

Cognitive ability tests are designed to measure different aspects of cognition. Specific domains assessed by tests include mathematical skill, verbal fluency, spatial visualization, and memory, among others. However, individuals who excel at one type of test tend to excel at other kinds of tests, too, while those who do poorly on one test tend to do so on all tests, regardless of the tests' contents. The English psychologist Charles Spearman was the first to describe this phenomenon. In a famous research paper published in 1904, he observed that children's performance measures across seemingly unrelated school subjects were positively correlated. This finding has since been replicated numerous times. The consistent finding of universally positive correlation matrices of mental test results (or the "positive manifold"), despite large differences in tests' contents, has been described as "arguably the most replicated result in all psychology." Zero or negative correlations between tests suggest the presence of sampling error or restriction of the range of ability in the sample studied.

Using factor analysis or related statistical methods, it is possible to compute a single common factor that can be regarded as a summary variable characterizing the correlations between all the different tests in a test battery. Spearman referred to this common factor as the *general factor*, or simply *g*. (By convention, *g* is always printed as a lower case italic.) Mathematically, the *g* factor is *a source of variance among individuals*, which entails that one cannot meaningfully speak of any one individual's mental abilities consisting of *g* or other factors to any specified degrees. One can only speak of an individual's standing on *g* (or other factors) compared to other individuals in a relevant population.

Different tests in a test battery may correlate with (or "load onto") the *g* factor of the battery to different degrees. These correlations are known as *g* loadings. An individual test taker's *g* factor score, representing his or her relative standing on the *g* factor in the total group of individuals, can be estimated using the *g* loadings. Full-scale IQ scores from a test battery will usually be highly correlated with *g* factor scores, and they are often regarded as estimates of *g*. For example, the correlations between *g* factor scores and full-scale IQ scores from David Wechsler's tests have been found to be greater than .95. The terms IQ, general intelligence, general cognitive ability, general mental ability, or simply intelligence are frequently used interchangeably to refer to the common core shared by cognitive tests.

The *g* loadings of mental tests are always positive and usually range between .10 and .90, with a mean of about .60 and a standard deviation of about .15. Raven's Progressive Matrices is among the tests with the highest *g* loadings, around .80. Tests of vocabulary and general information are also typically found to have high *g* loadings. However, the *g* loading of the same test may vary somewhat depending on the composition of the test battery.

The complexity of tests and the demands they place on mental manipulation are related to the tests' *g* loadings. For example, in the forward digit span test the subject is asked to repeat a sequence of digits in the order of their presentation after hearing them once at a rate of one digit per second. The backward digit span test is otherwise the same except that the subject is asked to repeat the digits in the reverse order to that in which they were presented. The backward digit span test is more complex than the forward digit span test, and it has a significantly higher *g* loading. Similarly, the *g* loadings of arithmetic computation, spelling, and word reading tests are lower than those of arithmetic problem solving, text composition, and reading comprehension tests, respectively.

Test difficulty and *g* loadings are distinct concepts that may or may not be empirically related in any specific situation. Tests that have the same difficulty level, as indexed by the proportion of test items that are failed by test takers, may exhibit a wide range of *g* loadings. For example, tests of rote memory have been shown to have the same level of difficulty but considerably lower *g* loadings than many tests that involve reasoning.

Theories

While the existence of *g* as a statistical regularity is well-established and uncontroversial among experts, there is no consensus as to what causes the positive intercorrelations. Several explanations have been proposed.

Mental Energy or Efficiency

Charles Spearman reasoned that correlations between tests reflected the influence of a common causal factor, a general mental ability that enters into performance on all kinds of mental tasks. However, he thought that the best indicators of *g* were those tests that reflected what he called *the eduction of relations and correlates*, which included abilities such as deduction, induction, problem solving, grasping relationships, inferring rules, and spotting differences and similarities. Spearman hypothesized that *g* was equivalent with "mental energy". However, this was more of a metaphorical explanation, and he remained agnostic about the physical basis of this energy, expecting that future research would uncover the exact physiological nature of *g*.

Following Spearman, Arthur Jensen maintained that all mental tasks tap into *g* to some degree. According to Jensen, the *g* factor represents a "distillate" of scores on different tests rather than a summation or an average of such scores, with factor analysis acting as the distillation procedure. He argued that *g* cannot be described in terms of the item characteristics or information content of tests, pointing out that very dissimilar mental tasks may have nearly equal *g* loadings. Wechsler similarly contended that *g* is not an ability at all but rather some general property of the brain. Jensen hypothesized that *g* corresponds to individual differences in the speed or efficiency of the neural processes associated with mental abilities. He also suggested that given the associations between *g* and elementary cognitive tasks, it should be possible to construct a ratio scale test of *g* that uses time as the unit of measurement.

Sampling Theory

The so-called sampling theory of *g*, originally developed by E.L. Thorndike and Godfrey Thomson, proposes that the existence of the positive manifold can be explained without reference to a unitary underlying capacity. According to this theory, there are a number of uncorrelated mental processes, and all tests draw upon different samples of these processes. The intercorrelations between tests are caused by an overlap between processes tapped by the tests. Thus, the positive manifold arises due to a measurement problem, an inability to measure more fine-grained, presumably uncorrelated mental processes.

It has been shown that it is not possible to distinguish statistically between Spearman's model of *g* and the sampling model; both are equally able to account for intercorrelations among tests. The sampling theory is also consistent with the observation that more complex mental tasks have higher *g* loadings, because more complex tasks are expected to involve a larger sampling of neural elements and therefore have more of them in common with other tasks.

Some researchers have argued that the sampling model invalidates *g* as a psychological concept, because the model suggests that *g* factors derived from different test batteries simply reflect the shared elements of the particular tests contained in each battery rather than a *g* that is common to all tests. Similarly, high correlations between different batteries could be due to them measuring the same set of abilities rather than *the* same ability.

Critics have argued that the sampling theory is incongruent with certain empirical findings. Based on the sampling theory, one might expect that related cognitive tests share many elements and thus be highly correlated. However, some closely related tests, such as forward and backward digit span, are only modestly correlated, while some seemingly completely dissimilar tests, such as vocabulary tests and Raven's matrices, are consistently highly correlated. Another problematic finding is that brain damage frequently leads to specific cognitive impairments rather than a general impairment one might expect based on the sampling theory.

Mutualism

The "mutualism" model of g proposes that cognitive processes are initially uncorrelated, but that the positive manifold arises during individual development due to mutual beneficial relations between cognitive processes. Thus there is no single process or capacity underlying the positive correlations between tests. During the course of development, the theory holds, any one particularly efficient process will benefit other processes, with the result that the processes will end up being correlated with one another. Thus similarly high IQs in different persons may stem from quite different initial advantages that they had. Critics have argued that the observed correlations between the g loadings and the heritability coefficients of subtests are problematic for the mutualism theory.

Factor Structure of Cognitive Abilities

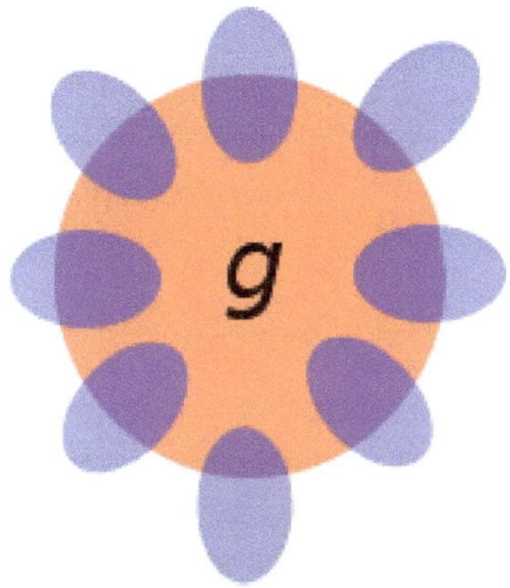

An illustration of Spearman's two-factor intelligence theory. Each small oval is a hypothetical mental test. The blue areas correspond to test-specific variance (s), while the purple areas represent the variance attributed to g.

Factor analysis is a family of mathematical techniques that can be used to represent correlations between intelligence tests in terms of a smaller number of variables known as factors. The purpose is to simplify the correlation matrix by using hypothetical underlying factors to explain the patterns in it. When all correlations in a matrix are positive, as they are in the case of IQ, factor analysis will yield a general factor common to all tests. The general factor of IQ tests is referred to as the g factor, and it typically accounts for 40 to 50 percent of the variance in IQ test batteries.

Charles Spearman developed factor analysis in order to study correlations between tests. Initially, he developed a model of intelligence in which variations in all intelligence test scores are explained by only two kinds of variables: first, factors that are specific to each test (denoted s); and second, a g factor that accounts for the positive correlations across tests. This is known as Spearman's two-factor theory. Later research based on more diverse test batteries than those used by Spearman demonstrated that g alone could not account for all correlations between tests. Specifically, it was found that even after controlling for g, some tests were still correlated with each other. This led to the postulation of *group factors* that represent variance that groups of tests with similar task demands (e.g., verbal, spatial, or numerical) have in common in addition to the shared g variance.

Through factor rotation, it is, in principle, possible to produce an infinite number of different factor solutions that are mathematically equivalent in their ability to account for the intercorrelations among cognitive tests. These include solutions that do not contain a *g* factor. Thus factor analysis alone cannot establish what the underlying structure of intelligence is. In choosing between different factor solutions, researchers have to examine the results of factor analysis together with other information about the structure of cognitive abilities.

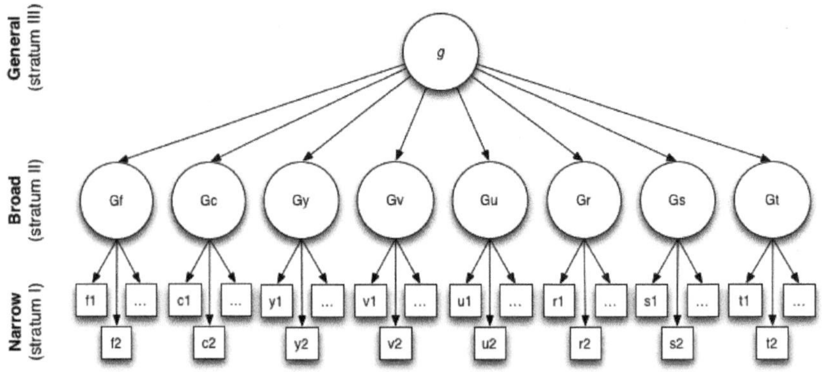

An illustration of John B. Carroll's three stratum theory, an influential contemporary model of cognitive abilities. The broad abilities recognized by the model are fluid intelligence (Gf), crystallized intelligence (Gc), general memory and learning (Gy), broad visual perception (Gv), broad auditory perception (Gu), broad retrieval ability (Gr), broad cognitive speediness (Gs), and processing speed (Gt). Carroll regarded the broad abilities as different "flavors" of *g*.

There are many psychologically relevant reasons for preferring factor solutions that contain a *g* factor. These include the existence of the positive manifold, the fact that certain kinds of tests (generally the more complex ones) have consistently larger *g* loadings, the substantial invariance of *g* factors across different test batteries, the impossibility of constructing test batteries that do not yield a *g* factor, and the widespread practical validity of *g* as a predictor of individual outcomes. The *g* factor, together with group factors, best represents the empirically established fact that, on average, overall ability differences *between* individuals are greater than differences among abilities *within* individuals, while a factor solution with orthogonal factors without *g* obscures this fact. Moreover, *g* appears to be the most heritable component of intelligence. Research utilizing the techniques of confirmatory factor analysis has also provided support for the existence of *g*.

A *g* factor can be computed from a correlation matrix of test results using several different methods. These include exploratory factor analysis, principal components analysis (PCA), and confirmatory factor analysis. Different factor-extraction methods produce highly consistent results, although PCA has sometimes been found to produce inflated estimates of the influence of *g* on test scores.

There is a broad contemporary consensus that cognitive variance between people can be conceptualized at three hierarchical levels, distinguished by their degree of generality. At the lowest, least general level there are a large number of narrow first-order factors; at a higher level, there are a relatively small number – somewhere between five and ten – of broad (i.e., more general) second-order factors (or group factors); and at the apex, there is a single third-order factor, *g*, the general factor common to all tests. The *g* factor usually accounts for the majority of the total common factor variance of IQ test batteries. Contemporary hierarchical models of intelligence include the three stratum theory and the Cattell–Horn–Carroll theory.

"Indifference of the Indicator"

Spearman proposed the principle of the *indifference of the indicator*, according to which the precise content of intelligence tests is unimportant for the purposes of identifying *g*, because *g* enters into performance on all kinds of tests. Any test can therefore be used as an indicator of *g*. Following Spearman, Arthur Jensen more recently argued that a *g* factor extracted from one test battery will always be the same, within the limits of measurement error, as that extracted from another battery, provided that the batteries are large and diverse. According to this view, every mental test, no matter how distinctive, calls on *g* to some extent. Thus a composite score of a number of different tests will load onto *g* more strongly than any of the individual test scores, because the *g* components cumulate into the composite score, while the uncorrelated non-*g* components will cancel each other out. Theoretically, the composite score of an infinitely large, diverse test battery would, then, be a perfect measure of *g*.

In contrast, L.L. Thurstone argued that a *g* factor extracted from a test battery reflects the average of all the abilities called for by the particular battery, and that *g* therefore varies from one battery to another and "has no fundamental psychological significance." Along similar lines, John Horn argued that *g* factors are meaningless because they are not invariant across test batteries, maintaining that correlations between different ability measures arise because it is difficult to define a human action that depends on just one ability.

To show that different batteries reflect the same *g*, one must administer several test batteries to the same individuals, extract *g* factors from each battery, and show that the factors are highly correlated. This can be done within a confirmatory factor analysis framework. Wendy Johnson and colleagues have published two such studies. The first found that the correlations between *g* factors extracted from three different batteries were .99, .99, and 1.00, supporting the hypothesis that *g* factors from different batteries are the same and that the identification of *g* is not dependent on the specific abilities assessed. The second study found that *g* factors derived from four of five test batteries correlated at between .95–1.00, while the correlations ranged from .79 to .96 for the fifth battery, the Cattell Culture Fair Intelligence Test (the CFIT). They attributed the somewhat lower correlations with the CFIT battery to its lack of content diversity for it contains only matrix-type items, and interpreted the findings as supporting the contention that *g* factors derived from different test batteries are the same provided that the batteries are diverse enough. The results suggest that the same *g* can be consistently identified from different test batteries.

Population Distribution

The form of the population distribution of *g* is unknown, because *g* cannot be measured on a ratio scale. (The distributions of scores on typical IQ tests are roughly normal, but this is achieved by construction, i.e., by normalizing the raw scores.) It has been argued that there are nevertheless good reasons for supposing that *g* is normally distributed in the general population, at least within a range of ±2 standard deviations from the mean. In particular, *g* can be thought of as a composite variable that reflects the additive effects of a large number of independent genetic and environmental influences, and such a variable should, according to the central limit theorem, follow a normal distribution.

Spearman's Law of Diminishing Returns

A number of researchers have suggested that the proportion of variation accounted for by *g* may not be uniform across all subgroups within a population. *Spearman's law of diminishing returns* (SLDR), also termed the *ability differentiation hypothesis*, predicts that the positive correlations among different cognitive abilities are weaker among more intelligent subgroups of individuals. More specifically, SLDR predicts that the *g* factor will account for a smaller proportion of individual differences in cognitive tests scores at higher scores on the *g* factor.

SLDR was originally proposed by Charles Spearman, who reported that the average correlation between 12 cognitive ability tests was .466 in 78 normal children, and .782 in 22 "defective" children. Detterman and Daniel rediscovered this phenomenon in 1989. They reported that for subtests of both the WAIS and the WISC, subtest intercorrelations decreased monotonically with ability group, ranging from approximately an average intercorrelation of .7 among individuals with IQs less than 78 to .4 among individuals with IQs greater than 122.

SLDR has been replicated in a variety of child and adult samples who have been measured using broad arrays of cognitive tests. The most common approach has been to divide individuals into multiple ability groups using an observable proxy for their general intellectual ability, and then to either compare the average interrelation among the subtests across the different groups, or to compare the proportion of variation accounted for by a single common factor, in the different groups. However, as both Deary et al. (1996). and Tucker-Drob (2009) have pointed out, dividing the continuous distribution of intelligence into an arbitrary number of discrete ability groups is less than ideal for examining SLDR. Tucker-Drob (2009) extensively reviewed the literature on SLDR and the various methods by which it had been previously tested, and proposed that SLDR could be most appropriately captured by fitting a common factor model that allows the relations between the factor and its indicators to be nonlinear in nature. He applied such a factor model to a nationally representative data of children and adults in the United States and found consistent evidence for SLDR. For example, Tucker-Drob (2009) found that a general factor accounted for approximately 75% of the variation in seven different cognitive abilities among very low IQ adults, but only accounted for approximately 30% of the variation in the abilities among very high IQ adults.

Practical Validity

The practical validity of *g* as a predictor of educational, economic, and social outcomes is more far-ranging and universal than that of any other known psychological variable. The validity of *g* is greater the greater the complexity of the task.

A test's practical validity is measured by its correlation with performance on some criterion external to the test, such as college grade-point average, or a rating of job performance. The correlation between test scores and a measure of some criterion is called the *validity coefficient*. One way to interpret a validity coefficient is to square it to obtain the variance accounted by the test. For example, a validity coefficient of .30 corresponds to 9 percent of variance explained. This approach has, however, been criticized as misleading and uninformative, and several alternatives have been proposed. One arguably more interpretable approach is to look at the percentage of test takers in each test score quintile who meet some agreed-upon standard of success. For example, if the correlation between test scores and performance is .30, the expectation is that 67 percent of those in the top quintile will be above-average performers, compared to 33 percent of those in the bottom quintile.

Academic Achievement

The predictive validity of *g* is most conspicuous in the domain of scholastic performance. This is apparently because *g* is closely linked to the ability to learn novel material and understand concepts and meanings.

In elementary school, the correlation between IQ and grades and achievement scores is between .60 and .70. At more advanced educational levels, more students from the lower end of the IQ distribution drop out, which restricts the range of IQs and results in lower validity coefficients. In high school, college, and graduate school the validity coefficients are .50–.60, .40–.50, and .30–.40, respectively. The *g* loadings of IQ scores are high, but it is possible that some of the validity of IQ in predicting scholastic achievement is attributable to factors measured by IQ independent of *g*. According to research by Robert L. Thorndike, 80 to 90 percent of the *predictable* variance in scholastic performance is due to *g*, with the rest attributed to non-*g* factors measured by IQ and other tests.

Achievement test scores are more highly correlated with IQ than school grades. This may be because grades are more influenced by the teacher's idiosyncratic perceptions of the student. In a longitudinal English study, *g* scores measured at age 11 correlated with all the 25 subject tests of the national GCSE examination taken at age 16. The correlations ranged from .77 for the mathematics test to .42 for the art test. The correlation between *g* and a general educational factor computed from the GCSE tests was .81.

Research suggests that the SAT, widely used in college admissions, is primarily a measure of *g*. A correlation of .82 has been found between *g* scores computed from an IQ test battery and SAT scores. In a study of 165,000 students at 41 U.S. colleges, SAT scores were found to be correlated at .47 with first-year college grade-point average after correcting for range restriction in SAT scores (the correlation rises to .55 when course difficulty is held constant, i.e., if all students attended the same set of classes).

Job Attainment

There is a high correlation of .90 to .95 between the prestige rankings of occupations, as rated by the general population, and the *average* general intelligence scores of people employed in each occupation. At the level of individual employees, the association between job prestige and *g* is lower – one large U.S. study reported a correlation of .65 (.72 corrected for attenuation). Mean level of *g* thus increases with perceived job prestige. It has also been found that the dispersion of general intelligence scores is smaller in more prestigious occupations than in lower level occupations, suggesting that higher level occupations have minimum *g* requirements.

Job Performance

Research indicates that tests of *g* are the best single predictors of job performance, with an average validity coefficient of .55 across several meta-analyses of studies based on supervisor ratings and job samples. The average meta-analytic validity coefficient for performance in job *training* is .63. The validity of *g* in the highest complexity jobs (professional, scientific, and upper management jobs) has been found to be greater than in the lowest complexity jobs, but *g* has predictive validity even for the simplest jobs. Research also shows that specific aptitude tests tailored for each job provide little or no increase in predictive validity over tests of general intelligence. It is believed that *g* affects job performance mainly by facilitating the acquisition of job-related knowledge. The predictive validity of *g* is greater than that of work experience, and increased experience on the job does not decrease the validity of *g*.

In a recent meta-analysis, researchers found that general cognitive ability (GCA) predicted job performance better than personality (Five factor model) and three streams of emotional intelligence. They examined the relative importance of these constructs on predicting job performance and found that cognitive ability explained most of the variance in job performance. Other studies suggested that GCA and emotional intelligence have a linear independent and complementary contribution to job performance. Côté and Miners (2015) found that these constructs are interrelated when assessing their relationship with two aspects of job performance: organisational citizenship behaviour (OCB) and task performance. Emotional intelligence is a better predictor of task performance and OCB when GCA is low and vice versa. For instance, an employee with low GCA will compensate his/her task performance and OCB, if emotional intelligence is high.

Although these compensatory effects favour emotional intelligence, GCA still remains as the best predictor of job performance. Several researchers have studied the correlation between GCA and job performance among different job positions. For instance, Ghiselli (1973) found that salespersons had a higher correlation than sales clerk. The former obtained a correlation of 0.61 for GCA, 0.40 for perceptual ability and 0.29 for psychomotor abilities; whereas sales clerk obtained a correlation of 0.27 for GCA, 0.22 for perceptual ability and 0.17 for psychomotor abilities. Other studies compared GCA – job performance correlation between jobs of different complexity. Hunter and Hunter (1984) developed a meta-analysis with over 400 studies and found that this correlation was higher for jobs of high complexity (0.57). Followed by jobs of medium complexity (0.51) and low complexity (0.38).

Job performance is measured by objective rating performance and subjective ratings. Although the former is better than subjective ratings, most of studies in job performance and GCA have been based on supervisor performance ratings. This rating criteria is considered problematic and unreliable, mainly because of its difficulty to define what is a good and bad performance. Rating of supervisors tends to be subjective and inconsistent among employees. Additionally, supervisor rating of job performance is influenced by different factors, such as halo effect, facial attractiveness, racial or ethnic bias, and height of employees. However, Vinchur, Schippmann, Switzer and Roth (1998) found in their study with sales employees that objective sales performance had a correlation of 0.04 with GCA, while supervisor performance rating got a correlation of 0.40. These findings were surprising, considering that the main criteria for assessing these employees would be the objective sales.

In understanding how GCA is associated job performance, several researchers concluded that GCA affects acquisition of job knowledge, which in turn improves job performance. In other words, people high in GCA are capable to learn faster and acquire more job knowledge easily, which allow them to perform better. Conversely, lack of ability to acquire job knowledge will directly affect job performance. This is due to low levels of GCA. Also, GCA has a direct effect on job performance. In a daily basis, employees are exposed constantly to challenges and problem solving tasks, which success depends solely on their GCA. These findings are discouraging for governmental entities in charge of protecting rights of workers. Because of the high correlation of GCA on job performance, companies are hiring employees based on GCA tests scores. Inevitably, this practice is denying the opportunity to work to many people with low GCA. Previous researchers have found significant differences in GCA between race / ethnicity groups. For instance, there is a debate whether studies were biased against Afro-Americans, who scored significantly lower than white Americans in GCA tests. However, findings on GCA-job performance correlation must be taken carefully. Some researchers have warned the existence of statistical artifacts related to measures of job performance and GCA test scores. For example, Viswesvaran, Ones and Schmidt (1996) argued that is quite impossible to obtain perfect measures of job performance without incurring in any methodological error. Moreover, studies on GCA and job performance are always susceptible to range restriction, because data is gathered mostly from current employees, neglecting those that were not hired. Hence, sample comes from employees who successfully passed hiring process, including measures of GCA.

Now researchers are questioning whether IQ test predicts job performance. Prior studies argued that IQ test had a low correlation with job performance, about 0.2 to 0.3. Many years later, Schmidt and Hunter (2003) suggested that these results were attenuated by different statistical errors and modifications. Hence, they proposed a methodology to correct these errors in a meta-analysis study, obtaining a corrected correlation of 0.5. However, some researchers are still sceptical of these findings because of quality of initial studies that were included in the meta-analysis. Moreover, some considerations about the correlation between IQ and job performance has been suggested. For instance, researchers suggested that interpretation of these correlations must be taken carefully when developing further studies that include IQ test or similar concepts. Similarly, many studies prior to 1970 found an inconsistent or low correlation between these constructs, but these findings are not reliable anymore. For this reason, several surrogate questionnaires for IQ test have been proposed in different studies. Arguably, these studies suggested that surrogate tests were measuring essentially the same as IQ test: general intelligence. For instance, they included working memory test and educational admission tests, such as GMAT, GRE and SATS. In some tests, they extracted general ability measures from special ability tests; while in others, they only renamed the construct as general mental ability. Although their similarity in results with IQ tests, these surrogate tests did not contemplate the "Flynn effect", which states that average scores significantly rise from one generation to another. This effect affects differently the variance, mean and distribution of each test.

Income

The correlation between income and g, as measured by IQ scores, averages about .40 across studies. The correlation is higher at higher levels of education and it increases with age, stabilizing when people reach their highest career potential in middle age. Even when education, occupation and socioeconomic background are held constant, the correlation does not vanish.

Other Correlates

The g factor is reflected in many social outcomes. Many social behavior problems, such as dropping out of school, chronic welfare dependency, accident proneness, and crime, are negatively correlated with g independent of social class of origin. Health and mortality outcomes are also linked to g, with higher childhood test scores predicting better health and mortality outcomes in adulthood.

Genetic and Environmental Determinants

Heritability is the proportion of phenotypic variance in a trait in a population that can be attributed to genetic factors. The heritability of g has been estimated to fall between 40 and 80 percent using twin, adoption, and other family study designs as well as molecular genetic methods. It has been found to increase linearly with age. For example, a large study involving more than 11,000 pairs of twins from four countries reported the heritability of g to be 41 percent at age nine, 55 percent at age twelve, and 66 percent at age seventeen. Other studies have estimated that the heritability is as high as 80 percent in adulthood, although it may decline in old age. Most of the research on the heritability of g has been conducted in the United States and Western Europe, but studies in Russia (Moscow), the former East Germany, Japan, and rural India have yielded similar estimates of heritability as Western studies.

Behavioral genetic research has also established that the shared (or between-family) environmental effects on g are strong in childhood, but decline thereafter and are negligible in adulthood. This indicates that the environmental effects that are important to the development of g are unique and not shared between members of the same family.

The genetic correlation is a statistic that indicates the extent to which the same genetic effects influence two different traits. If the genetic correlation between two traits is zero, the genetic effects on them are independent, whereas a correlation of 1.0 means that the same set of genes explains the heritability of both traits (regardless of how high or low the heritability of each is). Genetic correlations between specific mental abilities (such as verbal ability and spatial ability) have been consistently found to be very high, close to 1.0. This indicates that genetic variation in cognitive abilities is almost entirely due to genetic variation in whatever g is. It also suggests that what is common among cognitive abilities is largely caused by genes, and that independence among abilities is largely due to environmental effects. Thus it has been argued that when genes for intelligence are identified, they will be "generalist genes", each affecting many different cognitive abilities.

The g loadings of mental tests have been found to correlate with their heritabilities, with correlations ranging from moderate to perfect in various studies. Thus the heritability of a mental test is usually higher the larger its g loading is.

Much research points to g being a highly polygenic trait influenced by a large number of common genetic variants, each having only small effects. Another possibility is that heritable differences in g are due to individuals having different "loads" of rare, deleterious mutations, with genetic variation among individuals persisting due to mutation–selection balance.

A number of candidate genes have been reported to be associated with intelligence differences, but the effect sizes have been small and almost none of the findings have been replicated. No individual genetic variants have been conclusively linked to intelligence in the normal range so far. Many researchers believe that very large samples will be needed to reliably detect individual genetic polymorphisms associated with g. However, while genes influencing variation in g in the normal range have proven difficult to find, a large number of single-gene disorders with mental retardation among their symptoms have been discovered.

Several studies suggest that tests with larger g loadings are more affected by inbreeding depression lowering test scores. There is also evidence that tests with larger *g* loadings are associated with larger positive heterotic effects on test scores. Inbreeding depression and heterosis suggest the presence of genetic dominance effects for *g*.

Neuroscientific Findings

g has a number of correlates in the brain. Studies using magnetic resonance imaging (MRI) have established that *g* and total brain volume are moderately correlated (r~.3–.4). External head size has a correlation of ~.2 with *g*. MRI research on brain regions indicates that the volumes of frontal, parietal and temporal cortices, and the hippocampus are also correlated with *g*, generally at .25 or more, while the correlations, averaged over many studies, with overall grey matter and overall white matter have been found to be .31 and .27, respectively. Some but not all studies have also found positive correlations between *g* and cortical thickness. However, the underlying reasons for these associations between the quantity of brain tissue and differences in cognitive abilities remain largely unknown.

Most researchers believe that intelligence cannot be localized to a single brain region, such as the frontal lobe. Brain lesion studies have found small but consistent associations indicating that people with more white matter lesions tend to have lower cognitive ability. Research utilizing NMR spectroscopy has discovered somewhat inconsistent but generally positive correlations between intelligence and white matter integrity, supporting the notion that white matter is important for intelligence.

Some research suggests that aside from the integrity of white matter, also its organizational efficiency is related to intelligence. The hypothesis that brain efficiency has a role in intelligence is supported by functional MRI research showing that more intelligent people generally process information more efficiently, i.e., they use fewer brain resources for the same task than less intelligent people.

Small but relatively consistent associations with intelligence test scores include also brain activity, as measured by EEG records or event-related potentials, and nerve conduction velocity.

g in Non-humans

Evidence of a general factor of intelligence has also been observed in non-human animals. Studies have shown that *g* is responsible for 47% of the individual variance in primates and between 55% and 60% in mice. While not able to be assessed using the same intelligence measures used in humans, cognitive ability can be measured with a variety of interactive and observational tools focusing on innovation, habit reversal, social learning, and responses to novelty.

Non-human models of *g* such as mice are used to study genetic influences on intelligence and neurological developmental research into the mechanisms behind and biological correlates of *g*.

g (or c) in Human Groups

Similar to *g* for individuals, a new research path aims to extract a general collective intelligence factor *c* for groups displaying a group's general ability to perform a wide range of tasks. Definition, operationalization and statistical approach for this *c* factor are derived from and similar to *g*. Causes, predictive validity as well as additional parallels to *g* are investigated.

Other Biological Associations

Height is correlated with intelligence (r~.2), but this correlation has not generally been found within families (i.e., among siblings), suggesting that it results from cross-assortative mating for height and intelligence. Myopia is known to be associated with intelligence, with a correlation of around .2 to .25, and this association has been found within families, too.

Group Similarities and Differences

Cross-cultural studies indicate that the *g* factor can be observed whenever a battery of diverse, complex cognitive tests is administered to a human sample. The factor structure of IQ tests has also been found to be consistent across sexes and ethnic groups in the U.S. and elsewhere. The *g* factor has been found to be the most invariant of all factors in cross-cultural comparisons. For example, when the *g* factors computed from an American standardization sample of Wechsler's IQ battery and from large samples who completed the Japanese translation of the same battery were compared, the congruence coefficient was .99, indicating virtual identity. Similarly, the congruence coefficient between the *g* factors obtained from white and black standardization samples of the WISC battery in the U.S. was .995, and the variance in test scores accounted for by *g* was highly similar for both groups.

Most studies suggest that there are negligible differences in the mean level of *g* between the sexes, and that sex differences in cognitive abilities are to be found in more narrow domains. For example, males generally outperform females in spatial tasks, while females generally outperform males in verbal tasks. Another difference that has been found in many studies is that males show more variability in both general and specific abilities than females, with proportionately more males at both the low end and the high end of the test score distribution.

Consistent differences between racial and ethnic groups in *g* have been found, particularly in the U.S. A 2001 meta-analysis of millions of subjects indicated that there is a 1.1 standard deviation gap in the mean level of *g* between white and black Americans, favoring the former. The mean score of Hispanic Americans was found to be .72 standard deviations below that of non-Hispanic whites. In contrast, Americans of East Asian descent generally slightly outscore white Americans. Several researchers have suggested that the magnitude of the black-white gap in cognitive ability tests is dependent on the magnitude of the test's *g* loading, with tests showing higher *g* loadings producing larger gaps. It has also been claimed that racial and ethnic differences similar to those found in the U.S. can be observed globally.

Relation to other Psychological Constructs

Elementary Cognitive Tasks

Elementary cognitive tasks (ECTs) also correlate strongly with *g*. ECTs are, as the name suggests, simple tasks that apparently require very little intelligence, but still correlate strongly with more exhaustive intelligence tests. Determining whether a light is red or blue and determining whether there are four or five squares drawn on a computer screen are two examples of ECTs. The answers to such questions are usually provided by quickly pressing buttons. Often, in addition to buttons for the two options provided, a third button is held down from the start of the test. When the stimulus is given to the subject, they remove their hand from the starting button to the button of the correct answer. This allows the examiner to determine how much time was spent thinking about the answer to the question (reaction time, usually measured in small fractions of second), and how much time was spent on physical hand movement to the correct button (movement time). Reaction time correlates strongly with *g*, while movement time correlates less strongly. ECT testing has allowed quantitative examination of hypotheses concerning test bias, subject motivation, and group differences. By virtue of their simplicity, ECTs provide a link between classical IQ testing and biological inquiries such as fMRI studies.

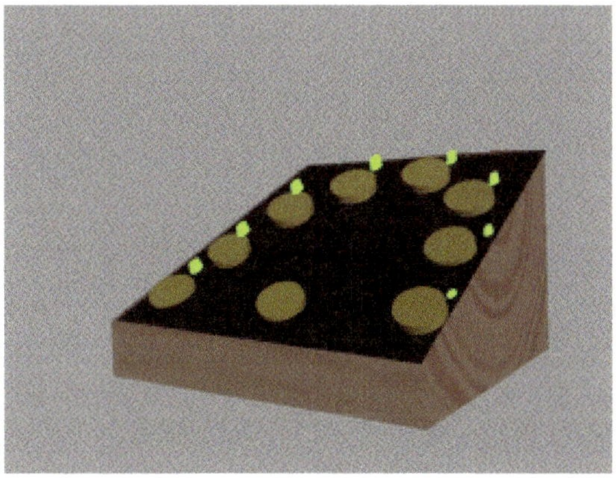

An illustration of the Jensen box, an apparatus for measuring choice reaction time.

Working Memory

One theory holds that *g* is identical or nearly identical to working memory capacity. Among other evidence for this view, some studies have found factors representing *g* and working memory to be perfectly correlated. However, in a meta-analysis the correlation was found to be considerably lower. One criticism that has been made of studies that identify *g* with working memory is that "we do not advance understanding by showing that one mysterious concept is linked to another."

Piagetian Tasks

Psychometric theories of intelligence aim at quantifying intellectual growth and identifying ability differences between individuals and groups. In contrast, Jean Piaget's theory of cognitive development seeks to understand qualitative changes in children's intellectual development. Piaget designed a number of tasks to verify hypotheses arising from his theory. The tasks were not intended to measure individual differences, and they have no equivalent in psychometric intelligence tests. For example, in one of the best-known Piagetian conservation tasks a child is asked if the amount of water in two identical glasses is the same. After the child agrees that the amount is the same, the investigator pours the water from one of the glasses into a glass of different shape so that the amount appears different although it remains the same. The child is then asked if the amount of water in the two glasses is the same or different.

Notwithstanding the different research traditions in which psychometric tests and Piagetian tasks were developed, the correlations between the two types of measures have been found to be consistently positive and generally moderate in magnitude. A common general factor underlies them. It has been shown that it is possible to construct a battery consisting of Piagetian tasks that is as good a measure of *g* as standard IQ tests.

Personality

The traditional view in psychology is that there is no meaningful relationship between personality and intelligence, and that the two should be studied separately. Intelligence can be understood in terms of what an individual *can* do, or what his or her *maximal* performance is, while personality can be thought of in terms of what an individual *will typically* do, or what his or her general tendencies of behavior are. Research has indicated that correlations between measures of intelligence and personality are small, and it has thus been argued that *g* is a purely cognitive variable that is independent of personality traits. In a 2007 meta-analysis the correlations between *g* and the "Big Five" personality traits were found to be as follows:

- conscientiousness -.04
- agreeableness .00
- extraversion .02
- openness .22
- emotional stability .09

The same meta-analysis found a correlation of .20 between self-efficacy and *g*.

Some researchers have argued that the associations between intelligence and personality, albeit modest, are consistent. They have interpreted correlations between intelligence and personality measures in two main ways. The first perspective is that personality traits influence performance on intelligence *tests*. For example, a person may fail to perform at a maximal level on an IQ test due to his or her anxiety and stress-proneness. The second perspective considers intelligence and personality to be *conceptually* related, with personality traits determining how people apply and invest their cognitive abilities, leading to knowledge expansion and greater cognitive differentiation.

Creativity

Some researchers believe that there is a threshold level of *g* below which socially significant creativity is rare, but that otherwise there is no relationship between the two. It has been suggested that this threshold is at least one standard deviation above the population mean. Above the threshold, personality differences are believed to be important determinants of individual variation in creativity.

Others have challenged the threshold theory. While not disputing that opportunity and personal attributes other than intelligence, such as energy and commitment, are important for creativity, they argue that *g* is positively associated with creativity even at the high end of the ability distribution. The longitudinal Study of Mathematically Precocious Youth has provided evidence for this contention. It has showed that individuals identified by standardized tests as intellectually gifted in early adolescence accomplish creative achievements (for example, securing patents or publishing literary or scientific works) at several times the rate of the general population, and that even within the top 1 percent of cognitive ability, those with higher ability are more likely to make outstanding achievements. The study has also suggested that the level of *g* acts as a predictor of the *level* of achievement, while specific cognitive ability patterns predict the *realm* of achievement.

Challenges

Gf-Gc Theory

Raymond Cattell, a student of Charles Spearman's, rejected the unitary *g* factor model and divided *g* into two broad, relatively independent domains: fluid intelligence (G*f*) and crystallized intelligence (Gc). G*f* is conceptualized as a capacity to figure out novel problems, and it is best assessed with tests with little cultural or scholastic content, such as Raven's matrices. Gc can be thought of as consolidated knowledge, reflecting the skills and information that an individual acquires and retains throughout his or her life. Gc is dependent on education and other forms of acculturation, and it is best assessed with tests that emphasize scholastic and cultural knowledge. G*f* can be thought to primarily consist of *current* reasoning and problem solving capabilities, while Gc reflects the outcome of *previously* executed cognitive processes.

The rationale for the separation of G*f* and Gc was to explain individuals' cognitive development over time. While G*f* and Gc have been found to be highly correlated, they differ in the way they change over a lifetime. G*f* tends to peak at around age 20, slowly declining thereafter. In contrast, Gc is stable or increases across adulthood. A single general factor has been criticized as obscuring this bifurcated pattern of development. Cattell argued that G*f* reflected individual differences in the efficiency of the central nervous system. Gc was, in Cattell's thinking, the result of a person "investing" his or her G*f* in learning experiences throughout life.

Cattell, together with John Horn, later expanded the G*f*-Gc model to include a number of other broad abilities, such as G*q* (quantitative reasoning) and G*v* (visual-spatial reasoning). While all the broad ability factors in the extended G*f*-Gc model are positively correlated and thus would enable the extraction of a higher order *g* factor, Cattell and Horn maintained that it would be erroneous to posit that a general factor underlies these broad abilities. They argued that *g* factors computed from different test batteries are not invariant and would give different values of *g*, and that the correlations among tests arise because it is difficult to test just one ability at a time.

However, several researchers have suggested that the G*f*-Gc model is compatible with a *g*-centered understanding of cognitive abilities. For example, John B. Carroll's three-stratum model of intelligence includes both G*f* and Gc together with a higher-order *g* factor. Based on factor analyses of many data sets, some researchers have also argued that G*f* and *g* are one and the same factor and that *g* factors from different test batteries are substantially invariant provided that the batteries are large and diverse.

Theories of Uncorrelated Abilities

Several theorists have proposed that there are intellectual abilities that are uncorrelated with each other. Among the earliest was L.L. Thurstone who created a model of *primary mental abilities* representing supposedly independent domains of intelligence. However, Thurstone's tests of these abilities were found to produce a strong general factor. He argued that the lack of independence among his tests reflected the difficulty of constructing "factorially pure" tests that measured just one ability. Similarly, J.P. Guilford proposed a model of intelligence that comprised up to 180 distinct, uncorrelated abilities, and claimed to be able to test all of them. Later analyses have shown that the factorial procedures Guilford presented as evidence for his theory did not provide support for it, and that the test data that he claimed provided evidence against *g* did in fact exhibit the usual pattern of intercorrelations after correction for statistical artifacts.

More recently, Howard Gardner has developed the theory of multiple intelligences. He posits the existence of nine different and independent domains of intelligence, such as mathematical, linguistic, spatial, musical, bodily-kinesthetic, meta-cognitive, and existential intelligences, and contends that individuals who fail in some of them may excel in others. According to Gardner, tests and schools traditionally emphasize only linguistic and logical abilities while neglecting other forms of intelligence. While popular among educationalists, Gardner's theory has been much criticized by psychologists and psychometricians. One criticism is that the theory does violence to both scientific and everyday usages of the word "intelligence." Several researchers have argued that not all of Gardner's intelligences fall within the cognitive sphere. For example, Gardner contends that a successful career in professional sports or popular music reflects bodily-kinesthetic *intelligence* and musical *intelligence*, respectively, even though one might usually talk of athletic and musical *skills*, *talents*, or *abilities* instead. Another criticism of Gardner's theory is that many of his purportedly independent domains of intelligence are in fact correlated with each other. Responding to empirical analyses showing correlations between the domains, Gardner has argued that the correlations exist because of the common format of tests and because all tests require linguistic and logical skills. His critics have in turn pointed out that not all IQ tests are administered in the paper-and-pencil format, that aside from linguistic and logical abilities, IQ test batteries contain also measures of, for example, spatial abilities, and that elementary cognitive tasks (for example, inspection time and reaction time) that do not involve linguistic or logical reasoning correlate with conventional IQ batteries, too.

Robert Sternberg, working with various colleagues, has also suggested that intelligence has dimensions independent of *g*. He argues that there are three classes of intelligence: analytic, practical, and creative. According to Sternberg, traditional psychometric tests measure only analytic intelligence, and should be augmented to test creative and practical intelligence as well. He has devised several tests to this effect. Sternberg equates analytic intelligence with academic intelligence, and contrasts it with practical intelligence, defined as an ability to deal with ill-defined real-life problems. Tacit intelligence is an important component of practical intelligence, consisting of knowledge that is not explicitly taught but is required in many real-life situations. Assessing creativity independent of intelligence tests has traditionally proved difficult, but Sternberg and colleagues have claimed to have created valid tests of creativity, too. The validation of Sternberg's theory requires that the three abilities tested are substantially uncorrelated and have independent predictive validity. Sternberg has conducted many experiments which he claims confirm the validity of his theory, but several researchers have disputed this conclusion. For example, in his reanalysis of a validation study of Sternberg's STAT test, Nathan Brody showed that the predictive validity of the STAT, a test of three allegedly independent abilities, was almost solely due to a single general factor underlying the tests, which Brody equated with the *g* factor.

Flynn's Model

James Flynn has argued that intelligence should be conceptualized at three different levels: brain physiology, cognitive differences between individuals, and social trends in intelligence over time. According to this model, the *g* factor is a useful concept with respect to individual differences but its explanatory power is limited when the focus of investigation is either brain physiology, or, especially, the effect of social trends on intelligence. Flynn has criticized the notion that cognitive gains over time, or the Flynn effect, are "hollow" if they cannot be shown to be increases in *g*. He argues that the Flynn effect reflects shifting social priorities and individuals' adaptation to them. To apply the individual differences concept of *g* to the Flynn effect is to confuse different levels of analysis. On the other hand, according to Flynn, it is also fallacious to deny, by referring to trends in intelligence over time, that some individuals have "better brains and minds" to cope with the cognitive demands of their particular time. At the level of brain physiology, Flynn has emphasized both that localized neural clusters can be affected differently by cognitive exercise, and that there are important factors that affect all neural clusters.

Other Criticisms

Perhaps the most famous critique of the construct of *g* is that of the paleontologist and biologist Stephen Jay Gould's, presented in his 1981 book *The Mismeasure of Man*. He argued that psychometricians have fallaciously reified the *g* factor as a physical thing in the brain, even though it is simply the product of statistical calculations (i.e., factor analysis). He further noted that it is possible to produce factor solutions of cognitive test data that do not contain a *g* factor yet explain the same amount of information as solutions that yield a *g*. According to Gould, there is no rationale for preferring one factor solution to another, and factor analysis therefore does not lend support to the existence of an entity like *g*. More generally, Gould criticized the *g* theory for abstracting intelligence as a single entity and for ranking people "in a single series of worthiness", arguing that such rankings are used to justify the oppression of disadvantaged groups.

Many researchers have criticized Gould's arguments. For example, they have rejected the accusation of reification, maintaining that the use of extracted factors such as *g* as potential causal variables whose reality can be supported or rejected by further investigations constitutes a normal scientific practice that in no way distinguishes psychometrics from other sciences. Critics have also suggested that Gould did not understand the purpose of factor analysis, and that he was ignorant of relevant methodological advances in the field. While different factor solutions may be mathematically equivalent in their ability to account for intercorrelations among tests, solutions that yield a *g* factor are psychologically preferable for several reasons extrinsic to factor analysis, including the phenomenon of the positive manifold, the fact that the same *g* can emerge from quite different test batteries, the widespread practical validity of *g*, and the linkage of *g* to many biological variables.

John Horn and John McArdle have argued that the modern *g* theory, as espoused by, for example, Arthur Jensen, is unfalsifiable, because the existence of a common factor like *g* follows tautologically from positive correlations among tests. They contrasted the modern hierarchical theory of *g* with Spearman's original two-factor theory which was readily falsifiable (and indeed was falsified).

Memory: Recapitulation

Till now our focus was on learning where the emphasis was on acquisition. We shall now have the recap of the deliberation on memory where the emphasis is on retention. Memory is studied in terms of mental processes involved in storage and retrieval of information. The three major types of memory are sensory, short-term, and long-term. The incoming sensory inputs can be stored for a very brief period of time ranging from 0.25-2 seconds. This is called sensory memory. Some of these items can further be retained for 20-30 seconds in our short-term storage. Some of them are stored for very long time, days, months, years, or even life time. This is diagrammatically represented below.

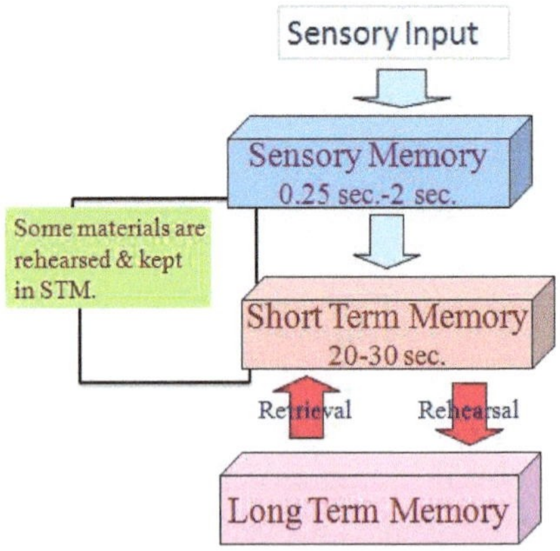

Further, there are various subtypes of these major types of memory.

The flow chart given below will help you recollect the subtypes of memory system.

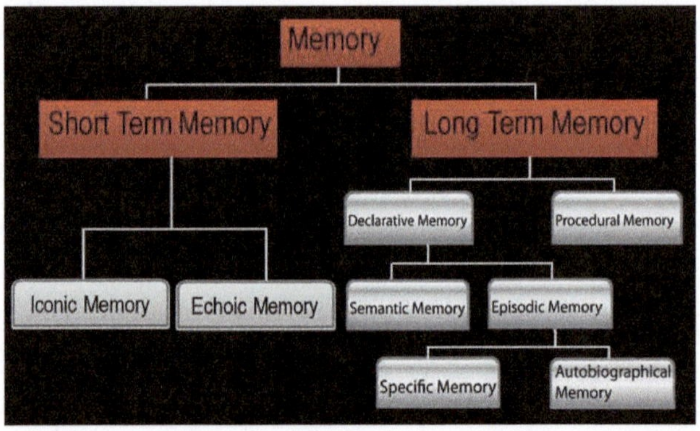

As such memory involves t hree distinct processes— encoding, storage and retrieval. Encoding is the p rocess of transformation of the physical stimulus into a form that human memory system accepts. Storage refers to retention of the encoded information, whereas recollecting information from storage is termed as retrieval.

Psychobiology of Memory

Our understanding of psychobiology of memory is largely dependent on the neuropsychological studies of humans and neurophysiological examinations of non-human primates. The knowledge about memory system has largely come from experimental studies, clinical cases, neuropsychological investigations, and brain imaging techniques. The findings indicate that human memory system is divisible. Different types of memory help us develop an exclusive sense of a personal history.

Other than the way memory has been classified above, people also classify long-term memory as explicit and implicit memories. Explicit memory has been further classified as semantic and episodic memory. Other forms of memory are typically implicit. Tulving (1984, 1985) has described memory as a hierarchically organized system with a set of correlated processes. The lower system supports the higher one. For example, implicit memory is at the lowest level in the hierarchy facilitating connections between stimuli and responses. Implicit memory does not depend upon conscious recollection of earlier experience whereas explicit memory involves conscious awareness. It is assumed that initially the semantic memory system develops making one understand the world and eventually it provides structure and meaning to the episodic memory system.

Episodic Memory

Episodic memory is the memory of autobiographical events (times, places, associated emotions, and other contextual who, what, when, where, why knowledge) that can be explicitly stated or conjured. It is the collection of past personal experiences that occurred at a particular time and place. For example, if one remembers the party on his or her 6th birthday, this is an episodic memory. They allow an individual to figuratively travel back in time to remember the event that took place at that particular time and place.

Semantic and episodic memory together make up the category of declarative memory, which is one of the two major divisions of memory – the other is implicit memory. The term "episodic memory" was coined by Endel Tulving in 1972. He was referring to the distinction between knowing and remembering. Knowing is more factual (semantic) whereas remembering is a feeling that is located in the past (episodic).

Tulving has seminally defined three key properties of episodic memory recollection. These are a subjective sense of time (or mental time travel), connection to the self, and autonoetic consciousness. Autonoetic consciousness refers to a special kind of consciousness that accompanies the act of remembering which enables an individual to be aware of the self in a subjective time. Aside from Tulving, others named the important aspects of recollection which includes visual imagery, narrative structure, retrieval of semantic information and the feelings of familiarity.

Events that are recorded into episodic memory may trigger episodic learning, i.e. a change in behavior that occurs as a result of an event. For example, a fear of dogs after being bitten by a dog is a result of episodic learning.

One of the main components of episodic memory is the process of recollection. Recollection is a process that elicits the retrieval of contextual information pertaining to a specific event or experience that has occurred.

Nine Properties

There are essentially nine properties of episodic memory that collectively distinguish it from other types of memory. Other types of memory may exhibit a few of these properties, but only episodic memory has all nine:

1. Contain summary records of sensory-perceptual-conceptual-affective processing.
2. Retain patterns of activation/inhibition over long periods.
3. Often represented in the form of (visual) images.

4. They always have a perspective (field or observer).
5. Represent short time slices of experience.
6. They are represented on a temporal dimension roughly in order of occurrence.
7. They are subject to rapid forgetting.
8. They make autobiographical remembering specific.
9. They are recollectively experienced when accessed.

Cognitive Neuroscience

The formation of new episodic memories requires the medial temporal lobe, a structure that includes the hippocampus. Without the medial temporal lobe, one is able to form new procedural memories (such as playing the piano) but cannot remember the events during which they happened.

The prefrontal cortex (and in particular the right hemisphere) is also involved in the formation of new episodic memories (also known as episodic encoding). Patients with damage to the prefrontal cortex can learn new information, but tend to do so in a disordered fashion. For example, they might show normal recognition of an object they had seen in the past, but fail to recollect when or where it had been viewed. Some researchers believe that the prefrontal cortex helps organize information for more efficient storage, drawing upon its role in executive function. Others believe that the prefrontal cortex underlies semantic strategies which enhance encoding, such as thinking about the meaning of the study material or rehearsing it in working memory.

Researchers do not agree about how long episodic memories are stored in the hippocampus. Some researchers believe that episodic memories always rely on the hippocampus. Others believe the hippocampus only stores episodic memories for a short time, after which the memories are consolidated to the neocortex. The latter view is strengthened by recent evidence that neurogenesis in the adult hippocampus may ease the removal of old memories and increase the efficiency of forming new memories.

Relationship to Semantic Memory

Endel Tulving originally described episodic memory as a record of a person's experience that held temporally dated information and spatio-temporal relations. A feature of episodic memory that Tulving later elaborates on is that it allows an agent to imagine traveling back in time. A current situation may cue retrieval of a previous episode, so that context that colours the previous episode is experienced at the immediate moment. The agent is provided with a means of associating previous feelings with current situations. Semantic memory, on the other hand, is a structured record of facts, concepts, and skills that we have acquired. Semantic information is derived from accumulated episodic memory. Episodic memory can be thought of as a "map" that ties together items in semantic memory. For example, all encounters with how a "dog" looks and sounds will make up the semantic representation of that word. All episodic memories concerning a dog will then reference this single semantic representation of "dog" and, likewise, all new experiences with the dog will modify the single semantic representation of that dog.

Together, semantic and episodic memory make up our declarative memory. They each represent different parts of context to form a complete picture. As such, something that affects episodic memory can also affect semantic memory. For example, anterograde amnesia, from damage of the medial temporal lobe, is an impairment of declarative memory that affects both episodic and semantic memory operations. Originally, Tulving proposed that episodic and semantic memory were separate systems that competed with each other in retrieval. However, this theory was rejected when Howard and Kahana completed experiments on latent semantic analysis (LSA) that supported the opposite. Instead of an increase in semantic similarity when there was a decrease in the strength of temporal associations, the two worked together so semantic cues on retrieval were strongest when episodic cues were strong as well.

Age Differences

Episodic memory emerges at approximately 3- to 4-years-of-age. Activation of specific brain areas (mostly the hippocampus) seems to be different between younger (aged 23–39) and older people (aged 67–80) upon episodic memory retrieval. Older people tend to activate both their left and right hippocampus, while younger people activate only the left one.

Relationship to Emotion

The relationship between emotion and memory is complex, but generally, emotion tends to increase the likelihood that an event will be remembered later and that it will be remembered vividly. Flashbulb memory is one example of this. An example of this would be an experience such as a close family member dying or the Christmas that you got the exact toy you wanted as a kid. The experience holds so much emotional significance that it is encoded as an extremely vivid, almost picture-perfect memory. However, whether the vividness of the flashbulb memory is due to a virtual "flash" that occurs because of the emotional experience has been hotly contested. Flashbulb memories may occur because of our propensity to rehearse and retell those highly emotional events, which strengthens the memory <McCloskey, Wibble & Cohen, 1988>.

Pharmacological Enhancement

In healthy adults, longterm visual episodic memory can be enhanced specifically through administration of the Acetylcholine esterase inhibitor Donepezil, whereas verbal episodic memory can be improved in persons with the val/val genotype of the val158met polymorphism through administration of the CNS penetrant specific catecholamine-O-methyltransferase inhibitor Tolcapone. Furthermore, episodic memory is enhanced through AZD3480, a selective agonist at the neuronal alpha4beta2 nicotinic receptor, which is developed by the company Targacept. Currently, there are several other products developed by several companies—including new catecholamine-O-methyltransferase inhibitors with fewer side effects—that aim for improving episodic memory. A recent placebo controlled study found that DHEA, which is a functional cortisol antagonist, improves episodic memory in healthy young men (Alhaj et al. 2006).

A 2015 meta-analysis of high quality evidence found that therapeutic doses of amphetamine and methylphenidate improve performance on working memory, episodic memory, and inhibitory control tests in normal healthy adults.

Damage

- Based on a review of behavioral studies, it is suggested that there may be selective damage to the limbic-prefrontal episodic memory system in some people with autism. Another study points to evidence of autistic deficits in the episodic or self-conscious memory of personally experienced events.
- The label "amnesia" is most often given to patients with deficits in episodic memory.
- Alzheimer's disease tends to damage the hippocampus before other brain areas.
- A rare type of shellfish poisoning called amnesic shellfish poisoning or "ASP" quite effectively and irreversibly damages the hippocampus, rendering one amnesic.
- Korsakoff's syndrome is caused by thiamine (vitamin B_1) deficiency, a form of malnutrition which can be precipitated by overconsumption of alcohol compared to foods.
- An acute cortisol level (by injection) has been found to significantly inhibit the recall of autobiographical memories which may contribute to memory deficits found in depression.
- The use of MDMA ("Ecstasy") has been associated with persistent deficits in episodic memory.

In Animals

Tulving (1983) proposed that to meet the criteria of episodic memory, evidence of conscious recollection must be provided. Demonstrating episodic memory in the absence of language, and thus in non-human animals, is impossible, because there are no agreed upon non-linguistic behavioral indicators of conscious experience (Griffiths et al., 1999).

This idea was first challenged by Clayton and Dickinson in their work with the western scrub jay (*Aphelocoma californica*). They were able to demonstrate that these birds may possess an episodic-like memory system as they found that they remember where they cached different food types, and discriminately recovered them depending on the perishability of the item and time that elapsed since caching. Thus, scrub-jays appear to remember the "what-where-and-when" of specific past caching events. The authors argued that such performance meets the behavioral criteria for episodic memory, but referred to the ability as "episodic-like" memory because the study did not address the phenomenological aspects of episodic memory.

After a study done by the University of Edinburgh (2006), hummingbirds were the first animal to demonstrate two of the aspects of episodic memory—the ability to recall where certain flowers were located and how recently they were visited. Other studies have demonstrated this type of memory in different animal species, such as dogs, rats, honey bees, and primates.

The ability of animals to encode and retrieve past experiences relies on the circuitry of the medial temporal lobe, a structure including the hippocampus. Animal lesion studies have provided significant findings related to the importance of particular brain structures in episodic-like memory. For example, hippocampal lesions have severely impacted all three components (what, where, and when) in animals, suggesting that the hippocampus is responsible for detecting novel events, stimuli, and places when forming new memories and on retrieving that information later on.

Despite similar neural areas and evidence from experiments, some scholars remain cautious about comparisons to human episodic memory (Suddendorf & Busby, 2003). Purported episodic-like memory often seems fixed to a particular domain or could be explained in terms of procedural or semantic memory. The problem may be better tractable by studying episodic memory's adaptive counterpart: the capacity to flexibly imagine future events. However, a recent experiment addressed one of Suddendorf and Busby (2003)'s specific criticisms (the Bischof-Köhler hypothesis, which states that nonhuman animals can only take actions based on immediate needs, as opposed to future needs). Correia and colleagues demonstrated that western scrub-jays can selectively cache different types of foods depending on which type of food they will desire at a future time, offering strong evidence against the Bischof-Köhler hypothesis by demonstrating that scrub-jays can flexibly adjust their behavior based on past experience of desiring a particular food. Similarities and differences between humans and other animals are currently much debated.

Autobiographical Memory

An autobiographical memory is a personal representation of general or specific events and personal facts. Autobiographical memory also refers to memory of a person's history. An individual does not remember exactly everything that has happened in one's past. Memory is constructive, where previous experience affects how we remember events and what we end up recalling from memory. Autobiographical memory is constructive and reconstructed as an evolving process of history. A person's autobiographical memory is fairly reliable; although, the reliability of autobiographical memories is questionable because of memory distortions.

Autobiographical memories can differ for special periods of life. People recall few personal events from the first years of their lives. The loss of these first events is called childhood or infantile amnesia. People tend to recall many personal events from adolescence and early adulthood. This effect is called the reminiscence bump. Additionally, people recall many personal events from their previous few years. For adolescents and young adults the reminiscence bump and the recent events can coincide.

It is known that autobiographical memories initially are stored as episodic memories, but it is currently unknown if autobiographical memories are the same as episodic memories or if the autobiographical memories become converted to semantic memories with time.

Types

- Specific events
    - When you first set foot in the ocean.
- General events
    - What it feels like stepping into the ocean in general. This is a memory of what a personal event is generally like. It might be based on the memories of having stepped

in the ocean, many times during the years.

- Personal facts
    - "Who was the Prime Minister of Italy when I was born?"
- Flashbulb memories
    - Flashbulb memories are critical autobiographical memories about a major event.

Neural Network Models

Episodic memories can be stored in autoassociative neural networks (e.g., a Hopfield network) if the stored representation includes information on the spatiotemporal context in which an item was studied.

Emotion and Memory

Memory of emotionally loaded information is mediated by amygdala. The memory of emotional items is better compared to neutral items. We have seen how reward facilitates human as well as animal learning. fMRI studies investigating brain mechanisms underlying reward induced episodic memory enhancement have shown better recall of pictures when monetary reward was anticipated (Adcock et al., 2006; Wittmann et al., 2005) with substantia nigra involved in reward anticipation and memory (Wittmann et al., 2005) and ventral tegmental area and nucleus accumbens related to memory facilitation by reward anticipation (Adcock et al., 2006). Memory and emotion are also interrelated. In an interesting study Tsukiura and Cabeza (2008) found that face-name associations were stronger for smiling face as compared to neutral expression.

Emotion: Recapitulation

Eysenck has defined emotion as "a complex state involving heightened perception of an object or situation, wide-spread bodily changes, an appraisal of felt attraction or repulsion, and behavior organized toward approach or withdrawal." It is a multifaceted process involving physiological, behavioural and expressive reactions as well as subjective experiences. Variation in the respiration rate is an example of physiological reactions. Behavioural reaction includes approach-avoidance reactions whereas smiling, frowning and so forth are our expressive reactions. Emotion always has subjective experience.

Emotional processes involve activation of both, the central and peripheral nervous systems. The emotional state gets depicted through face, body and voice and it further triggers certain psychological processes. As human beings we interact with the environment and mostly come forward with appropriate emotional response. An emotional state can be elicited by neuro-chemical, sensorimotor, motivational or cognitive factors.

Psychobiology of Emotion

Right in the beginning of this unit we extensively discussed the concept of conditioning. The procedures of classical and instrumental conditioning create multiple representations of the value of the stimuli in the brain. Motivational and emotional states are determined by the assessment of this value. Nucleus accumbens mediates the motivational effect of emotionally significant stimuli. Amygdala plays significant role in human emotional responses. Conditioning studies of emotional responses have examined freezing and fear-potentiated startle in rats. Freezing is considered a species-specific response to threat that makes the animal motionless. In fear-potentiated startle the presence of threat stimuli increases startle reflex. Central nucleus and basolateral amygdala (BLA) are the two functional units of amygdala that regulates emotional processes. BLA has reciprocal projections with polysensory neocortex and frontal lobe. It projects to the ventral striatum and the central nucleus. BLA is supposed to store the association that allows CS to retrieve the affective or motivational value of the US. This, in turn, controls central nucleus, hypothalamus, midbrain and brainstem to induce affective response. Freezing and fear-potentiated startle are examples of such affective response.

Brain damage and lesion studies also confirm these findings. A lesion of central nucleus impairs freezing conditioning. Damage to amygdala in human beings increases the threshold of perception and expression of emotion. Lesions in amygdala adversely affect emotional learning and memory of emotional events. Human beings with damaged orbito-frontal cortex damage resemble those with amygdala-lesion. They have impairment of reactions to emotional stimuli and decision making.

Another set of studies of emotional states primarily banks on the changes in the autonomic nervous system (ANS) functions. A large number of studies have measured ANS functions such as heart rate, pulse rate, blood pressure, and galvanic skin conductance to infer emotional state of an individual. Such studies are based on the premise that different emotions elicit distinctive patterns of physiological response. In an interesting study Hubert and Jong-Meyer (1991) screened cartoon film and recorded changes in the ANS functions. Cartoons inducing pleasant and amused state elicited very few changes in bodily sensations, temporary decrease in heart rate, and a rapid decrease in skin conductance. On the other hand, suspense film elicited marked changes in bodily sensations, increase in skin conductance and a temporary decrease in heart rate. Changes in heart rate are influenced by the sympathetic as well as the parasympathetic systems. Hence, psychological states determine the heart rate, which is otherwise a physiological process. On the other hand, skin conductance is entirely influenced by the sympathetic system. It reflects primary arousal in human beings.

Another set of studies of emotional states primarily banks on the changes in the autonomic nervous system (ANS) functions. A large number of studies have measured ANS functions such as heart rate, pulse rate, blood pressure, and galvanic skin conductance to infer emotional state of an individual. Such studies are based on the premise that different emotions elicit distinctive patterns of physiological response. In an interesting study Hubert and Jong-Meyer (1991) screened cartoon film and recorded changes in the ANS functions. Cartoons inducing pleasant and amused state elicited very few changes in bodily sensations, temporary decrease in heart rate, and a rapid decrease in skin conductance. On the other hand, suspense film elicited marked changes in bodily sensations, increase in skin conductance and a temporary decrease in heart rate. Changes in heart rate are influenced by the sympathetic as well as the parasympathetic systems. Hence, psychological states determine the heart rate, which is otherwise a physiological process. On the other hand, skin conductance is entirely influenced by the sympathetic system. It reflects primary arousal in human beings.

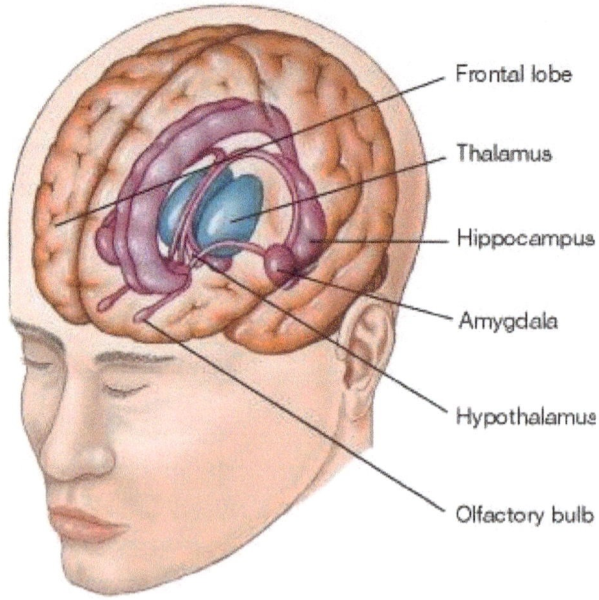

The illustration given above shows the brain structures responsible for emotions.

Another set of studies of emotional states primarily banks on the changes in the autonomic nervous system (ANS) functions. A large number of studies have measured ANS functions such as heart rate, pulse rate, blood pressure, and galvanic skin conductance to infer emotional state of an individual. Such studies are based on the premise that different emotions elicit distinctive patterns of physiological response. In an interesting study Hubert and Jong-Meyer (1991) screened cartoon film and recorded changes in the ANS functions. Cartoons inducing pleasant and amused state elicited very few changes in bodily sensations, temporary decrease in heart rate, and a rapid decrease in skin conductance. On the other hand, suspense film elicited marked changes in bodily sensations, increase in skin conductance and a temporary decrease in heart rate. Changes in heart rate are influenced by the sympathetic as well as the parasympathetic systems. Hence, psychological states determine the heart rate, which is otherwise a physiological process. On the other hand, skin conductance is entirely influenced by the sympathetic system. It reflects primary arousal in human beings.

Our emotional experiences as well as expressions are heavily influenced by bodily chemicals. For example, hormones secreted by various endocrine glands mixes-up with blood and travel to distant locations within the body. Although this is a relatively slow process to immediately affect the emotional state, it does play crucial role when one has to respond in similar situation in the future. Certain hormones, such as norepinephrine, epinephrine, cortisol, and thyroid hormones, increase during stress, whereas others, such as insulin and testosterone, decreases. We have different types of neurotransmitters that are instrumental in communicating signals across synaptic junctions. They act as chemical messengers. Catecholamines (such as epinephrine, norepinephrine, and dopamine) are involved in extreme emotional reactions. They have been considered potential factors for psychiatric symptoms such as schizophrenia and depression. Similarly, corticosteroids, endogenous opioid peptides and neuromodulators such as prostaglandins are associated with shyness, distress, aggression and fear. The other group of chemicals is the enzymes that are instrumental in m etabolism of endogenous chemicals or exogenous materials, thus indirectly altering mood states.

Emotional experiences also affect changes in the endocrine secretions. Contrarily, such secretions are relatively slow processes and might not directly influence emotional experiences. However, they are likely to predispose an individual to respond in a specific pattern in similar emotion eliciting situations in the future. For instance, elevation of cortisol is associated with anxiety, bereavement and sadness, whereas decrease in cortisol is associated with relaxation and meditation. The table given below highlights the emotional states such as lust, care and distress and the chemical bases of such states.

Endocrine secretions	Emotional states
Vasopressinergic and oxytocinergic system	Lust
Peripheral estrogen, progesterone, prolactin, and brain oxytocin [through subneocortical system]	Motherly care
Corticotrophin Releasing Factor, brain opioids, oxytocin, and prolactin	Panic/ distress

Personality Psychology

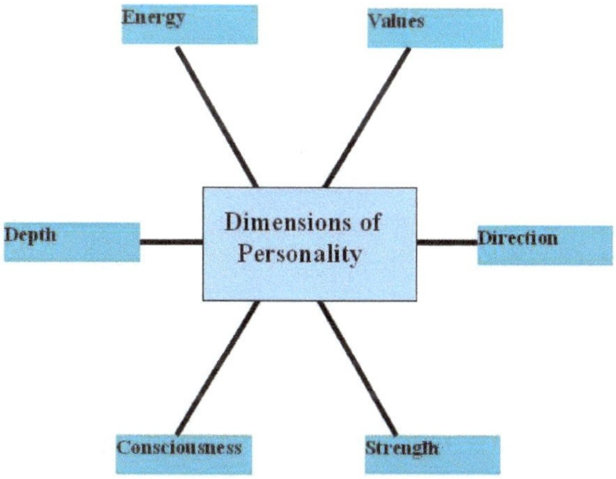

A picture of the depictions of personality dimensions.

Personality psychology is a branch of psychology that studies personality and its variation among individuals. Its areas of focus include:

- construction of a coherent picture of the individual and their major psychological processes
- investigation of individual psychological differences
- investigation of human nature and psychological similarities between individuals

"Personality" is a dynamic[clarification needed] and organized set of characteristics possessed by a person that uniquely[clarification needed] influences their environment, cognitions, emotions, motivations, and behaviors in various situations. The word "personality" originates from the Latin persona, which means mask.

Personality also refers to the pattern of thoughts, feelings, social adjustments, and behaviors consistently exhibited over time that strongly influences one's expectations, self-perceptions, values, and attitudes. It also predicts human reactions to other people, problems, and stress. There is still no universal consensus on the definition of "personality" in psychology. Gordon Allport (1937) described two major ways to study personality: the nomothetic and the idiographic. Nomothetic psychology seeks general laws that can be applied to many different people, such as the principle of self-actualization or the trait of extraversion. Idiographic psychology is an attempt to understand the unique aspects of a particular individual.

The study of personality has a broad and varied history in psychology with an abundance of theoretical traditions. The major theories include dispositional (trait) perspective, psychodynamic, humanistic, biological, behaviorist, evolutionary, and social learning perspective. However, many researchers and psychologists do not explicitly identify themselves with a certain perspective and instead take an eclectic approach. Research in this area is empirically driven, such as dimensional models, based on multivariate statistics, such as factor analysis, or emphasizes theory development, such as that of the psychodynamic theory. There is also a substantial emphasis on the applied field of personality testing. In psychological education and training, the study of the nature of personality and its psychological development is usually reviewed as a prerequisite to courses in abnormal psychology or clinical psychology.

Philosophical Assumptions

Many of the ideas developed by historical and modern personality theorists stem from the basic philosophical assumptions they hold. The study of personality is not a purely empirical discipline, as it brings in elements of art, science, and philosophy to draw general conclusions. The following five categories are some of the most fundamental philosophical assumptions on which theorists disagree:

- Freedom versus determinism – This is the question whether humans have control over their own behavior and understand the motives behind it or if their behavior is causally determined by forces beyond their control. Behavior is categorized as being either unconscious, environmental, or biological by various theories.
- Heredity versus environment – Personality is thought to be determined largely either by genetics and biology, or by environment and experiences. Contemporary research suggests that most personality traits are based on the joint influence of genetics and environment. One of the forerunners in this arena is C. Robert Cloninger, who pioneered the Temperament and Character model.
- Uniqueness versus universality – This question discusses the extent of each human's individuality (uniqueness) or similarity in nature (universality). Gordon Allport, Abraham Maslow, and Carl Rogers were all advocates of the uniqueness of individuals. Behaviorists and cognitive theorists, in contrast, emphasize the importance of universal principles, such as reinforcement and self-efficacy.
- Active versus reactive – This question explores whether humans primarily act through individual initiative (active) or through outside stimuli. Traditional behavioral theorists

typically believed that humans are passively shaped by their environments, whereas humanistic and cognitive theorists believe that humans are more active in their role. Most modern theorists agree that both are important, with aggregate behavior being primarily determined by traits and situational factors being the primary predictor of behavior in the short term.

- Optimistic versus pessimistic – Personality theories differ with regard to whether humans are integral in the changing of their own personalities. Theories that place a great deal of emphasis on learning are often more optimistic than those that do not.

Personality Theories

The study of personality is based on the essential insight that all people are similar in some ways, yet different in others. There have been many different definitions of personality proposed. However, many contemporary psychologists agree on the following defias differentiating the HEXACO model from other personality frameworks. Specifically, the H factor is described as sincere, honest, faithful/loyal, modest/unassuming, fair-minded, *VERSUS* sly, deceitful, greedy, pretentious, hypocritical, boastful, and pompous. The H factor has been linked to criminal, materialistic, power-seeking, and unethical tendencies.

Trait models have been criticized as being purely descriptive and offering little explanation of the underlying causes of personality. Eysenck's theory, however, proposes biological mechanisms as driving traits, and modern behavior genetics researchers have shown a clear genetic substrate to them. Another potential weakness of trait theories is that they may lead some people to accept oversimplified classifications—or worse, offer advice—based on a superficial analysis of personality. Finally, trait models often underestimate the effect of specific situations on people's behavior.

Traits are considered to be statistical generalizations that do not always correspond to an individual's behavior.

The importance that genetic influences have on personality characteristics can change across a five-year period. Age differences create more variables even within a family, so the best comparisons are found using twins. Twins typically share a family environment called a shared environment because they may share other aspects like teachers, school, and friends. A non-shared environment means completely different environment for both subjects. "Biologically related children who are separated after birth and raised in different families live in non-shared environments." Identical twins separated at birth and raised in different families constitute the best cases for heredity and personality because similarities between the two are due only to genetic influences. Vulnerability was a factor in this study that was taken into consideration regarding the issue of genetic influences on vulnerability. The study concluded that the monozygotic co-twins would be more similar than dizygotic co-twins in change over time. The data concluded that there were no significant differences for either variances between the monozygotic and dizygotic co-twins.

Another current open question is whether genetic influences are important for the likeliness of co-twins to change in the same way over a period of time. A link was found between the personality trait of neuroticism and a polymorphism called 5-HTTLPR in the serotonin transporter gene, but this association was not replicated in larger studies. Other candidate gene studies have provided weak evidence that some personality traits are related to *AVPR1A* ("ruthlessness gene") and *MAOA* ("Warrior gene"). Genotypes, or the genetic make up of an organism, influence but don't fully decide the physical traits of a person. Those are also influenced by the environment and behaviors they are surrounded by. For example, a person's height is affected by genetics, but if they are malnourished growth will be stunted no matter what their genetic coding says. Environment is also not completely responsible for an outcome in personality. An example from *Psychobiology of Personality* by Marvin Zuckerman is alcoholism: Studies suggest that alcoholism is an inherited disease, but if a subject with a strong biological background of alcoholism in their family tree is never exposed to alcohol, they will not be so inclined regardless of their genome.

It is also a question open to debate whether there are genetic influences on the tendency of the *co-twins to change, without keeping in mind the direction of the change. Another factor that can be addressed is biological versus adoptive relatives and can be clearly seen in what is a real-life experiment: adoption. This creates two groups: genetic relatives (biological parents and siblings) and environmental relatives (adoptive parents and siblings). After studying hundreds of adoptive families, researchers discovered that people who grow up together, whether biologically related or not, do not much resemble one another in personality. In characteristics such as extroversion and agreeableness, adoptees are more like their biological parents than their adoptive parents. However, the minute shared-environment effects do not mean that adoptive parenting is ineffective. Even though genetics may limit the family environment's influence on personality, parents do influence their children's attitudes, values, faith, manners, and politics. In adoptive homes, child neglect and abuse and even divorce between the parents is uncommon. This noted it is not surprising, despite a somewhat greater risk of psychological disorder, that most adopted children excel, especially when they are adopted as infants. In fact, seven out of eight have reported feeling a strong connection with one or even both of their adoptive parents.*

Type Theories

Personality type refers to the psychological classification of different types of people. Personality types are distinguished from personality traits, which come in different degrees. There are many types of theories regarding personality, but each theory contains several and sometimes many sub theories. A "theory of personality" constructed by any given psychologist will contain multiple relating theories or sub theories often expanding as more psychologist explore the theory. For example, according to type theories, there are two types of people, introverts and extroverts. According to trait theories, introversion and extroversion are part of a continuous dimension with many people in the middle. The idea of psychological types originated in the theoretical work of Carl Jung, specifically in his 1921 book *Psychologische Typen* (*Psychological Types*) and William Marston.

Building on the writings and observations of Jung during World War II, Isabel Briggs Myers and her mother, Katharine C. Briggs, delineated personality types by constructing the Myers–Briggs Type Indicator. This model was later used by David Keirsey with a different understanding from Jung, Briggs and Myers. In the former Soviet Union, Lithuanian Aušra Augustinavičiūtė independently derived a model of personality type from Jung's called socionics.

Theories could also be considered an "approach" to personality or psychology and is generally referred to as a model. The model is an older and more theoretical approach to personality, accepting extroversion and introversion as basic psychological orientations in connection with two pairs of psychological functions:

- *Perceiving functions:* sensing and intuition (trust in concrete, sensory-oriented facts vs. trust in abstract concepts and imagined possibilities)
- *Judging functions:* thinking and feeling (basing decisions primarily on logic vs. considering the effect on people).

Briggs and Myers also added another personality dimension to their type indicator to measure whether a person prefers to use a judging or perceiving function when interacting with the external world. Therefore, they included questions designed to indicate whether someone wishes to come to conclusions (judgment) or to keep options open (perception).

This personality typology has some aspects of a trait theory: it explains people's behavior in terms of opposite fixed characteristics. In these more traditional models, the sensing/intuition preference is considered the most basic, dividing people into "N" (intuitive) or "S" (sensing) personality types. An "N" is further assumed to be guided either by thinking or feeling and divided into the "NT" (scientist, engineer) or "NF" (author, humanitarian) temperament. An "S", in contrast, is assumed to be guided more by the judgment/perception axis and thus divided into the "SJ" (guardian, traditionalist) or "SP" (performer, artisan) temperament. These four are considered basic, with the other two factors in each case (including always extraversion/introversion) less important. Critics of this traditional view have observed that the types can be quite strongly stereotyped by professions (although neither Myers nor Keirsey engaged in such stereotyping in their type descriptions), and thus may arise more from the need to categorize people for purposes of guiding their career choice. This among other objections led to the emergence of the five-factor view, which is less concerned with behavior under work conditions and more concerned with behavior in personal and emotional circumstances. (It should be noted, however, that the MBTI is not designed to measure the "work self", but rather what Myers and McCaulley called the "shoes-off self.") Some critics have argued for more or fewer dimensions while others have proposed entirely different theories (often assuming different definitions of "personality"). Another criticism is that the MBTI dichotomizes continuous dimensions without a clear empirical justification for doing so.

Type A and Type B personality theory: During the 1950s, Meyer Friedman and his co-workers defined what they called Type A and Type B behavior patterns. They theorized that intense, hard-driving Type A personalities had a higher risk of coronary disease because they are "stress junkies." Type B people, on the other hand, tended to be relaxed, less competitive, and lower in risk. There was also a Type AB mixed profile.

John L. Holland's *RIASEC* vocational model, commonly referred to as the *Holland Codes*, stipulates that six personality types lead people to choose their career paths. In this circumplex model, the six types are represented as a hexagon, with adjacent types more closely related than those more distant. The model is widely used in vocational counseling.

Eduard Spranger's personality-model, consisting of six (or, by some revisions, 6 +1) basic types of *value attitudes*, described in his book *Types of Men* (*Lebensformen*; Halle (Saale): Niemeyer,

1914; English translation by P. J. W. Pigors - New York: G. E. Stechert Company, 1928).

The Enneagram of Personality, a model of human personality which is principally used as a typology of nine interconnected personality types. It has been criticized as being subject to interpretation, making it difficult to test or validate scientifically.

Perhaps the most ancient attempt at personality psychology is the personality typology outlined by the Indian Buddhist Abhidharma schools. This typology mostly focuses on negative personal traits (greed, hatred, and delusion) and the corresponding positive meditation practices used to counter those traits.

Psychoanalytic Theories

Psychoanalytic theories explain human behavior in terms of the interaction of various components of personality. Sigmund Freud was the founder of this school of thought. Freud drew on the physics of his day (thermodynamics) to coin the term psychodynamics. Based on the idea of converting heat into mechanical energy, he proposed psychic energy could be converted into behavior. Freud's theory places central importance on dynamic, unconscious psychological conflicts.

Freud divides human personality into three significant components: the id, ego and super-ego. The id acts according to the pleasure principle, demanding immediate gratification of its needs regardless of external environment; the ego then must emerge in order to realistically meet the wishes and demands of the id in accordance with the outside world, adhering to the reality principle. Finally, the superego (conscience) inculcates moral judgment and societal rules upon the ego, thus forcing the demands of the id to be met not only realistically but morally. The superego is the last function of the personality to develop, and is the embodiment of parental/social ideals established during childhood. According to Freud, personality is based on the dynamic interactions of these three components.

The channeling and release of sexual (libidal) and aggressive energies, which ensues from the "Eros" (sex; instinctual self-preservation) and "Thanatos" (death; instinctual self-annihilation) drives respectively, are major components of his theory. It is important to note that Freud's broad understanding of sexuality included all kinds of pleasurable feelings experienced by the human body.

Freud proposed five psychosexual stages of personality development. He believed adult personality is dependent upon early childhood experiences and largely determined by age five. Fixations that develop during the infantile stage contribute to adult personality and behavior.

One of Sigmund Freud's earlier associates, Alfred Adler, did agree with Freud that early childhood experiences are important to development and believed birth order may influence personality development. Adler believed that the oldest child was the individual who would set high achievement goals in order to gain attention lost when the younger siblings were born. He believed the middle children were competitive and ambitious. He reasoned that this behavior was motivated by the idea of surpassing the firstborn's achievements. He added, however, that the middle children were often not as concerned about the glory attributed with their behavior. He also believed the youngest would be more dependent and sociable. Adler finished by surmising that an only child loves being the center of attention and matures quickly but in the end fails to become independent.

Heinz Kohut thought similarly to Freud's idea of transference. He used narcissism as a model of how people develop their sense of self. Narcissism is the exaggerated sense of one self in which one is believed to exist in order to protect one's low self-esteem and sense of worthlessness. Kohut had a significant impact on the field by extending Freud's theory of narcissism and introducing what he called the 'self-object transferences' of mirroring and idealization. In other words, children need to idealize and emotionally "sink into" and identify with the idealized competence of admired figures such as parents or older siblings. They also need to have their self-worth mirrored by these people. These experiences allow them to thereby learn the self-soothing and other skills that are necessary for the development of a healthy sense of self.

Another important figure in the world of personality theory is Karen Horney. She is credited with the development of the "real self" and the "ideal self". She believes all people have these two views of their own self. The "real self" is how humans act with regard to personality, values, and morals; but the "ideal self" is a construct individuals implement in order to conform to social and personal norms.

Behaviorist Theories

Behaviorists explain personality in terms of the effects external stimuli have on behavior. The approaches used to analyze the behavioral aspect of personality are known as behavioral theories or learning-conditioning theories. These approaches were a radical shift away from Freudian philosophy. One of the major tenets of this concentration of personality psychology is a strong emphasis on scientific thinking and experimentation. This school of thought was developed by B. F. Skinner who put forth a model which emphasized the mutual interaction of the person or "the organism" with its environment. Skinner believed children do bad things because the behavior obtains attention that serves as a reinforcer. For example: a child cries because the child's crying in the past has led to attention. These are the *response*, and *consequences*. The response is the child crying, and the attention that child gets is the reinforcing consequence. According to this theory, people's behavior is formed by processes such as operant conditioning. Skinner put forward a "three term contingency model" which helped promote analysis of behavior based on the "Stimulus - Response - Consequence Model" in which the critical question is: "Under which circumstances or antecedent 'stimuli' does the organism engage in a particular behavior or 'response', which in turn produces a particular 'consequence'?"

Richard Herrnstein extended this theory by accounting for attitudes and traits. An attitude develops as the response strength (the tendency to respond) in the presences of a group of stimuli become stable. Rather than describing conditionable traits in non-behavioral language, response strength in a given situation accounts for the environmental portion. Herrstein also saw traits as having a large genetic or biological component, as do most modern behaviorists.

Ivan Pavlov is another notable influence. He is well known for his classical conditioning experiments involving dogs, which led him to discover the foundation of behaviorism.

Social Cognitive Theories

In cognitive theory, behavior is explained as guided by cognitions (e.g. expectations) about the world, especially those about other people. Cognitive theories are theories of personality that emphasize cognitive processes, such as thinking and judging.

Albert Bandura, a social learning theorist suggested the forces of memory and emotions worked in conjunction with environmental influences. Bandura was known mostly for his "Bobo doll experiment". During these experiments, Bandura video taped a college student kicking and verbally abusing a bobo doll. He then showed this video to a class of kindergarten children who were getting ready to go out to play. When they entered the play room, they saw bobo dolls, and some hammers. The people observing these children at play saw a group of children beating the doll. He called this study and his findings observational learning, or modeling.

Early examples of approaches to cognitive style are listed by Baron (1982). These include Witkin's (1965) work on field dependency, Gardner's (1953) discovering people had consistent preference for the number of categories they used to categorise heterogeneous objects, and Block and Petersen's (1955) work on confidence in line discrimination judgments. Baron relates early development of cognitive approaches of personality to ego psychology. More central to this field have been:

- Attributional style theory dealing with different ways in which people explain events in their lives. This approach builds upon locus of control, but extends it by stating we also need to consider whether people attribute to stable causes or variable causes, and to global causes or specific causes.

Various scales have been developed to assess both attributional style and locus of control. Locus of control scales include those used by Rotter and later by Duttweiler, the Nowicki and Strickland (1973) Locus of Control Scale for Children and various locus of control scales specifically in the health domain, most famously that of Kenneth Wallston and his colleagues, The Multidimensional Health Locus of Control Scale. Attributional style has been assessed by the Attributional Style Questionnaire, the Expanded Attributional Style Questionnaire, the Attributions Questionnaire, the Real Events Attributional Style Questionnaire and the Attributional Style Assessment Test.

- Achievement style theory focuses upon identification of an individual's Locus of Control tendency, such as by Rotter's evaluations, and was found by Cassandra Bolyard Whyte to provide valuable information for improving academic performance of students. Individuals with internal control tendencies are likely to persist to better academic performance levels, presenting an achievement personality, according to Cassandra B. Whyte.

Recognition that the tendency to believe that hard work and persistence often results in attainment of life and academic goals has influenced formal educational and counseling efforts with students of various ages and in various settings since the 1970s research about achievement. Counseling aimed toward encouraging individuals to design ambitious goals and work toward them, with recognition that there are external factors that may impact, often results in the incorporation of a more positive achievement style by students and employees, whatever the setting, to include higher education, workplace, or justice programming.

Walter Mischel (1999) has also defended a cognitive approach to personality. His work refers to "Cognitive Affective Units", and considers factors such as encoding of stimuli, affect, goal-setting, and self-regulatory beliefs. The term "Cognitive Affective Units" shows how his approach considers affect as well as cognition.

Cognitive-Experiential Self-Theory (CEST) is another cognitive personality theory. Developed by Seymour Epstein, CEST argues that humans operate by way of two independent information processing systems: experiential system and rational system. The experiential system is fast and emotion-driven. The rational system is slow and logic-driven. These two systems interact to determine our goals, thoughts, and behavior.

Personal construct psychology (PCP) is a theory of personality developed by the American psychologist George Kelly in the 1950s. Kelly's fundamental view of personality was that people are like naive scientists who see the world through a particular lens, based on their uniquely organized systems of construction, which they use to anticipate events. But because people are naive scientists, they sometimes employ systems for construing the world that are distorted by idiosyncratic experiences not applicable to their current social situation. A system of construction that chronically fails to characterize and/or predict events, and is not appropriately revised to comprehend and predict one's changing social world, is considered to underlie psychopathology (or mental illness.) From the theory, Kelly derived a psychotherapy approach and also a technique called *The Repertory Grid Interview* that helped his patients to uncover their own "constructs" with minimal intervention or interpretation by the therapist. The repertory grid was later adapted for various uses within organizations, including decision-making and interpretation of other people's world-views.

Humanistic Theories

Humanistic psychology emphasizes that people have free will and that this plays an active role in determining how they behave. Accordingly, humanistic psychology focuses on subjective experiences of persons as opposed to forced, definitive factors that determine behavior. Abraham Maslow and Carl Rogers were proponents of this view, which is based on the "phenomenal field" theory of Combs and Snygg (1949). Rogers and Maslow were among a group of psychologists that worked together for a decade to produce the *Journal of Humanistic Psychology*. This article was primarily focused on viewing individuals as a whole, rather than focusing solely on separate traits and processes within the individual.

Robert W. White wrote the book *The Abnormal Personality* that became a standard text on abnormal psychology. He also investigated the human need to strive for positive goals like competence and influence, to counterbalance the emphasis of Freud on the pathological elements of personality development.

Maslow spent much of his time studying what he called "self-actualizing persons", those who are "fulfilling themselves and doing the best they are capable of doing". Maslow believes all who are interested in growth move towards self-actualizing (growth, happiness, satisfaction) views. Many of these people demonstrate a trend in dimensions of their personalities. Characteristics of self-actualizers according to Maslow include the four key dimensions:

1. Awareness – maintaining constant enjoyment and awe of life. These individuals often experienced a "peak experience". He defined a peak experience as an "intensification of any experience to the degree there is a loss or transcendence of self". A peak experience is one in which an individual perceives an expansion of themselves, and detects a unity and meaningfulness in life. Intense concentration on an activity one is involved in, such as running a marathon, may invoke a peak experience.

2. Reality and problem centered – having a tendency to be concerned with "problems" in surroundings.

3. Acceptance/Spontaneity – accepting surroundings and what cannot be changed.

4. Unhostile sense of humor/democratic – do not take kindly to joking about others, which can be viewed as offensive. They have friends of all backgrounds and religions and hold very close friendships.

Maslow and Rogers emphasized a view of the person as an active, creative, experiencing human being who lives in the present and subjectively responds to current perceptions, relationships, and encounters. They disagree with the dark, pessimistic outlook of those in the Freudian psychoanalysis ranks, but rather view humanistic theories as positive and optimistic proposals which stress the tendency of the human personality toward growth and self-actualization. This progressing self will remain the center of its constantly changing world; a world that will help mold the self but not necessarily confine it. Rather, the self has opportunity for maturation based on its encounters with this world. This understanding attempts to reduce the acceptance of hopeless redundancy. Humanistic therapy typically relies on the client for information of the past and its effect on the present, therefore the client dictates the type of guidance the therapist may initiate. This allows for an individualized approach to therapy. Rogers found patients differ in how they respond to other people. Rogers tried to model a particular approach to therapy- he stressed the reflective or empathetic response. This response type takes the client's viewpoint and reflects back their feeling and the context for it. An example of a reflective response would be, "It seems you are feeling anxious about your upcoming marriage". This response type seeks to clarify the therapist's understanding while also encouraging the client to think more deeply and seek to fully understand the feelings they have expressed.

Biopsychological Theories

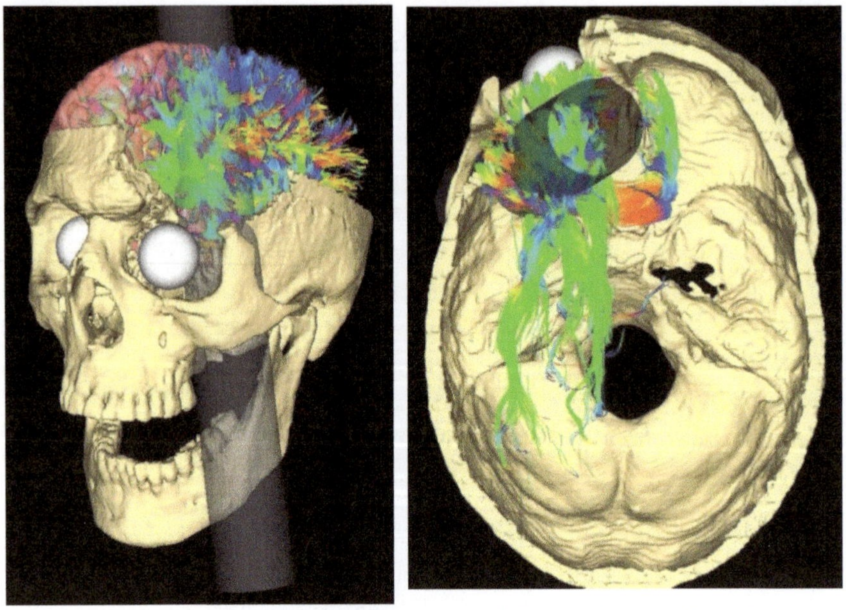

False-color representtations of cerebral fiber pathways affected in Phineas Gage's accident, per Van Horn et al.

Biology plays a very important role in the development of personality. The study of the biological level in personality psychology focuses primarily on identifying the role of genetic determinants and how they mold individual personalities. Some of the earliest thinking about possible biological bases of personality grew out of the case of Phineas Gage. In an 1848 accident, a large iron rod was driven through Gage's head, and his personality apparently changed as a result, although descriptions of these psychological changes are usually exaggerated.

In general, patients with brain damage have been difficult to find and study. In the 1990s, researchers began to use electroencephalography (EEG), positron emission tomography (PET), and more recently functional magnetic resonance imaging (fMRI), which is now the most widely used imaging technique to help localize personality traits in the brain.

Genetic Basis of Personality

Ever since the Human Genome Project allowed for a much more in depth understanding of genetics, there has been an ongoing controversy involving heritability, personality traits, and environmental vs. genetic influence on personality. The human genome is known to play a role in the development of personality. Previously, genetic personality studies focused on specific genes correlating to specific personality traits. Today's view of the gene-personality relationship focuses primarily on the activation and expression of genes related to personality and forms part of what is referred to as behavioral genetics. Genes provide numerous options for varying cells to be expressed; however, the environment determines which of these are activated. Many studies have noted this relationship in varying ways in which our bodies can develop, but the interaction between genes and the shaping of our minds and personality is also relevant to this biological relationship. DNA-environment interactions are important in the development of personality because this relationship determines what part of the DNA code is actually made into proteins that will become part of an individual. It has been noted that while different choices are made available by the genome, in the end, the environment is the ultimate determinant of what becomes activated. Small changes in DNA in individuals are what lead to the uniqueness of every person as well as differences in looks, abilities, brain functioning, and all the factors that culminate to develop a cohesive personality.

Cattell and Eysenck have proposed that genetics have a strong influence on personality. A large part of the evidence collected linking genetics and the environment to personality have come from twin studies. This "twin method" compares levels of similarity in personality using genetically identical twins. One of the first of these twin studies measured 800 pairs of twins, studied numerous personality traits, and determined that identical twins are most similar in their general abilities. Personality similarities were found to be less related for self-concepts, goals, and interests.

Twin studies have also been important in the creation of the five factor personality model: neuroticism, extraversion, openness, agreeableness, and conscientiousness. Neuroticism and extraversion are the two most widely studied traits. A person that may fall into the extravert category can display characteristics such as impulsiveness, sociability, and activeness. A person falling into the neuroticism category may be more likely to be moody, anxious, or irritable. Identical twins, however, have higher correlations in personality traits than fraternal twins. One study measuring genetic influence on twins in five different countries found that the correlations for identical twins were .50, while for fraternal they were about .20. It is suggested that heredity and environment interact to determine one's personality.

Evolutionary Theory

Charles Darwin is the founder of the theory of the evolution of the species. The evolutionary approach to personality psychology is based on this theory. This theory examines how individual personality differences are based on natural selection. Through natural selection organisms change over time through adaptation and selection. Traits are developed and certain genes come into expression based on an organism's environment and how these traits aid in an organism's survival and reproduction.

Polymorphisms, such as gender and blood-type, are forms of diversity which evolve to benefit a species as a whole. The theory of evolution has wide-ranging implications on personality psychology. Personality viewed through the lens of evolutionary psychology places a great deal of emphasis on specific traits that are most likely to aid in survival and reproduction, such as conscientiousness, sociability, emotional stability, and dominance. The social aspects of personality can be seen through an evolutionary perspective. Specific character traits develop and are selected for because they play an important and complex role in the social hierarchy of organisms. Such characteristics of this social hierarchy include the sharing of important resources, family and mating interactions, and the harm or help organisms can bestow upon one another.

Personality Tests

There are two major types of personality tests, projective and objective.

Projective tests assume personality is primarily unconscious and assess individuals by how they respond to an ambiguous stimulus, such as an ink blot. Projective tests have been in use for about 60 years and continue to be used today. Examples of such tests include the Rorschach test and the Thematic Apperception Test.

The Rorschach Test involves showing an individual a series of note cards with ambiguous ink blots on them. The individual being tested is asked to provide interpretations of the blots on the cards by stating everything that the ink blot may resemble based on their personal interpretation. The therapist then analyzes their responses. Rules for scoring the test have been covered in manuals that cover a wide variety of characteristics such as content, originality of response, location of "perceived images" and several other factors. Using these specific scoring methods, the therapist will then attempt to relate test responses to attributes of the individual's personality and their unique characteristics. The idea is that unconscious needs will come out in the person's response, e.g. an aggressive person may see images of destruction.

The Thematic Apperception Test (also known as the TAT) involves presenting individuals with vague pictures/scenes and asking them to tell a story based on what they see. Common examples of these "scenes" include images that may suggest family relationships or specific situations, such as a father and son or a man and a woman in a bedroom. Responses are analyzed for common themes. Responses unique to an individual are theoretically meant to indicate underlying thoughts, processes, and potentially conflicts present within the individual. Responses are believed to be directly linked to unconscious motives. There is very little empirical evidence available to support these methods.

Objective tests assume personality is consciously accessible and that it can be measured by self-report questionnaires. Research on psychological assessment has generally found objective tests to be more valid and reliable than projective tests. Critics have pointed to the Forer effect to suggest some of these appear to be more accurate and discriminating than they really are. Issues with these tests include false reporting because there is no way to tell if an individual is answering a question honestly or accurately.

Inner Experience

Psychology has traditionally defined personality through its behavioral patterns, and more recently with neuroscientific studies of the brain. In recent years, some psychologists have turned to the study of inner experiences for insight into personality as well as individuality. Inner experiences are the thoughts and feelings to an immediate phenomenon. Another term used to define inner experiences is qualia. Being able to understand inner experiences assists in understanding how humans behave, act, and respond. Defining personality using inner experiences has been expanding due to the fact that solely relying on behavioral principles to explain one's character may seem incomplete. Behavioral methods allow the subject to be observed by an observer, whereas with inner experiences the subject is its own observer.

Methods Measuring Inner Experience

Descriptive experience sampling (DES), developed by psychologist Russel Hurlburt. This is an idiographic method that is used to help examine inner experiences. This method relies on an introspective technique that allows an individual's inner experiences and characteristics to be described and measured. A beep notifies the subject to record their experience at that exact moment and 24 hours later an interview is given based on all the experiences recorded. DES has been used in subjects that have been diagnosed with schizophrenia and depression. It has also been crucial to studying the inner experiences of those who have been diagnosed with common psychiatric diseases.

Articulated thoughts in stimulated situations (ATSS): ATSS is a paradigm which was created as an alternative to the TA (think aloud) method. This method assumes that people have continuous internal dialogues that can be naturally attended to. ATSS also assesses a person's inner thoughts as they verbalize their cognitions. In this procedure, subjects listen to a scenario via a video or audio player and are asked to imagine that they are in that specific situation. Later, they are asked to articulate their thoughts as they occur in reaction to the playing scenario. This method is useful in studying emotional experience given that the scenarios used can influence specific emotions. Most importantly, the method has contributed to the study of personality. In a study conducted by Rayburn and Davison (2002), subjects' thoughts and empathy toward anti-gay hate crimes were evaluated. The researchers found that participants showed more aggressive intentions towards the offender in scenarios which mimicked hate crimes.

Experimental method: This method is an experimental paradigm used to study human experiences involved in the studies of sensation and perception, learning and memory, motivation, and biological psychology. The experimental psychologist usually deals with intact organisms although studies are often conducted with organisms modified by surgery, radiation, drug treatment, or long-standing deprivations of various kinds or with organisms that naturally present organic abnormalities or emotional disorders. Economists and psychologists have developed a variety of experimental methodologies to elicit and assess individual attitudes where each emotion differs for each individual. The results are then gathered and quantified to conclude if specific experiences have any common factors. This method is used to seek clarity of the experience and remove any biases to help understand the meaning behind the experience to see if it can be generalized.

Psychobiology of Personality

Several personality traits have been examined for their psychobiological relationships. For example, neuroticism is one of the well studies personality traits. A person high on neuroticism is susceptible to anxiety, depression, stress, and so forth. Benzodiazepine potentiates the effect of gama-aminobutyric acid (GABA) which has inhibitory effect on brain nuclei. Decreased amount of benzodiazepine in amygdala is related to high neuroticism. Similarly sensation seeking behaviour is another personality trait that has high social relevance. Those who are high on sensation seeking be likely to be under-aroused. Their Ascending Reticular Activation System (ARAS) is below the optimum level of arousal.

Studies examining autonomic nervous system (ANS) function differences introverts and extroverts have used skin conductance, heart rate and EEG measures. Studies have explored difference between introversion-extraversion and skin conductance level. Skin conductance level has been used to measure tonic arousal in the baseline resting condition or the period prior to stimulation in an experiment. Studies have found that simple sensory stimulation do not elicit any difference between introverts and extraverts in terms of tonic levels of electrodermal activity. However, when challenged by task demands, the s kin conductance level has been found to be higher for extraverts at higher stress levels. Contrarily the skin conductance level was higher in introverts for lower stress levels.

Cardiovascular measures are an important component of ANS function changes. Deceleration of the phasic heart rate is the cardiac depiction of orienting responses whereas phasic acceleration is the cardiac representation of the defensive responses. Studies examining difference between introverts and extraverts in terms of cardiovascular measures did not find any variation in the baseline or tonic heart rate. However, in vigilance conditions introverts show higher heart rate as compared to extraverts. Researchers studying sensation seeking behaviour have found heart rate deceleration when moderately intense novel stimuli are presented to high sensation seekers. The low sensation seekers display acceleration of heart rate.

The relationship between personality and electrical activities of the brain has also been studied. The introverts and extroverts have been found to be different with respect to alpha recording from the posterior regions of the skull. The amplitude and frequency of the alpha waves indicate the level of cortical activation. High arousal level is represented by low amplitude and high frequency ranging between 8-13 Hz.

Although the usage of imaging technique in personality studies is not new, there are still not many studies in this domain. Mathew *et al.* (1984) administered Eysenck Personality Inventory (Eysenck & Eysenck 1964) on 51 normal female volunteers and used the xenon inhalation technique to correlate regional blood flow with personality dimensions. They found inverse correlations between blood flow and extraversion. The correlation between blood flow and neuroticism was not significant. The findings suggest inverse relationship between extraversion and general cortical arousal. Couples of studies have correlated PET-glucose metabolic rate (GMR) and scores of Eysenck Personality Questionnaire. The findings show positive correlation between extraversion and GMR in frontal and temporal areas of the brain. Caudate and putamen areas were also correlated with extraversion.

Canli *et al.* (2001) used fMRI to study response to emotional stimuli and correlated them with personality. They found positive correlation between extraversion and increased activation to positive stimuli in the frontal and temporal lobes, and parts of the caudate, putamen, and amygdala. Similar results were found by Canli *et al.* (2002) where the degree of activation in the amygdala during presentation of happy stimuli correlated with extraversion.

Let us look at the boarder picture. Behaviour of an individual is under the control of executive functions. Our reaction to any stimuli involves planning, spatiotemporal segmentation and execution. It also entails self-regulation. Any given situation demands certain degree of attention, regulation of emotion and behaviour, and performance of psychomotor activity. All this are linked to the prefrontal cortex. Hence, it can be inferred that our executive functions are controlled by the prefrontal cortex. The amount of dopamine in the prefrontal cortex increases in response to stress. This, in turn, intensifies our attention towards the stressor. It is important to note that chronic stress might lead to extra amount of dopamine in the prefrontal cortex than what is functionally needed. This increase might impair the functions of the prefrontal cortex, thus leading to decreased attention, hypervigilance, and certain psychotic symptoms.

Deprivation and its psychological consequences has been a topic of interest for many psychologists. Studies of baby rats and monkeys confirm impaired executive function in those experiencing maternal deprivation. Now that we know the outcome of executive functions, we can infer the social and behavioral cost of maternal deprivation.

Adjustment of an individual is also appraised by their ability to understand and interpret behaviours of others in terms of deciphering other person's intentions and thoughts. The brain structures supposed to constitute the neural basis of this ability are amygdala and its projections to the superior temporal gyrus, thalamus, and prefrontal cortex. fMRI studies show that the superior temporal gyrus, amygdala and prefrontal cortex are involved in processing social information. Thus, they can be considered to constitute the neural basis of social intelligence.

Neuropsychological Assessment

Neuropsychological assessment was traditionally carried out to assess the extent of impairment to a particular skill and to attempt to determine the area of the brain which may have been damaged following brain injury or neurological illness. With the advent of neuroimaging techniques, location of space-occupying lesions can now be more accurately determined through this method, so the focus has now moved on to the assessment of cognition and behaviour, including examining the effects of any brain injury or neuropathological process that a person may have experienced.

A core part of neuropsychological assessment is the administration of neuropsychological tests for the formal assessment of cognitive function, though neuropsychological testing is more than the administration and scoring of tests and screening tools. It is essential that neuropsychological assessment also include an evaluation of the person's mental status. This is especially true in assessment of Alzheimer's disease and other forms of dementia. Aspects of cognitive functioning that are assessed typically include orientation, new-learning/memory, intelligence, language, visuoperception, and executive function. However, clinical neuropsychological assessment is more than this and also focuses on a person's psychological, personal, interpersonal and wider contextual circumstances.

Assessment may be carried out for a variety of reasons, such as:

- Clinical evaluation, to understand the pattern of cognitive strengths as well as any difficulties a person may have, and to aid decision making for use in a medical or rehabilitation environment.

- Scientific investigation, to examine an hypothesis about the structure and function of cognition to be tested, or to provide information that allows experimental testing to be seen in context of a wider cognitive profile.

- Medico-legal assessment, to be used in a court of law as evidence in a legal claim or criminal investigation.

Miller outlined three broad goals of neuropsychological assessment. Firstly, diagnosis, to determine the nature of the underlying problem. Secondly, to understand the nature of any brain injury or resulting cognitive problem and its impact on the individual, as a means of devising a rehabilitation programme or offering advice as to an individual's ability to carry out a certain tasks (for example, fitness to drive, or returning to work). And lastly, assessments may be undertaken to measure change in functioning over time, such as to determine the consequences of a surgical procedure or the impact of a rehabilitation programme over time.

Diagnosis of a Neuropsychological Disorder

Certain types of damage to the brain will cause behavioral and cognitive difficulties. Psychologists can start screening for these problems by using either one of the following techniques or all of these combined:

History Taking

This includes gathering medical history of the patient and their family, presence or absence of developmental milestones, psychosocial history, and character, severity, and progress of any history of complaints. The psychologist can then gauge how to treat the patient and determine if there are any historical determinants for his or her behavior.

Interviewing

Psychologists use structured interviews in order to determine what kind of neurological problem the patient might be experiencing. There are a number of specific interviews, including the Short Portable Mental Status Questionnaire, Neuropsychological Impairment Scale, Patient's Assessment of Own Functioning, and Structured Interview for the Diagnosis of Dementia.

Test-taking

The scores on standardized tests taken by children is a strong predictor of future or current neuropsychological problems. Standardized tests allow psychologists to compare a child's results with other children's because it has the same components and is given in the same way. It is representative of the child's behavior and cognition. The results of a standardized test are only a tool used to discover if there is a disorder. Further testing is needed to officially diagnose the patient.

Intelligence Testing

Testing one's intelligence can also give a clue to whether there is a problem in the brain-behavior connection. The Wechsler Scales are the tests most often used to determine level of intelligence. The variety of scales available, the nature of the tasks, as well as a wide gap in verbal and performance scores can give clues to whether there is a learning disability or damage to a certain area of the brain.

Testing other Areas

Other areas are also tested when a patient goes through neuropsychological assessment. These can include sensory perception, motor functions, attention, memory, auditory and visual processing, language, problem solving, planning, organization, speed of processing, and many others. Neuropsychological assessment can test many areas of cognitive and executive functioning to determine whether a patient's difficulty in function and behavior has a neuropsychological basis.

Information Gathered from Assessment

Tsatsanis and Volkmar believe that assessment can provide unique information about the type of disorder a patient has which allows the psychologist to come up with a treatment plan. Neuropsychological assessment can clarify the nature of the disorder and determine the cognitive functioning associated with a disorder. Assessment can also allow the psychologist to understand the developmental progress of the disorder in order to predict future problems and come up with a successful treatment package. Different assessments can also determine if a patient will be at risk for a particular disorder. It is important to remember, however, that assessing a patient at one time is not enough to go ahead and continue treatment because of the changes in behavior that can occur frequently. A patient must be retested multiple times in order to make sure that the current treatment is still the right treatment. For neuropsychological assessments, researchers discover the different areas of the brain that is damaged based on the cognitive and behavioral aspects of the patient.

Benefits of Assessment

The most beneficial factor of neuropsychological assessment is that is provides an accurate diagnosis of the disorder for the patient when it is unclear to the psychologist what exactly he/she has. This allows for accurate treatment later on in the process because treatment is driven by the exact symptoms of the disorder and how a specific patient may react to different treatments. The assessment allows the psychologist and patient to understand the severity of the deficit and to allow better decision-making by both parties. It is also helpful in understanding deteriorating diseases because the patient can be assessed multiple times to see how the disorder is progressing.

One area where neuropsychological assessments can be beneficial is in forensic cases where the defendant's competency is being questioned due to possible brain injury or damage. A neuropsychological assessment may show brain damage when neuroimaging has failed. It can also determine whether the individual is faking a disorder (malingering) in order to attain a lesser sentence.

Neuropsychological assessments usually do not take much time, with most testing completed in 6 to 12 hours or less. This time, however, does not include the role of the psychologist interpreting the data, scoring the test, making formulations, and writing a formal report.

Qualifications for Conducting Assessments

Neuropsychological assessments are usually conducted by doctoral-level (Ph.D., Psy.D.) psychologists trained in neuropsychology, known as clinical neuropsychologists. The definition and scope of a clinical neuropsychologist is outlined in the widely accepted Houston Conference Guidelines. They will usually have postdoctoral training in neuropsychology, neuroanatomy, and brain function. Most will be licensed and practicing psychologists in their particular field. Recent developments in the field allow for highly trained individuals such as psychometrists to administer selected instruments, though determinations regarding testing results remain the responsibility of the doctor.

Wechsler Adult Intelligence Scale

The Wechsler Adult Intelligence Scale (WAIS) is an IQ test designed to measure intelligence and cognitive ability in adults and older adolescents. The original WAIS (Form I) was published in February 1955 by David Wechsler, as a revision of the Wechsler–Bellevue Intelligence Scale, released in 1939. It is currently in its fourth edition (WAIS-IV) released in 2008 by Pearson, and is the most widely used IQ test, for both adults and older adolescents, in the world.

History

The WAIS is founded on Wechsler's definition of intelligence, which he defined as "... the global capacity of a person to act purposefully, to think rationally, and to deal effectively with his environment." He believed that intelligence was made up of specific elements that could be isolated, defined, and subsequently measured. However, these individual elements were not entirely independent, but were all interrelated. His argument, in other words, is that general intelligence is composed of various specific and interrelated functions or elements that can be individually measured.

This theory differed greatly from the Binet scale which, in Wechsler's day, was generally considered the supreme authority with regard to intelligence testing. A drastically revised new version of the

Binet scale, released in 1937, received a great deal of criticism from David Wechsler (after whom the original Wechsler–Bellevue Intelligence scale and the modern Weschler Adult Intelligence Scale IV are named).

- Wechsler was a very influential advocate for the concept of non-intellective factors, and he felt that the 1937 Binet scale did not do a good job of incorporating these factors into the scale (non-intellective factors are variables that contribute to the overall score in intelligence, but are not made up of intelligence-related items. These include things such as lack of confidence, fear of failure, attitudes, etc.).
- Wechsler did not agree with the idea of a single score that the Binet test gave.
- Wechsler argued that the Binet scale items were not valid for adult test-takers because the items were chosen specifically for use with children.
- The "Binet scale's emphasis on speed, with timed tasks scattered throughout the scale, tended to unduly handicap older adults."
- Wechsler believed that "mental age norms clearly did not apply to adults."
- Wechsler criticized the then existing Binet scale because "it did not consider that intellectual performance could deteriorate as a person grew older."

These criticisms of the 1937 Binet test helped produce the Wechsler–Bellevue scale, released in 1939. While this scale has been revised (resulting in the present day WAIS-IV), many of the original concepts Wechsler argued for, have become standards in psychological testing, including the point-scale concept and the performance-scale concept.

Wechsler–Bellevue Intelligence Scale

The Wechsler–Bellevue tests were innovative in the 1930s because they:

1. gathered tasks created for nonclinical purposes for administration as a "clinical test battery",
2. used the point scale concept instead of the age scale, and
3. included a non-verbal performance scale.

Point Scale Concept

In the Binet scales (prior to the 1986 version) items were grouped according to age level. Each of these age levels was composed of a group of tasks that could be passed by two-thirds to three-quarters of the individuals in that level. This meant that items were not arranged according to content. Additionally, an individual taking a Binet test would only receive credit if a certain number of the tasks were completed. This meant that falling short just one task required for the credit, resulted in no credit at all (for example, if passing three out of four tasks was required to receive credit, then passing two yielded no credit).

The point scale concept significantly changed the way testing was done by assigning credits or points to each item. This had two large effects. First, this allowed items to be grouped according to content. Second, participants were able to receive a set number of points or credits for each item passed. The result was a test that could be made up of different content areas (or subtests) with both an overall score and a score for each content area. In turn, this allowed for an analysis to be made of an individual's ability in a variety of content areas (as opposed to one general score).

The Non-Verbal Performance Scale

The non-verbal performance scale was also a critical difference from the Binet scale. Since the "early Binet scale had been persistently and consistently criticized for its emphasis on language and verbal skills," Wechsler made an entire scale that allowed the measurement of nonverbal intelligence. This became known as a performance scale. Essentially, this scale required a subject to do something (such as "copying symbols or point to a missing detail") rather than just answer questions. This was an important development as it attempted to overcome biases that were caused by "language, culture, and education." Further, this scale also provided an opportunity to observe a different type of behavior because something physical was required. Clinicians were able to observe how a participant reacted to the "longer interval of sustained effort, concentration, and attention" that the performance tasks required.

While the Wechsler–Bellevue scale was the first to effectively use the performance scale (meaning that (1) there was a "possibility of directly comparing an individual's verbal and nonverbal intelligence", and (2) that "the results of both scales were expressed in comparable units"), the idea had been around for a while. The Binet scale did have performance tasks (although they were geared towards children) and there were entire tests that were considered supplements or alternatives (an example of such a performance test is the Leiter International Performance Scale).

WAIS

The WAIS was initially created as a revision of the Wechsler–Bellevue Intelligence Scale (WBIS), which was a battery of tests published by Wechsler in 1939. The WBIS was composed of subtests that could be found in various other intelligence tests of the time, such as Robert Yerkes' army testing program and the Binet-Simon scale. The WAIS was first released in February 1955 by David Wechsler. Because the Wechsler tests included non-verbal items (known as *performance scales*) as well as verbal items for all test-takers, and because the 1960 form of Lewis Terman's Stanford–Binet Intelligence Scales was less carefully developed than previous versions, Form I of the WAIS surpassed the Stanford–Binet tests in popularity by the 1960s.

WAIS-R

The WAIS-R, a revised form of the WAIS, was released in 1981 and consisted of six verbal and five performance subtests. The verbal tests were: Information, Comprehension, Arithmetic, Digit Span, Similarities, and Vocabulary. The Performance subtests were: Picture Arrangement, Picture Completion, Block Design, Object Assembly, and Digit Symbol. A verbal IQ, performance IQ and full scale IQ were obtained.

This revised edition did not provide new validity data, but used the data from the original WAIS; however new norms were provided, carefully stratified.

WAIS-III

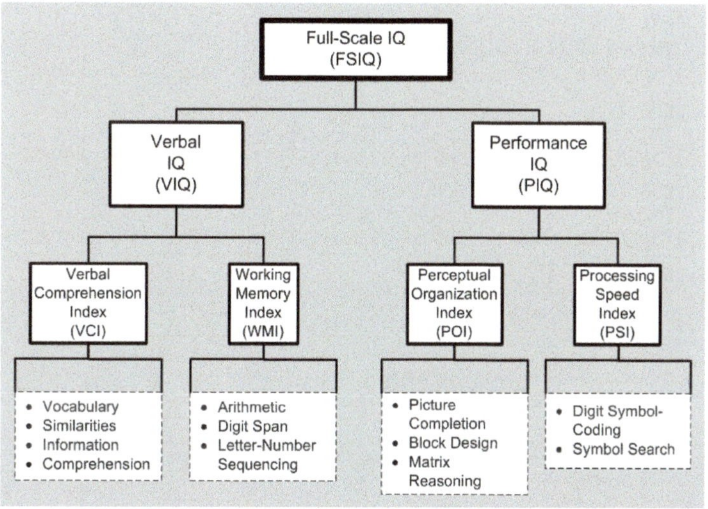

The WAIS-III, a subsequent revision of the WAIS and the WAIS-R, was released in 1997. It provided scores for Verbal IQ, Performance IQ, and Full Scale IQ, along with four secondary indices (Verbal Comprehension, Working Memory, Perceptual Organization, and Processing Speed).

Verbal IQ (VIQ)

Included seven tests and provided two subindexes; verbal comprehension and working memory.

The Verbal Comprehension Index (VCI) included the following tests:

- Information
- Similarities
- Vocabulary

The Working Memory Index (WMI) included:

- Arithmetic
- Digit Span

Letter-Number Sequencing and Comprehension are not included in these indices, but are used as substitutions for spoiled subtests within the WMI and VCI, respectively.

Performance IQ (PIQ)

Included six tests and it also provided two subindexes; perceptual organization and processing speed.

The Perceptual Organization Index (POI) included:

- Block Design
- Matrix Reasoning
- Picture Completion

The Processing Speed Index (PSI) included:

- Digit Symbol-Coding
- Symbol Search

Two tests; Picture Arrangement and Object Assembly were not included in the indexes. Object Assembly is not included in the PIQ.

WAIS-IV

The current version of the test, the WAIS-IV, which was released in 2008, is composed of 10 core subtests and five supplemental subtests, with the 10 core subtests comprising the Full Scale IQ. With the new WAIS-IV, the verbal/performance subscales from previous versions were removed and replaced by the index scores. The General Ability Index (GAI) was included, which consists of the Similarities, Vocabulary and Information subtests from the Verbal Comprehension Index and the Block Design, Matrix Reasoning and Visual Puzzles subtests from the Perceptual Reasoning Index. The GAI is clinically useful because it can be used as a measure of cognitive abilities that are less vulnerable to impairments of processing and working memory.

Index Scores and Scales

There are four index scores representing major components of intelligence:

- Verbal Comprehension Index (VCI)
- Perceptual Reasoning Index (PRI)
- Working Memory Index (WMI)
- Processing Speed Index (PSI)

Two broad scores, which can be used to summarize general intellectual abilities, can also be derived:

- Full Scale IQ (FSIQ), based on the total combined performance of the VCI, PRI, WMI, and PSI
- General Ability Index (GAI), based only on the six subtests that the VCI and PRI comprise.

Tasks grouped by index				
Index	**Task**	**Core?**	**Description**	**Proposed abilities measured**
Verbal Comprehension	**Similarities**	✓	Participants are given two words or concepts and have to describe how they are similar.	Abstract verbal reasoning; semantic knowledge
	Vocabulary	✓	Participants must name objects in pictures or define words presented to them.	Semantic knowledge; verbal comprehension and expression
	Information	✓	Participants are questioned about their general knowledge.	Degree of general information acquired from culture
	Comprehension			Ability to express abstract social conventions, rules and expressions
Perceptual Reasoning	**Block Design**	✓		Visual spatial processing and problem solving; visual motor construction
	Matrix Reasoning	✓		Nonverbal abstract problem solving, inductive reasoning
	Visual Puzzles	✓		Visual spatial reasoning
	Picture Completion			Ability to quickly perceive visual details
	Figure Weights			Quantitative reasoning
Working Memory	**Digit Span**	✓	Participants must recall a series of numbers in order.	Working memory, attention, encoding, auditory processing
	Arithmetic	✓		Quantitative reasoning, concentration, mental manipulation
	Letter-Number Sequencing		Participants must recall a series of numbers in increasing order and letters in alphabetical order.	Working memory, attention, mental control
Processing Speed	**Symbol Search**	✓		Processing speed
	Coding	✓		Processing speed, associative memory, graphomotor speed
	Cancellation			Processing speed

Standardization

The WAIS-IV was standardized on a sample of 2,200 people in the United States ranging in age from 16 to 90. An extension of the standardization has been conducted with 688 Canadians in the same age range.

Age Range and uses

The WAIS-IV measure is appropriate for use with individuals aged 16–90 years. For individuals under 16 years, the Wechsler Intelligence Scale for Children (WISC, 6–16 years) and the Wechsler Preschool and Primary Scale of Intelligence (WPPSI, 2½–7 years, 7 months) are used.

Intelligence tests may be utilized in populations with psychiatric illness or brain injury, in order to assess level of cognitive functioning, though some regard this use as controversial. Rehabilitation psychologists and neuropsychologists use the WAIS-IV and other neuropsychological tests to assess how the brain is functioning after injury. Specific subtests provide information on a specific cognitive function. For example, digit span may be used to get a sense of attentional difficulties. Others employ the WAIS-R NI (*Wechsler Adult Intelligence Scale-Revised as a Neuropsychological Instrument*), another measure published by Harcourt. Each subtest score is tallied and calculated with respect to neurotypical or brain-injury norms. As the WAIS is developed for the average, non-injured individual, separate norms were developed for appropriate comparison among similar functioning individuals.

Wechsler Intelligence Scale for Children

The WISC-V takes 45–65 minutes to administer and generates a Full Scale IQ (formerly known as an intelligence quotient or IQ score) which represents a child's general intellectual ability. It also provides five primary index scores (i.e., Verbal Comprehension Index, Visual Spatial Index, Fluid Reasoning Index, Working Memory Index, and Processing Speed Index) that represent a child's abilities in more discrete cognitive domains. Five ancillary composite scores can be derived from various combinations of primary or primary and secondary subtests.

The Wechsler Intelligence Scale for Children (WISC), developed by David Wechsler, is an individually administered intelligence test for children between the ages of 6 and 16. The Fifth Edition (WISC-V; Wechsler, 2014) is the most current version.

Five complementary subtests yield three complementary composite scores to measure related cognitive abilities relevant to assessment and identification of specific learning disabilities, particularly dyslexia and dyscalculia. Variation in testing procedures and goals can reduce time of assessment to 15–20 minutes for the assessment of a single primary index, or increase testing time to three or more hours for a complete assessment, including all primary, ancillary, and complementary indices.

History

The original WISC (Wechsler, 1949) was an adaption of several of the subtests which made up the Wechsler–Bellevue Intelligence Scale (Wechsler, 1939) but also featured several subtests designed specifically for it. The subtests were organized into Verbal and Performance scales, and provided scores for Verbal IQ (VIQ), Performance IQ (PIQ), and Full Scale IQ (FSIQ).

Each successive edition has re-normed the test to compensate for the Flynn effect, ensuring not only that the norms do not become outdated which is suggested to result in inflated scores on intelligence measures, but that they are representative of the current population (Flynn, 1984, 1987, 1999; Matarazzo, 1972). Additional updates and refinements include changes to the questions to make them less biased against minorities and females, and updated materials to make them more useful in the administration of the test. A revised edition was published in 1974 as the WISC-R (Wechsler, 1974), featuring the same subtests however the age range was changed from 5-15 to 6-16.

The third edition was published in 1991 (WISC-III; Wechsler, 1991) and brought with it a new subtest as a measure of processing speed. In addition to the traditional VIQ, PIQ, and FSIQ scores, four new index scores were introduced to represent more narrow domains of cognitive function: the Verbal Comprehension Index (VCI), the Perceptual Organization Index (POI), the Freedom from Distractibility Index (FDI), and the Processing Speed Index (PSI).

The WISC-IV was produced in 2003. The WISC-V was published in 2014. The WISC-V has a total of 21 subtests. It yields 15 composite scores.

Test Format

The WISC is one test in a suite of Wechsler intelligence scales. Subjects 16 and over are tested with the Wechsler Adult Intelligence Scale (WAIS), and children ages two years and six months to seven years and seven months are tested with the Wechsler Preschool and Primary Scale of Intelligence (WPPSI). There is some overlap between tests, with children aged 6 years 0 months through 7 years 7 months being able to complete the WPPSI or the WISC, and children aged 16 being able to complete the WISC-V or the WAIS-IV. Different floor effect and ceiling effect can be achieved using the different tests, allowing for a greater understanding of the child's abilities or deficits. This means that a 16-year-old child who has intellectual disability may be tested using the WISC-V so that the clinician may see the floor of their knowledge (the lowest level).

There are five primary index scores, the Verbal Comprehension Index (VCI), Visual Spatial Index (VSI), Fluid Reasoning Index (FRI), Working Memory Index (WMI), and Processing Speed Index (PSI). Two subtests must be administered to obtain each of the primary index scores; thus, a total of 10 subtests are primary subtests. The Full Scale IQ is derived from 7 of the 10 primary subtests: Both Verbal Comprehension subtests, one Visual Spatial subtest, two Fluid Reasoning subtests, one Working Memory subtest, and one Processing Speed subtest. Verbal Comprehension and Fluid Reasoning are weighted more heavily in the Full Scale IQ to reflect the importance of crystallized and fluid abilities in modern intelligence models (Wechsler, 2014).

The VCI is derived from the Similarities and Vocabulary subtests. The Verbal Comprehension scale subtests are described below:

- Similarities – (primary, FSIQ) asking how two words are alike/similar.
- Vocabulary – (primary, FSIQ) examinee is asked to define a provided word
- Information (secondary) – general knowledge questions.
- Comprehension – (secondary) questions about social situations or common concepts.

The VCI is an overall measure of verbal concept formation (the child's ability to verbally reason) and is influenced by semantic knowledge.

The VSI is derived from the Block Design and Visual Puzzles subtests. These subtests are as follows:

- Block Design (primary, FSIQ) – children put together red-and-white blocks in a pattern according to a displayed model. This is timed, and some of the more difficult puzzles award bonuses for speed.
- Visual Puzzles (primary) – children view a puzzle in a stimulus book and choose from among pieces which three could construct the puzzle.

The VSI is a measure of visual spatial processing.

The FRI is derived from the Matrix Reasoning and Figure Weights subtests. The Fluid Reasoning scale subtests are described below:

- Matrix Reasoning (primary, FSIQ) – children are shown an array of pictures with one missing square, and select the picture that fits the array from five options.
- Figure Weights (primary, FSIQ) – children view a stimulus book that pictures shapes on a scale (or scales) with one empty side and select the choice that keeps the scale balanced.
- Picture Concepts (secondary) – children are provided with a series of pictures presented in rows (either two or three rows) and asked to determine which pictures go together, one from each row.
- Arithmetic (secondary) – orally administered arithmetic questions. Timed.

The FRI is a measure of inductive and quantitative reasoning.

The WMI is derived from the Digit Span and Picture Span subtests. The Working Memory scale's subtests are as follows:

- Digit Span (primary, FSIQ) – children are orally given sequences of numbers and asked to repeat them, either as heard and in reverse order.
- Picture Span (primary) – children view pictures in a stimulus book and then select from among options to indicate the pictures they saw, in order if possible.
- Letter-Number Sequencing (secondary) – children are provided a series of numbers and letters and asked to provide them back to the examiner in a predetermined order.

The WMI is a measure of working memory ability.

The PSI is derived from the Coding and Symbol Search subtests. The Processing Speed subtests are as follows:

- Coding (primary, FSIQ) – children under 8 mark rows of shapes with different lines according to a code, children over 8 transcribe a digit-symbol code. The task is time-limited with bonuses for speed.
- Symbol Search (primary) – children are given rows of symbols and target symbols, and asked to mark whether or not the target symbols appear in each row.
- Cancellation (secondary) – children scan random and structured arrangements of pictures and marks specific target pictures within a limited amount of time.

The PSI is a measure of processing speed.

The 2014 publication of the WISC-V contained five ancillary index scores that may be derived for special clinical purposes or situations: the Quantitative Reasoning Index (QRI), the Auditory Working Memory Index (AWMI), the Nonverbal Index (NVI), the General Ability Index (GAI), and the Cognitive Proficiency Index (CPI). Three of these ancillary index scores (i.e., NVI, GAI, and CPI) can be derived from the 10 primary subtests. The QRI and the AWMI can each be derived by administering one additional subtest from subtests that are within one of the five primary scales (Verbal Comprehension scale, Visual Spatial Index, Fluid Reasoning scale, Working Memory scale, and Processing Speed scale) but are not primary. The set of these subtests is termed secondary subtests (Wechsler, 2014).

Two ancillary index scores termed the expanded index scores were released the year after the 2014 publication, so are not included in the published manuals. These are the Verbal (Expanded Crystallized) Index (VECI) and the Expanded Fluid Index (EFI) (Raiford, Drozdick, Zhang, & Zhou, 2015).

Three complementary index scores are available to measure cognitive processes that are important to achievement and are sensitive to specific learning disabilities. The complementary index scores are the Naming Speed Index (NSI), designed to measure rapid automatized naming, and the Symbol Translation Index, designed to measure visual-verbal associative memory, which is sometimes termed visual-verbal paired associate learning in the published literature (Wechsler, 2014). The Naming Speed scale contains Naming Speed Literacy, which measures rapid automatic naming, and Naming Speed Literacy, which is the only commercially published and normed measure of rapid quantity naming, also known as subitizing. Naming Speed Quantity is uniquely sensitive to math achievement and specific learning disabilities in mathematics (Raiford et al., 2016; Wechsler, Raiford, & Holdnack, 2014).

Psychometric Properties

The WISC–V normative sample consisted of 2,200 children between the ages of 6 and 16 years 11 months. In addition to the normative sample, a number of special group samples were collected, including the following: children identified as intellectually gifted, children with mild or moderate intellectual disability, children with specific learning disorders (reading, written expression, and math), children with ADHD, children with disruptive behavior, children who are English Language Learners, children with autism spectrum disorder with language impairment, children with autism spectrum disorder without language impairment, and children with traumatic brain injuries.

The WISC–V is also linked with measures of achievement, adaptive behavior, executive function, and behavior and emotion. Equivalency studies were also conducted within the Wechsler family of tests and with a Kaufman test (the KABC-II) enabling comparisons between various intellectual ability scores over the lifespan. A number of concurrent studies were conducted to examine the scale's reliability and validity. Evidence of the convergent and discriminant validity of the WISC–V is provided by correlational studies with the following instruments: WISC–IV, WPPSI–IV, WAIS–IV, WASI–II, KABC–II, KTEA–3, WIAT–III, NEPSY–II, Vineland–II, and BASC–II. Evidence of construct validity was provided through a series of factor-analytic studies and mean comparisons using matched samples of special group and nonclinical children.

Uses

The WISC is used not only as an intelligence test, but as a clinical tool. Some practitioners use the WISC as part of an assessment to diagnose attention-deficit hyperactivity disorder (ADHD) and learning disabilities, for example. This is usually done through a process called *pattern analysis*, in which the various subtests' scores are compared to one another (ipsative scoring) and clusters of unusually low scores in relation to the others are searched for. David Wechsler himself suggested this in 1958.

However, the research does not show this to be a very effective way to diagnose ADHD or learning disabilities. The vast majority of ADHD children do not display certain subtests substantially below others, and many children who display such patterns do not have ADHD. Other patterns for children with learning disabilities show a similar lack of usefulness of the WISC as a diagnostic tool. Although, when Cattell Horn Carrol (CHC) theory is used to interpret the WISC–V subtests, things tend to make a great deal more sense.

When diagnosing children, best practice suggests that a multi-test battery (i.e., multi-factored evaluation) should be used as learning problems, attention, and emotional difficulties can have similar symptoms, co-occur, or reciprocally influence each other. For example, children with learning difficulties can become emotionally distraught and thus have concentration difficulties, begin to exhibit behavior problems, or both. Children with ADD or ADHD may show learning difficulties because of their attentional problems or also have learning disorder or disability (or have nothing else). In short, while diagnosis of any childhood or adult difficulty should never be made based on IQ alone (or interview, physician examination, parent report, other test etc. for that matter) the cognitive ability test can help rule out, in conjunction with other tests and sources of information, other explanations for problems, uncover co-morbid problems, and be a rich source of information when properly analyzed and care is taken to avoid relying simply on the single summary IQ score (Sattler, Dumont, & Coalson, 2016).

The WISC can be used to show discrepancies between a child's intelligence and his/her performance at school (and it is this discrepancy that school psychologists look for when using this test). In a clinical setting, learning disabilities can be diagnosed through a comparison of intelligence scores and scores on an achievement test, such as the Woodcock Johnson III or Wechsler Individual Achievement Test II. If a child's achievement is below what would be expected given their level of intellectual functioning (as derived from an IQ test such as the WISC-IV), then a learning disability may be present. Other psychologists and researchers believe that the WISC can be used to understand the complexities of the human mind by examining each subtest and can, indeed, help in diagnosing learning disabilities.

Subsequently, the WISC can be used as part of an assessment battery to identify intellectual giftedness, learning difficulties, and cognitive strengths and weaknesses. When combined with other measures such as the Adaptive Behavior Assessment System–II (ABAS–II; Harrison & Oakland, 2003) and the Children's Memory Scale (CMS; Cohen, 1997) its clinical utility can be enhanced. Combinations such as these provide information on cognitive and adaptive functioning, both of which are required for the proper diagnosis of learning difficulties and learning and memory functioning resulting in a richer picture of a child's cognitive functioning.

The WISC–V is linked with the Kaufman Test of Educational Achievement–Third Edition (KTEA–3; Kaufman & Kaufman, 2014) and the Wechsler Individual Achievement Test-III (WIAT–III; Pearson, 2009), a measure of academic achievement. This linkage provides information on both cognitive ability and academic achievement in children. Tests of intellectual functioning are used extensively in school settings to evaluate specific cognitive deficits that may contribute to low academic achievement, and to predict future academic achievement. Using the WISC–V in such a manner provides information for educational intervention purposes, such as interventions that address learning difficulties and cognitive deficits.

The WISC–V can also be used to assess a child's cognitive development, with respect to the child's chronological age. Using such comparisons with other sources of data, the WISC can contribute information concerning a child's developmental and psychological well-being. Very high or very low scores may suggest contributing factors for adjustment difficulties in social contexts that present problems in accepting such developmental diversity (or that cannot accommodate more than a certain level of high cognitive functioning.)

Translations

WISC has been translated or adapted to many languages, and norms have been established for a number of countries, including Spanish, Portuguese (Brazil and Portugal), Arabic, Norwegian, Swedish, Finnish, Czech, Croatian, French (France and Canada), German (Germany, Austria and Switzerland), English (United States, Canada, United Kingdom, Australia), Welsh, Dutch, Japanese, Chinese (Hong Kong), Korean (South Korea), Greek, Romanian, Slovenian and Italian. Separate norms are established with each translation. (Norway uses the Swedish norms). India uses the Malin's Intelligence Scale for Children (MISIC), an adaptation of WISC. The fourth edition of WISC was adapted and standardized for India in 2012. The Japanese versions of the WISC-IV was developed by Japanese psychologists Kazuhiko Ueno, Kazuhiro Fujita, Hisao Maekawa, Toshinori Ishikuma, Hitoshi Dairoku, and Osamu Matsuda.

Luria-Nebraska Neuropsychological Battery

The Luria-Nebraska Neuropsychological Battery (LNNB) is a standardized test that identifies neuropsychological deficiencies by measuring functioning on fourteen scales. It evaluates learning, experience, and cognitive skills. The test was created by Charles Golden in 1981 and based on previous work by Alexander Luria that emphasizes a qualitative instead of quantitative approach. The original, adult version is for use with ages fifteen and over, while the Luria-Nebraska Neuropsychological Battery for Children (LNNB-C) can be used with ages eight to twelve; both tests take two to three hours to administer. The LNNB has 269 items divided among fourteen scales, which are motor, rhythm, tactile, visual, receptive speech, expressive speech, writing, reading, arithmetic, memory, intellectual processes, pathognomonic, left hemisphere, and right hemisphere. The test is graded on scales that are correlated to regions of the brain to help identify which region may be damaged.The Luria-Nebraska has been found to be reliable and valid; it is comparable in this sense to other neuropsychological tests in its ability to differentiate between brain damage and mental illness. The test is used to diagnose and determine the nature of cognitive impairment, including the location of the brain damage, to understand the patient's brain structure and abilities, to pinpoint causes of behavior, and to help plan treatment.

History

The purpose of early neuropsychological tests was simply to determine whether or not a person had a brain injury or brain damage. Although they can still perform this function, modern brain imaging has made it less necessary. Instead, these tests now serve to describe the injury, including its location and the degree of impairment. The ability to perform these functions began with Alexander Luria's original qualitative procedures. The work of this Russian neuropsychologist would become the basis for the theory behind the Luria-Nebraska Neuropsychological Battery. Compared to traditional tests, these procedures were better at determining patients' strengths and weaknesses; however, their standardization was prevented by their lack of fixed content and the fact they had no definite method of scoring or accuracy determination.

Luria's original method, released in 1966, was revised by Christensen in 1975 to describe the procedure more in-depth. This revision made possible a version that combined the qualitative and quantitative aspects of the procedures. In 1977 Charles Golden presented the Luria-South Dakota, a new version of the battery created at the University of South Dakota that combined Luria and Christensen's works. To develop this version and ensure it covered everything from both Luria and Christensen, Golden first created an exam that took approximately 18 hours to administer and contained nearly 2,000 procedures. From this base items were selectively removed if they were found to lack reliability or validity, be repetitive, be too long, or fail to accurately discriminate a brain injury. Existing interest in Luria's work made this battery instantly popular, and as it was circulated, demand and research only grew. Western Psychological Services created the current revision, the Luria-Nebraska Neuropsychological Battery. It was published in 1980 in the Journal of Consulting and Clinical Psychology and the International Journal of Neuroscience.

The Luria-Nebraska has been the subject of some debate that has split the neuropsychology field. It faced criticism for its combination of quantitative and qualitative methods, the wide variety of its fourteen scales, and the possibility that it did not include enough different neuropsychological skills or did not distinguish brain dysfunction adequately. Large empirical studies have suggested these criticisms are largely unfounded and based on misinformation or lack of understanding of how the test is interpreted. However, these concerns resulted in a decrease in use of the battery, and some negative views of it still persist despite evidence of its reliability and validity.

Administration and Scoring

For the adult version of this standardized test, used with ages 15 and above, there are 269 items that are scored from 0 to 2. On this continuum a score of 0 represents a normal non-damaged brain and a higher score near 2 depicts brain damage. None of these items measures exactly the same thing, although each of them may have alternative ways of measuring the same behavior. These 269 items are divided among fourteen scales, which are motor, rhythm, tactile, visual, receptive speech, expressive speech, writing, reading, arithmetic, memory, intellectual processes, pathognomonic, left hemisphere, and right hemisphere. The time it takes to administer the task is about 2 to 3 hours. The reason for the long length of time is the several items that need to be tested, and this is also why the test cannot be administered to very young children. By testing the limits of patients' performance, it is then able to make correlations between a normal and damaged brain. There is some discussion on the standardized interruption of the test. The children's version of the test is for 8-12 years old. This test has 149 different items that also measure on a continuum from 0 to 2. It also takes roughly 2 to 3 hours to administer and the same constructs are being measured.

Reliability and Validity

Studies have show that the LNNB is stable over time. A study has shown that the lowest test re-test reliability of the LNNB is a .77 and this is within the limitations of clinical tests. Also, studies have combined the Luria-Nebraska Battery with existing tests in psychology, speech, and education to look at the reliability of the battery. This version of the test had 33 scales and by comparing non-brain-injured control groups to brain-injured patients it was found that the test is very effective at discriminating between normal and brain-injured subjects. Studies have shown that the LNNB has yielded an 86% correct hit rate for identifying patients correctly. When looking at the left and right hemisphere scales, the test is based on the assumption that the left hemisphere is verbally dominant and composed of the motor and tactile scales that represent right-hand sensory/motor performance while the right hemisphere consists of items representing left-hand sensory/ motor performance. When looking at lateralization reports of the test, it yields an average hit rate of 78% on comparison of left and right scales with the highest hit rate being 92%. Also, when looking at localization of chronic hospitalized patients with injuries in the frontal, sensorimotor, temporal, and parietal-occipital areas, the test was 88% effective in localizing the brain damage, but the limit to this report was a small sample size of 60 patients.

Applications

Applications of the LNNB are generally seen in clinical settings such as hospitals, counseling, and research. Research has shown its shorter testing time, cost to administer, and effectiveness allow for cost-efficient and reliable results. The LNNB has been used to determine brain functions after trauma to the brain occurs and to pin-point what mental disorder is present. Through its development and revision, the battery has also been shown to aid in presenting other underlying ailments that could not be detected by other sources. In some cases the LNNB has been seen to show sensitivity to more subtle abnormalities in brain functioning, which researchers did not expect. Due to its ability to target the damage of the brain, if any, as well as the mental disorder, the LNNB is useful in finding treatment options, assessing research, and aiding in choosing research participants. Disorders that the LNNB has been seen to detect include schizophrenia, borderline personality, post-traumatic stress disorder, brain trauma, epilepsy tumor, metabolic problems, and degenerative disorders.

Rey–Osterrieth Complex Figure

The Rey–Osterrieth complex figure test (ROCF) is a neuropsychological assessment in which examinees are asked to reproduce a complicated line drawing, first by copying it freehand (recognition), and then drawing from memory (recall). Many different cognitive abilities are needed for a correct performance, and the test therefore permits the evaluation of different functions, such as visuospatial abilities, memory, attention, planning, and working memory (executive functions). First proposed by Swiss psychologist André Rey in 1941 and further standardized by Paul-Alexandre Osterrieth in 1944, it is frequently used to further explain any secondary effect of brain injury in neurological patients, to test for the presence of dementia, or to study the degree of cognitive development in children.

Conditions

Three *conditions* are most commonly used in the ROCF.

- Copy: In the Copy condition, the examinee is given a piece of paper and a pencil, and the stimulus figure is placed in front of them. They reproduce the figure to the best of their ability. The test is not timed, but the length of time needed to copy the figure is observed. Some administrators use a series of colored pencils, in order to preserve a record of the order in which design elements were reproduced. However, because of concerns that the use of color changes the nature of the test and makes it easier for the subject to remember the figure, the current test manual suggests that this should not be done. Instead, the evaluator should take notes on the process the examinee uses. Once the copy is complete, the stimulus figure and the examinee's copy are removed from view.
- Immediate recall: After a short delay, the examinee is asked to reproduce the figure from memory.
- Delayed recall: After a longer delay (20–30 minutes), the examinee may again be asked to draw the figure from memory. Examinees are not told beforehand that they will be asked to draw the figure from memory; the Immediate and Delayed Recall conditions are therefore tests of incidental memory. Each copy is scored for the accurate reproduction and placement of 18 specific design elements. Additionally, the test administrator can note their qualitative observations regarding the examinee's approach to the task and the effectiveness of any apparent strategy use.

History

André Rey

During the 1940s, psychologists throughout the world were facing difficulty in eliciting the specific deficits exhibited by individuals (both adults and children) who had experienced traumatic brain injury. In 1941, the Swiss psychologist André Rey was working at the University of Geneva and recognized the necessity of differentiating between "*primary effects, which are a direct result of the insult to the head, and the secondary effects, which develop out of subjective reactions determined by the loss of awareness from the physical impairments*". One of the many forms of assessment that Rey detailed in his 1941 report was a complex figure composed of many different shapes, line segments, and other elements.

Paul-Alexandre Osterrieth

In 1944, Paul-Alexandre Osterrieth, who had worked as a research assistant under André Rey at the University of Geneva, utilized the figure Rey had developed in his work with young children. Osterrieth proposed to subcategorize the figure into 18 elements and score them based on their presence, completeness, and correct placement. This 18-point scoring system is still commonly used today in evaluating an examinee's performance on the ROCF test.

Unlike Rey, Osterrieth was primarily interested in the measure as an assessment of whether or not children had developed the concept of a holistic or gestalt principle by various ages, as manifested by the way they approached the figure drawing. Based on his experimentation, Osterrieth recognized several important trends. Specifically, he noticed that the principle of *gestalt* seems to stabilize around the age of nine years in children. Also, he noted several different approaches that the children used in constructing the figure, each of which appears to be roughly correlated with a particular age group:

- Primitive forms that show "distorted integration" and "confabulations" in their drawings.
- Awareness of specific concepts while still remaining unaware of the overall figure.
- Complete awareness of the overall figure.

Additionally, Osterrieth noticed that strategy was a good predictor of the child's performance on all three of the various tasks.

Edith Meyer Taylor

In 1959 American (German immigrant) child psychologist Edith Meyer Taylor, who had been a student of Arnold Gesell and Jean Piaget, gave more elaborate descriptions on the 18-point scoring system initially proposed by Osterrieth. She had also briefly worked with Rey in Geneva and credited him with inspiring her to pursue this particular aspect of psychology.

Laughlin B. Taylor

In 1969, Laughlin B. Taylor developed a second complex figure that is comparable to Rey's and can be therefore used to eliminate the memory effect in a second evaluation. Explicit scoring criteria based on the Taylor-Osterrieth method have been developed for both the Rey-Osterrieth and Taylor Complex Figure Tests, although the Taylor figure has been found to be more easily remembered than the Rey-Osterrieth, calling into question their interchangeability.

References

- Dawson M, Gernsbacher MA, Mottron L (2011). "The level and nature of autistic intelligence II: What about Asperger Syndrome?". PLoS ONE. 6: 657–62. PMC 3182210 . PMID 21991394. doi:10.1371/journal.

pone.0025372. Lay summary – ScienceDaily (2011-09-02)

- Carlson, Neil R. (2010). Psychology: The Science of Behaviour. New Jersey, United States: Pearson Education Inc. pp. 599–604. ISBN 978-0-205-64524-4
- Flynn, James R. (March 1987). "Massive IQ Gains in 14 Nations: What IQ Tests Really Measure" (PDF). Psychological Bulletin. 101 (2): 171–191. doi:10.1037/0033-2909.101.2.171. Retrieved 13 May 2013
- O'Boyle Jr., E. H.; Humphrey, R. H.; Pollack, J. M.; Hawver, T. H.; Story, P. A. (2011). "The relation between emotional intelligence and job performance : A meta-analysis". Journal of Organizational Behavior. doi:10.1002/job
- Domino, George; Domino, Marla L. (2006-04-24). Psychological Testing: An Introduction. Cambridge University Press. ISBN 9781139455145
- Hoffman, Jascha (December 21, 2009). "Taking Mental Snapshots to Plumb Our Inner Selves". New York Times. Retrieved 3 April 2011
- Engler, Barbara (2008). Personality theories : an introduction (8th ed.). Boston, MA: Houghton Mifflin. ISBN 9780547148342
- "Neuropsychological Assessment". New York Assessment. December 2015. Retrieved February 2016. Check date values in: |access-date= (help)
- Vinchur, Andrew J.; Schippmann, Jeffery S.; S., Fred; Switzer, III; Roth, Philip L. "A meta-analytic review of predictors of job performance for salespeople.". Journal of Applied Psychology. 83 (4): 586–597. doi:10.1037/0021-9010.83.4.586
- Tapu, C.S. (2001). Hypostatic personality: psychopathology of doing and being made. Premier. pp. 28–31. ISBN 9738030595
- "Neuropsychological and Psychoeducational Testing for Children and Adults". New York Assessment. December 2015. Retrieved February 2016. Check date values in: |access-date= (help)
- Murphy, Kevin R.; Balzer, William K. "Systematic distortions in memory-based behavior ratings and performance evaluations: Consequences for rating accuracy.". Journal of Applied Psychology. 71 (1): 39–44. doi:10.1037/0021-9010.71.1.39
- Phares, E.J.; Chaplin, W.F. (1997). Introduction to personality (Fourth ed.). New York: Longman. pp. 8–9. ISBN 0-673-99456-2
- "THE HOUSTON CONFERENCE ON SPECIALTY EDUCATION AND TRAINING IN CLINICAL NEUROPSYCHOLOGY" (PDF). American Academy of Clinical Neuropsychology. September 1997. Retrieved February 2016. Check date values in: |access-date= (help)
- Stauffer, Joseph M.; Buckley, M. Ronald. "The Existence and Nature of Racial Bias in Supervisory Ratings.". Journal of Applied Psychology. 90 (3): 586–591. PMID 15910152. doi:10.1037/0021-9010.90.3.586
- Cartwright, Desmond (1979). Theories and Models of Personality (I ed.). Debuque, Iowa: Wm. C. Brown Company Publishers. p. 178. ISBN 0-697-06624-X
- "Wechsler Adult Intelligence Scale--Revised". LIST OF TESTS Available from the CPS Testing Library. Center for Psychological Studies at Nova Southeastern University. Retrieved 2009-03-31

5

Understanding Human Psychophysiological Activities

To study human psychophysiological activities, invasive and non-invasive techniques are used. Since non-invasive technologies were invented later, invasive techniques such as ablation, lesions, and knife cuts were used. The methods include electroencephalogram, computerized transaxial tomography, positron emission tomography, magnetic resonance imaging, magnetoencephalography and event-related potential. The section closely examines the key concepts of human psychophysiological activity to provide an extensive understanding of the subject.

Non-invasive Techniques

Our present understanding of the functions performed by the nervous system heavily depends upon the imaging techniques. This has literally made it possible to look into a function brain. Beginning with X-rays, which is not used for brain research, the non-invasive techniques available now, includes EEG, CT Scan, MRI (magnetic resonance imaging), PET (positron emission tomography), SPECT (single photon emission computerized tomography), and MEG (magnetoencephalography).

Minimally Invasive Procedures

Minimally invasive procedures (also known as minimally invasive surgeries) have been enabled by the advance of various medical technologies. Surgery by definition is invasive and many operations requiring incisions of some size are referred to as open surgery. Incisions made can sometimes leave large wounds that are painful and take a long time to heal. Minimally invasive surgery refers to surgical techniques that limit the size of incisions needed and so lessens wound healing time, associated pain and risk of infection. An endovascular aneurysm repair as an example of minimally invasive surgery is much less invasive in that it involves much smaller incisions, than the corresponding open surgery procedure of open aortic surgery. This minimally invasive surgery became the most common method of repairing abdominal aortic aneurysms in 2003 in the United States.

The front-runners of minimally invasive procedures were interventional radiologists. By the use of imaging techniques, interventional instruments could be directed throughout the body by the radiologists by way of catheters instead of large incisions needed in traditional surgery. So that many conditions once requiring surgery can now be treated non-surgically.

Diagnostic techniques that do not involve the puncturing of the skin or incision, or the introduction into the body of foreign objects or materials are known as *non-invasive* procedures. There are also several treatment procedures that are classed as non-invasive. A major example of a non-invasive alternative treatment to surgery is radiation therapy also called radiotherapy.

Medical Uses

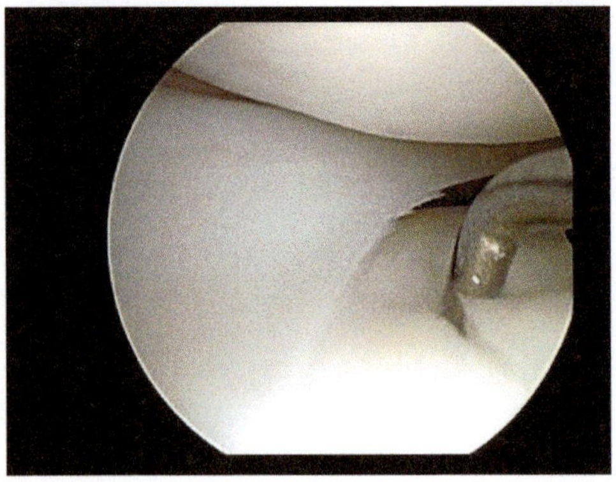

Arthroscopic surgery.

Minimally invasive procedures were pioneered by interventional radiologists who had first introduced angioplasty and the catheter-delivered stent. Many other minimally invasive procedures have followed where images of all parts of the body can be obtained and used to direct interventional instruments by way of catheters (needles and fine tubes). So that many conditions once requiring open surgery can now be treated non-surgically. A minimally invasive procedure typically involves the use of arthroscopic (for joints and the spine) or laparoscopic devices and remote-control manipulation of instruments with indirect observation of the surgical field through an endoscope or large scale display panel, and is carried out through the skin or through a body cavity or anatomical opening. Interventional radiology now offers many techniques that avoid the need for surgery.

By use of a MIP, a patient may require only a band-aid on the incision, rather than multiple stitches or staples to close a large incision. This usually results in less infection, a quicker recovery time and shorter hospital stays, or allow outpatient treatment. However, the safety and effectiveness of each procedure must be demonstrated with randomized controlled trials. The term was coined by John EA Wickham in 1984, who wrote of it in *British Medical Journal* in 1987. A minimally invasive procedure is distinct from a non-invasive procedure, such as external imaging instead of exploratory surgery. When there is minimal damage of biological tissues at the point of entrance of instrument(s), the procedure is called minimally invasive.

Specific Procedures

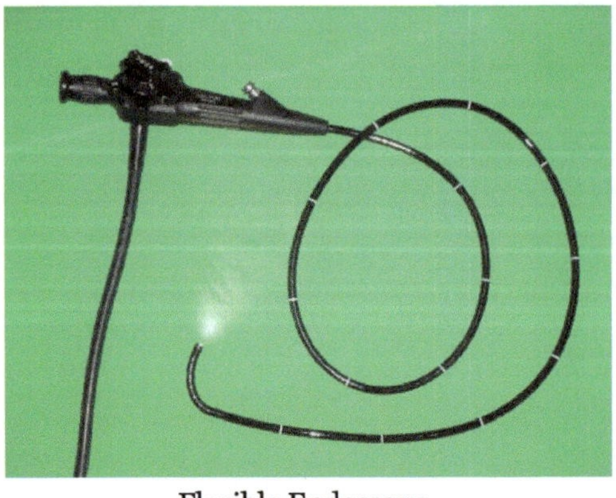

Flexible Endoscope.

Many medical procedures are called minimally invasive; those that involve small incisions through which an endoscope is inserted, end in the suffix *-oscopy*, such as endoscopy, laparoscopy, arthroscopy. Other examples of minimally invasive procedures include the use of hypodermic injection, and air-pressure injection, subdermal implants, refractive surgery, percutaneous surgery, cryosurgery, microsurgery, keyhole surgery, endovascular surgery using interventional radiology (such as angioplasty), coronary catheterization, permanent placement of spinal and brain electrodes, stereotactic surgery, the Nuss procedure, radioactivity-based medical imaging methods, such as gamma camera, positron emission tomography and SPECT (single photon emission tomography). Related procedures are image-guided surgery,and robot-assisted surgery.

Benefits

Minimally invasive surgery should have less operative trauma, other complications and adverse effects than an equivalent open surgery. It may be more or less expensive (for dental implants, a minimally invasive method reduces the cost of installed implants and shortens the implant-prosthetic rehabilitation time with 4–6 months). Operative time is longer, but hospitalization time is shorter. It causes less pain and scarring, speeds recovery, and reduces the incidence of post-surgical complications, such as adhesions and wound dehiscence (rupture). Some studies have compared heart surgery. However, minimally invasive surgery is not necessarily minor surgery that only requires local anesthesia. In fact, most of these procedures still require general anesthesia to be administered beforehand.

Risks

Risks and complications of minimally invasive procedures are the same as for any other surgical operation and include:

- Anesthesia or medication reactions
- Bleeding
- Infection
- Adhesions
- Internal organ injury
- Blood vessel injury
- Vein or lung blood clotting
- Breathing problems
- Death

There may be an increased risk of hypothermia and peritoneal trauma due to increased exposure to cold, dry gases during insufflation. The use of surgical humidification therapy, which is the use of heated and humidified CO_2 for insufflation, may reduce this risk.

Equipment

Special medical equipment may be used, such as fiber optic cables, miniature video cameras and special surgical instruments handled via tubes inserted into the body through small openings in its surface. The images of the interior of the body are transmitted to an external video monitor and the surgeon has the possibility of making a diagnosis, visually identifying internal features and acting surgically on them.

Invasive Procedures

Sometimes the use of non-invasive methods is not an option, so that the next level of minimally invasive techniques are looked to. These include the use of hypodermic injection (using the syringe), an endoscope, percutaneous surgery which involves needle puncture of the skin, laparoscopic surgery commonly called *keyhole surgery*, a coronary catheter, angioplasty and stereotactic surgery.

Open Surgery

"Open surgery" is any surgical procedure, where the incision made is enough to allow the surgery to take place. With tissues and structures exposed to the air, the procedure can be performed either with the unaided vision of the surgeon or with the use of loupes or microscopes. Some examples of open surgery used, are for herniated disc commonly called a "slipped disc", and most types of cardiac surgery and neurosurgery. These techniques have accelerated the healing process of otherwise larger wounds and so also have minimalised the pain associated with large wound healing. Also the more precise methods used, mean that damage to surrounding healthy tissues is greatly reduced.

Non-invasive Procedure

A medical procedure is defined as *non-invasive* when no break in the skin is created and there is no contact with the mucosa, or skin break, or internal body cavity beyond a natural or artificial body orifice. For example, deep palpation and percussion are non-invasive but a rectal examination is invasive. Likewise, examination of the ear-drum or inside the nose or a wound dressing change all fall outside the definition of *non-invasive procedure*. There are many non-invasive procedures, ranging from simple observation, to specialised forms of surgery, such as radiosurgery. Extracorporeal shock wave lithotripsy is a non-invasive treatment of stones in the kidney,gallbladder or liver, using an acoustic pulse. For centuries, physicians have employed many simple non-invasive methods based on physical parameters in order to assess body function in health and disease (physical examination and inspection), such as pulse-taking, the auscultation of heart sounds and lung sounds (using the stethoscope), temperature examination (using thermometers), respiratory examination, peripheral vascular examination, oral examination, abdominal examination, external percussion and palpation, blood pressure measurement (using the sphygmomanometer), change in body volumes (using plethysmograph), audiometry, eye examination, and many others.

Diagnostic Images

- Bioluminescence imaging
- Dermatoscopy
- Diffuse optical tomography

- Gamma camera
- Computed Tomography
- Infrared imaging of the body
- Magnetic resonance elastography
- Magnetic resonance imaging, using external magnetic fields
- Magnetic resonance spectroscopy
- Optical coherence tomography
- Posturography
- Radiography, fluoroscopy and computed tomography
- Ultrasonography and echocardiography

Diagnostic Signals

- Electrocardiography (EKG)
- Electroencephalography (EEG)
- Electromyography (EMG)
- Photoplethysmograph(PPG)
- Electrical impedance tomography (EIT)
- Electroneuronography (ENoG)
- Electroretinography (ERG)
- Electronystagmography (ENG)
- Magnetoencephalography (MEG)
- Evoked potentials
- Impedance phlebography
- Nuclear magnetic resonance spectroscopy

Therapy

In terms of therapy these include Radiation therapy, Brachytherapy, Lithotripsy, Defibrillation, Biofeedback, VPAP, BIPAP, Neurally Adjusted Ventilatory Assist, Biphasic Cuirass Ventilation, and Therapeutic ultrasound

Electroencephalogram (EEG)

Although Richard Caton recorded the electrical activity from the brain for the first time in 1875, Hans Berger was the first to record brainwaves from human beings in 1924. EEG recording is done by placing electrodes at designated places on the scalp or using cap fitted with electrodes. Each electrode is connected to an input of a differential amplifier and a common electrode is connected to the other input of each amplifier. Thus, the voltage between the active electrode and the reference gets amplified.

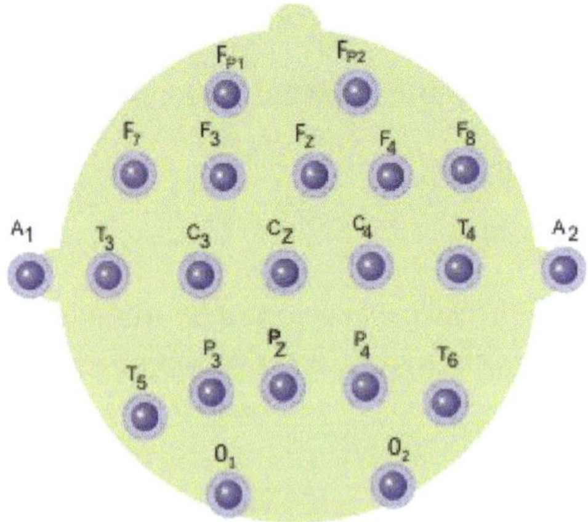

Sites of electrode placement.

Four types of brain waves are recorded from the scalp of normal human beings using EEG— a lpha waves (8-13 Hz), beta waves (>13 Hz), theta waves (4-7 Hz), and delta waves (<4 Hz). Each of these waves appears as a single line representing the summated electrical field resulting from the activity of the neurons. These records can be unipolar or bipolar in nature. When an electrode is placed on the scalp and another on some other part of the body the obtained potential differences are called unipolar records whereas potential fluctuations between two cortical electrodes are termed as bipolar records.

With a rate of 8-12 cycles per second alpha waves have the highest amplitude with an average of 50 microvolts. It is observed in the occipital, frontal and parietal regions of the cortex and cannot occur without the connection of RAS . It is prominent in darkness and/ or when eyes are closed and abolished with visual stimulation or mental concentration. Beta waves are usually found in parietal and frontal regions. It ranges between 18 and 60 (maximum) cycles per second with amplitude varying between 5-10 microvolts. Human scalp emits two types of beta waves- ß I and ß II. The frequency of ß I is twice that of a waves. While ß I disappears during mental activity ß II is apparent during stress and intense activation of CNS . Theta waves are primarily found in the parietal and temporal regions and are prominently observed in children between the ages of 2-5 years. Its rate ranges between 4-8 cycles per second with amplitude of 10 microvolts. With a rate of minimum 0.5-3.5 cycles per second and amplitude that varies between 20-200 microvolts, delta waves are rarely found in normal adults during working hours. It is observed during deep sleep, organic brain diseases, hypoxia and hypoglycemia. It is understood as a byproduct of separation of the cortex and RAS .

The table given below illustrates a comparative review of the four brain waves.

	Alpha waves	**Beta waves**	**Theta waves**	**Delta waves**
Frequency	8-13 Hz	14-30 Hz	4-7Hz	5-3.5 Hz
Amplitude	20-60 μV	2-20 μV	20-100μV	20-200μV
Easily produced when	Relaxed sitting position with closed eyes	During mental thought and activity	More common in children than adults	During deep sleep in most people

EEG has diagnostic application for epileptic cases. Before being replaced by CT scans and MRI , it was also used as first-line diagnosis for tumors and other brain disorders. It is useful as a n on-invasive technique and indicates the active brain area, but cannot precisely indicate where the signal came from. The EEG records electrical activities only from the cortical surface close to the skull and hence reflects the functional state of about 35% of the cortex only. The above description is of the normal EEG pattern. Minor differences have been observed in the EEG records of 5-7% of normal population but they have no clinical significance. EEG is also age-dependent; younger the child slower the activities. Elderly people have slower pattern indicating that with the increase in age the EEG pattern becomes slower.

Positron Emission Tomography (PET)

Positron Emission Tomography (PET) was developed by Michael Phelps. It depends on the introduction of tracers into the body by either injection or inhalation. PET shows images of the amount and localization of these radioactive molecules. It could be neurotransmitters, drugs, tracers for blood flow or glucose. As a matter of fact, it produces images of normal as well as diseased living biological processes in the body. The major application of PET is in the assessment of metabolic activities and neurotransmitters.

The PET of brain records the metabolism of radioactively labeled glucose (such as fluorodeoxyglucose) in different regions of the brain. As you know, glucose is the only source of energy that the brain uses. Since fluorine 18 has a half-life of about 17 minutes, it is quickly transported to the brain and positrons are emitted. The collision of these positrons with electrons generates gamma rays. A computer maps these rays and produces images of the brain. Given below are the PET images during visual stimulation.

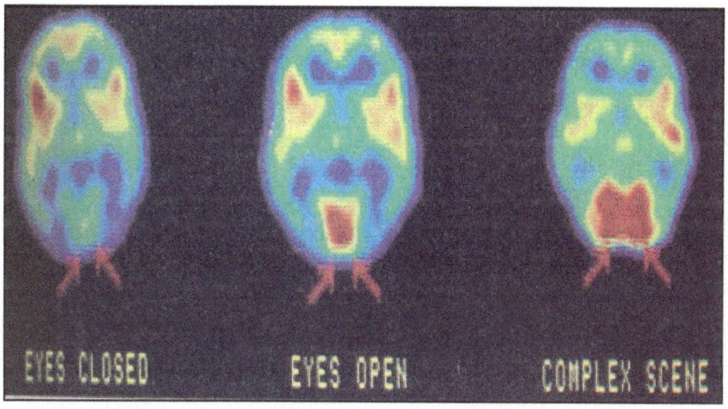

PET of visual stimulation (Source: UCLA School of Medicine).

A large number of published studies have used PET images and reported brain-behaviour association for whole range of activities.

Some examples of use of PET in behavioral studies are elaborated here.

Martin et al. (1996) conducted a study to explore the role of motor region of the neo cortex in observing, remembering and imagining movements. PET images were used to identify brain regions active while various words were silently rehearsed. An increase in blood flow was observed in the hand region of motor cortex when subjects named tools. The researchers concluded that a connection exist between the hand region of motor cortex and knowledge about the tools and its usage.

Frey et al. (2000) performed PET study where the participants heard sound of violent car crash or familiar abstract sounds generated from an electronic keyboard. In another study novel abstract visual designs were presented to the participants and they had to memorize or just view them. Increased activation was observed in area 13 as a response to the unpleasant auditory stimuli. This area is connected to amygdale and hypothalamus. On the other hand, new visual information activated area 11. This has medial temporal cortical connections. A generalized prediction based on the study was that those with damage to area 13 would show weak response to threatening stimuli.

Maguire et al. (1997) performed PET scan for imaging hippocampus of the London taxi drivers. The taxi drivers were supposed to describe the route between two points in greater London and recall landmark buildings not in London and not visited. PET scan was performed while this process was on. Occipitotemporal areas, medial parital cortex, posterior cingulate cortex, parahippocampal gyrus and right hippocampus were activated during this spatial test. These drivers were also supposed to recall plot of a film and the result indicated that the non-spatial task did not activate the right hippocampus. A very important finding of this study was that the right posterior hippocampus increased in size as a function of years spent as a taxi driver. This shows the effect of topographic memory on human brain.

Drevets et al. (1997) studied mood disorder using PET. Cerebral blood flow of unmedicated unipolar, bipola and control subjects was examined using PET. 12% decrease in cerebral blood flow was recorded in the medial frontal region below the anterior region of the corpus callosum. The largest difference was observed in control and depressive groups.

PET scans have also been used for diagnosis of Alzheimer's and Parkinson's disease. It has emerged that certain regions of the brain show reduced blood flow (and hence metabolism) in the early stage of the disease. This pattern can be recorded years before the patient is diagnosed by a physician. The advantage of PET is that it provides visual image analogous to the brain anatomy and is helpful for functional and biochemical studies. It can also be useful to identify specific receptors associated with certain neurotransmitters. However, it exposes you to low levels of radioactivity. Also, it is not able to trail changes faster than 30 seconds. In addition, it has poor resolution as compared to MRI .

Magnetic Resonance Imaging

Magnetic resonance imaging (MRI) is a medical imaging technique used in radiology to form pictures of the anatomy and the physiological processes of the body in both health and disease. MRI scanners use strong magnetic fields, radio waves, and field gradients to generate images of the organs in the body.

MRI does *not* involve x-rays, which distinguishes it from computed tomography (CT or CAT). While the hazards of x-rays are now well-controlled in most medical contexts, MRI can still be seen as superior to CT in this regard. MRI can often yield different diagnostic information compared with CT. There can be risks and discomfort associated with MRI scans. Compared with CT, MRI scans typically take far more time, are louder, and usually require that the subject go into a narrow, confined tube. In addition, people with some medical implants or other non-removable metal inside the body may be unable to safely undergo an MRI examination.

MRI is based upon the science of nuclear magnetic resonance (NMR). Certain atomic nuclei can absorb and emit radio frequency energy when placed in an external magnetic field. In clinical and research MRI, hydrogen atoms are most-often used to generate a detectable radio-frequency signal that is received by antennas in close proximity to the anatomy being examined. Hydrogen atoms exist naturally in people and other biological organisms in abundance, particularly in water and fat. For this reason, most MRI scans essentially map the location of water and fat in the body. Pulses of radio waves excite the nuclear spin energy transition, and magnetic field gradients localize the signal in space. By varying the parameters of the pulse sequence, different contrasts can be generated between tissues based on the relaxation properties of the hydrogen atoms therein. Since its early development in the 1970s and 1980s, MRI has proven to be a highly versatile imaging technique. While MRI is most prominently used in diagnostic medicine and biomedical research, it can also be used to form images of non-living objects. MRI scans are capable of producing a variety of chemical and physical data, in addition to detailed spatial images.

MRI is widely used in hospitals and clinics for medical diagnosis, staging of disease and follow-up without exposing the body to ionizing radiation.

Medical Uses

MRI has a wide range of applications in medical diagnosis and over 25,000 scanners are estimated to be in use worldwide. MRI affects diagnosis and treatment in many specialties although the effect on improved health outcomes is uncertain. Since MRI does not use any ionizing radiation, its use is generally favored in preference to CT when either modality could yield the same information. (In certain cases, MRI is not preferred as it can be more expensive, time-consuming, and claustrophobia-exacerbating).

MRI is in general a safe technique, although injuries can occur as a result of failed safety procedures or human error. Contraindications to MRI include most cochlear implants and cardiac pacemakers, shrapnel and metallic foreign bodies in the eyes. The safety of MRI during the first trimester of pregnancy is uncertain, but it may be preferable to other options. The sustained increase in demand for MRI within the healthcare industry has led to concerns about cost effectiveness and overdiagnosis.

Neuroimaging

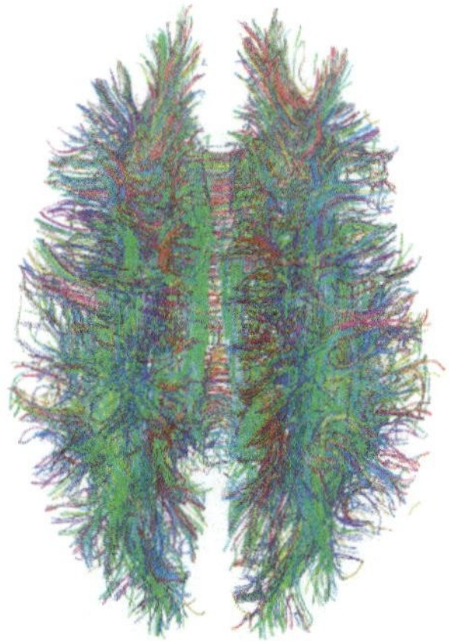

MRI image of white matter tracts.

MRI is the investigative tool of choice for neurological cancers, as it has better resolution than CT and offers better visualization of the posterior fossa. The contrast provided between grey and white matter makes it the best choice for many conditions of the central nervous system, including demyelinating diseases, dementia, cerebrovascular disease, infectious diseases and epilepsy. Since many images are taken milliseconds apart, it shows how the brain responds to different stimuli; researchers can then study both the functional and structural brain abnormalities in psychological disorders. MRI is also used in mri-guided stereotactic surgery and radiosurgery for treatment of intracranial tumors, arteriovenous malformations and other surgically treatable conditions using a device known as the N-localizer.

Cardiovascular

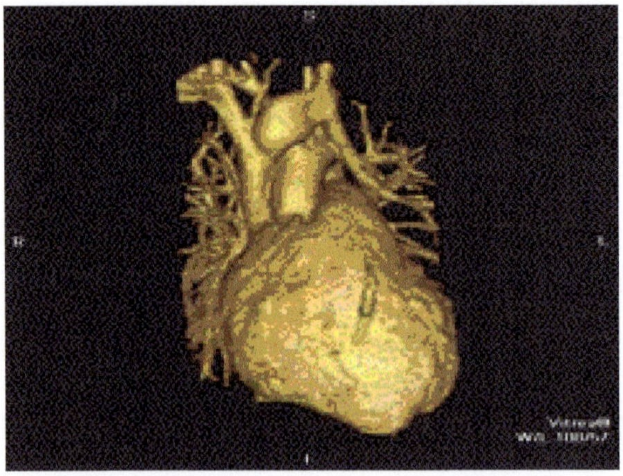

MR angiogram in congenital heart disease.

Cardiac MRI is complementary to other imaging techniques, such as echocardiography, cardiac CT and nuclear medicine. Its applications include assessment of myocardial ischemia and viability, cardiomyopathies, myocarditis, iron overload, vascular diseases and congenital heart disease.

Musculoskeletal

Applications in the musculoskeletal system includes spinal imaging, assessment of joint disease and soft tissue tumors.

Liver and Gastrointestinal Imaging MRI

Hepatobiliary MR is used to detect and characterize lesions of the liver, pancreas and bile ducts. Focal or diffuse disorders of the liver may be evaluated using diffusion-weighted, opposed-phase imaging and dynamic contrast enhancement sequences. Extracellular contrast agents are widely used in liver MRI and newer hepatobiliary contrast agents also provide the opportunity to perform functional biliary imaging. Anatomical imaging of the bile ducts is achieved by using a heavily T2-weighted sequence in magnetic resonance cholangiopancreatography (MRCP). Functional imaging of the pancreas is performed following administration of secretin. MR enterography provides non-invasive assessment of inflammatory bowel disease and small bowel tumors. MR-colonography can play a role in the detection of large polyps in patients at increased risk of colorectal cancer.

Functional MRI

Functional MRI (fMRI) is used to understand how different parts of the brain respond to external stimuli or passive activity in a resting state. Blood oxygenation level dependent (BOLD) fMRI measures the hemodynamic response to transient neural activity resulting from a change in the ratio of oxyhemoglobin and deoxyhemoglobin. Researchers use statistical methods to construct a 3D parametric map of the brain which indicates the regions of the cortex that demonstrate a significant change in activity in response to the task. fMRI has applications in behavioral and cognitive research, and in planning neurosurgery of eloquent brain areas.

Oncology

MRI is the investigation of choice in the preoperative staging of rectal and prostate cancer, and has a role in the diagnosis, staging, and follow-up of other tumors.

Phase Contrast MRI

Phase Contrast MRI (PC-MRI) is used to measure flow velocities in the body. It is mainly used to measure blood flow in the heart and throughout the body. PC-MRI can be considered a method of Magnetic Resonance Velocimetry. Since modern PC-MRI is typically time-resolved, it can also be referred to as 4D imaging (three spatial dimensions plus time).

Safety

Structure and Certification

In an effort to standardize the roles and responsibilities of MRI professionals, an international consensus document, written and endorsed by major MRI and medical physics professional societies from around the globe, has been formally published. The document outlines specific responsibilities for the following positions:

- *MR Medical Director / Research Director (MRMD)* - This individual is the supervising physician who has oversight responsibility for the safe utilization of MRI services.
- *MR Safety Officer (MRSO)* - Roughly analogous to a radiation safety officer, the MRSO acts on behalf of, and on the instruction of, the MRMD to execute safety procedures and practices at the point of care.
- *MR Safety Expert (MRSE)* - This individual serves in a consulting role to both the MRMD and MRSO, assisting in the investigation of safety questions that may include the need for extrapolation, interpolation, or quantification to approximate the risk of a specific study.

The American Board of Magnetic Resonance Safety (ABMRS) provides testing and board certification for each of the three positions, MRMD, MRSO, and MRSE. As most MRI accidents and injuries are directly attributable to decisions at the point of care, testing and certification of MRI professionals seeks to reduce the rates of MRI accidents and improve patient safety through the establishment of safety competency levels for MRI professionals.

Implants

The MRI environment may cause harm in patients with MR-Unsafe devices such as cochlear implants, aneurysm clips, and many permanent pacemakers. In November 1992, a patient with an undisclosed cerebral aneurysm clip reportedly died shortly after an MRI exam. Several deaths have been reported in patients with pacemakers who have undergone MRI scanning without appropriate precautions. MR Conditional pacemakers are increasingly available for selected patients.

MR-Safe sign

MR-Conditional sign

MR-Unsafe sign

All patients are reviewed for contraindications prior to MRI scanning. Medical devices and implants are categorized as MR Safe, MR Conditional or MR Unsafe:

- *MR-Safe* – The device or implant is completely non-magnetic, non-electrically conductive, and non-RF reactive, eliminating all of the primary potential threats during an MRI procedure.
- *MR-Conditional* – A device or implant that may contain magnetic, electrically conductive or RF-reactive components that is safe for operations in proximity to the MRI, provided the conditions for safe operation are defined and observed (such as 'tested safe to 1.5 teslas' or 'safe in magnetic fields below 500 gauss in strength').
- *MR-Unsafe* – Objects that are significantly ferromagnetic and pose a clear and direct threat to persons and equipment within the magnet room.

Ferromagnetic foreign bodies such as shell fragments, or metallic implants such as surgical prostheses and ferromagnetic aneurysm clips are also potential risks. Interaction of the magnetic and radio frequency fields with such objects can lead to heating or torque of the object during an MRI.

Titanium and its alloys are safe from attraction and torque forces produced by the magnetic field, though there may be some risks associated with Lenz effect forces acting on titanium implants in sensitive areas within the subject, such as stapes implants in the inner ear.

Projectile Risk

The very high strength of the magnetic field can cause projectile effect (or "missile-effect") accidents, where ferromagnetic objects are attracted to the center of the magnet. Pennsylvania reported 27 cases of objects becoming projectiles in the MRI environment between 2004 and 2008. There have been incidents of injury and death. In one case, a 6-year-old boy died during an MRI exam, after a metal oxygen tank was pulled across the room and crushed the child's head. To reduce the risk of projectile accidents, ferromagnetic objects and devices are typically prohibited near the MRI scanner, and patients undergoing MRI examinations must remove all metallic objects, often by changing into a gown or scrubs. Some radiology departments use ferromagnetic detection devices to ensure that no ferromagnetic objects enter the scanner room.

MRI-EEG

In research settings, structural MRI or functional MRI (fMRI) can be combined with EEG (electroencephalography) under the condition that the EEG equipment is MR compatible. Although EEG equipment (electrodes, amplifiers and peripherals) are either approved for research or clinical use, the same MR Safe, MR Conditional and MR Unsafe terminology applies. With the growth of the use of MR technology, the U.S. Food & Drug Administration [FDA] recognized the need for a consensus on standards of practice, and the FDA sought out ASTM International [ASTM] to achieve them. Committee F04 of ASTM developed F2503, Standard Practice for Marking Medical Devices and Other Items for Safety in the Magnetic Resonance Environment.

Genotoxic Effects

There is no proven risk of biological harm from any aspect of an MRI scan, including very powerful static magnetic fields, gradient magnetic fields, or radio frequency waves. Some studies have suggested possible genotoxic (i.e., potentially carcinogenic) effects of MRI scanning through micronuclei induction and DNA double strand breaks in vivo and in vitro. However, others have not been able to repeat or validate the results of these studies in most, if not all, cases, and the majority of research shows no genotoxic, or otherwise harmful, effects caused by any part of MRI. A recent study confirmed that MRI at some of the most potentially risky parameters tested to date (7-tesla static magnetic field, 70 mT/m gradient magnetic field, and maximum strength radio frequency waves) did not cause any DNA damage in vitro.

Peripheral Nerve Stimulation (PNS)

The rapid switching on and off of the magnetic field gradients is capable of causing nerve stimulation. Volunteers report a twitching sensation when exposed to rapidly switched fields, particularly in their extremities. The reason the peripheral nerves are stimulated is that the changing field increases with distance from the center of the gradient coils (which more or less coincides with the center of the magnet). Although PNS was not a problem for the slow, weak gradients used in the early days of MRI, the strong, rapidly switched gradients used in techniques such as EPI, fMRI, diffusion MRI, etc. are capable of inducing PNS. American and European regulatory agencies insist that manufacturers stay below specified $d\mathbf{B}/dt$ limits ($d\mathbf{B}/dt$ is the change in magnetic field strength per unit time) or else prove that no PNS is induced for any imaging sequence. As a result of $d\mathbf{B}/dt$ limitation, commercial MRI systems cannot use the full rated power of their gradient amplifiers.

Heating Caused by Absorption of Radio Waves

Every MRI scanner has a powerful radio transmitter that generates the electromagnetic field that excites the spins. If the body absorbs the energy, heating occurs. For this reason, the transmitter rate at which energy is absorbed by the body must be limited. It has been claimed that tattoos made with iron containing dyes can lead to burns on the subject's body. Cosmetics are very unlikely to undergo heating, as well as body lotions, since the outcome of the reactions between those with the radio waves is unknown. The best option for clothes is 100% cotton. The MRI System must attend to periodic maintenance from the manufacturer, Gradients and RF transmit must attend factory specifications. In some systems there are parts responsible for the measurement of the power absorption limiter that must be periodically replaced for a new one (or re-calibrated in the factory). There are several positions strictly forbidden during measurement such as crossing arms and legs, and the patient's body cannot create loops of any kind for the RF during the measurement. Unusual patient heating cases must be reported to the appropriate regulatory agency for further investigation.

Acoustic Noise

Switching of field gradients causes a change in the Lorentz force experienced by the gradient coils, producing minute expansions and contractions of the coil itself. As the switching is typically in the audible frequency range, the resulting vibration produces loud noises (clicking, banging, or beeping). This is most marked with high-field machines and rapid-imaging techniques in which sound pressure levels can reach 120 dB(A) (equivalent to a jet engine at take-off), and therefore appropriate ear protection is essential for anyone inside the MRI scanner room during the examination.

Radio frequency in itself does not cause audible noises (at least for human beings), since modern systems are using frequencies of 8.5 MHz (0.2 T System) or above.

Cryogens

As described in Physics of Magnetic Resonance Imaging, many MRI scanners rely on cryogenic liquids to enable the superconducting capabilities of the electromagnetic coils within. Though the cryogenic liquids used are non-toxic, their physical properties present specific hazards.

An unintentional shut-down of a superconducting electromagnet, an event known as "quench", involves the rapid boiling of liquid helium from the device. If the rapidly expanding helium cannot be dissipated through an external vent, sometimes referred to as a 'quench pipe', it may be released into the scanner room where it may cause displacement of the oxygen and present a risk of asphyxiation.

Oxygen deficiency monitors are usually used as a safety precaution. Liquid helium, the most commonly used cryogen in MRI, undergoes near explosive expansion as it changes from a liquid to gaseous state. The use of an oxygen monitor is important to ensure that oxygen levels are safe for patient/physicians. Rooms built for superconducting MRI equipment should be equipped with pressure relief mechanisms and an exhaust fan, in addition to the required quench pipe.

Because a quench results in rapid loss of cryogens from the magnet, recommissioning the magnet is expensive and time-consuming. Spontaneous quenches are uncommon, but a quench may also be triggered by an equipment malfunction, an improper cryogen fill technique, contaminants inside the cryostat, or extreme magnetic or vibrational disturbances.

Pregnancy

No effects of MRI on the fetus have been demonstrated. In particular, MRI avoids the use of ionizing radiation, to which the fetus is particularly sensitive. However, as a precaution, many guidelines recommend pregnant women only undergo MRI when essential, especially during the first trimester. The concerns in pregnancy are the same as for MRI in general, but the fetus may be more sensitive to the effects—particularly to heating and to noise. The use of gadolinium-based contrast media in pregnancy is an off-label indication and may only be administered in the lowest dose required to provide essential diagnostic information.

Despite these concerns, MRI is rapidly growing in importance as a way of diagnosing and monitoring congenital defects of the fetus because it can provide more diagnostic information than ultrasound and it lacks the ionizing radiation of CT. MRI without contrast agents is the imaging mode of choice for pre-surgical, in-utero diagnosis and evaluation of fetal tumors, primarily teratomas, facilitating open fetal surgery, other fetal interventions, and planning for procedures (such as the EXIT procedure) to safely deliver and treat babies whose defects would otherwise be fatal.

Claustrophobia and Discomfort

Although painless, MRI scans can be unpleasant for those who are claustrophobic or otherwise uncomfortable with the imaging device surrounding them. Older closed bore MRI systems have a fairly long tube or tunnel. The part of the body being imaged must lie at the center of the magnet, which is at the absolute center of the tunnel. Because scan times on these older scanners may be long (occasionally up to 40 minutes for the entire procedure), people with even mild claustrophobia are sometimes unable to tolerate an MRI scan without management. Some modern scanners have larger bores (up to 70 cm) and scan times are shorter. A 1.5 T wide short bore scanner increases the examination success rate in patients with claustrophobia and substantially reduces the need for anesthesia-assisted MRI examinations even when claustrophobia is severe.

Alternative scanner designs, such as open or upright systems, can also be helpful where these are available. Though open scanners have increased in popularity, they produce inferior scan quality because they operate at lower magnetic fields than closed scanners. However, commercial 1.5-tesla open systems have recently become available, providing much better image quality than previous lower field strength open models.

Mirror glasses can be used to help create the illusion of openness. The mirrors are angled at 45 degrees, allowing the patient to look down their body and out the end of the imaging area. The appearance is of an open tube pointing upwards. Even though one can see around the glasses and the proximity of the device is very evident, this illusion is quite persuasive and relieves the claustrophobic feeling.

For babies and other young children, chemical sedation or general anesthesia are the norm, as these subjects cannot be expected or instructed to hold still during the scanning session. Children are also frequently sedated because they are frightened by the unfamiliar procedure and the loud noises. To reduce anxiety, some hospitals have specially designed child-friendly approaches that pretend the MRI machine is a spaceship or other fun experience.

Obese patients and pregnant women may find the MRI machine a tight fit. Pregnant women in the third trimester may also have difficulty lying on their backs for an hour or more without moving.

MRI Versus CT

MRI and computed tomography (CT) are complementary imaging technologies and each has advantages and limitations for particular applications. CT is more widely used than MRI in OECD countries with a mean of 132 vs. 46 exams per 1000 population performed respectively. A concern is the potential for CT to contribute to radiation-induced cancer and in 2007 it was estimated that 0.4% of current cancers in the United States were due to CTs performed in the past, and that in the future this figure may rise to 1.5–2% based on historical rates of CT usage. An Australian study found that one in every 1800 CT scans was associated with an excess cancer. An advantage of MRI is that no ionizing radiation is used and so it is recommended over CT when either approach could yield the same diagnostic information. However, although the cost of MRI has fallen, making it more competitive with CT, there are not many common imaging scenarios in which MRI can simply replace CT, although this substitution has been suggested for the imaging of liver disease. The effect of low doses of radiation on carcinogenesis are also disputed. Although MRI is associated with biological effects, these have not been proven to cause measurable harm.

Iodinated contrast medium is routinely used in CT and the main adverse events are anaphylactoid reactions and nephrotoxicity. Commonly used MRI contrast agents have a good safety profile but linear non-ionic agents in particular have been implicated in nephrogenic systemic fibrosis in patients with severely impaired renal function.

MRI is contraindicated in the presence of MR-unsafe implants, and although these patients may be imaged with CT, beam hardening artefact from metallic devices, such as pacemakers and implantable cardioverter-defibrillators, may also affect image quality. MRI is a longer investigation than CT and an exam may take between 20–40 mins depending on complexity.

Guidance

Safety issues, including the potential for biostimulation device interference, movement of ferromagnetic bodies, and incidental localized heating, have been addressed in the American College of Radiology's *White Paper on MR Safety,* which was originally published in 2002 and expanded in 2004. The *ACR White Paper on MR Safety* has been rewritten and was released early in 2007 under the new title *ACR Guidance Document for Safe MR Practices.*

In December 2007, the Medicines and Healthcare Products Regulatory Agency (MHRA), a UK healthcare regulatory body, issued their *Safety Guidelines for Magnetic Resonance Imaging Equipment in Clinical Use.* In February 2008, the Joint Commission, a US healthcare accrediting organization, issued a Sentinel Event Alert #38, their highest patient safety advisory, on MRI safety issues. In July 2008, the United States Veterans Administration, a federal governmental agency serving the healthcare needs of former military personnel, issued a substantial revision to their *MRI Design Guide*, which includes physical and facility safety considerations.

The European Directive on Electromagnetic Fields

This Directive (2013/35/EU - electromagnetic fields) covers all known direct biophysical effects and indirect effects caused by electromagnetic fields within the EU and repealed the 2004/40/EC directive. The deadline for implementation of the new directive is 1 July 2016. Article 10 of the directive sets out the scope of the derogation for MRI, stating that the exposure limits may be exceeded during "the installation, testing, use, development, maintenance of or research related to magnetic resonance imaging (MRI) equipment for patients in the health sector, provided that certain conditions are met." Uncertainties remain regarding the scope and conditions of this derogation.

Procedure

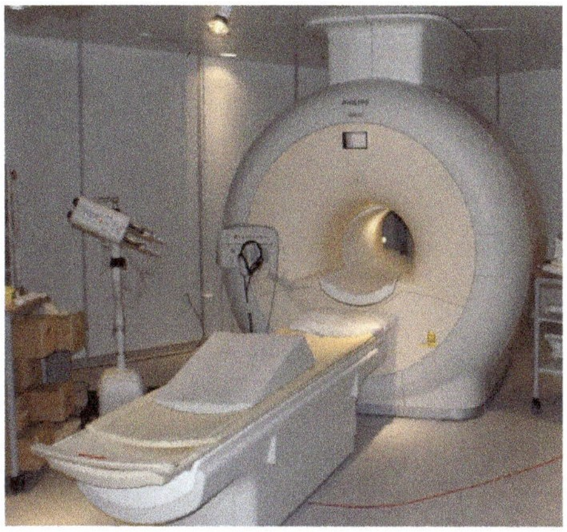

Medical MRI scanner.

To perform a study, the person is positioned within an MRI scanner that forms a strong magnetic field around the area to be imaged. In most medical applications, protons (hydrogen atoms) in tissues containing water molecules create a signal that is processed to form an image of the body. First, energy from an oscillating magnetic field is temporarily applied to the patient at the appropriate resonance frequency. The excited hydrogen atoms emit a radio frequency signal, which is measured by a receiving coil. The radio signal can be made to encode position information by varying the main magnetic field using gradient coils. As these coils are rapidly switched on and off they create the characteristic repetitive noise of an MRI scan. The contrast between different tissues is determined by the rate at which excited atoms return to the equilibrium state. Exogenous contrast agents may be given intravenously, orally or intra-articularly.

MRI requires a magnetic field that is both strong and uniform. The field strength of the magnet is measured in teslas – and while the majority of systems operate at 1.5 T, commercial systems are available between 0.2–7 T. Most clinical magnets are superconducting magnets, which require liquid helium. Lower field strengths can be achieved with permanent magnets, which are often used in "open" MRI scanners for claustrophobic patients. Recently, MRI has been demonstrated also at ultra-low fields, i.e., in the microtesla-to-millitesla range, where sufficient signal quality is made possible by prepolarization (on the order of 10-100 mT) and by measuring the Larmor precession fields at about 100 microtesla with highly sensitive superconducting quantum interference devices (SQUIDs).

Contrast

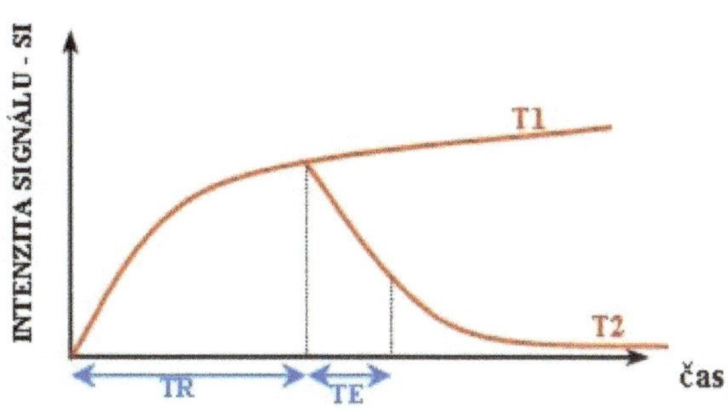

Effects of TR and TE on MR signal.

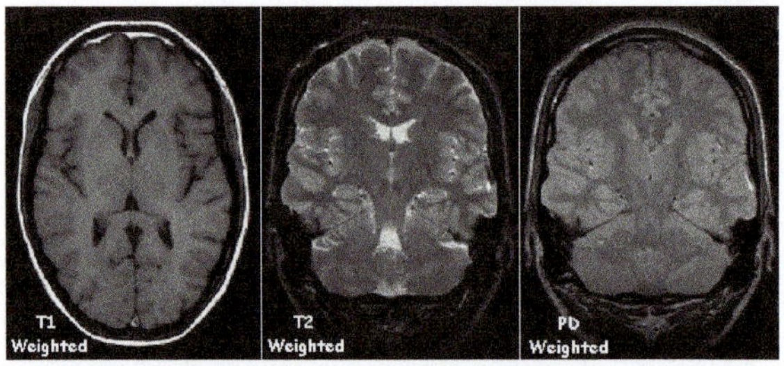

Examples of T1 weighted, T2 weighted and PD weighted MRI scans.

Image contrast may be weighted to demonstrate different anatomical structures or pathologies. Each tissue returns to its equilibrium state after excitation by the independent processes of T1 (spin-lattice) and T2 (spin-spin) relaxation. To create a T1-weighted image, magnetization is allowed to recover before measuring the MR signal by changing the repetition time (TR). This image weighting is useful for assessing the cerebral cortex, identifying fatty tissue, characterizing focal liver lesions and in general for obtaining morphological information, as well as for post-contrast imaging. To create a T2-weighted image, magnetization is allowed to decay before measuring the MR signal by changing the echo time (TE). This image weighting is useful for detecting edema and inflammation, revealing white matter lesions and assessing zonal anatomy in the prostate and uterus.

Contrast Agents

MRI for imaging anatomical structures or blood flow do not require contrast agents as the varying properties of the tissues or blood provide natural contrasts. However, for more specific types of imaging the most commonly used intravenous contrast agents are based on chelates of gadolinium. In general, these agents have proved safer than the iodinated contrast agents used in X-ray radiography or CT. Anaphylactoid reactions are rare, occurring in approx. 0.03–0.1%. Of particular interest is the lower incidence of nephrotoxicity, compared with iodinated agents, when given at usual doses—this has made contrast-enhanced MRI scanning an option for patients with renal impairment, who would otherwise not be able to undergo contrast-enhanced CT.

Although gadolinium agents have proved useful for patients with renal impairment, in patients with severe renal failure requiring dialysis there is a risk of a rare but serious illness, nephrogenic systemic fibrosis, which may be linked to the use of certain gadolinium-containing agents. The most frequently linked is gadodiamide, but other agents have been linked too. Although a causal link has not been definitively established, current guidelines in the United States are that dialysis patients should only receive gadolinium agents where essential, and that dialysis should be performed as soon as possible after the scan to remove the agent from the body promptly. In Europe, where more gadolinium-containing agents are available, a classification of agents according to potential risks has been released. Recently, a new contrast agent named gadoxetate, brand name Eovist (US) or Primovist (EU), was approved for diagnostic use: this has the theoretical benefit of a dual excretion path.

Interpretation

The standard display of MRI images is to represent fluid characteristics in black and white images, where different tissues turn out as follows:

	T1-weighted	T2-weighted
Bright	• Fat • Subacute hemorrhage • Melanin • Protein-rich fluid • Slowly flowing blood • Paramagnetic substances, such as gadolinium, manganese, copper • Cortical pseudolaminar necrosis	• More water content, as in edema, tumor, infarction, inflammation and infection • Extracellularly located methemoglobin in subacute hemorrhage
Inter- mediate	Gray matter darker than white matter	White matter darker than grey matter
Dark	• Bone • Air • More water content, as in edema, tumor, infarction, inflammation, infection, hyperacute or chronic hemorrhage • Low proton density as in calcification	• Bone • Air • Fat • Low proton density, as in calcification and fibrosis • Paramagnetic material, such as deoxyhemoglobin, intracelullar methemoglobin, iron, ferritin, hemosiderin, melanin • Protein-rich fluid

History

Magnetic resonance imaging was invented by Paul C. Lauterbur in September 1971; he published the theory behind it in March 1973. The factors leading to image contrast (differences in tissue relaxation time values) had been described nearly 20 years earlier by Erik Odeblad (physician and scientist) and Gunnar Lindström.

In 1950, spin echoes were first detected by Erwin Hahn and in 1952, Herman Carr produced a one-dimensional NMR spectrum as reported in his Harvard PhD thesis. In the Soviet Union, Vladislav Ivanov filed (in 1960) a document with the USSR State Committee for Inventions and Discovery at Leningrad for a Magnetic Resonance Imaging device, although this was not approved until the 1970s.

By 1959, Jay Singer had studied blood flow by NMR relaxation time measurements of blood in living humans. Such measurements were not introduced into common medical practice until the mid-1980s, although a patent for a whole-body NMR machine to measure blood flow in the human body was already filed by Alexander Ganssen in early 1967.

In the 1960s and 1970s the results of a very large amount of work on relaxation, diffusion, and chemical exchange of water in cells and tissues of all sorts appeared in the scientific literature. In 1967, Ligon reported the measurement of NMR relaxation of water in the arms of living human subjects. In 1968, Jackson and Langham published the first NMR signals from a living animal.

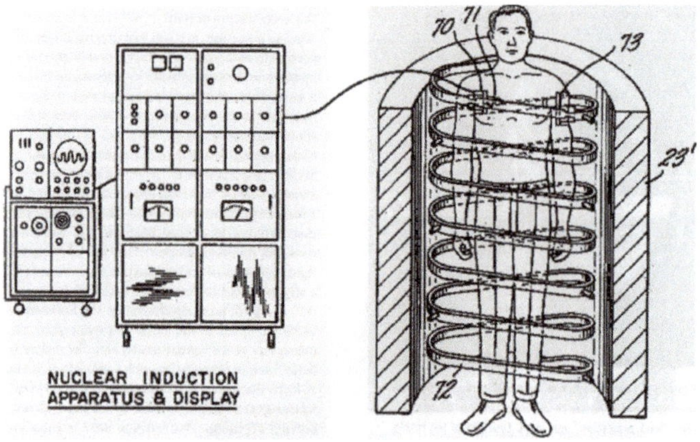

Raymond Damadian's "Apparatus and method for detecting cancer in tissue".

In a March 1971 paper in the journal *Science*, Raymond Damadian, an Armenian-American physician and professor at the Downstate Medical Center State University of New York (SUNY), reported that tumors and normal tissue can be distinguished in vivo by nuclear magnetic resonance ("NMR"). He suggested that these differences could be used to diagnose cancer, though later research would find that these differences, while real, are too variable for diagnostic purposes. Damadian's initial methods were flawed for practical use, relying on a point-by-point scan of the entire body and using relaxation rates, which turned out not to be an effective indicator of cancerous tissue. While researching the analytical properties of magnetic resonance, Damadian created a hypothetical magnetic resonance cancer-detecting machine in 1972. He filed the first patent for such a machine, U.S. Patent 3,789,832 on March 17, 1972, which was later issued to him on February 5, 1974. Zenuemon Abe and his colleagues applied the patent for targeted NMR scanner, U.S. Patent 3,932,805 on 1973. They published this technique in 1974.

Damadian Claims to have Invented the MRI.

MRI Scanner Mark One. The first MRI scanner to be built and used, in Aberdeen Royal Infirmary in Scotland.

The US National Science Foundation notes "The patent included the idea of using NMR to 'scan' the human body to locate cancerous tissue." However, it did not describe a method for generating pictures from such a scan or precisely how such a scan might be done. Meanwhile, Paul Lauterbur at Stony Brook University expanded on Carr's technique and developed a way to generate the first MRI images, in 2D and 3D, using gradients. In 1973, Lauterbur published the first nuclear magnetic resonance image and the first cross-sectional image of a living mouse in January 1974. In the late 1970s, Peter Mansfield, a physicist and professor at the University of Nottingham, England, developed the echo-planar imaging (EPI) technique that would lead to scans taking seconds rather than hours and produce clearer images than Lauterbur had. Damadian, along with Larry Minkoff and Michael Goldsmith, obtained an image of a tumor in the thorax of a mouse in 1976. They also performed the first MRI body scan of a human being on July 3, 1977, studies they published in 1977. In 1979, Richard S. Likes filed a patent on k-space U.S. Patent 4,307,343.

During the 1970s a team led by John Mallard built the first full-body MRI scanner at the University of Aberdeen. On 28 August 1980 they used this machine to obtain the first clinically useful image of a patient's internal tissues using MRI, which identified a primary tumour in the patient's chest, an abnormal liver, and secondary cancer in his bones. This machine was later used at St Bartholomew's Hospital, in London, from 1983 to 1993. Mallard and his team are credited for technological advances that led to the widespread introduction of MRI.

In 1975, the University of California, San Francisco Radiology Department founded the Radiologic Imaging Laboratory (RIL). With the support of Pfizer, Diasonics, and later Toshiba America MRI, the lab developed new imaging technology and installed systems in the US and worldwide. In 1981 RIL researchers, including Leon Kaufman and Lawrence Crooks, published *Nuclear Magnetic Resonance Imaging in Medicine*. In the 1980s the book was considered the definitive introductory textbook to the subject.

In 1980 Paul Bottomley joined the GE Research Center in Schenectady, NY. His team ordered the highest field-strength magnet then available — a 1.5 T system — and built the first high-field device, overcoming problems of coil design, RF penetration and signal-to-noise ratio to build the first whole-body MRI/MRS scanner. The results translated into the highly successful 1.5 T MRI product-line, with over 20,000 systems in use today. In 1982, Bottomley performed the first localized MRS in the human heart and brain. After starting a collaboration on heart applications with Robert Weiss at Johns Hopkins, Bottomley returned to the university in 1994 as Russell Morgan Professor and director of the MR Research Division. Although MRI is most commonly performed at 1.5 T, higher fields such as 3 T are gaining more popularity because of their increased sensitivity and resolution. In research laboratories, human studies have been performed at up to 9.4 T and animal studies have been performed at up to 21.1 T.

2003 Nobel Prize

Reflecting the fundamental importance and applicability of MRI in medicine, Paul Lauterbur of the University of Illinois at Urbana-Champaign and Sir Peter Mansfield of the University of Nottingham were awarded the 2003 Nobel Prize in Physiology or Medicine for their "discoveries concerning magnetic resonance imaging". The Nobel citation acknowledged Lauterbur's insight of using magnetic field gradients to determine spatial localization, a discovery that allowed rapid acquisition of 2D images. Mansfield was credited with introducing the mathematical formalism and developing techniques for efficient gradient utilization and fast imaging. The actual research that won the prize was done almost 30 years before while Paul Lauterbur was a professor in the Department of Chemistry at Stony Brook University in New York.

Economics

In the UK, the price of a clinical 1.5-tesla MRI scanner is around £920,000/US$1.4 million, with the lifetime maintenance cost broadly similar to the purchase cost. In the Netherlands, the average MRI scanner costs around €1 million, with a 7-T MRI having been taken in use by the UMC Utrecht in December 2007, costing €7 million. Construction of MRI suites could cost up to US$500,000/€370.000 or more, depending on project scope. Pre-polarizing MRI (PMRI) systems using resistive electromagnets have shown promise as a low-cost alternative and have specific advantages for joint imaging near metal implants, however they are likely unsuitable for routine whole-body or neuroimaging applications.

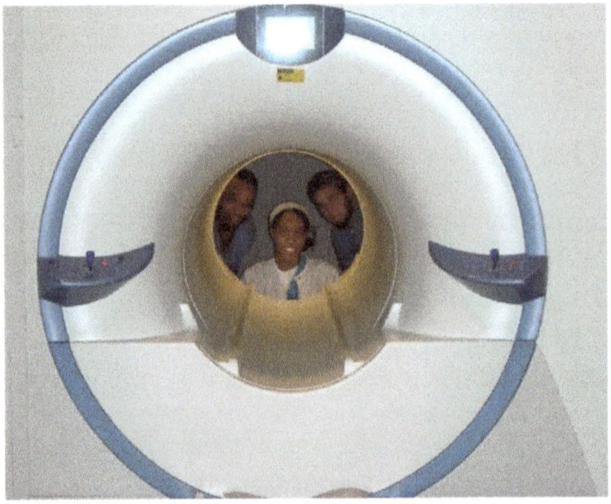

Looking through an MRI scanner.

MRI scanners have become significant sources of revenue for healthcare providers in the US. This is because of favorable reimbursement rates from insurers and federal government programs. Insurance reimbursement is provided in two components, an equipment charge for the actual performance and operation of the MRI scan and a professional charge for the radiologist's review of the images and/or data. In the US Northeast, an equipment charge might be $3,500/€2.600 and a professional charge might be $350/€260, although the actual fees received by the equipment owner and interpreting physician are often significantly less and depend on the rates negotiated with insurance companies or determined by the Medicare fee schedule. For example, an orthopedic surgery group in Illinois billed a charge of $1,116/€825 for a knee MRI in 2007, but the Medicare reimbursement in 2007 was only $470.91/€350. Many insurance companies require advance approval of an MRI procedure as a condition for coverage.

In the US, the Deficit Reduction Act of 2005 significantly reduced reimbursement rates paid by federal insurance programs for the equipment component of many scans, shifting the economic landscape. Many private insurers have followed suit.

In the United States, an MRI of the brain with and without contrast billed to Medicare Part B entails, on average, a technical payment of US$403/€300 and a separate payment to the radiologist of US$93/€70. In France, the cost of an MRI exam is approximately €150/US$205. This covers three basic scans including one with an intravenous contrast agent as well as a consultation with the technician and a written report to the patient's physician. In Japan, the cost of an MRI examination (excluding the cost of contrast material and films) ranges from US$155/€115 to US$180/€133, with an additional radiologist professional fee of US$17/€12.50. In India, the cost of an MRI examination including the fee for the radiologist's opinion comes to around Rs 3000–4000 (€37–49/US$50–60), excluding the cost of contrast material. In the UK the retail price for an MRI scan privately ranges between £350 and £700 (€405–810).

Overuse

Medical societies issue guidelines for when physicians should use MRI on patients and recommend against overuse. MRI can detect health problems or confirm a diagnosis, but medical societies often recommend that MRI not be the first procedure for creating a plan to diagnose or manage a patient's complaint. A common case is to use MRI to seek a cause of low back pain; the American College of Physicians, for example, recommends against this procedure as unlikely to result in a positive outcome for the patient.

Specialized Applications

Diffusion MRI

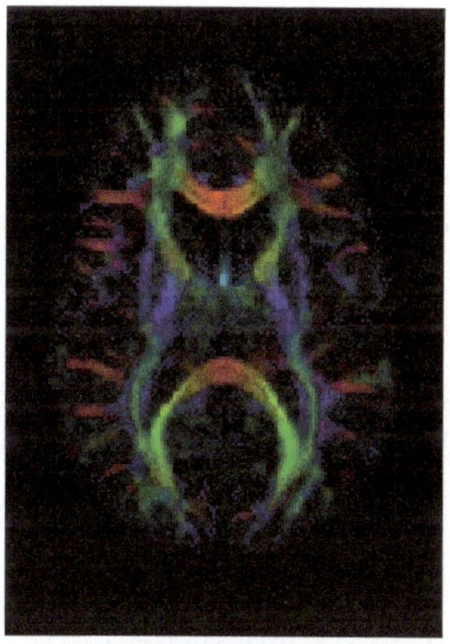

DTI image.

Diffusion MRI measures the diffusion of water molecules in biological tissues. Clinically, diffusion MRI is useful for the diagnoses of conditions (e.g., stroke) or neurological disorders (e.g., multiple sclerosis), and helps better understand the connectivity of white matter axons in the central nervous system. In an isotropic medium (inside a glass of water for example), water molecules naturally move randomly according to turbulence and Brownian motion. In biological tissues however, where the Reynolds number is low enough for laminar flow, the diffusion may be anisotropic. For example, a molecule inside the axon of a neuron has a low probability of crossing the myelin membrane. Therefore, the molecule moves principally along the axis of the neural fiber. If it is known that molecules in a particular voxel diffuse principally in one direction, the assumption can be made that the majority of the fibers in this area are parallel to that direction.

The recent development of diffusion tensor imaging (DTI) enables diffusion to be measured in multiple directions, and the fractional anisotropy in each direction to be calculated for each voxel. This enables researchers to make brain maps of fiber directions to examine the connectivity of different regions in the brain (using tractography) or to examine areas of neural degeneration and demyelination in diseases like multiple sclerosis.

Another application of diffusion MRI is diffusion-weighted imaging (DWI). Following an ischemic stroke, DWI is highly sensitive to the changes occurring in the lesion. It is speculated that increases in restriction (barriers) to water diffusion, as a result of cytotoxic edema (cellular swelling), is responsible for the increase in signal on a DWI scan. The DWI enhancement appears within 5–10 minutes of the onset of stroke symptoms (as compared to computed tomography, which often does not detect changes of acute infarct for up to 4–6 hours) and remains for up to two weeks. Coupled with imaging of cerebral perfusion, researchers can highlight regions of "perfusion/diffusion mismatch" that may indicate regions capable of salvage by reperfusion therapy.

Like many other specialized applications, this technique is usually coupled with a fast image acquisition sequence, such as echo planar imaging sequence.

Magnetic Resonance Angiography

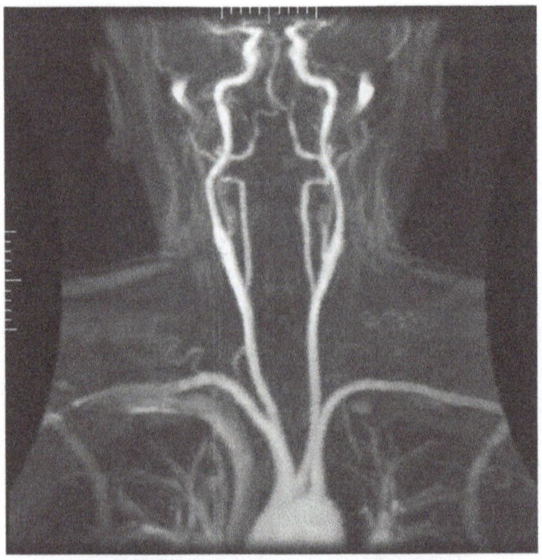

Magnetic resonance angiography.

Magnetic resonance angiography (MRA) generates pictures of the arteries to evaluate them for stenosis (abnormal narrowing) or aneurysms (vessel wall dilatations, at risk of rupture). MRA is often used to evaluate the arteries of the neck and brain, the thoracic and abdominal aorta, the renal arteries, and the legs (called a "run-off"). A variety of techniques can be used to generate the pictures, such as administration of a paramagnetic contrast agent (gadolinium) or using a technique known as "flow-related enhancement" (e.g., 2D and 3D time-of-flight sequences), where most of the signal on an image is due to blood that recently moved into that plane, see also FLASH MRI. Techniques involving phase accumulation (known as phase contrast angiography) can also be used to generate flow velocity maps easily and accurately. Magnetic resonance venography (MRV) is a similar procedure that is used to image veins. In this method, the tissue is now excited inferiorly, while the signal is gathered in the plane immediately superior to the excitation plane—thus imaging the venous blood that recently moved from the excited plane.

Magnetic Resonance Spectroscopy

Magnetic resonance spectroscopy (MRS) is used to measure the levels of different metabolites in body tissues. The MR signal produces a spectrum of resonances that corresponds to different molecular arrangements of the isotope being "excited". This signature is used to diagnose certain metabolic disorders, especially those affecting the brain, and to provide information on tumor metabolism.

Magnetic resonance spectroscopic imaging (MRSI) combines both spectroscopic and imaging methods to produce spatially localized spectra from within the sample or patient. The spatial resolution is much lower (limited by the available SNR), but the spectra in each voxel contains information about many metabolites. Because the available signal is used to encode spatial and spectral information, MRSI requires high SNR achievable only at higher field strengths (3 T and above).

Functional MRI

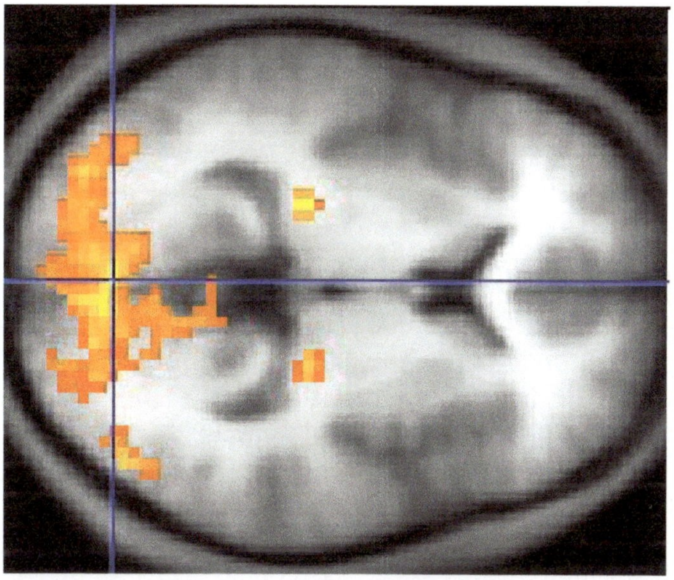

A fMRI scan showing regions of activation in orange, including the primary visual cortex (V1, BA17).

Functional MRI (fMRI) measures signal changes in the brain that are due to changing neural activity. Compared to anatomical T1W imaging, the brain is scanned at lower spatial resolution but at a higher temporal resolution (typically once every 2–3 seconds). Increases in neural activity cause changes in the MR signal via T^*2 changes; this mechanism is referred to as the BOLD (blood-oxygen-level dependent) effect. Increased neural activity causes an increased demand for oxygen, and the vascular system actually overcompensates for this, increasing the amount of oxygenated hemoglobin relative to deoxygenated hemoglobin. Because deoxygenated hemoglobin attenuates the MR signal, the vascular response leads to a signal increase that is related to the neural activity. The precise nature of the relationship between neural activity and the BOLD signal is a subject of current research. The BOLD effect also allows for the generation of high resolution 3D maps of the venous vasculature within neural tissue.

While BOLD signal analysis is the most common method employed for neuroscience studies in human subjects, the flexible nature of MR imaging provides means to sensitize the signal to other aspects of the blood supply. Alternative techniques employ arterial spin labeling (ASL) or weighting the MRI signal by cerebral blood flow (CBF) and cerebral blood volume (CBV). The CBV method requires injection of a class of MRI contrast agents that are now in human clinical trials. Because this method has been shown to be far more sensitive than the BOLD technique in preclinical studies, it may potentially expand the role of fMRI in clinical applications. The CBF method provides more quantitative information than the BOLD signal, albeit at a significant loss of detection sensitivity.

Real-time MRI

Real-time MRI refers to the continuous monitoring ("filming") of moving objects in real time. While many different strategies have been developed over the past two decades, a recent development reported a real-time MRI technique based on radial FLASH and iterative reconstruction that yields a temporal resolution of 20 to 30 milliseconds for images with an in-plane resolution of 1.5 to 2.0 mm. The new method promises to add important information about diseases of the joints and the heart. In many cases MRI examinations may become easier and more comfortable for patients.

Interventional MRI

The lack of harmful effects on the patient and the operator make MRI well-suited for interventional radiology, where the images produced by an MRI scanner guide minimally invasive procedures. Such procedures must be done with no ferromagnetic instruments.

A specialized growing subset of interventional MRI is intraoperative MRI, in which doctors use an MRI in surgery. Some specialized MRI systems allow imaging concurrent with the surgical procedure. More typical, however, is that the surgical procedure is temporarily interrupted so that MRI can verify the success of the procedure or guide subsequent surgical work.

Magnetic Resonance Guided Focused Ultrasound

In MRgFUS therapy, ultrasound beams are focused on a tissue—guided and controlled using MR thermal imaging—and due to the significant energy deposition at the focus, temperature within the tissue rises to more than 65 °C (150 °F), completely destroying it. This technology can achieve precise ablation of diseased tissue. MR imaging provides a three-dimensional view of the target tissue, allowing for precise focusing of ultrasound energy. The MR imaging provides quantitative, real-time, thermal images of the treated area. This allows the physician to ensure that the temperature generated during each cycle of ultrasound energy is sufficient to cause thermal ablation within the desired tissue and if not, to adapt the parameters to ensure effective treatment.

Multinuclear Imaging

Hydrogen is the most frequently imaged nucleus in MRI because it is present in biological tissues in great abundance, and because its high gyromagnetic ratio gives a strong signal. However, any nucleus with a net nuclear spin could potentially be imaged with MRI. Such nuclei include helium-3, lithium-7, carbon-13, fluorine-19, oxygen-17, sodium-23, phosphorus-31 and xenon-129. ^{23}Na and ^{31}P are naturally abundant in the body, so can be imaged directly. Gaseous isotopes such as ^3He or ^{129}Xe must be hyperpolarized and then inhaled as their nuclear density is too low to yield a useful signal under normal conditions. ^{17}O and ^{19}F can be administered in sufficient quantities in liquid form (e.g. ^{17}O-water) that hyperpolarization is not a necessity.

Moreover, the nucleus of any atom that has a net nuclear spin and that is bonded to a hydrogen atom could potentially be imaged via heteronuclear magnetization transfer MRI that would image the high-gyromagnetic-ratio hydrogen nucleus instead of the low-gyromagnetic-ratio nucleus that is bonded to the hydrogen atom. In principle, hetereonuclear magnetization transfer MRI could be used to detect the presence or absence of specific chemical bonds.

Multinuclear imaging is primarily a research technique at present. However, potential applications include functional imaging and imaging of organs poorly seen on ^1H MRI (e.g., lungs and bones) or as alternative contrast agents. Inhaled hyperpolarized ^3He can be used to image the distribution of air spaces within the lungs. Injectable solutions containing ^{13}C or stabilized bubbles of hyperpolarized ^{129}Xe have been studied as contrast agents for angiography and perfusion imaging. ^{31}P can potentially provide information on bone density and structure, as well as functional imaging of the brain. Multinuclear imaging holds the potential to chart the distribution of lithium in the human brain, this element finding use as an important drug for those with conditions such as bipolar disorder.

Molecular Imaging by MRI

MRI has the advantages of having very high spatial resolution and is very adept at morphological imaging and functional imaging. MRI does have several disadvantages though. First, MRI has a sensitivity of around 10^{-3} mol/L to 10^{-5} mol/L, which, compared to other types of imaging, can be very limiting. This problem stems from the fact that the population difference between the nuclear spin states is very small at room temperature. For example, at 1.5 teslas, a typical field strength for clinical MRI, the difference between high and low energy states is approximately 9 molecules per 2 million. Improvements to increase MR sensitivity include increasing magnetic field strength, and hyperpolarization via optical pumping or dynamic nuclear polarization. There are also a variety of signal amplification schemes based on chemical exchange that increase sensitivity.

To achieve molecular imaging of disease biomarkers using MRI, targeted MRI contrast agents with high specificity and high relaxivity (sensitivity) are required. To date, many studies have been devoted to developing targeted-MRI contrast agents to achieve molecular imaging by MRI. Commonly, peptides, antibodies, or small ligands, and small protein domains, such as HER-2 affibodies, have been applied to achieve targeting. To enhance the sensitivity of the contrast agents, these targeting moieties are usually linked to high payload MRI contrast agents or MRI contrast agents with high relaxivities. A new class of gene targeting MR contrast agents (CA) has been introduced to show gene action of unique mRNA and gene transcription factor proteins. This new CA can trace cells with unique mRNA, microRNA and virus; tissue response to inflammation in living brains. The MR reports change in gene expression with positive correlation to TaqMan analysis, optical and electron microscopy.

Other Specialized Sequences

New methods and variants of existing methods are often published when they are able to produce better results in specific fields. Examples of these recent improvements are T^* 2-weighted turbo spin-echo (T_2 TSE MRI), double inversion recovery MRI (DIR-MRI) or phase-sensitive inversion recovery MRI (PSIR-MRI), all of them able to improve imaging of brain lesions. Another example is MP-RAGE (magnetization-prepared rapid acquisition with gradient echo), which improves images of multiple sclerosis cortical lesions.

Magnetization Transfer MRI

Magnetization transfer (MT) is a technique to enhance image contrast in certain applications of MRI.

Bound protons are associated with proteins and as they have a very short T2 decay they do not normally contribute to image contrast. However, because these protons have a broad resonance peak they can be excited by a radiofrequency pulse that has no effect on free protons. Their excitation increases image contrast by transfer of saturated spins from the bound pool into the free pool, thereby reducing the signal of free water. This homonuclear magnetization transfer provides an indirect measurement of macromolecular content in tissue. Implementation of homonuclear magnetization transfer involves choosing suitable frequency offsets and pulse shapes to saturate the bound spins sufficiently strongly, within the safety limits of specific absorption rate for MRI.

The most common use of this technique is for suppression of background signal in time of flight MR angiography. There are also applications in neuroimaging particularly in the characterization of white matter lesions in multiple sclerosis.

T1rho MRI

T1ρ (T1rho): Molecules have a kinetic energy that is a function of the temperature and is expressed as translational and rotational motions, and by collisions between molecules. The moving dipoles disturb the magnetic field but are often extremely rapid so that the average effect over a long time-scale may be zero. However, depending on the time-scale, the interactions between the dipoles do not always average away. At the slowest extreme the interaction time is effectively infinite and occurs where there are large, stationary field disturbances (e.g., a metallic implant). In this case the loss of coherence is described as a "static dephasing". T2* is a measure of the loss of coherence in an ensemble of spins that includes all interactions (including static dephasing). T2 is a measure of the loss of coherence that excludes static dephasing, using an RF pulse to reverse the slowest types of dipolar interaction. There is in fact a continuum of interaction time-scales in a given biological sample, and the properties of the refocusing RF pulse can be tuned to refocus more than just static dephasing. In general, the rate of decay of an ensemble of spins is a function of the interaction times and also the power of the RF pulse. This type of decay, occurring under the influence of RF, is known as T1ρ. It is similar to T2 decay but with some slower dipolar interactions refocused, as well as static interactions, hence $T1\rho \geq T2$.

Proton Density Weighted

A proton density (PD) weighted images are created by having a long repetition time (TR) and a short echo time (TE). On images of the brain, this sequence has a more pronounced distinction between gray matter (bright) and white matter (darker gray), but with little contrast between brain and CSF.

Fluid Attenuated Inversion Recovery (FLAIR)

Fluid Attenuated Inversion Recovery (FLAIR) is an inversion-recovery pulse sequence used to nullify the signal from fluids. For example, it can be used in brain imaging to suppress cerebrospinal fluid (CSF) so as to bring out periventricular hyperintense lesions, such as multiple sclerosis (MS) plaques. By carefully choosing the inversion time TI (the time between the inversion and excitation pulses), the signal from any particular tissue can be suppressed.

Susceptibility Weighted Imaging (SWI)

Susceptibility weighted imaging (SWI), is a new type of contrast in MRI different from spin density, T_1, or T_2 imaging. This method exploits the susceptibility differences between tissues and uses a fully velocity compensated, three dimensional, RF spoiled, high-resolution, 3D gradient echo scan. This special data acquisition and image processing produces an enhanced contrast magnitude image very sensitive to venous blood, hemorrhage and iron storage. It is used to enhance the detection and diagnosis of tumors, vascular and neurovascular diseases (stroke and hemorrhage), multiple sclerosis, Alzheimer's, and also detects traumatic brain injuries that may not be diagnosed using other methods.

Neuromelanin Imaging

This method exploits the paramagnetic properties of neuromelanin and can be used to visualize the substantia nigra and the locus coeruleus. It is used to detect the atrophy of these nuclei in Parkinson's disease and other parkinsonisms, and also detects signal intensity changes in major depressive disorder and schizophrenia.

References

- Colletti, P.M.; Shinbane, J; S, Shellock; F. G. (2011). "MR-conditional" pacemakers: the radiologist's role in multidisciplinary management". AJR Am J Roentgenol. 197 (4): 1024. doi:10.2214/AJR.11.7120
- Ahmed K, Khan MS, Vats A, et al. (October 2009). "Current status of robotic assisted pelvic surgery and future developments". International Journal of Surgery. 7 (5): 431–40. doi:10.1016/j.ijsu.2009.08.008. PMID 19735746
- Daniel Albert (2012). Dorland's illustrated medical dictionary. (32nd ed.). Philadelphia, PA: Saunders/Elsevier. p. 1573. ISBN 978-1-4160-6257-8
- Sethi RK, Henry AJ, Hevelone ND, Lipsitz SR, Belkin M, Nguyen LL (September 2013). "Impact of hospital market competition on endovascular aneurysm repair adoption and outcomes.". J. Vasc. Surg. 58 (3): 596–606. PMID 23684424. doi:10.1016/j.jvs.2013.02.014
- "Managing high value capital equipment in the NHS in England" (PDF). National Audit Office (United Kingdom). Retrieved 30 November 2013
- Leksell L; Leksell D; Schwebel J (1985). "Stereotaxis and nuclear magnetic resonance". Journal of Neurology, Neurosurgery & Psychiatry. 48 (1): 14–18. doi:10.1136/jnnp.48.1.14. PMC 1028176 . PMID 3882889
- Health risks from exposure to low levels of ionizing radiation : BEIR VII Phase. Washington, D.C.: National Academies Press. 2006. ISBN 978-0-309-09156-5
- Watson, Robert E. (2015-10-01). "Lessons Learned from MRI Safety Events". Current Radiology Reports. 3 (10): 37. ISSN 2167-4825. doi:10.1007/s40134-015-0122-z
- "Magnetic Resonance, a critical peer-reviewed introduction". European Magnetic Resonance Forum. Retrieved 17 November 2014

- Thomas DG; Davis CH; Ingram S; Olney JS; Bydder GM; Young IR (1986). "Stereotaxic biopsy of the brain under MR imaging control". AJNR American Journal of Neuroradiology. 7 (1): 161–163. PMID 3082131
- McRobbie, Donald W. (2007). MRI from picture to proton. Cambridge, UK ; New York: Cambridge University Press. ISBN 0-521-68384-X
- Brown RA, Nelson JA (2016). "The invention and early history of the N-localizer for stereotactic neurosurgery". Cureus. 8 (6): e642. PMC 4959822 . PMID 27462476. doi:10.7759/cureus.642
- "Nephrogenic Systemic Fibrosis" (PDF). ACR Manual on Contrast Material. American College of Radiology. Retrieved 13 October 2012
- Haacke, E Mark; Brown, Robert F; Thompson, Michael; Venkatesan, Ramesh (1999). Magnetic resonance imaging: Physical principles and sequence design. New York: J. Wiley & Sons. ISBN 0-471-35128-8 Retrieved
- Heeger DJ; Ress D (2002). "What does fMRI tell us about neuronal activity?". Nat. Rev. Neurosci. 3 (2): 142–51. PMID 11836522. doi:10.1038/nrn730
- "Response to the FDA's May 23, 2007, Nephrogenic Systemic Fibrosis Update1 — Radiology". Radiology.rsna.org. 2007-09-12. Retrieved 2010-08-02
- Stankovic, Zoran; Allen, Bradley D.; Garcia, Julio; Jarvis, Kelly B.; Markl, Michael (2014). "4D flow imaging with MRI". Cardiovascular diagnosis and therapy. 4 (2): 173–192. doi:10.3978/j.issn.2223-3652.2014.01.02
- "A SHORT HISTORY OF MAGNETIC RESONANCE IMAGING FROM A EUROPEAN POINT OF VIEW". emrf.org. Archived from the original on 2007-04-13. Retrieved 2016-08-08
- Keith A. Johnson. "Basic proton MR imaging. Tissue Signal Characteristics". Harvard Medical School. Retrieved 2016-03-14
- Murphy KJ; Brunberg JA; Cohan RH (October 1996). "Adverse reactions to gadolinium contrast media: a review of 36 cases". AJR Am J Roentgenol. 167 (4): 847–9. PMID 8819369. doi:10.2214/ajr.167.4.8819369

Permissions

All chapters in this book are published with permission under the Creative Commons Attribution Share Alike License or equivalent. Every chapter published in this book has been scrutinized by our experts. Their significance has been extensively debated. The topics covered herein carry significant information for a comprehensive understanding. They may even be implemented as practical applications or may be referred to as a beginning point for further studies.

We would like to thank the editorial team for lending their expertise to make the book truly unique. They have played a crucial role in the development of this book. Without their invaluable contributions this book wouldn't have been possible. They have made vital efforts to compile up to date information on the varied aspects of this subject to make this book a valuable addition to the collection of many professionals and students.

This book was conceptualized with the vision of imparting up-to-date and integrated information in this field. To ensure the same, a matchless editorial board was set up. Every individual on the board went through rigorous rounds of assessment to prove their worth. After which they invested a large part of their time researching and compiling the most relevant data for our readers.

The editorial board has been involved in producing this book since its inception. They have spent rigorous hours researching and exploring the diverse topics which have resulted in the successful publishing of this book. They have passed on their knowledge of decades through this book. To expedite this challenging task, the publisher supported the team at every step. A small team of assistant editors was also appointed to further simplify the editing procedure and attain best results for the readers.

Apart from the editorial board, the designing team has also invested a significant amount of their time in understanding the subject and creating the most relevant covers. They scrutinized every image to scout for the most suitable representation of the subject and create an appropriate cover for the book.

The publishing team has been an ardent support to the editorial, designing and production team. Their endless efforts to recruit the best for this project, has resulted in the accomplishment of this book. They are a veteran in the field of academics and their pool of knowledge is as vast as their experience in printing. Their expertise and guidance has proved useful at every step. Their uncompromising quality standards have made this book an exceptional effort. Their encouragement from time to time has been an inspiration for everyone.

The publisher and the editorial board hope that this book will prove to be a valuable piece of knowledge for students, practitioners and scholars across the globe.

Index